SILENT YEARS

No. 7 Eccles Street, Dublin. J. F. Byrne's residence
before coming to America in 1910, the site designated
by Joyce as the home of the two great protagonists,
Leopold and Mollie Bloom, in *Ulysses*.

SILENT YEARS

*An Autobiography with Memoirs of
James Joyce and Our Ireland*

by

J. F. BYRNE

*Tempora labuntur, tacitisque senescimus annis,
Et fugiunt freno non remorante dies.*

OVID

OCTAGON BOOKS

A DIVISION OF FARRAR, STRAUS AND GIROUX

New York   1975

Reprinted 1975

OCTAGON BOOKS
A Division of Farrar, Straus & Giroux, Inc.
19 Union Square West
New York, N. Y. 10003

Library of Congress Cataloging in Publication Data

Byrne, John Francis, 1880-
    Silent years.

        1. Byrne, John Francis, 1880-   2. Joyce, James, 1882-1941
        —Biography.   I. Title.
[CT808.B9A3   1975]   973.91'092'4 [B]   75-11682
ISBN 0-374-91144-4

Manufactured by Braun-Brumfield, Inc.
Ann Arbor, Michigan

Printed in the United States of America

To HARVEY BREIT

In melancholy mood I wandered forth
Alone.
For I had left the fetich of life behind,
And in the darkness stumbled wearily on,
Going I knew not whither. Things I did
That to myself seemed strange and meaningless,
But still pursued my erring, lonely way.
Much did I yearn to know—nor got reply.
So, worse than sad, I felt that I had dreamed,
Was dreaming, and would dream till the end of all—
If end there be.
Just then I sat me down awhile to rest;
And with my heavy eyes I vainly sought
A refuge from the gloom, but all was dark.
Despairingly I turned and looked behind,
The way that I had come, and there beheld
A bower illumined with soft, rosy light.
Instinctively I knew it was the home
Of living love; and thither I resolved
To wend my way.
Whilst thinking thus I heard the heart-born sigh
Of one approaching slowly through the night,
Seeking, like me, the distant bower of love.
Weary she was; so having come quite near,
She sat beside me, and in sympathy
I took her hand, but spoke not any word,
For ours was sorrow kindred. She but came
Nearer to me, until with joy I felt
Her loosened tresses fluttering at my cheek—
Then did I boldly take YOU in my arms,
And kiss your yielding lips; whereat behold,
WE stood illumined in soft rosy light!
Wonderingly we saw, till that we gazed
Each in the other's eyes; then we both knew
That HERE was LOVE.

J. F. BYRNE

Written August 1898 after visiting
Lugnaquilla and Vinegar Hill

CONTENTS

FOREWORD

IN A WORLD SO specialized as the one we are living in today, it may cause surprise that "this mere painstaking burrower and grub-worm of a poor devil of a Sub-Sub" should be the author of a foreword to a book subtitled *Memoirs of Joyce and Our Ireland*. He never saw Joyce plain and the nearest he came to Dublin was London. Consider the staggering number of people who have made Joyce and Ireland their favorite subject, consider this Sub-Sub who knows so little of either that he cannot even be fanatic, and you have Justifiable Surprise. But there you also have J. F. Byrne.

Let it be said at the outset that Mr. Byrne is not an orthodox man. He does things in his own way. Even my meeting with him, a year ago, had its decisive quota of unorthodoxy. He came to the sedate and conservative offices of *The New York Times* a white-haired man, unjacketed, his trousers held up by braces that ran over the shoulders of a short-sleeved, open-collar shirt. I was, from the outset, charmed by his appearance and touched by his conversation, and I am glad that I experienced these reactions before I knew that J. F. Byrne was Joyce's *Cranly*.

Mr. Byrne left his manuscript with me on the very day that Frank O'Connor came by to take me off to lunch. I told him about my Irish adventure. Mr. O'Connor was delighted, amazed, excited. I remember that he said, "Don't tell the Joyce experts. They will tear you apart, and tear the book away from you." More significantly, he told me that Byrne was the last important bridge between the present and the schoolboy days of the author of *Ulysses*, that many interested hands had been after Byrne to do a book but that he had chosen to remain silent, that he had literally disappeared from the scene, and that Byrne had written a book, whatever kind of book, was sufficient cause for jubilation. Mr. O'Connor's parting words were: "Tell Byrne he has an admirer."

I know little enough about Mr. Byrne. My meetings with him, the telephone conversations I had with him, have without exception revealed to me that he is an honest man. Is it a basic criticism of experience to be forced to say how extraordinary a thing it was to discover that here was an honest man? There are many men who are honest, there are degrees and nuances of honesty; what is rare is to experience it as the dominating attribute in a human being. The impact of Byrne was honesty; not wit, or intelligence, or kindness, or shyness, or malevolence, but honesty. There was some deep gratification for me in that; there still is. I can almost laugh aloud with pleasure and amusement when I construct for myself the invariable image of our talks: the question asked, the short intense pause, the question answered, as simple as you could want it without it falling into insufficiency, as direct and candid, as bearing the stamp of himself, the blood of his being.

I find this in the book too. Even when I disagree with some thought of Byrne's, or an attitude, or a tone, or a pitch, or even with the mechanics of the thinking, I recognize this rooted, deep-down honesty. Why, this is the very man himself, with his anger, his memory (which I would guess is the next thing to total recall), his scrupulousness, his gentleness, his ill-temper, his detachment, his faith. I like to read about a man like that, a man who has resisted—unlike most of us—those historic forces and currents that alienate us from ourselves. I wish I had known him in those early days too, and seen him with the young Joyce's eyes, as well as with my own; watched him playing chess, waited alongside Joyce as Joyce waited for him to finish the game; played against him at handball; walked alongside him as he walked with Joyce through the Dublin streets and heard Joyce test his esthetic against the cryptic, subtle responses of Cranly-Byrne. I look at the famous photo showing Clancy and Joyce in sitting positions and Byrne standing between them, and I am envious. I recall no such dedicated faces in my own youth, not in myself or in my friends.

I am filled with some emotion about Byrne, or perhaps about a life like Byrne's. It isn't love, or even friendship. It is something more important. Some lives are lived out in the way that a work of art unfolds, whether tragic or comic—and there is a mixture of both in Byrne's life. These lives bring you closer to the nature of life, to the basic issues and engagements, to the mystery of death, to the tragedy of being alive and to the wonderfulness of each day. I recall that when Franklin D. Roosevelt died, I felt that my life had suffered some serious deprivation. It wasn't that I was sad, or that I held the president in such high esteem, or believed in his idealism and ideas; no, it wasn't that. He was an abstraction to me, yet in some mysterious way his life, his ways, his design, had touched the mainspring of my being and I felt a deprivation more surely than when my own father had died. This is what I mean about Byrne: you may disagree about him, you may find some of his notions disagreeable and some of his findings ludicrous, and yet he will bring you closer to life in the way that a work of art does; you will see the lineaments and structure of a life that unfolded without superfluity, and through this contact with innocence and seriousness you are brought close to the whole business of being alive. That is a great deal—and I am delighted that J. F. Byrne is unorthodox enough to ask me to write this foreword to his book.

HARVEY BREIT
June 5, 1953

CHAPTER ONE

Anna Liffey—I "woke on its breast"

JUDGING FROM old maps of Dublin City, it seems that the house in which I was born on East Essex Street stood on ground which some three hundred years ago must have formed part of the bed of the River Liffey—James Joyce's *Anna Livia Plurabelle*.

To me, in my early childhood, and that was before the main-drainage system, the Liffey of my little world in Dublin City was just a stream put there for the primary purpose of carrying the city sewage out to the Dublin Bay prawns and herrings, both of which marine creatures were nevertheless among the most delectable edibles in the world. A secondary purpose for which my infant mind may have thought the Liffey had been put there was to provide a waterway on which the half-dozen Guinness' steamers could ply between the brewery wharves up near Kingsbridge and the cargo vessels moored along the north and south walls in the general vicinity of the Custom House. These little steamers—one of the swiftest was named "Anna Liffey"—were about one hundred feet long by fifteen wide, with about a five-foot draught, and they transported their cargoes of full barrels from the brewery to the vessels, and the empties from the vessels to the brewery.

As for the name "Anna Liffey," the word "Anna," meaning river, is an Aryan derivative; Sanskrit "Avani"; Irish "Abhainn," which has three different forms: Abhaim, Abhanna, and Aibhne. The origin of the name "Liffey" is obscure, but possibly it derives from liob,-ibe, which, according to Dinneen, means a wet rag, anything sodden; Taim im lib, I am drenched, a form of leadhb.

About one hundred yards from my residence was the "mouth" of the Poddle on Wellington Quay (not Wood Quay, as *Ulysses*

1

has it), facing Jervis Street on the other, and northern, side of the river. This Poddle river, a man-made one, and so named about the year 1490, derived some of its water from rivulets, but mostly from the Dodder. Its purpose was to drain sewage from the south, and oldest, part of Dublin City and you can take my word for it that the dear old smelly old Poddle functioned fluently in the adequate performance of this catharsis. When I was a very little boy, I used to climb the Liffey wall to look down into the filthy flood gushing through the thick iron bars that guarded the mouth of the Poddle; and I would marvel at the mysterious ways of nature as revealed in the presence of the hundreds of screeching gulls that "dropt and lifted, dropt and lifted" over this their happy hunting ground.

In December, 1883, when I was not yet four years old my father came home earlier than usual one evening and said to my mother: "Biddy, I don't feel very well—I think I'll go up and lie down for awhile." Five minutes afterwards my mother went up to him, and found him dead.

Two months later I went to school for the first time—it was to King's Inn Street School. Why I was lugged off so far away from my home I don't know. However, the period of my scholarship in that secular institution was extremely brief; it lasted only till the afternoon of the first day; for an accident happened, one not uncommonly associated with nervous and sensitive childhood, so it was decided to send me to some other abode of learning nearer home. Accordingly, on the following day, I was enrolled under the care of the nuns in their "Infants' School" in Clarendon Street. The spiritual directors of this school were the priests of the Carmelite Order, discalced, in the neighboring church on Clarendon Street.

Coincidental with my first going to school and while I was still in petticoats, I became an altar boy in the Carmelite Church, Whitefriars' Street, the priests in this church being of the O.C.C., or calced Carmelites. In this church there were about seven altars, including the High Altar, and often in the early morning Masses were being said on all of them at one time. Generally, I was favored by the priests, but one of them, Father Tom Doyle, really took me under his wing. He personally taught me the few requisite Latin responses at Mass, and in a couple of months I was able to repeat a few longer bits including the "Confiteor." From that time for many years I served Father Doyle's Mass—he would have no one else—and he would patiently prompt my faltering Latin, and, of course, he always had to move the massive gilt leather-bound missal with its heavy mahogany stand from either side of the altar to the other.

Father Doyle was around sixty years of age; he was of medium height, slim and ascetic looking. He was a first-rate musician, speaking and singing in a full, resonant and musical baritone voice. He was choir leader and music master for the altar boys and confraternity men, and probably also trained his fellow priests individually and collectively. Many of them, noticeably Father Felix Cullen, and Father Moore, had excellent voices, and the priests' choir was one of the best I ever heard. Attired in soutane and surplice, I was at the foot of the High Altar on every night the Tenebrae were sung during Holy Week, in my first year as an altar boy, and the ceremonies, especially the priests' choir, moved me indescribably. When the priests sang the "Miserere," I thought it beautiful; particularly when they came to the verse, "Asperges me hyssopo et mundabor: labavis me et super nivem dealabor." This was sung in what was to me a thrilling outpouring of melodious harmony.

For a considerable time about this period, I suffered from tender "plum-tree gum" eyes. Cousin Mary brought me to Vincent's Hospital where I was treated, but to no avail. Father Doyle suggested applying tea that had been prepared as you would to drink it, but of course his advice was just pisherogue. Mary then brought me at different times to two specialists on Merrion Square, but they didn't do me any good. Then someone suggested I should be brought to Father Charles, the Redemptorist, at Harold's Cross. I had heard, of course, about Father Charles, for you couldn't have lived in the Dublin of these years without hearing of his sanctity and his miraculous good works. Indeed, he was the uncanonized saint of the city of Dublin. Well, to Father Charles Mary brought me. As we approached along the avenue and neared the church, Mary pointed out to me Father Charles who was strolling with another priest in the grounds. Young as I was, or maybe because I was so young, the sight of Father Charles impressed me indelibly. Aged and thin and frail, his face and appearance gave me instantly to understand why he was referred to by all who spoke of him as a saint. When we went on into the church there were several other persons waiting for the touch of Father Charles. Soon he came in, and began at once his prayerful ministration, and when he came to me and stood before me and I looked up into his rapt face, I beheld a vision of unutterable holiness, and as I felt the soft caress of the tips of his emaciated fingers all over my closed eyes I was in a state of near ecstasy. I think it is needless to say that my eyes got well; the next day they were normal, and I have never suffered from them since.

I remained in the "Infants" school for two years; and then the Prioress sent for my cousin Mary, the daughter of my father's sister, to tell her I was no longer to be considered an "infant," and that I would have to enter the adjacent "Big Boys" school. But Mary wouldn't listen to such a suggestion; so she compromised by having me admitted to the "Academy for Young Ladies and Gentlemen" conducted by the same nuns in the house next door. I don't recall the names of many of my childhood "academicians," but there was one young lady (she was my own age, 6 to 8 years) whose name I never forgot. As a child, I was partial to fizzy drinks, and there was one I especially liked, it was a "Lemonade" manufactured and bottled in Dublin by the firm of Cantrell & Cochrane. The young lady, whom I remember, was a daughter of the Cochrane owner of the soft drink firm.

About the time I was being adjudged by the Prioress of the Infants' School to be no longer an infant, I made my "first confession"—to Father Doyle. Whether it had anything to do with this emotional experience I don't know, but I suffered excruciating toothache, and I had a big back tooth extracted by a "dentist" who had his dirty little "office" on York Street, about half a furlong east of Whitefriars' Street Church. Soon thereafter I took very sick, and Mary went to tell Father Doyle, who came immediately to see me. He recommended applying a hot camomile poultice to my puffed-up face, and this being done, I soon fell into a coma and was unconscious for the better part of two days. A Doctor Barton who meanwhile had been called by Mary to see me diagnosed my trouble as erysipelas; and when he was told about the camomile application he muttered, "The worst thing in the world you could have done." Anyhow, whatever was the trouble, I was very sick and spent the next three weeks in bed.

In Whitefriars' Street Church at this time there were approximately a dozen priests. All of them knew me and almost all were kindly, but there was one of them who had been a boyhood friend of my father's in Wicklow, and he had for me always a roguish smile. He was Father Hall, the Carmelite Provincial, a real and true priest and gentleman with a host of personal friends, most of them influential, and many of them "diggers with the left foot."

On the feast of Corpus Christi in 1888, I made my first communion, receiving the Host from the fingers of Father Doyle. It was at the side altar to the right, the one nearest the rails. On the following Sunday evening, June 3, kneeling at the foot of the High Altar, I had an experience which could be described as ecstatic. What this was doesn't matter—it is of no consequence. On one occasion, a year before this I had had another, but definitely different, experience. This previous one had been very unpleasant and had nothing of an ecstatic character. It happened one Friday night in the church which was dubbed affectionately in the local vernacular, "Mickey and Jack's," the parish church of Michael's and John's. Mary Fleming who was all her life very devout, and a daily communicant up to the day of her death, always went to this church Friday nights to do the Stations of the Cross, and I often went with her. I rather liked to go, although I didn't do the stations. It was always late at night just before the church was locked up, and I enjoyed the dark solitude of the otherwise empty place as Mary proceeded slowly round it. On this night I fell to thinking on, of all subjects, the notion of Eternity; and as I contemplated and endeavored to catch up with the ever elusive and receding thought, I felt myself growing faint, and I got very sick. After that, I never again went on Friday nights to "Mickey and Jack's."

All things considered, it is not surprising that during the summer ending my second year in the Academy, it came to be arranged that I should be transferred to the Carmelite Seminary, 41 Lower Dominick St. In this institution I was enrolled in September, 1888, in the very month James Joyce was entering the illustrious Jesuit College of "Clongowes Wood." The President of the Carmelite Seminary was one Father Donegan, a nondescript little man, chiefly distinguished by being Chaplain to the Lord Mayor of Dublin. In the Dominick Street School the old system of first, second, and so on to the sixth book prevailed. I had already read all the books up to and including the fourth—knew them almost by heart, as well as the "second" and "third-sized" catechisms. On my first day in school, I was brought in to be "evaluated" by the president. After I had read a little aloud, Father Donegan said to the old attendant who had ushered me into his presence: "This boy goes into the Fifth Book, bring him up to Mr. Scanlan, and tell him I said he's got the best reader in the school."

When I entered Mr. Scanlan's classroom, the place was in an uproar, which, I quickly discovered, had nothing to do with my coming. It was that way when I entered because it was never any other way. There were about fifteen pupils in the class, and they were all doing just what they pleased, and what most of them pleased to do was to climb up on the teacher's back, on his lap, under his chair, knock his biretta off, scamper to get it, put it on again and knock it off again. It was all "great gas," and the absolutely unbelievable part of this utterly hilarious pandemonium was that Mr. Scanlan showed every sign of enjoying himself more than anybody else. Mr. Scanlan was a Carmelite novice; and I don't think he was yet out of his teens. He was blond and of medium size. In my life I have met many easy-going, smiling, good-humored, tolerant people, but not one of them fit to hold a candle to this young cleric Scanlan.

I remember a few of the names of the boys in this class. There were two Italian brothers, Dominick and Luigi Pisani. There was a boy Foley, son of a publican whose place of business was a few doors east of the subsequent site of the Abbey Theatre. (This boy was the brother of a lovely brunette, whom I recall seeing act "Red Riding Hood" in the Rotunda; in after life she became much better known as Mrs. John McCormack.) There was also a friend of Foley's whose name was Joe McGrane. He was son of another publican whose place was exactly opposite Foley's in Abbey Street. McGrane was nicknamed "Gout," for at least twice every hour he would raise his hand in class and ask, "Plaze, sir, may I gout to the yard?" Then there was a George Porter, whom I remember chiefly because he was a chum of another boy in the class, Bob Power. Bob was an older boy, about eleven, and we were close friends in Dominick Street, and later in Whitefriars' Street Church, where he became an altar boy.

So far as education is concerned—well, the Seminary has been defunct for a great many years, so we'll forget all about that, but there were a few incidents that occurred in this school that left their mark on my memory. At the rear of the school and on a level with the basement there was a large area which ran the full width of the house and about twenty feet in depth. This area had been roughly converted into a passable ball alley, and it was in this place that I first learned to love the game of handball. Back of the area there was a playground, approximately sixty by thirty, in which we used to play a game I also greatly enjoyed. We called it rounders, and it was probably like primitive baseball.

One day during lunch, when I had been in the school about a month, I was playfully seized by a big boy named Delaney, about five years my senior. He was one of the Blanchardstown Mill people. Anyway this lad grasped me and in a make-belief wrestling gesture tripped me, but as I fell he tried to save me and instead of doing this he fell himself with his full weight on top of me. When I was lifted up my right ankle was broken. They brought me into the priests' parlor, took off my shoe and stocking and looked at my damaged foot; they kept me there for two hours, hoping, perhaps, for a miracle, but there was none. Not a doctor was called; nor was there any notification sent to my mother or my cousins, and after two o'clock that day they let me out to drag myself as best I could all the way from Dominick St. to Essex St. One six-penny-bit would have paid the fare at that time for two persons on an outside car or cab; one penny would have paid my fare on the horse tram that ran down Bolton and Capel Streets and passed the corner of West Essex St. Neither the six-penny-bit nor the penny was offered, and having no money, I had to crawl home. In retrospect now this incident seems to be like a bad dream—something that just could not have happened to an eight-year-old boy.

After this incident I did not leave the house for six weeks, four of them spent in bed. Many of the priests, including Father Hall, and all bearing little gifts, came to see me, but my most attentive and frequent visitor was Father Doyle, who brought me Jaffa oranges and large purple hothouse grapes. He regaled me with tales of his small adventures and travels. He told me how once when a young priest he had been chased by a wicked bull on Howth Hill; and as the bull was rapidly gaining on him, the thought struck him to open his umbrella and turn, keeping the open umbrella before the bull, and the ruse worked: the bull was baffled and stopped in his tracks.

By his narration of his experiences in his frequent wanderings on "the continent" he stirred my imagination. He described incidents in Holland, Belgium, Switzerland, France, Spain, Malta (where the Carmelites had a "house"), and, above all, Italy, the Alps, Venice and Rome.

"Oh," I cried out fervently, "wouldn't I love to go there!"

And he said simply, "Hurry up and get well, John, and the next time I go to Italy I'll take you along with me."

And I, little fool that I was, believed him. I should have known better, but I was only eight years young, and at the time I was generally referred to as "the boy who wouldn't tell a lie." Let it not be inferred that I am imputing untruth to poor old Father Doyle. He spoke merely as grownups often chatter with children. He couldn't have realized as he set out for Italy a few months later, without so much as a remark to me, that he was leaving behind him something shattered.

In this Seminary there was one stinkpot—a dirty little moronic tippling sadist. How he ever came to be ordained a priest was to me then, as it is now, a mystery. I shall not disclose his name. As I have said, this man was little. With a cocked hat on his head and his arm stuck under his scapular, he could have posed as a comic-opera Napoleon Buonaparte. He was moronic; indeed submoronic. He never taught anything, he wouldn't be let; and the one plausible explanation for his presence in the school may be simply that he was one of the principal and most productive of the collectors, his clients being almost exclusively publicans, or saloon-keepers, a considerable number of whose sons he lured to the school.

He was scarcely ever sober, and went staggering round the yard with a stick, not a cane, in his hand during playtime. When recreation was over he would line a group of us boys against the playground wall, asking to look at our hands to see if they were dirty. If you were a saloon-keeper's son, your hands were all right even if they were filthy; but if you were not a saloon-keeper's son, or better still, if you were an orphan without a father, then you got rapped sadistically on your bare knuckles. I have already mentioned that there was a handball alley of sorts in the area back of the school. I loved the game and played it rain or shine;

and there was another boy of my own age, George Reynolds, of the "Golden Ball," who also loved the game and was my constant opponent. Whenever the handball alley was wet, which, being in Dublin, it was more often than not, our hands would get muddied, and as there was nothing but a water cock in the area— no soap, brush, or towel—our hands would not be immaculate. So George and I got it—plenty of it—from this stickler for cleanliness. And what about this tippling sadist himself; what about his own hands? Many a time I served his Mass in Whitefriars' Street. He would go to the altar bleary and unwashed, and the hands he held out so that I might pour wine and water over his fingers, were unspeakably dirty.

Just one more incident about this boyo. During recreation time one day in the early summer of 1889, I saw him in the yard with a great leaf of large succulent strawberries. These he distributed one by one to several of the boys. I pretended not to notice what was going on. After a little while he came over to me and offered me a particularly luscious berry, but I refused to take it. He coaxed me; then pressed me, but I still refused. He put the leaf aside, caught me with his left arm round my shoulders and with both hands he tried to force open my mouth to stuff the strawberry in it. I resisted with all the vigor I had and being balked in his design, he pressed the large berry against my lips till it was squashed and scattered cayenne pepper, with which it had been filled, all over my face.

This fellow wasn't typical of the Seminary; he was the exception. However, there was, indeed, a terrible looking layman, Hanratti, the music teacher—"Hamrasher," of course, was his nickname. He was a middle-aged burly fellow who wielded without stint something like a potstick that had been burned at both ends. The music lessons he inflicted on us might have emanated from Hades; the part singing, the harmony and the resultant discordant shrilling from the throats of about thirty reluctant boys all intent on doing violence to some dismal composition like the *Canadian Boat Song*. It was awful! But I don't suppose it was unique, for I think there were few schools in those days, particularly among the so-called "more exclusive" group, that did not inflict similar tortures on their sensitive adolescents.

For the rest, the Carmelite Seminary wasn't bad at all, and there were some splendid fellows among the priests and novices who taught there; men like Father Dunne who succeeded Donegan as President; Father Michael Byrne, a young strapping, almost bald-headed blond priest, who had just returned after some years in New York, and who at that time always said Mass in a loud voice making every syllable of the Latin he read plainly audible. And there was Father Doyle, who for a very brief period gave French lessons, and thought it a cute trick to put a finger to the side of one's nose to produce the required nasal effect.

Also a Mr. McCabe, a young novice; tall, blond and athletic, with the figure and face of an Adonis. He invited me to spend a day with him in the playgrounds of Terenure College. When I arrived with cousin Mary in Terenure that morning, I was ushered into a waiting room, where there were logs burning in an open fireplace. At one side of this room there was a small Chippendale table covered with green baize, and in the centre of this table there was a chessboard, with red and white carved ivory chessmen. I was thrilled, and for the second time in my life I fell in love with—well, I was going to say a game, but it couldn't have been the game I fell in love with for I didn't become proficient in it till I was eighteen. I suppose what I fell in love with that cool spring morning was just chess.

In the Seminary there was also Father Felix Cullen who taught Latin, and who was the only teacher in my life who would seem to have aroused in me the desire to emulate in school or college studies. I say "seem" because it was not so—my one motive for improving my studies was to please Father Felix. There still existed in this school the old system of having pupils in a class move bottomwards or topwards in accordance with their ignorance or knowledge. When Father Cullen first came to teach us Latin, I stood at the bottom of the class, but after school one day he took me to the parlor and talked kindly and understandingly to me—and from that day until the day he ceased to be our Latin teacher, no one ever displaced me from the top of the class.

It was around this time that Father Doyle asked me to join the choir at all services. Being himself a devoted and talented musician, he wished to have me follow in his footsteps. In my home there were two musical instruments; one a pianoforte, and the other, a very beautiful piece of work, an eighteenth century "Clementi" piano, on which from the time I was six years old Cousin Mary used to have me finger some of her favorites like, *Minnie, dear Minnie, come o'er the lea,* and *Under the willow* with golden hair. For myself, I was partial to some of *Moore's Melodies,* as well as to some other tunes that were less melodic than they were menacing and portentous, tunes like *We'll hang James Carey on the sour apple tree.* In Whitefriars' Street, Father Doyle had given me lessons on the harmonium, and had once had me play *Adeste Fideles* on the lowest keyboard of the three-manual organ. So when he asked me to join the choir and I demurred, he was shocked. I did consent to go to the choir at ordinary ceremonies like Vespers and evening Benedictions, but I could not bring myself to mingle with the "swells" and "toffs," some of them professionals, who made up the choir on all special occasions. Among these professionals at that time, was one, J. C. Doyle, who achieved a national reputation for his baritone rendering of folk songs like *The Ould Plaid Shawl.*

Every Sunday evening the routine was Vespers, sermon, and Benediction. When the Vespers were over, I must record in all truthfulness that the choir members, to a man, all took occasion to go away from there while the sermon was being delivered. I, however, not being a man, invariably stayed on to listen. And I did this not because of any sense of obligation to do so, but for the perhaps quaint reason that I liked to listen. And in this way I made a lot of discoveries. For example, I discovered to my own amazement, that after listening to a sermon I could have re-delivered it virtually word for word, and with almost the fidelity of a gramophone record. Then I began to recognize the individual in the sermon he preached; so that if anyone had given me a few phrases of the sermon together with their rate of delivery, I could have named the preacher; and I discovered, too, that the simulation of sincerity in a preacher was something that he could not hide by such devices as emphasis, gesturing or shouting. A case in point was one ignorant man, a Father Behan, who, for some obscure reason, was elected Prior at least for one term. This gentleman constituted himself a raucous authority on his favorite topic, impurity. In every sermon he preached, he always worked up to a point where he shouted: "Those who" and "Those who" and "Those who" in a crescendo of excoriation. Those "Thoses" were all made up of groups of despicable wretches, each succeeding "Those" being worse and still worse than the "Thoses" preceding; until the last "Those," which included only human reptiles richly deserving of being consigned for all eternity to that lower deep within the lowest depth.

CHAPTER TWO

"How much are your penny oranges?"

ONE SATURDAY in the spring of 1890, when I had just
turned ten, I was thurifer at Benediction after the
last Mass. Father Felix Cullen was the celebrant. As he faced the
congregation making the Sign of the Cross with the Monstrance
held in his elevated hands, it was my part in the ceremony to
wave the thurible in keeping with the movement of the Monstrance, and the thurible would make that tinkling sound as it
fell back against the looped chain. After the Benediction was
over, and as I was about to assist Father Cullen in taking off his
veil, he stooped down; took my head in his hands and whispered
gently into my ear, "Johnny, me boy, you're a sceptic!" Of course,
I knew how he knew, and he knew that I knew how he knew. But
neither of us ever said a word about it. I was greatly relieved to
know that he knew, for I liked him very much, and at that time
he was the one person I would have accepted with least reluctance into my confidence. The fact, too, that he had whispered as
he had, and had addressed me as "Johnny" was comforting. No
other person except my mother had ever called me "Johnny."

Only on one occasion after that did he ever again broach the
subject, and that was on the next day, Sunday, while we were
walking in the garden back of the confraternity chapel; and all
he said on that day was to suggest that maybe I would like to
read Balzac's *Letters to a Sceptic*. Now, in regard to the name of
the author of this book, I may have been wrong at the time in
thinking Father Felix said "Balzac," or maybe the priest erred.
For I have only recently looked up this point, and I can find no
trace of Balzac's having written such a work. That Sunday in the
garden, however, I had no doubt about the name being Balzac;

and I had no desire then nor since to read anything that gentleman had to say about sceptics or any other subject.

During my time in Whitefriars' Street, the altar boys were
under special charge of Father Wheatley, pale, thin, wrinkled and
dyspeptic. Normally the altar boys were enrolled in two societies,
Children of the Angels, and Children of Mary, but in Father
Wheatley's regime, there was another society, Children of the
Blessed Sacrament, which, I believe, was introduced to Whitefriars' Street first by him. Only the older boys were enrolled in
this society; and on the altar they were easily distinguished by
their special regalia, consisting of a long Italian-cloth soutane,
with white braid on sleeves and on the stand-up collar; a white
cincture, with suspending white braid and tassel, and a two-and-
one-half-inch wide red poplin ribbon round the neck; and from
this ribbon there was pendant over the chest a three-inch diamond
shaped rhinestone-studded bronze reliquary, with a little oval
glass-covered case in the center in which there was a relic. The
relic in the little case I had, with the name written in almost micro-
scopic scroll, was of St. Angela.

Father Wheatley was a holy little man. Generally, he appeared
sad, but on some occasions he could be joyous, this being notably
so whenever one or more of his boys would be about to be received into the order. And these occasions were not infrequent;
for there were four boys whom I knew well became novices in a
space of about five years; they were Denis Devlin; some seven
years my senior, his younger brother Hugh Devlin; Bob Power,
and Paddy Wade, who was for a great many years in the Carmelite Church in 29th Street, Manhattan. When I landed from the
"Baltic" on May 8, 1910, Paddy was on the pier to meet me, and
he was the only person I then knew in the United States.

One afternoon when I was about eleven or twelve, I was playing ball with Paddy in the yard of the church. While we played
a small group of boys looked on; in this group there was one
little fellow, about nine years of age who was a protégé of mine.
His name was Charlie Ronayne. He was black-haired, diminutive,
thin and delicate, but always with a keen sense of humor and
ready for a laugh. After we had been playing for a little while two
novices, who apparently had the same idea, came out to the yard,
and one of them, Mr. Peter Magennis, an advanced novice, caught
my ball on a hop, and with never a word to me, began to play

"handball" with the other novice. I have put the word in inverted commas because at that game, young as I was, I could have licked the two of them together. I didn't relish having my handball confiscated, and if it had been anyone other than a cleric I would have made that fact known and would have done something about it. Since it was two clerics who were playing with my ball, I didn't say or do anything. So these two novices went on playing this game they were playing, and which, no doubt, they would have called handball, when suddenly, Mr. Peter Magennis, the lout, rushed after the ball, made a swipe at it with his hand; missed it, and stumblingly kicked it into the yard of the adjoining old National School.

Did Mr. Magennis come to me with assurance that he would either have my ball retrieved, or that he would replace it? He did not. Did he apologize to me, or did he say anything to me at all? Again, he did not. He and his companion just footed it back in silence to the cloister from which I would have preferred they had not emerged. As Mr. Magennis retreated to the House that afternoon, he could not foresee that he was destined to be the first Irishman ever to be elected General of the Carmelite Order; and neither could he foresee that little Charlie Ronayne, who had witnessed the whole incident, and who was doubled up in laughter at the fun of it, was destined to be his own Assistant General of the Carmelite Order.

One of the oddities in Whitefriars' Street was a person named Dillon Cosgrave, an advanced novice who remained that way. He had been ordained deacon, but there he stopped. He either wouldn't, or wouldn't be let, go on; and he couldn't go back. Apparently he had reached the point where "returning were more tedious than go o'er." For Dillon even the most elementary mathematics and physics had no meaning; and possibly on that account, he was in a way the most extraordinary genius I have ever met. His knowledge of general literature and of the arts, including the literature of music, was extraordinarily comprehensive. He knew such tomes as *Burke's Peerage,* and *Thom's Dublin Directory* from cover to cover. Whenever a street band struck up, he couldn't resist following it. Occasionally, he asked me to go on one of these peregrinations; and on our way through the city he would keep up a ceaseless prattle about incidents, historic, memorable, notorious or infamous, connected with the neighborhood we were in, or even individual houses we passed.

Dillon Cosgrave was an elder brother of the "Lynch" in Joyce's *Ulysses* and the *Portrait*. He was of medium size, blond, and near-sighted; and always he remained as simple and trusting as an unspoiled child. At sacerdotal ceremonies he was a complete failure. Often when they tried him out at the 7 o'clock First Friday High Mass on the side altar to the left of the church, he would literally fumble and tumble, himself and missal, all over the steps of the altar.

I was told that it was his practice when eating dinner always to eat his potatoes first. His fellow novices were constantly playing practical jokes on him, like the time they said to him, when they saw a formidable-looking female at a fruit stand, "Dillon, ask the woman how much are the penny oranges." And Dillon did. He went over and, peering at the lady, enquired, "How much are your penny oranges." She gazed at him sharply, and being quite certain that he, cleric or no cleric, was trying to cod her, she stooped and picked up from a bucket a green-moldy orange and holding it menacingly in her hand she screamed, "Go 'long wid yerself, y' unholy spalpeen. If ye don't get out o' me sight at wanst, here's a penny orange I'll let ye have, where ye won't like it, fer nawthin."

In September, 1892, I entered Belvedere College, then under the rectorship of Father Tom Wheeler. The room I was first put in was No. 4, at the end of a long corridor that ran east and west in the north side of the building. The teacher's dais in this room was near its southeast corner; and in the northwest corner there was a door leading down to the chemistry and physics laboratory, in which a teacher named P. Bertram Foy held sway. Opening on the corridor I have mentioned were four classrooms numbered 1 to 4; being respectively for the senior, middle, junior and preparatory grades. All four rooms were "connected" by folding doors, and when these doors were all open at once, as they always were during lunch-time, a proctor could, and did, oscillate uninterruptedly from No. 1 to No. 4, and back; preserving a modicum of order in all the classes.

The teacher of English in my first year was one Father Fagan, who liked me, and whom I liked. It was interesting, and indicative, that Father Fagan asked me one day shortly after I had joined his class, whether I was of Scotch origin or parentage. Perhaps he was thinking of Bobby Burns and confused our names, but this is most unlikely. The fact is that Father Fagan, and indeed the great majority of the Jesuits in Dublin, had few friends or acquaintances among persons who were born and bred on one of the banks of the Liffey.

In my early days my parents had their place of business and residence on the south side of Essex Street next door to the big workshop of Donegan's, the famous Dublin jewelers. On the opposite side of this street, Mary and Cicely Fleming occupied the upper part of 20 East Essex Street. Cicely was an expert dressmaker, employed for years in Cameron's, Grafton Street, and later with Switzer's. Mary was in business partnership with an Emily Pentland who lived with us for years as one of the family. The business in which Mary and Emily engaged, and in which Cicely helped out on occasions, was the manufacture (using this word in its strictly literal sense) of everything pertaining to sacerdotal vesture, including copes, vestments, surplices, birettas, and the rest, and also in the sale of all kinds of church ornaments, statues and appurtenances. The premises for this business were at 25 Wellington Quay, where we occupied the whole of that house, except the shop.

Emily Pentland had an elder sister, Julia, who was a highly placed and highly prized employe of Bull's extensive church supplies warehouse in Suffolk Street, and from this connection the sisters benefitted mutually. Both Julia and Emily were well educated and well bred. Emily had suffered an accident to her left leg which deprived her of its use; she walked on a wooden leg, without a crutch, but with the aid of an umbrella. The wooden leg was strapped to her thigh and waist; and as no part of her injured leg had been amputated, the portion from her knee to her foot stuck out behind her and was a continuous occasion of accident and discomfort. However, she was always cheerful, enjoyed excellent health, including a perfect set of teeth, till her death at 73, in 1903. She died in our home at 100 Phibsboro Road, after an eight months' siege of cancer, which apparently gave her no pain. Indeed, she died without knowing what was wrong with her. Emily had been a novice in a nunnery in France but could not quite make it. After leaving the convent, and as she was proceeding home, she was enmeshed in Paris during its frightful siege in the war of 1870. Emily was a close lifelong friend of the Allingham family, the immensely rich wine and spirit merchants of 99 and 100 Capel Street, Dublin. Two or three nights a week, and every week-end, she spent with them in their mansion, Seafield, Dollymount, facing the Bull Wall. Oweson Allingham was the second-last survivor of the family, and when he died in the last years of the nineteenth century he bequeathed all his property to his sister Jane (who was already wealthier than Oweson had been) with a written expression to her of his wishes for its disposition. Jane carried out her brother's wishes to the letter. Among them was one that four hundred pounds should be given to Emily Pentland, and another of his wishes was that a sum of eighty thousand pounds sterling be put aside as a nucleus for a fund to build a Catholic Cathedral in Dublin. I don't know what ever came of this.

In such circumstances it will be clear that Mary Fleming was the active partner in the business with Emily. Mary was not educated in the sense that Emily was; neither did she possess her polish. But Mary was vastly more shrewd in business matters and was recognized as one of the best judges in Dublin of all goods, particularly cloths, required in church usage. As a business woman, however, Mary had one terrible drawback—she had no idea of the value of time. She would walk from shop to shop and spend hours of effort to save a farthing. A consequence of this which affected me personally as a child was that almost every day when I returned from school I found the fire out, with many a household chore left for me.

The shop on 25 Wellington Quay was the business office and showplace of Kane Brothers, church decorators and house painters, and the shop on 20 East Essex Street was the workshop of these same Kanes. The Kane family, consisting of father, mother, uncle, son and two daughters, resided on one floor in 26 Wellington Quay. They were the landlords of that house and of many others in the neighborhood, including 25 Wellington Quay and 20 East Essex Street.

At the extreme rear of the hall in 20 East Essex Street there were two doors, one opening to the north and the other to the east. The door opening to the north gave entry to a small cellar; and then down a few steps to the large basements of 25 Wellington Quay. One night when I was five years old I was passing in the dark from 20 East Essex Street to 25 Wellington Quay; and when I stepped down from the cellar to the basement I found myself in water to above my knees; and I was almost immersed in the waters of Anna Liffey as she was revisiting her ancient domain on an occasion of exceptionally high tide. This was the first time I had ever observed the phenomenon or had come into personal contact with it, but although intensely surprised, I was not frightened.

When you opened the door to the east at the back of the Essex Street hall, you went down about three stone steps to a yard in which, on its north side, there was a water closet that had to serve for three houses—and which was always filthy. Twice I had typhoid fever. During my first year in Belvedere I had one attack, and nine years later I suffered another. To make matters worse Mary got it too, and during her illness she would permit no one except me who had barely recovered, to do anything for her.

From this yard there was another door, which we never used, leading to 25 Wellington Quay; and at the east side of the w.c. there was a passage leading to 26 Wellington Quay. Walking through this passage and up to the hall of 26, you found as you passed through the hall that you were in a book shop, which had been constructed by tearing down the east wall of the hall and partitioning off a portion of the main shop. This portion had also a part of the main window in front of it, and was about six feet wide and about fourteen feet in depth. Thousands of times as child and boy have I passed through that hall with its bookshop. When I was very young, I was rather leery of its proprietor —a stout, greying, reddish-faced, loud-voiced man, with glaring, protruding grey eyes. But as I grew in boyhood I found that he was just a harmless gasbag.

In *Ulysses,* Chapter X, there is a short description of the man: "The shopman's uncombed grey head came out and his unshaven reddened face, coughing. He racked his throat rudely . . . and bent, showing a raw-skinned crown, scantily haired."

Josh Strong was the name of the man who owned the bookshop, and he was a Jew. In the little window of the shop the passersby on Wellington Quay could see a few selected books which had been hung in the window with their pages spread at some illustration with popular appeal. You would see, if you looked, not a few books which have since become collectors' pieces—*Penny Horribles; Ha'penny Dreadfuls; Deadwood Dicks; The Mysteries of Paris; Hell Open to Christians* (referred to in *Ulysses,* Chapter X) and *The Newgate Calendar.* There was also the *Apocalypse*

of St. John, of which I often heard Josh shout to a customer or
browser, "Here's something for ye—the ravin's of a madman in
the horrors." And hanging prominently in the window with its
pages open at a colored illustration of a fecund uterus, was a
small, thick book called *Aristotle's Masterpiece.* This little shop
presided over by Josh Strong was the shop which, in Joyce's
Ulysses, Bloom frequents in search of various pieces of literature
for his Molly, and from which he had procured a copy of the
book which Molly called the "Aristocrat's Masterpiece."

Josh Strong came to "work" every morning at eight thirty, and
closed shop at about five thirty in the evening. During the day
he never went out to lunch, but he had a little finish-burning
lamp on which he cooked vittles of a sort a couple of times each
day. Josh was a real "card"—a veritable oddity even among
owners of second-hand bookshops in Dublin—and he didn't seem
to care about anything or anybody. Why he lived as he did, I
cannot say, but it was not because of poverty. He was a wealthy
man and owned house property appraised at several thousand
pounds. Josh had an elder bearded brother who ran a bookshop,
situated about a furlong to the east, in Merchant's Arch right
across the quay from the entrance to the Metal Bridge. This shop
is also menioned in *Ulysses,* Chap. X, "A dark backed figure under
Merchant's Arch scanned books on the hawker's car." This is
inaccurate in that there was no car in the Arch; the books were
on shelves. This older Strong was a different kind of person from
the younger. Generally he was taciturn, and when he did speak
he spoke softly. Also, he did not feature the species of literature
Josh liked most to peddle.

The main shop at 26 Wellington Quay, from which Josh's
cubbyhole had been partitioned, was rented by one Figatner,
another wealthy Jew and jeweler. Fig was altogether a different
character from Josh. He had the reputation of being well versed
in Oriental languages. I was told he had lectured in these languages in Trinity College, but this I never verified. He always
wore a black hat, frock coat, flamboyant waistcoat with a gold
chain like a hawser, and spats. Somewhere around 1894 he was
married to a young Irish girl, daughter of the caretaker of the
local Workmen's Club on Wellington Quay. In *Ulysses,* Chapter
XV, Josh Strong and Figatner are referred to, the former as "the
bookseller of *Sweets of Sin.*"

On Wellington Quay, about midway between the bookshops of the brothers Strong, there was another divided shop run by people named Moulang and Goyer, the latter selling pictures, frames, etc. In Goyer's window there were featured Currier and Ives and "Darktown" pictures—including "Fire Brigade," "Cock Fights" and "Dog Fights." One of the last named groups had a legend reading, "She'd have won the money only for the other dog" (*Ulysses*, Chapter XII). Another picture of this series that I recall bore the legend "It's pickin' up money backin' does yer pup."

When I was young I often heard people in my neighborhood refer to and talk about Dean Swift as if he had been up and around the day before yesterday. In Belvedere some of the boys were what we denizens of the Liffey bank would, at that time, have called West Britishers, hailing as they did from places on the outskirts of the city where the letter "R" had been flattened out to "W," and where the word "door" no longer rhymed with "poor."

Many a night in my home I went to sleep literally on the bosom of Anna Liffey. On occasions when the tide was unusually high she would spread herself out over her ancient bed, and flood our cellars with a foot or so of aqua not so pura. Whenever this occurred you could hear the water bubbling and gurgling merrily in the numerous crevices through which it reascended, and as the flood subsided it made sucking sounds which later softened to sighs and kisses expressive of its sorrow at parting. However, I had often heard that "to the pure all things are pure"; and one of cousin Mary's most frequently uttered of her numerous maxims was, "Cleanliness is next to Godliness," and to her, of course, the notion of Godliness was the highest possible form of beauty.

It was easy for me therefore to come to regard the river as tending through cleanliness to beauty; a thought which, as I later realized, was what Keats had expressed when he spoke of:
> *The moving waters at their priestlike task*
> *Of pure ablution round earth's human shores.*

Yes, as a little boy I learned to love the river for its dual and blended attributes of utility and beauty; and after nightfall when the sandman came to visit me I could lull myself to sleep by listening to the fancied music of the bubbling, gurgling, sighing, and kissing waters of our "Anna Liffey."

CHAPTER THREE

Ivanhoe—My God—a NOVEL!

IN JANUARY, 1893, just four months after I entered Belvedere, my mother died, and I remember appreciatingly the kind things Father Fagan said to the assembled class about me and my bereavement when I returned to school after her burial. This friendliness on his part was of short duration, ceasing abruptly in the next month, February, when I became thirteen years old; and its cessation was due to his flagrant injustice to me. It was Father Fagan's practice in his English class once or twice a week to read for a quarter of an hour from some story book. During that month he was reading *Eugene Aram,* and he advised us boys to improve our English by reading other books ᶜ a similar character; among these mentioning the name of *Ivanhoe.* Now the very name *Ivanhoe* attracted me, and I went to the Confraternity Library in Whitefriars' Street, where one Tommy Hickey, a personal friend of my cousins and a frequent visitor to our home, was librarian. Tommy was thin and lanky; and he seemed to me not very far from seven feet in height. He was so tall, and so conscious of it, that he always walked stooped forward. Of course, he couldn't escape being joked about as "here's me head, and me heels are comin'." After last Mass one Sunday, when the library was open, Tommy lent me a copy of *Ivanhoe,* which I took home with me, and read hungrily during the whole afternoon. Cousin Mary, seeing me reading a book and obviously enjoying it, was naturally interested, because she knew it couldn't be a school book. So she asked me what it was, and I told her about it enthusiastically. She then looked over my shoulder at the book, and as it happened, on the open page there was something about friars that Mary didn't approve of.

"That isn't a school book," says Mary. "What's the name of it—who wrote it?"

I turned to the front of the book, and on the title page I pointed out to her:

Ivanhoe
A NOVEL
By
Sir Walter Scott

"My God—a NOVEL!" exclaimed Mary, and the way she said it you would have thought it was a SPIDER. "Where did you get that thing?"

"I got it in the Confraternity Library—Tommy Hickey lent it to me."

"Why did he do that, did you ask him for it?"

"Yes, I did."

"And how did you know anything about a thing like that, who told you about it?"

"Father Fagan told us boys to read some good books, books like . . ."

"Like *Ivanhoe*," she interrupted, "a NOVEL—by Sir Walter Scott—whoever the wretch is. So Father Fagan, a Jesuit, tells you to read NOVELS. I'll see about that the first thing in the morning."

And next morning before school opened she stood, personifying outraged Christian womanhood, confronting Father Wheeler in his rectorial office, demanding to know if it was true that the priests in Belvedere encouraged the boys in their school to read NOVELS?

What was the result of this pitiable little tragi-comedy? That same day when Father Fagan entered the English class he was plainly abashed. He sat down before his desk on the dais, and as he did so I saw his face was purple. Looking down at his hands, he remained silent for a minute, and then he said solemnly, "I have been informed that a boy in this class has been telling his people at home that the priests in this college advise the pupils to read novels. I won't mention the boy's name" he went on, looking straight down at me sitting in the back row, "he should be thoroughly ashamed of himself for his conduct. It has come as a great shock to me."

And during the remainder of that school year while I was in his class there was no more reading. *Eugene Aram* remained unfinished; and to Father Fagan I was as the slug in his rosy apple.

This incident occurred in February 1893. Two months later a frail-looking lad named James Augustine Joyce was entered in Belvedere College.

That experience I had with Father Fagan stands out as my one big memory of my three years in Belvedere College. The corroding injustice of it was to me inexplicable. There was, however, one mitigating circumstance. The boys in my class sympathized with me, and many of them came to me after class to comfort me and urge me to cheer up. "What's he so angry about," they wondered, "he did advise us to read *Ivanhoe*." As a late commentary on this experience, it may be worth mentioning that *Ivanhoe* always has remained one of my favorites among the comparatively few books I have enjoyed.

During my time in Belvedere, the teachers could not have been characterized as outstanding members of their profession. Indeed, it might well be questioned whether there ever was, or ever could be, such a thing as a great teacher. I have my own opinion on this point. I think none of the clerical teachers in Belvedere was deserving of a high rating as a teacher; and, assuming my judgment in this to be correct, I think the explanation is that they had been assigned to the kind of work they didn't like. There was one lay teacher, P. Bertram Foy, who seemed the best. But I realized even at the time that my higher opinion of him as a dominie was due not so much to his own greater efficiency, as to the fact that he taught subjects in which I was then interested, drawing, physics, and chemistry. These two last-named subjects stirred my imagination, and, indeed, it was in Foy's class in 1895 that I first conceived the story, *The Throne of Chaos,* that we come to later on.

* * *

One day every summer the altar boys in Whitefriars' Street were taken on an "excursion." Two or three drags, into each of which about twenty boys could be packed, were hired from Flanagan's livery stable in Aungiers Street. Hampers and baskets laden with food, fruit and soft drinks were swung underneath the drags, and the boys would be off to spend a day in some popular resort, usually Powerscourt Waterfall. These expeditions I detested, for whenever I was on one I invariably suffered from frightful headache, superinduced by the ceaseless noise made by the cheering, shouting and singing.

One of these excursions I did enjoy, and it left a deep impression on me; it was in the summer of 1893. When we set out that early morning for Powerscourt, Erin had a smile in her eye; but by the time we reached the Scalp, her smile had been washed away by a flood of tears. The rain poured down on us, and as we had passed the point of no return, it was decided to camp for the day in a wayside hotel in the lovely village of Stepaside. Of this little hotel we took full possession, including its kitchen. In the capacious diningroom a huge fire was lit, and here we took turns drying ourselves before dinner. After the dinner things had been cleared away, we improvised a variety entertainment of dancing, musical instrument playing, recitals and singing, and it is of this last-named that I will forever entertain the fondest memory. Among the clerics who were with us that day was a young, dark, very good looking, unpretentious novice by the name of Larkin. He possessed the most strikingly beautiful tenor voice I have ever heard. He sang selection on selection, and melody after melody with the abandon and "full throated ease" of a nightingale. I could see that he loved to sing. I took my courage in my hands: "Mr. Larkin, I asked, "would you please sing *The Coulun* for us?" And without saying a word, and playing his own accompaniment, without script, on the piano, he broke into: "The last glimpse of Erin." I was enchanted. It was my favorite melody and when he came to the words "one chord from that harp or one lock from that hair," I knew that I had heard something I would remember forever.

Not long afterwards young Larkin was ordained in Rome; and it was with more regret than surprise I heard he had been "se-lected" for the Vatican Choir. I never had a chance to ask him how he felt about the "honor," because I never saw him again. In about a year he was dead of tuberculosis.

I have previously referred to my boyhood friend and school-mate, Bob Power, who was also a fellow altar boy in Whitefriars' Street. In 1894, Bob and I were walking home from night services in Whitefriars' Street. It was a solemn occasion, for he was going home that night for the last time. On the morrow, the only child of doting parents, he would enter the Carmelite novitiate in Terenure College. Bob was a truly splendid fellow. As we walked home that night, he did most of the talking. However, I did ex-press my sorrow at the prospect of losing a companion. I was quick to add I felt glad for his sake that he was about to fulfill his vocation. Then he turned to me and said very earnestly, and rather surprisingly, "John, don't think for a minute I'm under any delusion that when I join the Carmelite Order I'll be lying on a bed of roses."

A few mornings later, Bob was received together with three others into the Order. One of them was also a long-time altar-boy friend of mine, Hugh Devlin. The two others were named Canavan and Farrell. After the reception, at which Father Hall officiated, there was a reception breakfast. I was the only lay person invited, and at the table was seated directly opposite Father Hall. The murmur of a young lector who was reading on a perch away to my right was barely audible in the room, and no one seemed to pay any attention to what he read. Just as we were about to break bread, Father Hall looked over at me with his usual rogueish smile, saying slowly and pleasantly, "I think I know who will be the next young gentleman I'll have the pleasure of receiving into the Order."

* * *

Later that year, when the time for the Forty Hours' Adoration was approaching, Father Wheatley asked three of us to be on hand to assist in the decoration of the High Altar. In those years the floral arrangements were under the supervision of an elderly buxom lady named McGrath; and she always had some ladies working under her direction in the disposition of plants and flowers which were provided in cartfuls. As I was performing some chores in the vestry I saw the door open and something fascinating happened. A girl entered and crossed the room to the buxom lady. She was young and fair and like an opening flower. Her eyes were large and blue, her lips full, and nut-brown ringlets veiled her neck and fell profusely below her shoulders. She was laden down with roses, beautiful red roses, but the most beautiful rose of all was in the blush in her oval face brought there by her shyness. Instantly I loved her. But long afterwards, I knew that it was not love—it was worship. Her first name was Norah. She and her two brothers, both younger, had been made wards of a Father Ward, who was Prior of the Order, and they had been put in residence with a Miss Noonan who owned a house in Whitefriars' Street opposite the western or "body" entrance to the church. In the shop of this house Miss Noonan sold religious appurtenances; she ran another shop on York Row with similar merchandise opposite the southern entrance to the sanctuary. Since Norah lived beside the church I frequented, we saw each other constantly, but we did not speak. It was one late afternoon in May, 1895, a few days before her fifteenth birthday, that I encountered Norah, and a girl friend of hers, Kitty. We both happened to be putting letters into the same drop at the G. P. O. in O'Connell Street. Neither of us spoke, however, and we turned to go to our respective homes. I stopped to look in a shop window, and the girls stopped to look, not in that window, but the one beyond it. I moved from the window in which I was closely scrutinizing nothing; passed the girls at their window where they were similarly engaged, and stopped at the next window, to examine nothing with still greater diligence. The girls left their window and passed me at my window but stopped at the next window where they were likewise enthralled by nothing. The three of us played this little nameless game till, finally, we came to Chancellor's shop, and there I saw Kitty nudge Norah, who then approached me, and in a scarcely audible voice said, "Excuse me, sir, but could you tell us the correct time?" I turned my eyes upwards to the large, double-faced clock that was projecting over our heads, and then hoping that I would be able to find utterance, I ventured faintly, "It is a quarter to six."

For a full two minutes Norah and I looked at each other without a word, becoming more and more selfconscious and embarrassed until at last I began to fear that the blushing girl might run from me in fright. I managed to say to her, "I have seen you often around Whitefriars' Street, and since I first saw you I have wanted to know you; and I think you must know me, by sight. You are Norah Hogan and my name is John Francis Byrne—let me introduce myself to you." And Norah said simply, "Yes, of course, I know you, John, and I am very glad to meet you. I've been hoping for a long time that we would meet." Norah then introduced me to her companion, Kitty K., and we all three sauntered slowly by Westmoreland Street and Dame Street to the corner of George's Street, where, most reluctantly, I had to part from them, because it was now dinnertime and it was my chore to get it ready.

I got home to find the fire out, as usual, but I proceeded to light it in preparation for dinner, and for the second time in my life I was near ecstasy. After I had the fire going and the table set, I took down an old green cloth-covered volume of Shakespeare's complete works (I had bought it for sixpence from Josh Strong), and in the front of it wrote some little thing, including a hope-fully prophetic J. F. B., and N. B., and I made up my mind to go to Skerry's School and begin grinding for a job, preferably, a tele-graph operator, because the age limit for that, which was sixteen, was lower than for any other civil service job. To this end I decided to quit Belvedere after the June intermediate exami-nation, and to effect this beyond peradventure I determined to enter, and to pass, the autumn matriculation exam in the old Royal University; for if I should pass this, I would automatically cease to be a pupil in Belvedere. My scheme looked good and was good, insofar as it went.

That autumn I took the matric exam., and then went down to Wicklow, where a short time later I received word that I had passed. I was jubilant. Let me make it clear that it was not because Belvedere was ended, but because Skerry's would begin; and through that school I hoped to enter a job, make lots of money, so that by the time I was twenty-one I would have "lashins" for everybody and everything, but mainly for a little place where I would have Norah by me—in a tabernacle.

On my return to Dublin, I resumed my practice as an altar boy. For years it had been my habit to serve Mass at seven o'clock; sometimes, but very rarely, I would accompany Mary home. One morning in the first week of November, Mary asked me to wait for her after Mass. As we walked home together, who do you think we should meet, by some extraordinary coincidence, as I fully believed, at the corner of Dame Street and Eustace Street? It was Father Tom Wheeler, the priest to whom Mary had protested about *"Ivanhoe."* Father Wheeler was now Rector in University College, Saint Stephen's Green.

"Oh good morning, Miss Fleming, I'm very glad I met you. How are you? And how are you, John? I'm sorry for your trouble." He was referring to the death of my stepbrother Peter the week before.

"Thank you, sir," I said.

"Now that he has matriculated, Miss Fleming, what is he going to do?"

"Oh he wants to go to Skerry's."

"Send him round to University College. Come to see me there tomorrow morning, John."

Reluctantly I went to University College the next morning.

But when I walked up the steps and into the large hall I no longer regretted coming. I felt, perhaps for the first time, at home.

An attendant came up to me. "Are you looking for anybody?"

"I'd like to see Father Wheeler."

"What is your name?"

"My name is Byrne."

"Oh yes, Mr. Byrne. Father Wheeler is expecting you."

We went a few steps to the back of the hall, and along a passage way where I was ushered into Father Wheeler's office.

"Good morning John. I'm glad to see you. Just take a seat for a moment, I want to introduce you to our Dean of Studies, Father Darlington. He will be here in a moment." And sure enough, in a moment the Dean of Studies, brisk, genial and radiating culture, walked quickly into the room.

"Father Darlington, this is John Byrne. He is going to join the First Arts class here with us today."

"Delighted, Mr. Byrne, to meet you, and to welcome you to University College. Kindly come along with me." And this is how I ceased to be "John" and became officially for the first time, "Mister."

To Father Darlington I cottoned at once. He was a gentleman. In height and build he was something more than medium. Quick of movement, but not impetuous, he definitely gave me the impression of having been an athlete, although I never verified this. He was balding; pale, and his face was heavy, so it did not strike me that he was ascetic, though he may well have been. He had a high forehead; large grey-blue quizzical eyes; and a long—one might add, massive—chin, which may have been elongated more than nature intended by his persistent habit of stroking it downward with his right hand, while at the same time sucking his breath through puckered lips and usually winding up this gesture by ejaculating, " 'Pon my word!" His voice was soft baritone; and he spoke and lectured well, but not fluently. In moments of conversational pleasantry, he would start "washing his hands with invisible soap in imperceptible water." He was affable and keenly appreciative of wit or a humorous situation. He was pious, but his piety did not obtrude. I think that by nature he was self-conscious and prone to embarrassment, but if this was so he had schooled himself so well that it could only have been detected by a close observer. His education was wide and profound; his mentality alert, and he was richly endowed with common sense. He was a great educationalist, and in this capacity he was one of the very few I ever met who seemed thoroughly to enjoy his work.

The first class I entered at University College was one in English conducted by Tommy Arnold, brother of Matthew Arnold. Tommy was old not alone in years; he was old, and feeble, in fact. The class had begun a few minutes earlier, so Father Darlington knocked on the door, and without waiting for an answer opened it, nodded to Tommy, motioned me into the room, and closed the door behind me. I tiptoed forward and seated myself noiselessly at the nearest bench in front of a long table. Whether Tommy actually saw me come in, I don't know, he gave no sign. He kept his eyes on the little book of Gray's poems open in front of him, and he was calling on each member of the class to read a couple of verses from Gray's exquisite "Elegy." It happened to be the turn of a slim young man, about eighteen years of age, sitting across from me and facing me at the table. He couldn't have weighed more than ninety pounds. He was thin, rosy-cheeked, and strangely girlish, in appearance, in mannerism and voice—which was high-pitched, musical, and clear. The two verses which it was his turn to read were:

> "Th' applause of listening senates to command,
> The threats of pain and ruin to despise,
> To scatter plenty o'er a smiling land,
> And read their history in a nation's eyes,
>
> Their lot forbade: nor circumscribed alone
> Their growing virtues, but their crimes confined;
> Forbade to wade through slaughter to a throne,
> And shut the gates of mercy on mankind;"

I particularly noticed the way he glided, as the poet intended, from the first quatrain to the second, laying the proper emphasis on "Their lot forbade." It is strange that a little incident should impress one so and become indelible in one's memory. But so it is. This lissom youth, who at that time had a penchant for smirking, was one of several children of a prominent Dublin physician whose residence was a few doors west of Belvedere College. He had never been to school, but whether this was cause or effect I didn't know. Anyway, my pencil sketch of him will surprise many thousands of persons in the United States as well as in Ireland, who came to know him in after life as the first Chief Justice of the Irish Free State, Hugh Boyle Kennedy.

Only a few minutes after this recital there was another knock on the door, which again was opened without waiting for a "Come in." All eyes, except mine, were directed to the door, but I being so newly come, hesitated to show curiosity. After a minute had elapsed without anything happening, I did turn to look towards the door, and standing there, apparently in perfect composure, was a tall young man with round face, black hair, and large dark eyes. His eyes met mine, and he came over with assured deliberation and sat beside me. This tall young man became one of my closest friends in University College. He was Jim O'Toole, who established a reputation as the best pure mathematician to have been in the college up to his time. But despite this, and I am not being flippant, Jim O'Toole was one of the most widely and deeply intelligent men, as well as one of the most noble, I have known.

To me, and to one other, my attendance at University College had a beautiful circumstance. Norah was a pupil in Loretto College on Stephen's Green, scarcely more than a furlong away; and every morning, rain or shine, I met her at eight o'clock near Whitefriars' Street and walked with her to the Green, where we would stroll on the south walk in the Green in front of University College till about five to nine.

As I was about to leave the college one afternoon at the end of my first month, a priest, with whom I had not before spoken, Father Henry Browne, professor of Latin, came to me at the foot of the broad staircase and said, "Mr. Byrne, if you are not in a hurry away, I'd like to have a little chat with you, may I?"

"I'm not in a hurry, Sir, I'll be delighted."

"Then let us look for some place where we can have our talk without being disturbed." We opened the door of the dim and beautiful oratory, and went in. Father Browne did not beat about the bush. "Mr. Byrne, I have been asked to talk with you about your plans for your future. What we want to know is whether you have any thought of entering the priesthood."

At this moment the oratory door was opened and Father Darlington peered in. "I beg your pardon," he said, and made as if to go out. But Father Browne said, "Oh, Father Darlington, Mr. Byrne and I were just having a chat. I'm sure he won't mind if you join us, will you, Mr. Byrne?"

"Quite the contrary," I replied truthfully.

Father Darlington closed the door and came in. Father Browne continued, "We have been told that the Carmelites have long been expecting you as a novice, and we know that it is the fondest ambition of your cousin, Miss Fleming, that you become a priest. Is not that correct?"

"Yes, Sir, it is."

"Well, are you under any kind of pledge, or promise, or understanding with the Carmelites?"

"No, Sir, I am not; several of them especially Father Wheatley and Father Hall have for a long time taken it for granted I would enter Terenure, but that is all. I have never promised anything to them."

"Well then we would be glad to have you enter our Jesuit novitiate. Would you think of doing that?"

I looked up at both priests for a long time without saying a word. First at Father Browne, then at Father Darlington; then again at Father Browne, and then once more at Father Darlington, and addressing myself to the latter I said something which I was sure would close the conversation. "But, Father Darlington, I must tell you that I have not the faith, I am not a believer."

And Father Darlington said quietly, "We know that." And from this point Father Darlington was the one who spoke to me. He went on. "Faith is the gift of God to man. Man may lose that gift in many ways, but so long as he does not deliberately and of his own free will throw it away, God may recover the gift for him and bestow it on him again. You are an unbeliever, but you are not invincibly so, are you?"

I thought this question over intently, and then I answered, "No."

"That's what we felt sure of, and we are confident that if you come to us your faith will return to you. You must remember that you are very young; you are only fifteen. God gave you two great gifts, the gift of Faith and the gift of a good mind; your gift of Faith has become mislaid, but the gift of a good mind you still possess, and you cannot but realize that at such a tender age your mind has not become permanently closed."

"Thank you, Father Darlington. I am very grateful to you; but there would be one other impediment to my entering your novitiate."

"And what is that?"

"My two cousins. I owe them a lot for what they have done for me, it is my duty, I believe, to do what I can for them."

And then Father Darlington gave me my one big surprise in this conversation. With deliberation he said, "We are in a position to give you assurance that if you enter the Jesuit Order, the welfare of your cousins will be provided for if either or both should be in need."

Once more I said, "Thank you again very much, Father Darlington, but there is still another obstacle. You know there is a girl. . . ."

Both of the priests smiled when I said this, and Father Darlington continued: "Yes, yes, of course, we know. There's no secret about that, the whole college knows it, but—well, you are young and she is younger. Anyway, we would like you to consider what we have said. We ask you to do that, and we want you to remember that if at any time within a year or so you might like to take up this matter again, we shall be delighted to have you come to us about it."

That was the one time this subject was broached. Never again during my connection of several years with the college was it even remotely referred to.

CHAPTER FOUR

The White Bishop

ONE MORNING, a few weeks after the "chat" in the oratory, I waited for Norah at our usual meeting place near York Street. It was a bitterly cold, raw morning a few days before the Christmas vacation. Having waited in the cold for more than a half-hour, I decided to go on to the college and to keep a look-out for her passing my window. It was about twenty minutes to nine when I came up to the first-arts class; and I was disappointed to find that it was nearly as cold in the room as it had been outside. The fire in the open grate had been lit carelessly, and it had gone out.

Just as I had taken my stand at the window watching for Norah, Father Darlington came swiftly into the room, looked at me, said "Good morning, Mr. Byrne, you're early aren't you?" To which I replied, "Yes, Sir, I'm earlier in class than usual." He then went over to the cold grate, peered into it, stood away from it, looked at me again, said nothing, and went out. Five minutes later, Father Darlington re-entered the room; looked at me; then around the room; then went over to the inhospitable grate; scrutinized it, looked at me and seemed about to say something, thought better of it and went out. At ten minutes to nine he returned to the room, and this time his manner and entry were different, it could be said that he came breezing in confidently. I was still at the window, for Norah had not yet come, but he appeared now not to be in the slightest degree disconcerted; he smiled at me and winked his right eye; and went straight to the fireplace. Stooping down before it, he picked out the singed coal putting it on the fender, then he pulled up his soutane and brought to view a paper bag which he rapidly tore open on the hearth, exposing a few "Evening Telegraphs" and a good supply of firewood. The papers he tore up and wisped and deposited in the grate, superimposing the bits of firewood, on which he redeposited the pieces of charred coal he had shortly before taken out. Then he lit a match, which he applied to the paper in the grate at each side and in the middle; and then he stood up hastily and looked over at me, still posted right at the window, but not with undivided attention. Lifting up his soutane once more, Father Darlington drew forth from somewhere a wee paper package containing three candle ends; these he placed strategically amid the coals on top of the fire, one at each side and one in the middle. When the melting candle grease burst into flame at all three places, he stood erect to survey his work and saw that it was good. Thereupon he produced his handkerchief, wiped his hands with it, replaced it, and in embarrassed but none the less boyish exultation, he turned to look at me. Being thoroughly pleased with himself and his achievement, he stroked his chin downward with his right hand; sucked his breath, and coming over to me said, " 'Pon my word, Mister— Mister Byrne, there's quite an art in lighting a fire, is there not!"

And all I said in reply was an emphatic assent. "Yes, sir, there certainly is." I did not offer any comment about his own exposition of the art, especially in the employment of candle ends. In fact, I said nothing more, for at this moment I saw Norah walking rapidly in the Green to school. She turned her face to look over at my classroom window, where she could see Father Darlington standing beside me. She waved to me with her right hand, and I waved to her, and she hurried on. Father Darlington was silent for a moment, and then with a wistful tone in his voice, he said: "I thought so. She's late, isn't she. Lovely child."

It was now a few minutes to nine, and already some of the pupils had entered the room. I didn't say anything, nor did Father Darlington. He just smiled at me benignly and left the room.

I have already made it plain that I liked Father Darlington, but after this incident the word "like" would have been altogether too feeble to express my regard for him. This was not alone for his remark about Norah, it was perhaps more for the fact that I believed he had admitted me as nearly to him as it would ever be possible for him to permit anyone to come. I felt sure that there was no one else in the college, lay or cleric, in whose presence he would have lit that fire as he did—candle ends and all.

It was not until seven years afterwards, in 1902, that I committed the blunder of telling Joyce about this incident of Father Darlington and the fire, and years later I regretted my indiscretion when I read how he used, or rather abused, the story in his *Portrait of the Artist*. When I visited Joyce in Paris in 1927, I criticized him for this, and I told him that instead of being an ornament to his book, the incident, as he narrated it, was a disfigurement. The reader of his book, I said, is left with the impression that, because of some "private griefs," Joyce was venting his spleen on Father Darlington. I reminded Joyce that he should have remembered what the fishwives in Mary's Abbey used to say to a fiddling and fingering customer. "If ye want the cod, ma'am, take it, but if ye don't want the cod, don't maul it." Joyce agreed with me, saying he was sorry he had written it as he had, and that he was sorry for certain other things he had written. So I said no more.

I assumed at that time that he had simply let himself go in a moment of fluent literary effusion, and that he had been for that moment "inebriated with the exuberance of his own verbosity." However, in 1944, when *Stephen Hero*, Joyce's first draft of the *Portrait of the Artist*, was published, I realized how wrong I had been in my assumption. For, in *Stephen Hero* the incident of Father Darlington's lighting the fire had been told by Joyce with approximate accuracy in fewer than two hundred words, whereas in the *Portrait of the Artist*, written long after the first draft, the incident has been elongated and elaborated to almost two thousand words of twaddle; in which Joyce labors to narrate a flat-footed conversational minuet à deux danced by himself and the dean of studies with all the grace and agility of a pair of sawdust dolls. In *Stephen Hero* Joyce had played exactly the same melody entitled "Pulchra sunt quae visa placent," and had indulged to its accompaniment in similar terpsichorean conversational antics—but with a different partner. His first partner had not been the dean of studies, but the President of the College, Father William Delaney.

Through what oversight has it happened that this passage at arms between Stephen and the dean has escaped the penetrating elucidation of Joyce's interpreters? To an exegete the passage should have been a magnet with irresistible attraction for his analytical prowess. One cannot but be amazed that no one appears to have realized the full significance of the *place* chosen by Joyce as the locale for his renditions. Reference has been made to Joyce's predilection for places "with Greek sounding names"; and what place could have a more Greek sounding name than "Physics Theatre," which not merely sounds Greek, but is in fact pure Greek?

Of course, when it comes to the interpretation of numbers, the subject might have been found a little more recondite than the number of that house of myth on Eccles Street. For, in the first draft, Joyce says the dean took out *three* "dirty" candle-butts, whereas in the *Portrait* the dean extracted *four* candle-butts, all of which must have been different from the *three,* because none of them is described as "dirty." Now what made Joyce change the number of "butts" from three, which is considerable of a mystic number in its own right—to such a vulgar and unmystic number as four? Puzzling, is it not? Not at all! The explanation is simple; for, mark you, if to the "three dirty" candle-butts which in *Stephen Hero,* the dean "produced from the most remote pockets of his chalkey soutane," you add "the four candle butts from the side pockets of his soutane," as detailed in the *Portrait,* you get a total of what? You get a total of *seven*—the very number of the mysterious house on "the street with the Greek sounding name," Eccles Street.

Furthermore, it may be observed that when Stephen perceived the figure of the dean "crouching before the large grate" in his act of lighting the fire, he opened the conversation with, "Good morning, sir! Can I help you?" And here it should well be noted that Stephen offered to help the dean to light the fire, forgetting what he had previously had reason a thousand times to remember that he himself could not light a fire. As he says only thirty seconds later "to fill the silence" in this arthritic conversation "I am sure I could not light a fire." And to this admission by Stephen what could be the only adequate comment one could make? Why, the only comment that would fill the bill here would be "Freudians please note!"

Pursuing the examination of this conglomeration of piffle, see how the archaic meaning of the word "detain" is laboriously introduced, and how Stephen himself misapplies the word when he says "I hope I am not detaining you." Observe also that word "tundish," of which the dean is made to say, "I never heard the word in my life," and yet Stephen goes on to say "The language in which we are speaking is his before it is mine . . . His language . . . will always be for me an acquired speech. I have not made or accepted his words," and Stephen admits that he "felt with a smart of dejection that the man to whom he was speaking was a countryman of Ben Jonson." Ben Jonson and Shakespeare were contemporaries and pals; and Shakespeare used the word "tundish"; and yet the Dean of Studies, a born Englishman and Oxford graduate, is depicted by Joyce as ruminating in infantile amazement over this Anglo-Saxon word, and saying that he had never before heard it in his life.

How or why Joyce wrote such stuff as this is a question I do not answer. But I do say that these mythical talks of Stephen with the President of the College, and with the Dean of Studies, are really interesting in that they reveal Joyce's immanent and abiding simplicity. In his own way, Father Darlington, too, was a simple man—and a strange man. But, I repeat, he was a good man —honest and sincere. Having already referred to his sense of humor, and now to his simplicity, I think that a little anecdote told in his own words will fully illuminate my two points.

In a book entitled *A Page of Irish History* Father Darlington is quoted as reminiscing about John Casey, who was professor of mathematics in the earlier days of University College. Here in his own words is a brief quotation from Father Darlington's yarns about Casey:

"In 1884 I joined his class of spherical trigonometry, and there saw the famous mathematician for the first time. . . . about every ten minutes he stopped talking, and rolling his pencil between his two hands in front of his face, he told us some amusing little anecdote. This, he believed, kept the attention of his hearers fresh—kept them wide awake. . . . During another interval of teaching I remember him telling us something more ludicrous. At a Conversazione in the college an eminent mathematician was standing near the buffet, holding in his hand a glass of soda-water. Seeing Casey he whispered, putting the glass behind his back, 'For heaven's

sake put something into it unbeknown to me.' The poor
man had taken the pledge!"

Do you want any better proof of Father Darlington's in-
genuous sense of humor!

Joseph Darlington was an alumnus of Brasenose College, Oxford, matriculated 1869, at nineteen, and M.A. 1876, and he had
been an Anglican minister. In University College he was always
on the go, and on the *qui vive;* and his one big aim in life seemed
to be to constitute himself a kind of perpetual and ubiquitous
lubricant against friction. Constantly he was trying to rectify the
errors or wrongdoings of others. In the college there was a full-
sized billiard table, reserved chiefly for the use of the boarders,
among whom there were sometimes to be found a couple of
bounders. And what these latter fellows could, and did, do to
the billiard table and the balls and the cues and the chalk was
disgusting. But it didn't seem to disgust Father Darlington. I saw
him frequently go into that room, pick up the billiard balls, and
cubes of green chalk from all over the floor; put tips on the cues,
and produce a curved needle with green thread to mend rips that
had been made maliciously in the green baize cloth on the
billiard table. I say I frequently saw him do these things, but I
could say that there was a period when he did them daily; and
the oftener I saw him do them, the more I wondered. Never did
I say anything to him about it, but I didn't have to tell him my
thoughts—he could read them in my face.

On one occasion a slippered boarder, this one being no
bounder, came down the broad staircase holding two boots in
his hand. To Father Darlington who was at the foot of the stairs,
he showed the boots and complained that they had not been
cleaned. Father Darlington looked at the boarder and then at
the muddy boots; stroked down his chin with his hand, the while
sucking his breath with more than usual force, as if gasping with
indignation. Then he exclaimed, " 'Pon my word, Mister, Mister
X, this certainly is outrageous. I must speak to the fellow and
see that this doesn't occur again." Young X was quite satisfied and
went immediately up to his room; and Father Darlington started
to go downstairs—with me following him. As we went along the
short passage I called out to him, "Father Darlington." He did
not turn nor answer, but started down the flight of steps. I called

out louder "Father Darlington," and again he ignored me. I went down the steps after him and was behind him on the lower passage when I called out for the third time "Father Darlington." He didn't say anything, but stopped and turned to me, whereupon I demanded, "Give me those shoes. I know what you're going to do, and I don't think it's right for you to do it. Give them to me and I'll polish them. I can do them well and I'd much rather do them than have you polish them." He looked at me, and was silent for a moment. Then, without any gestures he said, "Thank you, Mr. Byrne, but you know I couldn't do that. That would be wrong." "Well," I countered, "I think it's wrong for you to do them."

"Perhaps—perhaps it is," he said musingly. "But I am acting for what I think is best."

"Why didn't you tell X to do them himself?"

"The boarder is within his rights in expecting the service."

"Why not get the man to do them."

"He's—he's—not well," said Father Darlington, and I knew he meant the fellow was drunk.

"Well I think that if this man behaves that way, something ought to be done about it."

"Yes, maybe there should, but—well, there are complications."

I knew what he meant, and as there was nothing more for me to say I stood there silent. Immediately he went to a little press; and took out blacking, brushes, and cloths, and began cleaning the boots. I went away from him then without another word.

It was not until the beginning of the academic year 1898-9 that Joyce entered University College; and during that year I did not attend classes because I had been appointed tutor to the two Mooney boys, aged twelve and ten, of Elm Green, Castleknock. It was Father Darlington who asked me to take this job, which I was glad to do. The Mooneys had a beautiful residence on a large estate, and Mrs. Mooney, in her early thirties, was dark, poised and altogether charming. It was not until comparatively recently that I learned her name was Gretta, and the person who told me this was the late Thomas F. Woodlock, who had been an intimate friend of the Mooney family before he came to the United States.

I had made the acquaintance of Woodlock in 1911, when he was board member of the New York Stock Exchange firm of S. N.

Warren & Co. Later he was for many years an Interstate Commerce Commissioner, and still later, for many years until he died in 1945, columnist on the Wall Street Journal. His father owned a valuable residence and property at Chapelizod, on the Liffey, only about three miles from Elm Green, Castleknock. Woodlock had been an undergraduate student with the Jesuits in University College. His name is on the College Register for 1883.

On four days a week I cycled through the Phoenix Park to Elm Green and was there from ten to two-thirty. The boys were tractable, clever and good. After "school" was out, they used to walk with me down a stony and rutted path, and one day they asked me could I leap across it. I said I could, and I did, but in landing I stubbed my toe against a hidden rock and muttered something. The two lads were delighted, and when a little later we met Mrs. Mooney down the path, the elder boy, Willie, shouted out to her, "Oh Mother, Mr. Byrne said 'damn' he really did. He thought we wouldn't hear him but we did." And this was his way of telling his mother I was all right in his estimation.

When Joyce entered University College in September 1898, it was only natural for him to cleave to me. We had been together in Belvedere, and in the intervening years had maintained acquaintanceship. Joyce was nearly two years younger than I, and at our respective ages, eighteen and sixteen, these two years meant a lot, at least in physical and muscular equipment. Moreover, I was unusually strong, much stronger than anyone would have thought from my appearance, whereas Joyce was thin, light and weak. Due to this, my attitude toward him became, and to a great degree remained, protective.

Towards the end of 1896, I had been instrumental in arousing a certain degree of chess consciousness in a small group in University College. We raised some funds by passing the hat; and John Hooper, Skeffington and I were delegated to buy the required equipment. This we did in Lawrence's on Grafton Street, where we bought a half dozen sets of leaden-based Staunton chessmen, at three half crowns a set, with six large boards. The chess coterie had its sessions on Saturday afternoons and evenings, and once in a while some of the Jesuits, including Father Darlington, would participate. However, the group never amounted to anything as a chess center, this being partly due to the fact that there was only one person in it who seemed to have any idea of what the game was about. This person was Hugh MacNeill, and he was erratic. Francis J. C. Skeffington and I did continue on rare occasions to go through the motions of playing chess, and he was well aware of my keen desire to learn the game. It was he who told me of a newly-opened center for chess players in the smoke-room of the D. B. C. on Dame Street, and I decided to go there to see what it was like. I went one afternoon, and found the place was comfortably appointed, with about a dozen oval green tables, each having a chessboard inlaid in its center. In the drawer of each table there was a set of "Staunton" chessmen, and a set of draughts, and at each table there were two players, and almost every table had its fringe of kibitzers. On the bill of fare I read that one could get a pot of tea, with bread and butter, for three pence, or a "regular" tea, including a little ham or beef or tongue, with bread and butter, and a piece of cake or pastry for sixpence. I decided the threepenny one would do me, and it would be well within my means a few times a week.

On my third afternoon in the place, as I was standing intently, but quite uncomprehendingly, watching a game, a bearded gentleman came to me and inquired in a soft drawling voice, "Would you care to play a game of chess?" I replied eagerly, "Yes, sir, I would, but unfortunately I'm only a beginner."

"Everybody has to begin," he said, "there's no royal road to chess. Let's try a game. I'm a fairly good player, and if you care to accept it we can fix a handicap."

We sat down opposite each other at a table; and he ordered the sixpenny tea, only it was not tea but "cawf-ee" he asked for. His pronunciation of the word was something I had never heard, and I did not know what he meant till the waitress brought him coffee. I asked her to bring me the threepenny tea, and proceeded to set up the chessmen. Having played for a little while he could see I really knew next to nothing about the game, but he could also sense that I was most eager to learn. He tried me out in three or four games, giving me odds of the queen, and demolished me. However, he seemed to enjoy having me for an opponent; and he asked me to play with him again next afternoon.

This experience I was having in the D. B. C. was something entirely new and enjoyable in my life. I liked the atmosphere of the smokeroom, too; I mean the social, not the physical, atmosphere; for the latter to me, who did not smoke, was rank and almost stifling. But even in this respect the smokeroom couldn't compare with the room I had entered a short time previously in University College, when, on knocking at the door of the great Father Hogan's cubicle, I heard a welcoming "Come in." Obediently I turned the handle and went in, to find myself in an impenetrable and choking fog of tobacco smoke. As I stood groping inside the open door a voice to my right, which I realised later came from the throat of the illustrious priest lying on his couch, said gruffly but kindly, "It's all right, you'll get used to it, young man. Leave the door open and you can open the window wide for a bit if you like. I was just taking a pull."

The company in the D. B. C. smokeroom was heterogeneous; made up as it was of persons of various pursuits and professions, and of several religious and ethnological shades. For the greater part they addressed one another by their first names. All the men in it were mature, and almost all were financially well heeled. As for me, they must have thought I was a bit of a freak, because I certainly was different; and I didn't know anbody there. Even the flabby-faced, rather ponderous but courtly gentleman who had preempted me for his opponent remained a stranger until I had been playing with him for more than a week. Then one afternoon just as he had checkmated me, a gentleman in tall hat, frock coat, striped trousers, spats, and umbrella leaned over my shoulder and smiling at my opponent greeted him: "Hello Jack, who is your young friend—won't you introduce me?"

My opponent looked smilingly at me, and then he said to the gentleman in the tall hat. "I'd be delighted to, Porterfield, but—" then he said to me—"This is Mr. Porterfield Rynd, I don't know your name."

"Oh, my name is J. F. Byrne."

"How do you do, Mr. Byrne," said Rynd.

"Now, Porterfield," said my opponent, "I have introduced you —why not do the same for me?"

"Permit me, Mr. Byrne," said Porterfield Rynd grandiloquently and jocularly "to present Mr. John Howard Parnell."

I bowed to Mr. Parnell, and then looked over to the corner of the room where there was a slim lad, sixteen years young sitting near the window patiently and very much alone. I beckoned to him, and when he had come over I said to the two gentlemen,

"Mr. Parnell and Mr. Rynd, let me introduce my friend, Mr. James A. Joyce."

And John Howard Parnell said to him, "Are you a chess enthusiast, Mr. Joyce, like your friend, Mr. Byrne?"

"I'm afraid not, Mr. Parnell. I fear I should never master the intricacies of the game."

If Joyce had spoken what was really in his mind it would have sounded something like this: "No, Mr. Parnell, I don't play chess—and I don't want to play chess. In fact, I detest even the look of the damn game. I come in here to see Byrne, and not to gaze at chess, nor at chess players. And I wish to heaven Byrne wouldn't keep me so long waiting for him to finish his nauseating game."

Joyce did not know one chess piece from another, but in *Ulysses,* Stephen reflects esoterically,

> "John Howard Parnell translated a white bishop quietly and his grey claw went up again to his forehead whereat it rested.
>
> "An instant after, under its screen, his eyes looked quickly ghostbright, at his foe."

It was late in October 1898, that Joyce first dubbed me Cranly. This was one of the months during which he sat waiting for me, session after session while I played chess with Parnell.

After one of these sessions Joyce came over and stood beside me, waiting impatiently for us to go. For perhaps a minute or two I held a post mortem with John Howard on the game we had just played; when Joyce, taking me by the arm, intoned softly into my ear " 'Ite missa est,' your Grace. Come on, Cranly; as you say yourself 'Let us eke go.' "

On the footpath outside, Joyce, still linking me, asked, "Did you hear what I called you?"

"Yes, of course I did. You called me Cranly."

"I like that name," he said, "do you mind me calling you by it?"

"No, I don't mind—only I'd just as lief be called Byrne or J. F."

"Very well, then, I'll go on calling you J. F., but I'll think of you as Cranly. Do you know where I got that name?"

"Yes, I do. Since you came to University College last month you have heard me occasionally referred to as the "White Bishop." And in the past few weeks there have been a couple of notices

about a White Bishop who came here as Archbishop of Dublin '
five hundred years ago this very month of October. The other
night I saw you reading about him in John D'Alton's book, the
Memoirs of the Archbishops of Dublin."

That is how I became Cranly to Joyce. He liked the name, the
word, the sound of it. He liked the word "Cranly" as much as, if
not more than, any other word spoken or written. As for anything
else about it, or connected with it, he didn't really care. Joyce was
not interested in Cranly, or his times, but I was, and for that
reason I digress here to ruminate on them briefly.

D'Alton notes that Thomas Cranly of the Carmelite Order
(succ. 1397; ob. 1417) was Archbishop of Dublin. He was a native
of England; Doctor of Divinity; Fellow of Merton College, Oxford; Warden of New College, and for a time Chancellor of the
University of Oxford. Cranly did not arrive in Dublin till October 1398, when he came there in company with the Duke of Sur-
rey, Lord Lieutenant of Ireland. Cranly was also Lord Chancellor
of Ireland. In 1398 he had letters of protection on proceeding to
"foreign parts" in the service of the king, and in the following
year had power to treat with the Irish. In view of these facts it is
a practical certainty that Cranly must have had, among his other
accomplishments, a thorough knowledge of Gaelic.

> "At the end of April, 1417," D'Alton says, "he went into Eng-
> land where he died at Farringdon on the 25th of May fol-
> lowing, in the 80th year of his age, and not more full of years
> than honors. His body was conveyed to Oxford, and there
> interred in New College, of which he had been first warden.
> A monument was erected to him there. Marleburgh writes,
> 'He was fair, magnificent, of a sanguine complexion, and tall
> of stature, so that in his time it might be said to him, thou
> art fair beyond the children of men, grace is diffused through
> thy lips because of thy elegance.' "

In the notorious Statute of Laborers the following passage
occurs on September 26, 1390, and again on March 15, 1391:

> "Dominus rex mandavit litteras suas patentes in hec uerba:
> Ricardus dei gracia rex Anglie & Francie & dominus Hibernie
> delecto sibi in Cristo Thome Craule cancellario universitatis
> Oxonie, etc."

One question that interested me was this: Cranly was appointed Archbishop of Dublin in 1397; he did not arrive there till October 1398, and only a few months later King Richard II went over to Ireland on an idiotic expedition which proved his direct undoing and forced his abdication and formal deposition by parliament in 1399. Now it must be borne in mind that Cranly was not only Archbishop of Dublin, but also Lord Chancellor of the Pale; and he had been furnished with letters of protection to proceed to "foreign parts" and he was empowered to "treat with the Irish." Does it seem plausible to assume that Cranly had nothing whatever to do with Richard's abortive "expedition" to Ireland? Or does it seem extravagant to suppose that Richard, who was generally credited with being a "fellow traveler" of the Lollards, may have floundered right into a trap? I did make an effort at one time to find an answer to this question, but all I discovered was that the research involved would be prodigious and possibly fruitless, and my interest in the question was not strong enough to goad me to the effort. Source material for English history in the fourteenth and early fifteenth centuries is rare and widely scattered; so much so that I was unable to locate a reliable account of what became of Richard II, after his historic dethronement.

Shakespeare had no qualms in giving his detailed account of Richard the Second's death at the hands of "Sir Pierce of Exton," but William was drawing on his imagination, which was probably stimulated by the story of Henry the Second and Thomas à Becket. Of Richard's mysterious expedition to Ireland Shakespeare talks a lot but says nothing. But he does put in Richard's mouth a couple of funny remarks which might aptly be called the before-thought and the after-thought. Immediately on hearing of John of Gaunt's death, Richard blathers:

> ". . . Now for our Irish wars;
> We must supplant those rough rug-headed kerns,
> Who live like venom where no venom else
> But only they have privilege to live."

And a short while later, when he had perhaps realised that some wily cat charmer must have lured him away so that the mice might play, Richard, standing in the shadow of Barkloughly Castle in Wales, gives us a flashlight glimpse of what he was thinking of the rug-headed kerns in their venomous habitat when he denounces:

> ". . . this thief, this traitor, Bolingbroke
> Who all this while hath revelled in the night
> While we were wandering with the antipodes."

Alas, "Poor Richard!" He could now realise how deplorably accurate he himself had been in giving Cranly letters of protection on proceeding to "foreign parts" in the service of the King.

Richard landed in Waterford on June 1st, 1399, and after encountering severe hardships, with heavy losses in men in the mountains, bogs and woods of Wexford and Carlow, he reached Dublin on July 1. He did nothing, nor did he attempt anything, except to negotiate with Art MacMurrough Kavanagh; and this attempted negotiation having failed, he made the futile gesture of offering one hundred marks for the body of Kavanagh "alive or dead." Having performed this dauntless deed of knightly valor, the benighted Richard crawled back to Waterford, from which, having heard of Henry's landing at Ravenspur, he sailed on August 13 of the same year to Milford Haven and his impending doom.

Here, indeed, is a case where a "pale king" with his "princes, too" could have cried "La Belle Dame sans Merci hath us in thrall." But Shakespeare shows no suspicion of a plot, nor does any other commentator that I know of; and it may be noted that in his play he does not lay even one simple small scene in Ireland. He could, an' if he would, have given us his dramatic record of a conversation between Richard, Exeter, Albemarle and Gloucester as they floundered through some venomous bog, or as they trudged a tortuous path through a wood infested by rough, rug-headed kerns.

But in retrospect it seems to me that the period in which Cranly flourished, 1338-1417, was one of the most terrible, destructive, and yet formative in recorded history. During that time there were three visitations of the Black Death, the first which occurred in 1348-49 wiping out in England an estimated 30 per cent of a possible total population of five million people.

In Cranly's lifetime there were fourteen Popes, six of whom sat in Avignon, and Cranly also lived under four kings of England, surviving as he did till two years after the overrated victory of

Henry V in the battle of Agincourt; and to within a few months of the same Henry's horrible siege of Rouen, where he was frustrated in the infamous demand for the "unconditional surrender" of that city. When Cranly died, Joan of Arc was about five years old, and fourteen years later she was to be rewarded for her sanctity and patriotism by being burned to death by the English in the market place of this same city of Rouen.

Cranly was a contemporary of three great figures in English history; John Wyclif, Chaucer, and "Long Will" Langland, and it can be fairly assumed that he was personally acquainted with all three of them. Wyclif did as much as any one man for the development of English prose, and was posthumously honored more than thirty years after his death, when by order of the Council of Constance his body was dug up and burnt, and his ashes thrown into the River Swift. Chaucer and his Canterbury Tales everybody knows about; but not so many are aware of the far greater significance of the work of Will Langland in his *The Vision of William concerning Piers the Plowman, and The Vision of the Same Concerning Do Wel, Do Bet, and Do Best.* These poems are narrated as dreams, the poet telling us that on a fine morning in May he fell asleep on the Malvern Hills and had a "marveilous sweuene."

> "In a somer season when soft was the sonne,
> I shope me in shroudes as I a shepe were,
> In habite as an heremite unholy of workes
> Went wide in this world wondres to hear."

Langland's poem ranks high among the greatest of man's didactic efforts; and it was the source of inspiration for those who fought for, and achieved, an amelioration of the plight of the peasant and laborer in the dismal fourteenth century England. Langland says:

> "I was wery forwandered and went me to rest
> under a broad bank by a burn side, and as I
> lay and leaned and looked in the water I
> slumbered in a sleeping, it sweyved so merry."

"What chains one to the poem," says Green, "is its deep undertone of sadness. . . . His poem covers indeed an age of shame and suffering such as England had never known, and its final issue preceded but by a single year the Peasant Revolt."

CHAPTER FIVE

Congress v. House of Commons at Chess

I T WAS A strange assortment of humanity that frequented the D. B. C. in Dame Street; coming from so many walks of life, they were all attracted to one another by the same lodestone, chess. Easily the most colorful personage in the place was Porterfield Rynd, one of the ablest members of the Dublin bar—a man who, if he had been half as devoted to the drudgery of work as he was to the allurement of play, could easily have attained the highest honors in the judiciary. When I first met him he was about fifty-five years of age, and in top physical condition. He was of medium size, ruddy and powerfully strong and active. He had been champion skuller and rackets player; and he was a great chess player. He was fond of the piano and many an evening I heard him perform for hours while at the same time playing blindfold chess with some one of those present. I knew Rynd well and admired him.

Another striking figure in the group was the octogenarian Parker Dunscombe, a well-to-do land owner from Cork, with white hair and beard and pink jovial face in traditional Santa Claus style. This old man boasted of having kept a record of all the games he had played for a half century. Then there was Hobson, a great odds giver at chess and, after Rynd, the best player in the room. Another frequent visitor and ardent chess devotee was Monsignor Murphy of Maryborough. Two other habitués were John White and Daniel O'Connell Miley, both prominent Dublin solicitors.

Also there was a gentlemanly little wealthy Jew named Solomon, who for some reason or another, chose to confide in me toward the end of 1898 that he was worried about his South

African stock holdings, particularly De Beers. Trouble was brewing between England and the Boers, and I had no doubt the scoundrelly Joe Chamberlain would do his damndest to bring it to a head. But with all my contempt for the monocled Joe, and my sympathy with the Boers, I reluctantly gave Solomon my opinion, "Hold on to your South African stock. I deeply regret to say I think they're perfectly safe."

For three months, I played chess on three or four afternoons a week for occasionally as long as three hours at a sitting. John Howard Parnell rapidly dropped the odds from a queen to a rook; and, by the end of a month, from a rook to a knight. A few weeks later, he was giving me pawn and two; then pawn and move, and then we played on even terms. Before the end of the third month, in the second week of December, I was beating him regularly.

Did this make John Howard mad? It did not. Did it disturb his customary equanimity? It did. For when I played with him now, there would sometimes be a deep fringe of onlookers, and when I checkmated him, he would gesture toward me with his right hand and say beamingly, "My pupil!" And during the subsequent twelve years till my coming to the United States, he held me in friendship, often inviting me to his home for dinner.

In his own right, it may be said, John Howard was noteworthy. When I first knew him, I could thrill to the recent memory of his great brother, Charles Stewart Parnell, of whom I had many a vivid boyhood memory. One day in the spring of 1890 an outside car was driven rapidly westward on Wood Quay, and then past Hoey's public house about sixty yards west of the Merchant's Arch. In this pub at the time you could get a pint o' plain for threeha'pence; and leaning up against it on the outside, as if to prevent the edifice from collapse were some half-dozen coal porters. As the jaunting car went rapidly by, they all tipped their hats to the pale-faced, black-bearded "Charlie" sitting on the near side of the hack, on his way to Kingsbridge. When the figure of Charlie was fading towards the corner of Eustace Street, one of the coal porters stalked to the curb, spat out, and then turning to face his companions called out to them in a loud voice: "Do ye know what it is, mates! Be the livin' jingo I think every man in Ireland ought to stand that man a pint!"

John Howard Parnell was for some years a fruit farmer in the

United States, which, of course, accounted for his drawl. In a brochure entitled "Charles Stewart Parnell, a Memoir, by John Howard Parnell" he narrates in part:

"Sir John Parnell (Bart.) member of Irish Parliament 1776 onwards, he held in succession the offices of Commissioner of Customs and Excise and Chancellor of the Exchequer. A sturdy supporter and defender of Grattan he resisted to his utmost Pitt's scheme of legislative union. His death followed closely on the merging of the Irish Parliament into the British one.

"His son, Sir Henry Parnell, created Lord Congleton in 1841, warmly opposed the continuance of the Irish Insurrection Act, opposed the Bill for the repression of the Catholic Emancipation. He died in 1842, after having held the offices of Minister for War (under Lord Grey), and Paymaster-General of the Forces (under Lord Melbourne).

"By his wife, Lady Caroline Elizabeth Dawson, daughter of the Earl of Portarlington, he had five children, the youngest of whom, William, was our grandfather.

"Our mother, Delia Stewart, was the daughter of the American Nelson, Commodore Charles Stewart. His countless exploits, his indomitable bravery and his many conflicts with and victories over the English fleet during the American War of Independence, are such that to recount them with any justice would need a volume to itself."

When I was introduced to John Howard, I recalled that in the preceding year, 1897, he had been a member of a team representing the British House of Commons in the one cable chess match ever played by that legislative body with members of the United States Congress. For refreshing my memory on this event I thank Mr. Dwyer W. Shugrue, Counsel to United States Senator Ives of New York, who wrote me:

"A chess match by cable was contested between the American House of Representatives and the British House of Commons on May 31, 1897. The principal promoter was a Mr. Henniker Heaton, M.P. Messages of greeting were exchanged between the two Speakers and between Ambassadors Hay and Pauncefote. The American team consisted of Richmond

Pearson, a North Carolina Republican, John F. Shafroth, a
Colorado Democrat (later Senator), Robert N. Bodine, a
Missouri Democrat, Thomas S. Plowman, an Alabama Democrat, and Levin I. Handy, a Delaware Democrat. The result
was as follows:

House of Commons		House of Representatives	
Plunkett	1	Pearson	0
Parnell	0	Shafroth	1
Strauss	0	Bodine	1
Atherly-Jones	1	Plowman	0
Wilson	½	Handy	½
	2½		2½

This is the only such match of which we have found any record. Of the American team, three members (Bodine, Plowman, and Handy) served only during this Fifty-fifth Congress,
and Plowman was unseated before its close as the result of
a contested election."

In a dispatch from London, the New York Tribune on June 1,
1897, reports:

"John Howard Parnell is in some respects like his famous
brother, Charles. Before the match began he complained of
not feeling well, but he played very deliberately . . . Sir
Horace C. Plunkett is also a small man, with gentle voice
and manner. He is a brother of Lord Dunsany, started the
Irish Agricultural Scheme, has written for the 'Pall Mall
Gazette,' and lived for a long time in Wyoming, where he
has large interests."
"Mr. Parnell wore a look of concentrated anxiety, again
strikingly recalling his famous brother in fateful moments.
. . . Arthur J. Balfour, First Lord of the Treasury, 'looked
in.'
"Mr. Henniker Heaton promptly wired to Washington that
Arthur J. Balfour was present (Mr. Heaton 'who has talents
for such an occasion that the late P. T. Barnum might have
envied'). This drew forth the retort that Mr. Shafroth of
Colorado is also an ardent bimetalist and felt inspired to

greater exertions on learning that the distinguished leader of the House of Commons was present. There was a hearty round of laughter in which Arthur J. Balfour joined with evident relish."

Why Mr. Pearson was chosen to play first board on the American team is a mystery. He could not play chess, as any chess player will see from the transcript of his game with Plunkett. It may be recalled, however, that only a few weeks before the match took place, the Republicans, under the leadership of McKinley, had recovered power from the Democrats—and Pearson was the only Republican on the team. I know John Howard Parnell did not do himself justice in his game with Shafroth; he could play better chess. He and Shafroth played a double Micawber game— both of them waiting and hoping for something to turn up— Parnell should have resigned ten moves before he did.

Here are the scores of Plunkett's and Parnell's games. They will interest chess playing readers of Joyce's *Ulysses,* in which frequent reference is made to John Howard Parnell.

	Plunkett (white)	Pearson (black)		Plunkett (white)	Pearson (black)
1	P — K4	P — K4	9	Q — Q3	Q — Q
2	P — KB4	P x P	10	R — K	Kt — K2
3	B — B4	B — B4	11	P — K5	P — KB4
4	P — Q4	Q — R5ch	12	KKt — Kt5	R — B
5	K — B	B — Kt3	13	Kt x P	R — R
6	Kt — KB3	Q — K2	14	Q — R3	R x Kt
7	Kt — B3	P — QB3	15	Q x R	Kt — Q4
8	QB x P	P — KB3	16	Q — Kt8ch	Resigns

	Shafroth (white)	Parnell (black)		Shafroth (white)	Parnell (black)
1	P — K4	P — K3	31	Q — KB3	Q — K3
2	P — Q4	P — Q4	32	K — B2	B — B3
3	Kt — QB3	KKt — B3	33	R x P	B — R5ch
4	B — Q3	P — B4	34	K — K2	R x R
5	QP x P	B x P	35	Q x R	Q x Q
6	P — KR3	Kt — B3	36	R x Q	B — B3
7	P x P	Kt x P	37	K — B3	K — B2
8	KKt — K2	Castles	38	R — Q7ch	R — K2
9	Castles	QKt — K2	39	R x Rch	B x R
10	Kt — K4	B — Kt3	40	K — K4	K — K3

11	QB	— Kt5	P	— B3	41	B	— Q4	B	— Q
12	B	— Q2	Q	— B2	42	P	— B5ch	P	x Pch
13	P	— QB4	P	— B4	43	P	x Pch	K	— B2
14	P	x Kt	P	x Kt	44	B	— K5	P	— QR3
15	B	x P	P	x P	45	K	— Q5	P	— Kt4
16	B	— Q3	Q	— Q3	46	P	— QR4	P	x P
17	B	— K3	B	— B2	47	P	x P	B	— R4
18	Kt	— Kt3	B	— B4	48	K	— B6	B	— K8
19	P	— B4	P	— QKt3	49	K	— Kt6	P	— QR4
20	R	— B3	QR	— Q	50	K	— Kt5	P	— R4
21	QR	— B	B	— Kt	51	K	— B4	P	— R5
22	R	— KB2	Q	— Kt3	52	K	— Kt5	B	— Q7
23	Kt	x B	Kt ·	x Kt	53	B	— B7	K	— B3
24	Q	— KB3	Q	— KB3	54	B	x P	B	— B5
25	B	x Kt	Q	x B	55	B	— Q8ch	K	x P
26	P	— KKt4	Q	— B2	56	P	— R5	B	— Kt6
27	P	— Kt3	B	— K4	57	P	— R6	B	— Kt
28	QR	— Q	P	— Kt3	58	K	— Kt6	K	— K5
29	Q	— Kt2	B	— Kt2	59	K	— Kt7	Resigns	
30	KR	— Q2	KR	— K					

About the time I began to beat Parnell consistently, I decided to quit frequenting the Dame Street D. B. C. In making this decision I was yielding to the importunities of Joyce. He came to the smokeroom at almost every one of my chess sessions, and waited for me till I finished. Always he sat alone and remained aloof. And he did this not because of shyness, but because he did not want to mix with the company even to the extent of a "Good afternoon" or "How de do!" Every minute I gave to chess was sheer waste to him, and he was frankly jealous of John Howard who was my partner in profligacy. He was jealous of the few to whom I gave my time or attention; and these few to him were just interlopers.

This attitude of Joyce towards me is depicted clearly by himself in *Stephen Hero* when he says:

"Stephen repaired to the Library where he was supposed to be engaged in serious work. As a matter of fact he read little or nothing in the Library. He talked with Cranly by the hour either at a table, or, if removed by the librarian or by the indignant glances of students, standing at the top of the staircase. At ten o'clock when the library closed the two re-

turned together through the central streets exchanging banalities with the other students. . . . Cranly's chosen companions represented the rabblement in a stage of partial
fermentation when it is midway between vat and flagon and
Cranly seemed to please himself in the spectacle of this cari-
cature of his own unreadiness."

I had very few "chosen companions" in University College,
and with one exception the few I had were, from the point of
view of scholastic attainment all of outstanding brilliancy. Indeed
from this viewpoint much more brilliant than Joyce himself.
There was Jim O'Toole, whom I have already mentioned, who
always won first honors and place in mathematics; and who might
have developed into one of the world's greatest mathematicians
had he not died of consumption in his twenties. Then there was
Alphonsus O'Farrelly, first honors and place in physics and
chemistry. Alphy was blond, powerfully built and stocky. He was
always good-humored and ready to laugh. He could have been
one of the best handball players in the college. His style, especially his stroke was beautiful. If the ball came anywhere near
him, he handled it all right, but if the ball were coy and distant,
it could go to hell for all he cared—he wasn't going to run after
it. Alphy was later my best man, and has long been a distinguished professor in Dublin. There was also the bearded Joe
Skeffington (the McCann in Joyce's books) who invariably took
first place in English, and who won the prize with the resounding
title of "The Chancellor's Gold Medal for English Prose Composition." In those days Skeffington and Alphy were close friends.
During the Easter uprising in 1916 Skeffington was murdered by
the British in Portobello Barracks, Dublin.

Another of my companions was George Clancy (Davin in
Joyce's books), a fine young fellow and a great Irishman, with a
flair for complicated but none the less fluent imprecations in
mixed Celtic and English uttered in the soft brogue of Kilmal-
lock. George was the one other person besides myself in University College whose companionship Joyce courted. (There was one
other whose company Joyce accepted and in whom, to his later
regret, he partially confided.) George Clancy always called Joyce
"Jebh," as if the "b" were aspirated. The little tale in the *Portrait* about Davin's midnight adventure when returning home

from the hurling match, is almost exactly as George told it himself. During the infamous British military occupation in Ireland, George was Mayor of Limerick, the renowned city of the "Treaty Stone," and while in that capacity was foully murdered in 1921 by the Black and Tans at night in his home before the eyes of his family.

One other student who rounded out the group of my "chosen companions" was Paddy Merriman, with whom I was in some respects on terms of closer mental intimacy than with anyone else in the college. Like Jim O'Toole, Paddy was a Christian Brothers' boy from Richmond Street school. He came of humble parents, and nature had not been over-kind to him in the matter of physique or appearance. But where nature had been niggardly in some things of the body she had been lavish in her bestowal on Paddy of the vastly greater attributes of mind and spirit. In October 1898, one of the months when I was playing chess, Paddy was up for his B.A. degree. His subject was "Modern Literature," including English, German, and French. One late evening two weeks before his exam, he and I were walking through the Green, and I asked him how he felt about it. "I wish the examination were on tomorrow," he answered. For a fellow to tell me a fortnight before an important exam that he wished it were on the next day, was something new; and something which I myself could never have uttered.

During the ten preceding years, first place with first class honors in Modern Literature had always been captured by a female; and that year there was an unusually brilliant young lady taking the exam. She was Miss Mary Bowler of Loreto College. Well, Paddy was ungallant enough to beat Mary, and he won first place with first class honors, and was very happy about it. But on this afternoon of the conferring of degrees, as I sauntered with him very slowly from the Leeson Street Gate towards Grafton Street, he was no longer in merry mood; he was glum and I was not surprised. Paddy was then twenty-two years of age, and for the preceding eight years, through the Intermediate and through college, he had learned to look upon examinations and the acquisition of "exhibitions" and scholarships as the main purpose of existence. And now here he was with his B.A. achievement behind him, and nothing in front of him. Of course there was the M.A. to go for next year, but, as it happened, there would be no

Studentship to aim at in connection with it. Studentships, worth one hundred pounds a year for two years, were offered every year in major groups, but in the "Modern Literature" group it was given in alternate years, and there would be none next year in his group. So Paddy was sad. As we were crossing the rustic bridge, I halted and went over to the low, wide rocky wall to lean there and to look unseeingly at the lake and the water fowl; for I was intent on Paddy's problem, as he leaned woebegone, alongside me. Then a bright thought flashed, and I said to him, "Paddy, there's no studentship in your course next year, but there will be a studentship in the Political Economy course. You could easily take that in the year, even though it's intended to be a two year course and to include the B.A. What is there to the subject of Political Economy that you couldn't prepare for the M.A. in a year? Nobody knows anything about it anyway. And as for Jurisprudence, that subject is so interesting in itself you could read it for recreation."

Paddy instantly accepted my suggestion; and his mood just as quickly changed. He saw once more before him the accustomed vision of an annual exam with concomitant prize money, and he was happy. So Paddy studied his Political Economy and his Jurisprudence and History and went for his M.A. in that group; and in the M.A. he won first place in Ireland, with first class honors, but the powers that were withheld the studentship and did not give it to him. First place in Ireland Paddy won, and first class honors he was awarded, but to award the studentship meant—well, that meant money—and they weren't giving away any of that, especially not to a poor man's son like Paddy if they could possibly find some loophole for getting out of what was undoubtedly a clear obligation. I was furiously indignant and I told Paddy I would try to call a big student meeting to frame a protest to Father Delaney, President of the College, on whose shoulders as Senator of the University, I believed, rightly or wrongly, the blame for the injustice done to Paddy should be placed. Paddy was dead against this, however, so I desisted. And in later years I had reason to know that Paddy's resignation and patience in this matter had been as "bread cast upon the waters."

In October 1899, Joe Chamberlain finally succeeded, even over the opposition of two future Prime Ministers, Lloyd George, and Ramsey MacDonald, in his vicious purpose of subjugating the

Boers. As for Paddy Merriman and I, we didn't even want to talk about it. Up to the outbreak of the war we had argued the Boer cause with many, and I remember making one of the few conversions I ever made in the person of a dark haired, mild mannered, bespectacled Hinch, one of the minor librarians in the National Library. Sean O'Kelly will remember him. Hinch had been ardently pro-British, but after I had given him a few heart to heart talks, he became a much more ardent pro-Boer. But neither Padraig MacGiolla Mhuire (meaning Patrick the son of Mary's man), as at that time Paddy Merriman was signing himself, nor I wanted to do any more arguing with anybody about the merits of the war. We both wanted to fight for the Boers. On investigation we found this to be impracticable.

A few years later Paddy won a Junior Fellowship in the University, and one of his unsuccessful competitors in that examination was Joe Skeffington. Shortly after that event Paddy was married from my residence at 100 Phibsboro Road, and I was Paddy's best man. Not long afterwards, Patrick Joseph Merriman became the President of the National University College in Cork, a position he adorned until his death a few years ago.

CHAPTER SIX

"Diseases of the OX"

IN THE *Portrait of the Artist* Joyce writes of "Stephen pointing to the title page of Cranly's book on which was written 'Diseases of the Ox.'" This apparently trivial incident affords much material for rumination. Here is the story.

In July, 1899, something occurred to a cow owned by my farming friends in the County Wicklow; in the National Library I sought for, and with the help of the librarian, Mr. Lyster, finally located a book in which I hoped to find some information that might be useful should a similar emergency occur. When the librarian handed me the book at the counter, he indicated a section or chapter in it with the title "Diseases of the Ox," and although I was in serious mood, I immediately smiled. "Diseases of the Ox" I read aloud, and remarked to Lyster, who also had a broad smile on his visage, "Sounds funny, somehow, that title." "Yes, it does," he agreed, "but maybe it covers what you are looking for."

I took the book with me and sat down at a table near the balcony door, and I had just begun to peruse it when Joyce came in and sat down beside me. At that period Joyce was cramming himself with the Norwegian language, and he had brought with him to our table a pile of books on Ibsen including some of his plays, a Norwegian dictionary and a Norwegian grammar. For a moment he was silent, but then he leaned over to look at the large book I had open before me. "Good Lord, Byrne," he ejaculated, "what *are* you reading?" I didn't say anything but I turned the pages to the title of the chapter where printed in large type was "DISEASES OF THE OX." The instantaneous affect on James Joyce was the detonating expulsion of a howl that reverberated through

58

the reading room; and no Assyrian ever came down more swiftly on a fold than did Lyster on Joyce, who was in a convulsion of laughter.

"Mr. Joyce," the librarian ordered, "please leave the reading room." By way of calling attention to an ameliorating circumstance, I pointed to the title, but Lyster snapped, "Yes, Mr. Byrne, I know, but Mr. Joyce should learn to control himself, and I must ask him to leave the reading room, and to stay out of it, until he does." Compliantly Joyce struggled to his feet, and I got up to go with him. "I don't mean you, Mr. Byrne. Of course, you can stay." "That's all right, thank you, Mr. Lyster, but I'm afraid I'll have to help my friend out of the room. He would never be able to navigate as far as the turnstile."

Outside of the library Joyce slowly regained his composure, but neither of us felt inclined to make an immediate return to the vicinity of that book. Instead, we went for a walk through the Green and, needless to say, we talked; and the one big question that interested us was why that title was so funny. Why, for instance, was it that if that title had been "Diseases of Cattle," or "Bovine Diseases," we would not have thought it a bit funny? But "Diseases of the Ox" yes; for some obscure reason, it was funny.

The consideration of this question suggests two other questions which, being more closely related than might appear at first sight, we may take up here in connection with the mammoth *Ulysses*. In that book Joyce employs three elemental four-letter words. According to Hanley's *Word Index to James Joyce's Ulysses* these words, with variations, are employed by Joyce in that book a total of thirty times; and the two questions that arise are "What effect did the employment of these words have on the book considered as a work of art?", and "What effect did the appearance of these three words in the book have on its sales?"

I have already told how I took up with Joyce the matter of that yarn he had written in the *Portrait* about the "conversation" between Stephen and Father Butt in the Physics Theatre, and as a corollary to our talk on this point, we had gone on to mull over his use of the three four-letter words. The upshot was that I found Joyce not at all positive about the artistic value of the words; but inflexibly positive about their sales or popularity value. And with this judgment of Joyce's I could largely agree.

Two points in this general connection I want to stress: The first of these is that Joyce rarely, indeed scarcely ever, uttered orally any of these words; and it is all the more strange, therefore, that he had a leaning to write them, and it is also a little strange that he was so addicted to putting a plethora of expletives and fulminations into the mouths of some of his characters. In this regard, he made another mistake of over-embellishment, but the reason he did this was simply that he believed it was becoming for strong men, or strong characters, to talk that way.

To illustrate my point, let us look at and note the language in a letter he wrote to his brother, and which is reproduced in part in Mr. Gorman's book. In it Joyce fulminates, "For the love of the Lord Christ change my curse-o'-God state of affairs. Give me for Christ's sake a pen and an ink bottle . . . and then, by the crucified Jaysus, if I don't . . ., send me to hell. . . . Whoever the hell you are . . . I'm darned to hell if. . . . For your sake I refrained from taking a little black fellow from Bristol by the nape of the neck and hurling him into the street. . . . But my heroic nature urged me to do this because he was smaller than I."

Let me stress the fact that Joyce was no coward; but muscularly he was weak and he knew it. It would have taxed his strength to take a one-year-old baby "by the nape of the neck." In writing this letter Joyce was consciously posing as the eldest and strongest of the brothers—mentally, physically, and muscularly. And he wrote as he fancied a man of his "heroic nature" should thunderously express himself.

And now coming to the second of my two points, it is that I believe one of Joyce's principal purposes in insisting on the use of elemental words in his works was in protest against popular insincerity, cant, and hypocrisy; and against a puritanical prudery which is essentially prurient.

Harking back to that "conversation" between Stephen and Father Butt, I reminded Joyce that toward the end of his *Portrait* he made Stephen say, "That tundish has been in my mind for a long time. I looked it up and find it English and good old blunt English too." I asked Joyce where did he look up the word tundish and he told me in the dictionary. Then I asked him, "Did you ever look up the word in Shakespeare, you know he uses it once in that piffly *Measure for Measure?*" "Probably I did, but I couldn't say for certain."

"Well, the point I am getting at is this: In that play the Duke says to Lucio, 'Why should he die, sir?' And Lucio replies, 'Why? For filling a bottle with a tundish.' Now we can well imagine the guffaw that went up from the surrounding audience when it heard these words issue with ribald flippancy from the mouth of a character whom Shakespeare was depicting as the lowdown skunk, Lucio."

"I see what you're driving at," interrupted Joyce. "Your point is that if Lucio had used all three of the elemental words in this seven-word sentence, as he could have done, he would have expressed himself with less indecency. This never occurred to me before, but if that is your point I fully agree."

"Yes," I said, "that is my point."

There is another aspect to this matter to which I will advert briefly. James Joyce valued many words for their sounds and for their own sake as much as he did for their connotation. Indeed the meaning of a word or group of words often was less important to Joyce than the word itself, or the grouping. Milton could say, and did, when he was imprecating—of all things—Urania, "The meaning, not the name, I call." Joyce could scarcely ever have so spoken. He would have insisted on his Urania—and a rose to him by any other name would have been just another weed.

To retrace my steps once more after this digression, that incident in the National Library of Joyce's outburst of mirth at the title, "Diseases of the Ox," occurred during the period when he was studying Ibsen and preparing his essay on that playwright—an essay which found prompt acceptance, on its very first offering, in the *Fortnightly Review*. While Joyce was writing it, a period of about two months, he sat as usual beside me in the Library, and at his insistence I read it and re-read it as it progressed, and when it was finished I could have recited it verbatim. Whether it was a good thing for Joyce that his essay was accepted by the *Fortnightly*, and that it was accepted so promptly, is a point I won't discuss here.

It must, however, in this connection be emphasized that it would be impossible for a young collegiate of the present day to realise the importance attached in Joyce's time by some persons, in certain circles, to the *Fortnightly Review*. Joyce was well aware, however, that this was not my attitude; and he knew that my opinion of him, or of the essay he wrote, would not be modified in the slightest degree by the *Fortnightly* acceptance. To some extent *Blackwood's* mantle, or to speak more aptly, *Blackwood's* "muddy vesture of decay" had fallen on the *Fortnightly*. Joyce knew that I was a reader of Poe's works and that I admired the great American; and he knew that whereas Poe's opinion of *Blackwood's* stood at freezing point on Poe's thermometer, my opinion of the literary importance of that magazine, or, indeed, of any other magazine with similar pretensions, stood down near absolute zero.

More than a year before the *Fortnightly* acceptance, I had been reading Poe's "Review of Elizabeth Barrett Browning's Poems," and I had expressed to Joyce my unstinted admiration for it and for the selected excerpts illustrating what Poe called "her wild and magnificent genius." I cull here a few lines chosen by him from her *Drama of Exile:*

> "With his calm massive face turned full on thine,
> And his mane listening.
>
> *   *   *
>
> As if the new reality of death
> Were dashed against his eyes,—and roared so fierce,
> (Such thick carnivorous passion in his throat
> Tearing a passage through the wrath and fear)—
> And roared so wild, and smote from all the hills
> Such fast keen echoes crumbling down the vales
> To distant silence,—that the forest beasts,
> One after one, did mutter a response
> In savage and in sorrowful complaint
> Which trailed along the gorges."

And then Poe goes on to write anent *Blackwood's* literary critic:

> "But, perhaps, we are guilty of a very gross absurdity ourselves, in commenting *at all* upon the whimsicalities of a reviewer who can deliberately *select* for special animadversion the second of the four verses we here copy:
>
> > 'Eyes,' he said, 'now throbbing through me! are ye
> >   eyes that did undoe me?
> >   *Shining eyes like antique jewels set in Parian*
> >   *statue-stone!*

Underneath that calm white forehead are ye ever
    burning torrid
O'er the desolate sand desert of my heart and
    life undone?'

". . . when we take into consideration the moral designed, the weirdness of effect intended, and the historical adaptation of the fact alluded to in the line italicized (a fact of which it is by no means impossible that the critic is ignorant), we cannot refrain from expressing our conviction—and we here *express it* in the teeth of the whole horde of the Ambrosianians—that from the entire range of poetical literature there shall not, in a century, be produced a more sonorous— a more vigorous verse—a juster—a nobler—a more ideal—a more magnificent image—than this very image, in this very verse, which the most noted magazine of Europe has so especially and so contemptuously condemned."

In his recent biography of his grandfather, Lord Alfred Tennyson, Charles Tennyson tells us that Alfred was driven into nine years of public silence by the cruelty of a sneering review in the *Quarterly Review*. It sounds almost incredible that anyone should have been so deeply affected by such a cause; but the fact is only too well established that many persons were, and Tennyson was more than ordinarily sensitive. He was, fortunately for himself, not so sensitive or so delicate as Keats, whom the damnable reviewers almost literally stoned to death.

Down through the years, from ". . . Scotch Reviewers" through Keats' killers, and from *Blackwood's* through the *Quarterly,* and through the *Fortnightly,* gross ignorance pontificated incessantly from the pulpit of some "magazine" or "review."

After his article on Ibsen had been published, Joyce's relationship with his few associates became impaired by either their jealousy or sycophancy; and so it happened that Joyce was forced during the next couple of years to rely more than ever on me for companionship.

Immediately after the publication of the Ibsen article, Joyce began occasionally, and when in the mood, to seek expression in writing short poems. In the production of these he was not prolific; and even as he sat beside me in the library he would write and rewrite and retouch, it might almost seem interminably, a bit of verse containing perhaps a dozen or a score of lines. When he had at last polished his gem to a satisfying degree of curvature and smoothness, he would write out the finished poem with slow and stylish penmanship and hand the copy to me. Many a time he said to me as he did this: "Keep all these, J. F.—some day they'll be worth a pound a piece to you." Joyce always said this jokingly; but I never took his remark as a joke for I was even then quite sure that, no matter what my own personal opinion of his bits of verse might be, these bits of polished verse in Joyce's equally polished handwriting would some day be collector's pieces.

The finished poems were invariably done on slips of good quality white paper provided free and in abundance to the readers of the National Library. The slips were approximately 7⅝ inches in length by 3⅜ inches in width. Joyce gave me copies of all the poems he wrote prior to October, 1902; and I kept all of them, as well as I could, for more than twenty years. Then, finding that many had been either lost, or, more likely, pilfered, and realizing that they would probably be safer in a collection, I yielded to the importunities of John Quinn and sold him the few originals I had left. With these I also sold to Mr. Quinn a signed copy of Joyce's *The Holy Office,* which he gave to me on one of his visits to my place at 100 Phibsboro Road. The price I got for these several items averaged about six dollars. That certainly wasn't much; but still it was more than even Joyce had jokingly told me they would some day be worth.

One day late in March, 1902, Joyce said to me, "I have another poem for you."

"Good," I said, "give it to me."

"I have it in the rough here, but I'll write it out for you."

"You know I told you I had an appointment at four o'clock in connection with the handball tournament, and it is nearly that now. Give me the rough, and I'll copy it myself in one-quarter the time it would take you to write it."

He did; and I did. And that copy of Joyce's poem written by me with a pencil on two library slips so many years ago is still in my possession. On the second slip where the word "sorrow" occurs in the poem, Joyce drew a mark over that word, and he wrote in the margin "Accent divided equally."

Here is a reproduction of the poem, verbatim et literatim, as I copied it from Joyce's rough:

I

O, it is cold and still—alas!—
The soft white bosom of my love,
Wherein no mood of guile or fear
But only gentleness did move.
She heard as standing on the shore,
A bell above the water's toll,
She heard the call of, "come away"
Which is the calling of the soul.

II

They covered her with linen white
And set white candles at her head
And loosened out her glorious hair
And laid her on a snow-white bed.
I saw her passing like a cloud,
Discreet and silent and apart.
O, little joy and great sorrow
Is all the music of the heart

III

The fiddle has a mournful sound
That's playing in the street below.
I would I lay with her I love—
And who is there to say me no?
We lie upon the bed of love
And lie together in the ground:
To live, to love and to forget
Is all the wisdom lovers have.

Joyce was fond of music, and at that time I was even fonder of it than he was. During the far-flung visits of the Rouseby, and Carl Rosa Opera Companies, we went to as many operas as we could afford. In our very youthful days we enjoyed such popular favorites as "Trovatore"; "Maritana"; "The Bohemian Girl"; "Lily of Killarney," and such like; but as we grew older, it was Wagner who attracted us—especially by such of his music dramas as "Tristan and Isolde," and "Lohengrin."

In the dramatic field we looked forward to the occasional visits of, for instance, Osmond Tearle, whose repertory was chiefly, but not exclusively, Shakespearean. Tearle's locale was always the Gaiety Theatre; and in that theatre, whether we were attending opera, play, or pantomime, Joyce had the peculiar whim to sit at the extreme right of the top gallery (the gods). From this vantage point you looked down almost vertically on the players. I did not like the spot at all, but Joyce was so childishly eager to sit there that, of course, I agreed to sit with him.

Once in a while during the period of which I have been writing, Joyce developed an urge to set something to music. Usually it was one of his own pieces of verse, but at one time in 1902 he labored lovingly over composing an accompaniment for James Clarence Mangin's beautiful poem "Dark Rosaleen." Toward the south end of the Aula Maxima in University College, and on its west side, there was a door leading to a small room in which was a pianoforte. Joyce and I went there on many a night so that I could hear him sing the airs he had in mind and then play them for him. And sometimes on these nights, in order not to attract attention, we stayed in that room in pitch darkness— Joyce singing almost *sotto voce* and I playing the piano *pianissimo*. Whether Joyce's accompaniment to Mangin's "Dark Rosaleen" has ever been published I do not know. But I do know that after all these years I remember perfectly the air for it which he sang to me, and which I played for him, in the dark.

CHAPTER SEVEN

"Ghosts" in House on Cork Hill

Towards the end of 1902, a house on Cork Hill became vacant. This house was about 150 yards from the entrance to the Castle Yard. It stood almost directly opposite the City Hall, and next door to the "Mail" office which was on the corner of Parliament Street. For a considerable time before this, my cousin Mary had entertained the idea of renting a house in a good business district; a house large enough to provide dwelling accommodation for the four of us, together with at least two rooms for her own church business, and also a floor, preferably on the street level, suitable to be sublet as a business office.

When Mary saw this vacant house on Cork Hill, she thought it was just what she was looking for, and having talked the matter over with the rest of us, we all decided that she and I should have a look at it. On inquiry, we learned that the owner of the house was one Walter Butler, who at that time was Dublin City Architect. Mary and I had a talk with Mr. Butler in his residence, and he arranged to have a man meet us at the house at 9 A.M. the following morning and let us view it.

Next morning, Mary and I met a young man at the hall door of the house, and he let us in to see it. We found it was in very fair condition, but requiring, of course, the customary cleaning, painting, renovation of wall paper, and some minor improvements. One thing we noticed, with very little concern more than thinking it odd, was that on the front of the mantelpiece in the top back room was written very prominently, in several places, the one word "Ghosts."

Altogether Mary and I spent nearly an hour inspecting the place, and making tentative plans how we would fix it up and settle in it. We decided that the ground floor should be sublet for an office, or offices; that the second floor should be the "church warerooms"; that the top floor should be our living and sleeping quarters, and that we would cook and eat in the basement, where one of the rooms was fitted out as a comparatively comfortable kitchen.

While we were looking, cogitating and planning, we twice heard the footsteps of other people, apparently, like ourselves, looking over the house, and we assumed that the owner had also arranged to let other prospective tenants view the place simultaneously with us. So when Mary and I, having concluded our inspection and planning, were taking leave of the young man who was standing at the open hall door, I said to him just for talk sake, "You had other people in to look over the house; how do you think they liked it?" He answered with more emphasis than seemed to be required, "Nobody entered this house since you went into it. I have stood here all the time without moving a step from this open hall door, and I have let nobody but you two into the place."

Mary had two more interviews with Mr. Butler, as a result of which he agreed to accept her as tenant on a monthly basis, but he refused to do any renovation or improvement in the house unless we would give him a full year's rent of sixty pounds in advance.

Well, after deliberating the project for a few days, we scraped together the required sixty pounds, which Mary gave in cash to Mr. Butler. He in turn gave her a receipt, with a comprehensive memorandum of the whole transaction. He also gave her the keys of the house. In the early afternoon of the day on which this occurred, Mary went to the house to make a thorough final study of what she wanted done, and how she wanted it. While in the house alone, she again heard footsteps of people walking through it; these footsteps being especially loud on the stairs from the basement to the top. These noises were so real that she went down to the hall door to see whether she had inadvertently failed to close it properly. But the hall door was closed tight.

When she had finished her study of the house, Mary prepared to come home, first making sure that the back door and any accessible windows were firmly closed. Then when she emerged from the hall door, she turned and locked it carefully, and as she did so, a man whom she had noticed for some time standing outside on the footpath came over to her and said, "Miss Fleming, I'd like to talk to you." Mary took in at a glance that this man was a decent fellow. He seemed like a prosperous tradesman, of about her own age, and his manner was gentlemanly. So when Mary nodded, "Yes, you may," he said, "You don't know me, ma'am, but I know you; for years ago I was a friend of your Uncle Matt Byrne; and I want to advise you that if you're thinking of taking this house here, don't do it. The place is haunted. I know what I'm talking about—and it's not hearsay."

"But," said Mary, "I have already taken the house and got the keys."

"Well then, ma'am, all I can say is I'm terribly sorry. It was in the basement of this very house here that the Invincibles used to meet before the Phoenix Park murders. I saw them here myself, often and often—James Carey, young Tim Kelly, Joe Brady, and the rest of them. It's an awful pity you should have anything to do with a house like this. But I wish ye all the luck in the world, and of course I don't think very much wrong can happen to a good woman like you."

That night at dinner and later, we did not lack subjects for conversation and speculation. Mary was positive she had never before met the man who had claimed friendship with my father; and she was full of regret that, as she explained, she was so preoccupied with their conversation, she never thought of asking him for, and he did not give, either his name or address. Her description of him, of his dress, appearance, manner and talk, was very detailed and minute, but neither Cicely nor Emily could place him. About this I said nothing, but I did reflect that there are more things in heaven and earth than are to be found in anyone's philosophy.

On the morning of the day after, which was a Saturday, I went round alone to the house, bringing along with me a candlestick, candles, and wax matches. I went through the house, without a microscope, it's true, but in much the same way as Sherlock Holmes might have done. In the whole house I saw nothing out of the ordinary except one thing, and that was in the west wall of the back kitchen in the basement. In this wall there was a recession, as if there had been a small opening into another smaller cellar, or apartment, or possibly, tunnel. This opening, into whatever had been there, or may have still been there, was about four and one-half feet high and about the same in width, but it was bricked up, and no attempt had ever been made to conceal this former opening; just the plain bricks and mortar, with no plaster or other covering.

In all other respects, so far as I saw, there was nothing in the house out of the ordinary; and moreover during the half-hour or so it took me to scrutinize the place from bottom to top, nothing out of the ordinary occurred. I decided then to postpone further investigation till that night. None of us had ever been in the house late at night, and I wanted to see what would happen; so I left the candlestick, candles, and a box of vestas just inside the hall door, which I locked carefully from the outside.

After dinner, I went to the National Library, carrying with me, as I occasionally did, a stout ash plant, which was one of several I had uprooted long before in Carrigmore. When the Library closed at about five minutes to ten, I walked from there with Paddy Merriman and Skeffington to the entrance to Trinity College on College Green. Here I said good night to my two companions and walked straight west on Dame Street to the house on Cork Hill, which I entered at about ten fifteen.

When inside, I lit my candle, and locked and bolted the hall door. I then went once more through the house from bottom to top, giving special attention to the back door and to two windows in the back of the house which might have been accessible from outside. Then I continued up to the top floor of the house where I had decided to keep my vigil. Up here I put out my candle, afterwards trimming the wick by the light of a wax vesta, so that it could be relit quickly when required.

My purpose in putting out the candle was perhaps a little vague. But I was of the firm opinion that the noises in the house were due to natural and not to spiritual causes. It was part of my thought that perhaps someone had found a way of getting into the house for some purpose or another and that if there was a light, he would be warned.

I stood there in the top front room of the house; but I was not completely in the dark. For through the two windows some light did enter the room from the tall electric arc-burner street lamps. It was very cold that night, but that didn't trouble me much because I was warmly clad, and with a frieze overcoat. I stood looking out of the windows watching the few vehicles and pedestrians outside, and noting the infrequent passing of the well-lit Inchicore trams. From time to time I looked at my watch, and as one tram climbed the hill on its way to Inchicore, I said to myself that must be the last tram tonight from Nelson's Pillar.

At this very moment, there arose, apparently from the basement, a sudden loud noise as of many persons tramping the kitchen floor and up the stairway to the hall. It was but the work of an instant for me to take off my cumbersome overcoat; throw it on the floor between the two windows; hang my ash plant by its crook over my left forearm; seize the candlestick with candle and vestas, and go out to the top lobby.

At this point, standing still in the darkness, the din of the scuffle in the basement was much louder, and for perhaps thirty seconds continued unabated. Then suddenly I heard a thud which seemed to shake the whole house to its foundations, and this thud was followed immediately by the sound of heavy bumping on the stairway from the hall to the basement. Then, after a complete silence for about ten seconds, there was the sound of a heavy footstep mounting the first flight of stairs up from the hall. These footsteps continued slowly but heavily up to the first lobby directly beneath me.

When the footsteps continued to ascend, I lit my vesta, which gave nearly as much light as would the candle, and looked over the horizontal balustrade to the flight immediately below, but there was no one in sight. I then applied my burning vesta to the candle, the while the footsteps reached the top landing and were coming up the last flight to the lobby on which I stood.

Holding my candlestick in my left hand I grasped my ashplant near its ferrule, with the intention of laying about with its sturdy crook, but this I remembered from experience was no way to handle my stick because it would give my adversary a chance to grab it by the crook and pull it away from me. So I let my stick drop in my fist till I grasped the crook, and meanwhile the heavy steps continued till they sounded right beside me on the lobby where I stood, and then they passed through the open door into the top back room. Instantly I followed, but there was nothing out of place in the room, and I found myself standing there, with my lit candle in my left hand and my ashplant in my right, alone in utter silence. The sound of the footsteps had ceased.

This was a small room, about thirteen feet square, and for

perhaps five seconds I stood still in its center, listening. But there was no sound. Then I swished my ashplant, this way and that, all round the room, but it encountered nothing. Looking towards the mantelpiece I observed the word "Ghosts" splattered over it, and at the sight of this I became incensed. I stepped over and slashed viciously with my ashplant on the many places where the word was written, as if in slashing at the word I was slashing at the thing it connoted.

Suddenly I realised what I was doing and I was mortified. I recalled in a flash the soliloquy of Hamlet, in which he berates himself that he should "fall a-cursing, like a very drab, a scullion." I had not fallen a-cursing in words, but the futile whacks of my plant were an outward manifestation of exactly the same mood which the Dane decried, and my principal feelings became at once both shame and disgust.

I left the room without further ado, went into the front room, put on my overcoat, descended to the hall and then to the cellar, looking rather perfunctorily to see if there was anything untoward. There wasn't anything out of the way, as I knew well there wouldn't be. And then I stepped out of the house into the bleak night and a deserted street. That night and early morning I walked out to Rathfarnham by way of Harold's Cross, returning through Rathmines. I turned into Harcourt Street and around Stephen's Green, and then home. I wanted to make up my mind what was best to do.

None of us spoke about the matter that day until, as we sat around after dinner, I brought the matter swiftly to a head by saying that I had decided we should not move into the house. I narrated very briefly and without detail my visit of the preceding night. I made it clear that, speaking for my part, I hated to come to this decision, but that there was nothing else for us to do but stay out.

Cicely was the first of the female trinity to say anything, and then, flicking a couple of non-existent crumbs on the tablecloth, she countered with, "Oh, that's all rubbish. Maybe there is noise in the place, and maybe there isn't—maybe it comes from outside— next door, or somewhere, and anyway even if there is something in the place, we can hang relics around and sprinkle holy water everywhere, and then we'll be safe." I had known perfectly well that this would be Cicely's reaction. The whole realm of her religion was fortressed on the North, South, East, and West, by holy water, relics, miraculous medals, and scapulars, with an occasional agnus dei scattered strategically here and there like pillboxes round a frontier. But if Cicely were in the house and anything took place she'd go tottering round the room woebegone and helpless, mooning and moaning and mumbling, "Oh, Mhuire 's truagh—Mhuire 's truagh, what's goin' to become of us, at all, at all!"

As for Emily, she said nothing; but I knew from the look of relief on her face that she thoroughly agreed with me. And then the very practical Mary said, "What about our sixty pounds? We'll never get that back." "No," I admitted, "I don't think there's the slightest chance of that, but you and I can go to Mr. Butler in his office first thing in the morning, and see what he'll do about it."

Well, we went to Mr. Butler, but he wasn't in his office, so we didn't see him until that evening in his home. When Mary told him she had changed her mind about taking the place and why, I could see that he wasn't a bit surprised. But he said he couldn't, and he didn't, give us any assurance about returning the money. Mary ended the interview by saying to him: "Well, Mr. Butler, I hope your conscience will be your guide as to what you ought to do. As for us, although we surely can't afford to lose that money, we don't want the house, so I'm giving you back the keys and washing my hands of the whole transaction."

Now let me ask you, what would you have done, had you been in my place?

Well, we didn't go into the house; and we did forfeit our badly needed sixty pounds. So that was that—but it wasn't the end of it.

On the night of February 26-27, 1903, just a couple of months after these incidents, there occurred one of the heaviest storms to which Ireland has ever been subjected. Damage and ruin over the City of Dublin were widespread. It was during this storm that the world-famed Chesterfield elms—scores of them—along the main road of the Phoenix Park were uprooted and destroyed.

On Cork Hill, too, there was a sight of destruction. The house we had decided not to enter, and which was still unrented, stood in ruins. A chimney stack which had been blown down on its roof, had gone down to the basement, bringing down every floor in the house along with it.

CHAPTER EIGHT

"Prodigal Medical Stew-Gents"

EARLY IN 1902, Father Darlington was made Dean of the Medical School, and in March of that year I organised the first handball tournament for college students, including the students of the Medical School. This meant my making many visits to the Medical School to confer with some of the students, especially O'Connell Sullivan who was secretary to the Registrar; and to solicit the support, cooperation, and financial assistance of the professors to many of whom I thus became well known.

These professors included Ambrose Birmingham, Registrar of the Medical School, and co-author of Cunningham's famous text book on anatomy. "Ambie" Birmingham was a brilliant man and a great educationalist. When making his anatomical sketches on the blackboard, veins were done in blue chalk, and arteries in red; sometimes the chalks got mixed, and it was amusing to a newcomer to the class to see Ambie hold up a stick of chalk and hear him ask, "What color is this?" Ambie was color-blind.

Another I came to know well, and to like, was Denis J. Coffey, professor of Physiology, and afterwards first President of the National University. Coffey always smoked his cigarette by taking about three puffs and throwing it away. Then there was Johnny McArdle, who had achieved, somehow or other, a far-flung reputation as a surgeon, and who looked like a he-man but talked in a squeak. On the side, Johnny was a petty lothario, and he spent a lot of money in the ownership of a few nags that almost always helped to swell the ranks of the "also rans." And then there was E. J. McWeeney, the distinguished pathologist who, because he stuttered badly, often sounded like a sitting goose protecting its nest.

I anticipate here by a couple of years to come a tragic incident with which E. J. was professionally connected. One afternoon as I was walking along Berkeley Road towards my home, there was a commotion outside a tailor shop right across the road from the entrance to the parish church. The proprietor of the shop, a man named Lowry, and his daughter, had had their throats cut by young Lowry who only a couple of weeks before had been liberated from the Dundrum Lunatic Asylum. Both the father and daughter had been brought to the Mater Hospital in which, at that hour, there was only one resident surgeon on duty. Seeing that the father was the more gravely wounded, the young surgeon started to attend him first, but the father waved him aside and told him to care first for the daughter. The surgeon complied, and while he was so engaged the father died.

The following day in the Mater Hospital, I was present at the post-mortem, made by E. J. McWeeney. He gave a most instructive object lesson on the purpose of a post-mortem and its comprehensive procedure. On this subject I will not elaborate, but there was one detail that was especially interesting to me because I learned about it then for the first time. This was when McWeeney pointed out to us the presence of a pearl-like object, about the size of a pea, in the victim's lung. This object, the pathologist told us, indicated that the man had suffered at some time from tuberculosis, but the white leucocytes of the blood had beaten the attack of the tubercular bacilli and had imprisoned them forever in an impenetrable chitinous-like cell.

Shortly afterwards I was also present at the coroner's inquest on this victim, in the same hospital, at which Dr. McWeeney testified. Needless to say, the inquest was gloomy, and everyone at it was grave and solemn-faced until McWeeney came to that part of his testimony in which he attempted to describe the extent of the cut "from the carotid artery on one side to the zygomatic process on the other." The first part of this sentence the professor negotiated with difficulty, but when he came to the words "zygomatic process" he was stumped. "ZZZ. . . . ," he essayed, and stopped; and then again he uttered "ZZZZ. . . . ," and again he balked; once more he attempted belligerently to negotiate the hurdle, and having filled his lungs he hissed forth a long blast, "ZZZZZZ. . . ."

By this time the courtroom was in convulsions, but the coroner, who was tactful and sympathetic with McWeeney, rapped violently for order. Shouting above the din, he yelled "Order—Order —this is an unseemly, untimely, and disgraceful exhibition. Dr. McWeeney, I'm afraid the bedlam of this pack of laughing hyenas may have prevented the shorthand reporter from hearing what you said. You told us that the incision in the victim's throat was from the left carotid to the zygoma on the right; I want to thank you for your detailed and clarifying testimony." The coroner was really sorry for Edmund J., and that was nice of him, but it was sorrow wasted—McWeeney wasn't in the least perturbed.

In March, 1902, I told Dr. Birmingham that there were three acquaintances of mine in University College who were toying with the idea of going for medicine, and who had asked me to make general enquiries about it, chiefly about the matter of maximum expenses. Dr. Birmingham said immediately, "Bring them here some afternoon to see me—come any time before six o'clock." One late afternoon early in April I accompanied the three men to the Medical School. They were John Bassett, Vincent Cosgrave, and James Augustine Joyce.

I introduced the three to Dr. Birmingham and acted most of the time as spokesman for them. They appeared well satisfied with what they learned, and two of them, Cosgrave and Joyce, applied there and then for registration as medical students. When this had been done, Ambrose Birmingham said to me, "What about you—would you think of going for medicine?" And I replied flippantly, but laughingly, "I might consider that, if you'd pay my fees." He looked at me sharply for a second or so, and then he said smilingly, "Come in to see me here some afternoon soon—what about this time tomorrow?"

We all stood up, and Cosgrave and Bassett left right away, but I stayed to talk with Ambie, and Joyce remained. After chatting a minute, Ambie suggested showing us around the place. "It isn't a big place; in fact we're hampered for lack of room, but I'd like you to see what there is of it." One of the first rooms we went into was a little one at the back of the hall, where Nolan, the porter, had set up his primitive apparatus for injecting formaline and arsenic into the femoral arteries of the corpses. But Nolan invariably did this gruesome job after the school was closed. Nolan was a mild-mannered, falsetto-voiced, elderly, white-haired man.

He always wore a cap, and his general appearance, particularly his face, faintly suggested Bismarck.

Ambie then led us up to the dissecting room, where he brought us around from one "subject" to another. At one table there was a grey-eyed, rough-looking, middle-aged man, helping a group of students to put a "subject" in position. This man had all the outward appearance of being a porter, probably assistant to Nolan. When Ambie drew near this group, Joyce and I got a surprise, for he said to us as he smiled at the "assistant porter," "Boys, let me introduce you to Surgeon Fagan, one of the ablest surgeons in Ireland." And this was no empty eulogy uttered by Ambie. As we learned later, Fagan fronted for McArdle on many of the most difficult of his operations.

At a table directly under the large northeast window in the room a florid, muscular, middle sized, athletic-looking and balding man in his early thirties stood bending in concentrated intentness over an open abdomen. On a rack nearby hung a shiny topper and a frock coat, these being obviously part of the attire of the athletic-looking man, whose striped trousers, spats and highly polished expensive shoes were not concealed by his working smock. As we came near this man, Ambie said to us, "Remain here a moment, I want to speak to. . . ." and then, without finishing, he went over to the man, saying, "Hello, Alec, what is the prospect?"

The man looked up, and concern was visible in his face as he replied simply, "Ambie, look here." For a full ten minutes the two men conversed in low voice; and then Ambie came back to us as we stood waiting intensely interested in, but intensely ignorant of, what had been going on. And then Ambie said to us, "That is Dr. Alexander Blaney. He is one of the best surgeons in the world today. If you enter a medical career you will meet him as a professor in several capacities. I could not introduce you to him just now because he is so intent on his work. He has an extremely critical operation scheduled for tomorrow and he is here 'rehearsing' for the event."

Less than two years after that, I saw the same Alec day after day in the same old spot in the dissecting room; he was rehearsing for an extremely rare operation, one which had never before been performed in Ireland, and this was the removal of the fifth ganglion as a radical and last-resort treatment for chronic neuralgia.

Alec performed this operation with meticulous devotion to detail on six subjects in the dissecting room, so that on the morning fixed for the operation in the Mater Hospital he was thoroughly prepared.

I was present that morning in the operating theatre, which was filled with interested surgeons from near and far—two of them hailing from the continent. The patient had been brought up from Kerry, and his family physician had come up with him and was in the operating theatre. Blaney worked quickly and surely, with anaesthetics and antiseptics, of course, but without gloves or mask. Indeed, these latter were not worn by anyone at that time, and the only surgeon I knew of who wore gloves was Lentaigne, and of his cases it was rumored, whether correctly or not I don't know, that they showed a higher than average percentage of "second intentions."

After perhaps a half-hour Blaney excised the ganglion and then held it up at the end of a forceps for all to see, whereupon there was the pounding of feet and clapping of hands in applause. At that moment the little bearded practitioner from Kerry asked permission to look into the operational cavity of his patient. This permission was granted, so he came to the operating table, peered down for a moment into the cavity—and dropped to the floor in a dead faint.

And now after this anticipation, let me get back to the dissecting room where Ambie had begun to give Joyce and me an elementary talk on various medical subjects, including the action of the human heart. He mentioned as particularly noteworthy the reputed record of Napoleon's heartbeat in repose being as slow as forty to the minute. To this I remarked, "That surely cannot be an extremely rare phenomenon, for my heartbeat in repose is scarcely ever as high as forty." Ambie did not say anything, but I knew he wasn't convinced. As we entered the anatomy room I said to him, "I'll sit down here for a minute, and then you can take my pulse."

He went across the hall into his office and came back with a stethoscope, then taking out a beautiful gold repeater, he said, "All right, open your shirt and we'll see." For three consecutive minutes Ambie held the stethoscope to my fifth intercostal space, and at the end of that time he declared, "Well, this is certainly remarkable. Your total beat for the whole three minutes was one hundred and ten." Then looking at my chest again, he asked me, "Would you mind taking off your shirt?" I did so, and he looked at me and fingered me fore and aft. Then he said, "I wonder would you let me use you in class to demonstrate superficial anatomy?" And I rejoined emphatically, "No, I would not like that at all." After putting on my shirt, Joyce and I started to go. As we went out Ambie said to me, "Don't forget—I'll expect you tomorrow afternoon."

The next day I went to see him. He said to me, "Lots of young men come in here wanting to become medical students, but, as you know, they cannot be medical students until they have passed either their First Arts for the Royal University, or a preliminary examination for the College of Surgeons, or for Edinburgh University. Of course, there are the regular classes in the Green for the Royal University students, but there are at present no established classes for students wanting to take the preliminary examinations. Now most of these young men have more money than brains, and they are willing to pay well for grinding, and it seems to me that you are the very man I have been looking for to do this work. What do you think? Of course, if you do this work you will have no difficulty in paying medical fees—you'll make much more than enough money for that."

What could I do but thank Dr. Birmingham cordially? I filled a formal application to become a medical student, knowing well as I did so, that I would never be a medical practitioner.

In the autumn beginning the academic year 1902-3, Joyce attended a few first-medical lectures in University College. These lectures included biology by Professor Sigerson, and chemistry and physics given respectively by Professors Ryan and McClelland in the chemistry lab at the sunken rear of the college, the lab building being a converted stable. But for two reasons, the less impelling of which was financial, Joyce decided to defer his medical studies and take a trip to Paris, in which city he remained till Holy Saturday, April, 1903. It was during his stay in Paris that the incidents relating to the "haunted" house on Cork Hill took place.

Also in this period there was an interesting social development brought about largely by the efforts of Dean Darlington. In *A Page of Irish History* we read:

"One matter in which he (Father Darlington) cooperated was in starting the Cecilian dinners which were intended to bring the Medical Staff and their students into closer touch. Incidentally also, these helped to unite the Medical School with the Staff of St. Stephen's Green, at least in so far as members of the latter could be entertained at the dinners as guests. We read that on January 22, 1903, the function came off at the Dolphin Hotel, that it was very successful, being attended by Dr. McGrath, Sir Christopher Nixon, Dr. Coffey (who complimented "St. Stephen's" for the good work it was doing) . . ."

One late afternoon, a few days subsequent to this first Cecilian dinner in Nugent's Dolphin Hotel, I was in the Medical School where I watched Nolan for a while injecting a fluid mixture of arsenic and a red-colored clay into the femoral arteries of corpses. When I had observed a few injections, I left Nolan still at his chore, and it was already evening, with the street lights lit, when I went out to the hall door and stood for a couple of minutes in idle thought. The neighborhood was deserted, and not a soul was to be seen on Cecilia Street or on nearby Temple Lane, nor even on the normally busy short and narrow Crow Street that ran from right in front of the Medical School entrance to Dame Street.

Then before leaving to go home I went upstairs and entered the dissecting room, where, in the gloaming, I could see dimly the scattered tables, with the "subjects" on them in various stages of disintegration, and as I looked my thoughts went back to that night, only a month earlier, when I held vigil in the house on Cork Hill. I then walked slowly from table to table ruminating on the fate—the earthly fate—of man, as exemplified here by the sprawling cadavers and dismembered bodies of men and of women, who had suffered the last indignity of dying in a poorhouse. Mostly old they had been when they passed away, but all of them had once been young, as I was then, and at one time, no doubt, they had been inspired by hope and desire, which in their cases, however, had led only to the blind alley of a pauper's death. And here they were now—unknown and unnamed. No, I'm wrong in saying this; they had a name—a group name given to them in death. By the medical students they were all called "stiffs."

At home that night I began a bit of verse telling of an imaginary experience I had in the dissecting room. This versified yarn was intended for presentation to "St. Stephen's," the college magazine extolled by Dr. Coffey, professor of physiology, but I never submitted it to that magazine nor to any other publication; it comprised some fifteen eight-line stanzas of which I here present seven; the first four, one from the middle, and the last two.

> Philosophy teaches us much, I trow,
> Of a great many things we desire to know;
> And we sometimes, therefore, elated grow
> When we think on the Fundamental;
> And from Physiology much we may glean
> If our brain's stimulated by some *Caffeine;*
> But naught can explain some things I've seen—
> For our Knowledge is but elemental.

> One evening last week I went down to the School,
> As a medical student should do as a rule,
> Where I, having a mind to dissect, seized a stool,
> And sat by my subject *reflecting.*
> But a feeling strange I felt o'er me creep;
> For I had a peculiar desire to sleep,
> So I shortly fell into a slumber deep,
> My subject quite neglecting.

> Now, when I awoke 'twas the dead of night,
> And the room was half lit by a greenish light;
> Oh you'll shudder to think of the ghastly sight
> Which to gaze on then I was fated.
> Of the corpses which lately lay stiff and stark
> Some argued and talked in the semi-dark;
> Some sat gravely listening to every remark,
> And some—that had limbs—ambulated!

> As I looked on the group I observed with dread
> That a little old gent whom I'd known to be dead
> Came smilingly near me, and, nodding his head,
> Spoke to me with great complacency.
> He averred that the weather was then very cold—

Avowed he'd have felt the great cold, being so old,
Were it not for one thing which, he genially told,
Was his wonderful *heat of latency.*

At this point, influenced by the geniality of the revivified stiff,
I grow quite pally with him, and ask him how do he and his
friends make out. He tells me, quite cheerfully, that they do very
well indeed, and are quite happy about the whole thing, and he
adds,

"For although we can't have a Cecilian din-
Ner, nor go to rest quite as full as a bin
Of chartreuse and kummel had at the Dolphin
Of the best provided by Nugent's,
Yet we sport ourselves in our own mild way,
For we're fed on arsenic and red-colored clay,
And we smoke cigarette butts left during the day
By prodigal medical *stew-gents.*"

Feeling at this point much the same way as Dante must have
felt when talking to his guide Virgil, I asked the complacent gent
to tell me how they got along in the "gloom," and whether any
one of them had ever made a successful effort to escape. He told
me there was one who had boasted he would, and who finally did,
escape, from the gloom, but of this person he said:
"His name I can't tell for a *cause grave.*"
Compare here Stephen's ejaculation in *Ulysses,* nearly twenty
years later:
"Exit Judas et laqueo se suspendit."
And my guide goes on to tell about this boaster who made good
on his promise to escape.

"His words came true, sir, but think on the doom
Which befell that poor wretch who "escaped" from the
gloom;
He's the skeleton now in th'anatomy room,
And his bones from his soul shall ne'er sever—
Unprotesting and speechless and heartless and dull;
He's condemned to hang there with a hook through his
skull,

And—to fill up his measure of misery full—
He hears all the lectures for *ever!*

"But my time's getting short, sir, methinks to mine ear
Comes a warning note which you scarce can hear;
But if on some future occasion you're here
Many more things I'll give you to know."
Then the thin shrill sound of a chanticleer
Came floating up from a street very near,
And I mused on my friend as he flitted in fear—
But I knew why that street's name was *"Crow"!*

*   *   *

The handball tournament I organized in 1902 was so successful
and popular, especially in bringing the medical and art students
together, that I was importuned by many, including professors,
to organize another tournament in the following spring of 1903.
With this request I complied willingly, and proceeded to do the
job, on the tacit understanding that the handball alley at University College would again be available for the event. But when
I had organized the tourney, and it was ready to start, some prigs
and bounders among the boarders at University College objected
to the use of what they claimed was *their* ball-alley; and, to my
astonishment, the objections of these dogs in a manger among
the boarders was sustained by the College authorities, and the
use of the handball alley for the tournament was denied. This
unexpected and thoroughly unsportsmanlike development was
one which I could not leave unchallenged. I had to meet it.

I am dealing with this incident briefly because it is told in
detail in *A Page of Irish History*. I will only say that I went to
the head of the Dublin Metropolitan Police, Sir John Ross of
Bladensburg, and asked him for permission to hold the tournament in the splendid ball-alley attached to the Mountjoy police
station. Sir John was most agreeable and immediately granted my
request, stipulating only that there should be no play during
certain hours when the night-duty bobbies were sleeping. This
proviso was entirely acceptable; indeed, it proved a fortunate circumstance in that it prolonged the tournament—which turned
out to be just as popular with the bobbies and prison warders as
it was with the students.

During the progress of the tournament we engaged in athletic competition including some weight-lifting stunts. One of these stunts was the repeated lifting from the ground with one hand two 56-pound dumbbells to arm's length above the head. In this event I easily outlifted all competitors; a result which vastly surprised me because the bobbies in Mountjoy were the C Division, the athletic pick of the metropolitan police. Joyce arrived back in Dublin from Paris at this time, and the superiority of "Cranly's arm" (*Ulysses*), in the weight-raising event was no surprise to him.

During Joyce's absence in Paris something had occurred which hurt me deeply. I cannot go into detail about this, but I felt so badly about it that I wanted to break with him. In long rambles about Dublin during the week after Easter, I talked the matter over with him exhaustively, but it seemed to me that his explanation explained nothing, and I would not agree to a continuation of our friendship. With this understanding, we parted finally on Friday night. On the following Sunday morning, the postman delivered to me this letter from James A. Joyce:

Dear Byrne:

Would you care to meet me tomorrow (Sunday) in Prince's St. at one o'clock? Perhaps you will not get this tomorrow morning as the post is upset.

J A J

7 S Peter's Terrace, Cabra

Saturday night

In writing this letter to me Joyce proved that, in a way, he knew me better than I knew myself. We had said goodbye to each other —definitely; and yet only twenty-four hours later he wrote to ask me to meet him. And, of course, I did meet him—in Prince's Street at one o'clock.

That Sunday afternoon, evening, and night, we walked through all the southern suburbs of Dublin. And as we walked we talked; and gradually James Joyce won, in substantial part, his battle for a continued friendship.

Towards the end of *A Portrait of the Artist*, Joyce writes about this long walk and talk. As usual, however, he mixes this event with events of other times and places. In one passage, he writes:

"Their minds, lately estranged, seemed suddenly to have
been drawn closer, one to the other."

I would distinguish here that it was not our minds that were
estranged. Indeed, Joyce's mind was at one with mine in ap-
prehending the cause of my grievance. He knew and admitted
that he was at fault; he tried to explain, and he told me he was
sorry. His explanation I did not accept—at that time; but he did
succeed in convincing me of the earnestness of his sorrow. Looking back on this incident in the light of maturity, I think now
that I was wrong—I should have realised more clearly his difficulty in formulating an explanation, and if I had realised this
I would have been able more adequately to interpret the one he
gave me.

Notwithstanding our reconciliation, there was a modification in
our relationship. This condition persisted for more than twelve
months, but became gradually ameliorated, and by the time Nora
Barnacle came into his life, James Joyce and I were again at one.

Harking back to Joyce's account of our walk and talk in *A
Portrait of the Artist* there are some passages in which Joyce tells
of my trying to get him to yield to the wish of his ailing mother.
Of Cranly he says:

"His hat had come down on his forehead. He shoved it back:
and in the shadow of the trees Stephen saw his pale face,
framed by the dark, and his large dark eyes. Yes. His face
was handsome: and his body was strong and hard. He had
spoken of a mother's love."

And in another passage he quotes Cranly:

"Whatever else is unsure in this stinking dunghill of a world
a mother's love is not."

The point at issue between Joyce and his mother was her wish
that he would make his Easter duty, and his refusal to do so. In
his narration of our discussion of this point, Joyce reports on
Cranly:

"It is a curious thing, do you know—Cranly said dispassion-
ately—how your mind is supersaturated with the religion in
which you say you disbelieve."

And in *Stephen Hero* he quotes Cranly as remarking:

> "You say you're emancipated but, in my opinion, you haven't
> got beyond the first book of Genesis yet."

Joyce would have been more accurate had he reported me as
saying "chapter" instead of "book" of Genesis. In commenting
thus I am not making the merely captious point that Genesis is
not divided into books—my point is that, as Joyce quoted me,
my remark implies my opinion that in order to become "eman-
cipated" you have to read "beyond" the Book of Genesis. That
wasn't what I had in mind at all. For I was satisfied that a perusal
of the Book of Genesis was in itself sufficient to lead one to
"emancipation."

Joyce's attitude towards his mother affected me keenly as had
his attitude a short time back to his dying sister Isabel. I thought
he was callous, and did not hesitate to tell him so; and when he
sought to defend himself on religious grounds, while at the same
time proclaiming his freedom from religion, and his emancipation, I was doubly angered. Look at one bit of the conversation
between Cranly and Stephen, as told in *A Portrait,* which for academic purposes, I accept as he reported it.

"Let me ask you a question. Do you love your mother?—
Stephen shook his head slowly.

—I don't know what your words mean—he said simply.

—Have you never loved anyone?—Cranly asked.

—Do you mean women?—

—I am not speaking of that—Cranly said in a colder tone.

—I ask you if you ever felt love towards anyone or anything.—
Stephen walked on beside his friend, staring gloomily at the
footpath."

Let me make it clear that this incident of Joyce and his mother
was not the cause of the near rupture in our relationship. But I
did feel deeply his refusal to comply with what he knew was practically her dying wish; and my feeling, I repeat, was further
deepened by the explanation he gave for his refusal. To quote
once more from *A Portrait:*

"—Cranly, I had an unpleasant quarrel this evening.—

—With your people?—Cranly asked.

—With my mother.—

—About religion?—

—Yes—Stephen answered.

After a pause Cranly asked:

—What age is your mother?—

—Not old—Stephen said.—She wishes me to make my easter duty.—

—And will you?—

—I will not—Stephen said.

—Why not?—Cranly said.

—I will not serve—answered Stephen.

—That remark was made before—Cranly said calmly.

—It is made behind now—said Stephen hotly.

Cranly pressed Stephen's arm, saying:

—Go easy, my dear man. You're an excitable bloody man, do you know.—

He laughed nervously as he spoke and, looking up into Stephen's face with moved and friendly eyes, said:

—Do you know that you are an excitable man?—

—I daresay I am—said Stephen, laughing also."

As partly bearing on, and undoubtedly stemming from, Joyce's attitude towards his mother, it is noteworthy that in his youth and early manhood his attitude towards older people, generally, was distant, unresponsive, unwelcoming, guarded and cold—to the point of frigidity. I do not recall one older person in whose company he was at ease.

With my cousin Cicely he could sit for a while without being in obvious discomfort, but this was because Cicely would wait for him to say something, or else nothing would be said. But with my cousin Mary he didn't get along at all. Mary was a little bit of a gusher; she wouldn't let many gaps occur in a conversation, and she would always be trying to cap a story told by anyone else; or cap even a simple statement of fact, with something better, or funnier, or more strangely factual. Mary was an oddity; she was as unselfish a person as ever lived, and although she was capable and brainy she never learned even the elementary facts of life.

One evening when Joyce was in number 7 Eccles St., a lady friend of my two cousins came in to pay them a visit; and during the conversation, which was confined almost entirely to Mary and the visiting lady, there was a bit of dialogue which was truly stereoscopic in the light it threw on Mary—her deep ignorance of life, and her desire to go one better. The visitor was lugubriously telling us about the troubles in a family she knew: the husband had just died leaving his widow with three children, and, what was much worse, there was a posthumous child that would not be born for a full six months.

And to this what did Mary say? Did she express her sympathetic commiseration? She did not. She said:

"Why that's nothing. *My* father was dead years before I was born."

Mary did not like Joyce, partly because, as she said of him once, "When he holds out his hand for you to shake, you feel nothing but five little, raw, cold sausages." And Joyce did not like Mary. And that is why in his *Ulysses,* Mrs. Fleming is the lady who cooks and darns socks for Poldy and Molly Bloom in number 7 Eccles Street.

CHAPTER NINE

I Leave No. 7 Eccles Street

ON APRIL 23, 1910, my two cousins being fairly comfortably fixed in a small flat a few doors away from our former residence in No. 7 Eccles Street, I sailed from Dunleary via Holyhead to Hull, where I stayed for a week near Anlaby College.

A couple of days after my arrival in Hull, I received from Frank Sheehy Skeffington (the original of the MacCann in Joyce's *Stephen Hero* and *Portrait of the Artist*) a letter which I reproduce here.

11, Grosvenor Place,
Rathmines.
25—IV—10.

My Dear Byrne,

I hope you are not one of those finicky persons who object to typewritten letters. The ground generally alleged for such objection is the absence of the personal note which one associates with individual bad writing. But of course this is nonsense; everything a man does must be steeped in his personality; and the people who can't find the personality of their correspondent behind a typewritten document are irritated only at their own denseness. I have no doubt that you will be able, a la Sherlock Holmes, to deduce from this typewritten letter everything that you already knew with regard to my character and habits. And as further evidence of good faith, I will append my name in my own beautiful calligraphy at the end.

I felt quite triumphant at having succeeded in seeing you off on Saturday, considering the obstacles which you threw in my way! On Wednesday I was at Westland Row at eight;

and then sent the wire which you received. Not getting any wired reply, I went again to Westland Row at one; and as you did not call or wire in the afternoon, I went again at eight in the evening. After my return from this third trip, I got your letter asking me to fix a time for your farewell visit on Thursday. I sent a card mentioning the hours at which we would be found; I suppose you never got it. Anyhow, as you didn't turn up, I went to Westland Row on Friday morning, as that was the revised time of departure you mentioned. Not finding you there, I despatched, from the station, a telegram to you, in the words *"Encore une fois quand donc."* My previous telegram I had, you will remember, addressed to "7 or 53" Eccles St., as your remarks on Monday evening had left me quite uncertain where you were to be found. But, your reply having come from 7 Eccles St., I sent Friday morning's wire to that address only. Then I came home, and found awaiting me your letter-card, saying you were not going till Saturday, and would call at 3:30 on Friday. I at once went out and despatched another wire, (again to 7 Eccles St.,) saying "Three thirty will suit excellently." I had just returned from dispatching it and had sat down to breakfast, when I received the customary official form, informing me that my wire of an hour previous had not been delivered, owing to house being vacant. And of course a similar intimation reached me in due course as to the second wire. I gave it up at that and didn't repeat the attempt to 53. For the first wire was sent because I hadn't heard from you; and the second was necessary in order to show that I had heard from you since dispatching the first. I was in from 3:30 to 6:30, and Hanna for an hour longer, when we had respectively to go out, I to the Young Ireland Branch meeting, she to the School of Commerce. Of course I'd have cut the meeting if I had had any certainty, even then, that you would actually come; but I was quite prepared to receive a further intimation of postponement. We are both very sorry to have missed the chance of a final chat. I thought I'd be able to dodge your cousin by going to Kingstown; I anticipated she would bid farewell to you at Westland Row. So I left Westland Row by the train which starts fifteen minutes before the boat train, with the result you know. I waved my parti-coloured neckerchief (which I won as a prize from "Chums" about sixteen years ago, and which I never wore until Hanna discovered it and commanded its use, and which grievously offends my esthetic friends by its brightness) until I could see you no longer;

then I departed and left your cousin still waving. "He's gone in good spirits," said she. One for you!

I had been considering whether I should go over to Holyhead with you; had you departed on Wednesday morning I should almost certainly have gone. But the postponements make it difficult for me to keep every day free; and then I always had at the back of my mind the fear that I might be seasick, in which case I could hardly be an exhilarating companion. I hope you got the sleep on deck which you anticipated, and which was doubtless more restorative than my chatter could have been—though not much, of course; I can't admit that!

Do you know that you set out for England on St. George's Day—Shakespeare's Day? I celebrated it by going down to the police courts to hear the chalking case. You know, Mrs. Garvey Kelly, of the Irish Women's Franchise League, was summoned for chalking on the pavements announcements of the Christabel Pankhurst meeting. She was charged with causing an obstruction in the public highway "by placing thereon some words in chalk"! Healy, who defended her, argued that the summons was bad, as words in chalk could not obstruct anybody. On this ground he got the summons dismissed without having to call any evidence to show that there was no actual obstruction. Two columns in all the papers; a good advertisement for the League.

Do you know that Father Eugene Sheehy is going to America soon? He starts today, but will be in London for some time, and likely will call here on his way to America. He has been very restless in Belvedere Place, and the family rows have made things disagreeable for him. The American lecturing life will suit him far better.

Yesterday Cruise O'Brien and I went up the Liffey for the first time this year. There were not many hail showers. But the wind was with the current, and both were strong. We rowed down from Chapelizod to Islandbridge with great success. We spent about two hours trying to get back. We did cover nearly half the distance before we had to abandon the task and the boat. The gale was terrific, and our efforts to make headway against it quite unavailing. I haven't seen Cruise since. Personally I am alive. But I did not go to the lecture on "John Mitchell, Socialist" last night.

I don't expect you to reply to this letter while you are enjoying sweet sorrow at Hull. I expect the reply to be written on board the Baltic and posted on your arrival in New York.

Tell me if the dietary is up to the prospectus.

With all good wishes for your success from self and Hanna, I am

Yours as ever,

F. Sheehy Skeffington

On Saturday, April 30, I embarked at Liverpool as a second-class passenger on the Baltic, my fare being approximately eleven pounds sterling. The following day, Sunday, I watched the Mauretania, which had left Cobh a couple of hours after we did, swiftly overhaul and pass us, giving one the impression that the Baltic was moving in the opposite direction. On Friday night, May 6, there was the usual ship's Concert, which was followed on this occasion by a noisy row in the second-class bar. The real cause of the row was too much liquor, but the belligerents in the row would have sworn that the fight was due solely to the fact that the ship's orchestra had wound up the concert with "God Save the King," and not "The Star Spangled Banner."

As the fight, mostly vocal, was proceeding lustily and growing in intensity, a steward came to me and told me that the Assistant Purser, with whom I had become friendly, would like to have a word with me in his office. I went with the steward immediately, and the youngish Purser solemnly informed me: "Mr. Byrne, we have just picked up a wireless message in transit; it was not sent to us, but it is so important I want to tell you about it. The message said that King Edward had just passed away tonight." I went back to the smokeroom, where the row was then about to enter the Donnybrook Fair stage, and waving my right arm, I shouted loud enough to make myself heard: "You are fighting about 'God Save the King.' Well, the King is dead. King Edward died tonight a little while ago." Instantly, the belligerents became silent; bottles and glasses and smokestands, and even chairs, which had been gripped ready for assault were quietly put down, and in little more than a minute I was standing a lone passenger among a few frightened stewards, on the deserted battlefield.

On Sunday, May 8, I arrived in New York, where I was met at the pier by a boyhood chum, Paddy Wade, who had become a priest of the Carmelite Order, and was stationed in East 29th Street, Manhattan. Paddy had secured for me a room in East 30th Street, just around the corner from the Carmelite Church, and that night after I had chatted with him and a couple of other priests whom I had known in Dublin, I went around to my boarding house and got into bed. Almost immediately I fell asleep, and I began to dream that I, like Gulliver in Lilliput, was being enmeshed and made prisoner by thousands of little beings who paraded over me longitudinally and latitudinally in their concerted effort to truss me as a living victim in inescapable toils. I awoke, jumped immediately out of bed, went to my pocket for matches, and lit the gas. When I looked at the bed I realized that my dream had not been a total hallucination, for the bed was carpeted with bugs. I went to the bathroom; washed myself; went back to my room; put on my clothes, and spent my first night in these United States sleeping in a chair at my window.

*   *   *

In July, 1912, Mary and Cicely Fleming came to join me in New York. As they were both over 65 years of age at that time, and as I, being only a cousin, could not be held legally responsible for their welfare, they were held up by the immigration authorities, and, after a hearing at Ellis Island, it was ordered that they be held there for deportation. I went at once to my friend Joseph I. C. Clarke, and, through him, I sought and obtained the aid of Senator O'Gorman, who, in turn went to Charles Nagel, the Secretary of Commerce and Labor. Mr. Nagel canceled the order of deportation, and admitted my two cousins under a $500 bond, the bond to be put up by someone owning at least that amount in real estate. J. I. C. Clarke, having no real estate in his own name, asked for and got the cooperation of two friends of his who had. These men furnished the bond for the $500 and when I brought it to Ellis Island, the immigration authorities there were a little bit impressed—for the names of my two bondsmen were John D. Crimmins, the multi-millionaire contractor who constructed the first New York subways, and Thomas Mulry, president of the Emigrant's Industrial Savings Bank.

From the moment she set foot on terra firma, cousin Mary hankered to be at her old church business, and for a while she attempted to make a go of it in private enterprise. But seeing that this was uphill work, especially for one of her age, she attached herself to a couple of large establishments catering to ecclesiastical requirements, and for these, especially for McEvoy's of Barclay

Street, Manhattan, she executed orders for various items of clerical garb for several religious denominations, including Jewish. As
a matter of fact, if there is at present hanging from the ceiling
over the altar in St. Patrick's Cathedral, a couple of caps that
belonged to Cardinals Farley and Hayes, these caps were almost
certainly made by Mary and Cicely Fleming.

Both of my cousins were devout Catholics, and Mary, as I
have already said, was a daily communicant till the day she died.
In the early afternoon of Oct. 15, 1925, when she was in her
eightieth year, she became faint and weak, and she told me she
was sure she was about to die. I telephoned for a priest and a
doctor; and when I came back to tell her I had done this she asked
me to take her on my lap and to put my arms around her because
she was feeling cold. While she was sitting in my arms, I tried to
comfort her by the assurance that the priest and doctor would
soon arrive, but she said, "When the doctor comes I will be gone,
and as for the priest I don't care. All my life I have tried to do
my best, and I have never neglected my prayers, and I am very
glad and grateful for this because now that I am dying I don't
feel like praying."

For a little while she said nothing more, but then she whispered, "Ever since you were a little boy, John, I have prayed that
you would regain your faith; and I always hoped my prayers
would be answered, as they were, after long years, to Monica,
mother of Augustine. And my last wish now is that this prayer
of mine may some day be granted."

I whispered back, "Mary, you may take it that your wish has
been granted." She raised her eyes to look at me and there was in
them a real glow of happiness; and almost immediately she passed
away in my arms.

Often down through the years had Mary told me about her
prayers for me, like Monica for her son; and always she had told
me she was sure that some day her prayer would be answered. I
never made any reply to her in this connection; and she never
knew that Augustine, particularly after his conversion, was a
person for whom I had scant respect.

Cicely Fleming remained here till 1928, when she returned to
Ireland, where she died two years later in La Bergerie, Leix.

*   *   *

On May 29, 1915, Sheehy Skeffington was arrested in Dublin for a speech he made a week before, in which, according to the Crown prosecution, "passive resistance to Conscription was more strongly emphasized," and he was charged under the Defence of the Realm Act with "Statements likely to be prejudicial to recruiting." Skeffington, with two co-defendants, Milroy and Mc-Dermott, were denied the right of trial by either jury or court martial. Co-defendant McDermott was destined to be in the following year one of the seven signers (Sean MacDiarmada) to the "Declaration of the Irish Republic," posted in Dublin on Monday, April 24, 1916. The seven signers of the Declaration were: Thomas I. Clarke; Sean MacDiarmada; Thomas MacDonagh; P. H. Pearse; Eamonn Ceannt; James Connolly; and Joseph Plunkett. All seven were executed during the first two weeks of May 1916.

On June 9, 1915, Skeffington was tried before Magistrate Mahoney in the Dublin Police Court. At this trial he made a speech from the dock in which the following passage occurred:

> Sheehy-Skeffington: It is not necessary for me to refer to the cases of passive resisters in England, who refused to obey the law at the dictates of their consciences. It is not necessary for me to refer to the imprisonment of Mr. Redmond and Mr. Dillon on behalf of the welfare of the people. It is only necessary for me to refer to Sir Edward Carson—
>
> Mr. Mahoney: It will do you no good to talk about that. It will not affect your position.
>
> Sheehy-Skeffington: It may not affect my position as regards your Worship, but it may have a great effect on my position as regards the people. If Sir Edward Carson, as a reward for saying that he would break every law possible, gets a Cabinet appointment, what is the logical position as regards myself? (Laughter and Applause.) Your Worship cannot make me Attorney-General for England, nor even Lord Chancellor for Ireland, and it may even happen that your Worship may think it necessary to send me to prison for a small breach of an infamous law—
>
> Mr. Mahoney: Strike out the word "infamous" and I accept your description as accurate.
>
> Sheehy-Skeffington: I think the word "infamous" adds to the accuracy of the description. You may think it necessary to add to the eleven days I have spent in prison a few days more. If

so I will serve them, provided I can do so under conditions
suitable to political offenders, but I wish it clearly understood
that I will serve no long sentence under any conditions, and
I will serve no sentence whatever which does not recognize
my rights as a political prisoner. . . . I have done what I
regarded both as a duty and a right, both in opposing recruiting and conscription, and in the latter case I have broken no
law. This prosecution would be intelligible in a country ruled
by an autocrat, in a country under the iron heel of military
despotism; in a country ruled by a narrow oligarchy fearing
the smallest breath of criticism. It would be intelligible above
all in a country held by force by another country, the rulers
of which would fear to allow any expression of opinion
amongst the subject people. If you condemn me, you condemn the system you represent as being some or all of these
things. Any sentence you may pass on me is a sentence upon
British rule in Ireland.

Mr. Mahoney: Mr. Skeffington admits the offence and
glories in it. The chances are that he will repeat the offence
when he gets his liberty. I know nothing of political offences.
I am a long time here, but I do not know what a political offence is. The only offence I know is an offence against the
law, and this is a grave offence. I will sentence him to six
months' imprisonment with hard labor; and, at the expiration of that period, he will have to find bail in fifty pounds
or, in default, go to prison for another period of six months.

Skeffington: I will serve no such sentence. I will eat no food
from this moment, and long before the expiration of the
sentence I shall be out of prison, alive or dead!"

Referring to Sheehy-Skeffington's sentence in this case, George
Bernard Shaw wrote to Mrs. Sheehy-Skeffington a letter in which
he said in part:

"Dear Mrs. Sheehy-Skeffington:
    I have naturally been interested in your husband's case,
and have carefully read not only the newspaper accounts of
the proceedings before the magistrates, but the transcript of
the speech which you have sent me. I have also noted the references that have been made in Parliament and elsewhere in
England to the contrast between the Government's treatment of Mr. Sheehy-Skeffington and the complete immunity

with which Lord Northcliffe . . . endeavoured to stop vol-
untary recruiting by refusing to insert the War Office appeals
. . . .

However there is nothing to be done. The Defence of the
Realm Act abolishes all liberty in Great Britain and Ireland,
except such as the authorities may and have to leave us. Even
if the powers given by the Act were insufficient, the Government could act arbitrarily without the least risk, as there is
no remedy for such arbitrariness except a revolution. It may
be within your recollection that before the Act was amended
it did not give the Government power to put German spies to
death. Nevertheless, they shot one and amended the Act
afterwards. Therefore, if they should decide for any reason
to hang your husband you will not have any practical
remedy. . . .

As for me, personally, I should only make matters worse by
interfering, even if I had any effective means of doing so. As
it happens I am not afraid of the Germans, and have very
little patience with the Englishmen who are. If they cannot
win at the present odds without putting Mr. Sheehy-Skeffington in prison for depleting the British army to the extent of
half-a-dozen men or so they deserve to be beaten. Unfortunately this confidence of mine sends the British alarmists into
ecstacies of fright. They commonly allude to me as a Pro-
German; and if they knew that I sympathized with your husband they would declare that nothing but his imprisonment
for life could save England. I can fight stupidity; but nobody
can fight cowardice.

Yours faithfully,
G. Bernard Shaw."

Skeffington was released under the "Cat and Mouse Act" on the
Tuesday following his trial, June 15th, in a state of collapse on
the seventh day of his Hunger Strike. The following month he
arrived in New York City, and I alone met him at the pier and
escorted him to my residence in Long Island City, where he made
his headquarters with me during his stay in the United States.
His expressed purposes in coming here (and these were subordinate to a purpose which he did not express) were to raise
funds for the little weekly he edited and published in Dublin, and
to gain passage on Henry Ford's rather notorious "peace ship,"

Oscar II, which was scheduled to sail from New York to the European maelstrom with a cargo of "peacemakers," whose announced aim was "to get the boys out of the trenches by Christmas." That the "peacemakers" themselves became mortal enemies with one another before the "peace ship" reached Cobh is an historic fact which would have been laughable had it taken place, say, in a Gilbert and Sullivan opera, but which taking place as it did, was only disgusting. When Skeffington came here I introduced him to several of my friends or acquaintances, including the brothers Ford, of The Irish World, John Devoy of The Gaelic American, Senator O'Gorman, Daniel F. Cohalan, J. I. C. Clarke, Tom Woodlock, Garet Garrett, of the editorial staff of The New York Times, and many others.

During his stay in this country, Skeffington addressed numerous meetings; each of these meetings was presided over by a prominent American, one of whom was Bainbridge Colby, who was slated some years later to be Secretary of State under President Wilson. At these meetings Skeffington was outspoken, one of his favorite quips being to declare in his broad northern Irish accent, "In this war the Irish people are neutral—we don't care who licks England."

Skeffington wrote a great deal while in this country, but although his contributions' appeared in many publications he did not derive much of an income therefrom, not enough to meet his expenses. In The New York Times he had a couple of two-column articles published in the form of letters, on the editorial page; and the usual rate for such contributions was ten dollars a column. On Oct. 5, 1915, there was a two-column "letter" from Skeffington on the editorial page of The Times, the caption to this being:

FREEDOM WAS IN IRELAND'S LAP

But, of course, the man who should have seized it boggled—
Redmond committed his country to the war for nothing.

On The Times editorial page of the same date, the first paragraph of the Topics of the Times had this to say:

"Valuable and needed help toward an understanding of Germany's submarine warfare in the past and its practical suspension in the present was given by the letter from J. S. Rendy, printed on this page yesterday. He showed that the progress of events, as is so often the case—as geographers say is almost always the case—was largely determined by the physical configuration of the various lands and waters held or covered by the several antagonists."

This paragraph referred to one of my two-column "letters" in The Times, the name J. S. Rendy, being a mistake for my customary pen name, J. F. Renby.

Toward the end of 1915, Skeffington decided to go back to Ireland, but as a matter of record it may be said that he at least toyed with the idea of remaining in the United States. This was when Robert Ford of The Irish World asked him to take an editorial job on that paper at, what was then, a not unattractive salary of $40 a week. The two brothers Ford were splendid fellows whom few could help liking and none could help admiring; and they and Skeffington were mutually attracted. Moreover, the job they offered would have been an unexacting stint, which would have allowed Skeffington plenty of time for other work. However, he decided, with a trace of ruefulness, to return and "face the music." And in order that the music he would inevitably face might not be too dirgeful, Skeffington had his father-in-law, David Sheehy the M.P., approach the Crown authorities in Dublin. The Chief Secretary for Ireland at the time was nominally Augustine Birrell, who had held that office since 1907. But, seeing that Birrell spent most of his time away from Ireland, the duties of the Chief Secretary had mainly devolved on the Under-Secretary, Sir Matthew Nathan. I reproduce two letters from Nathan to Sheehy, one which spoke for itself, and the other, written by Nathan four days later, which failed utterly to speak for itself.

Under-Secretary's Lodge,
Phoenix Park,
Dublin.
Nov. 14, 1915

Dear Mr. Sheehy,

I have been in communication with Mr. Birrell on the subject of Mr. Skeffington's return. We think that his speeches in the United States have aggravated his original offence and that no assurance can be given him if he returns during the War.

Yours sincerely,
Matthew Nathan

CHIEF SECRETARY'S OFFICE,
DUBLIN CASTLE.
18th November 1915.

Dear Mr. Sheehy,

Thank you for your letter of yesterday. I hope the necessity will not arise of putting into force any action that may be determined on in the event of Mr. Sheehy-Skeffington returning to Ireland during the course of the War.

Yours sincerely,
Matthew Nathan

David Sheehy, Esq., M.P.
Springfield,
Leixlip,
Co. Kildare.

Notwithstanding the unencouraging outlook, Skeffington determined to return to Ireland; so he sailed from New York on Dec. 11, 1915. That day was bleak, windy and very cold, and I was the only person at the pier to bid him farewell when he sailed.

By the time Skeffington was leaving New York, I had already resolved to go over to Ireland in order to be there for developments that were plainly coming to a head. I emphasize here the point, which I develop later, that despite the professed ignorance of almost all the British authorities concerned, including Mr. Birrell, regarding the real state of affairs in Ireland, there was nothing secret or covert in either the words or deeds of those who participated in the rising. In numerous publications and public statements they reiterated their intentions, purposes, plans, and reasons, and instead of seeking anonymity, ambiguity, or silence, they demonstrated their courage, determination and honesty by making a point of frankness and courting publicity.

I was fully aware of the situation and of the possible personal danger involved in going to Ireland. At that time I was still a "British subject," for I had not yet become a citizen of the United States, so as Bernard Shaw said in relation to Skeffington, "if they should decide for any reason to hang" me, I would "not have any practical remedy."

With the purpose of providing myself with a little cloak, however tenuous, of immunity, I had a talk, late in January, 1916, with Garet Garrett of The New York Times, as a result of which Garrett went to the Managing Editor, Carr Van Anda, who cabled to Marshall, the Times correspondent in the London office, that I was coming over. On Feb. 19, 1916, I sailed on board the old St. Paul, the ship which, on her return visit to New York, subsided wearily at the pier.

On Wednesday, March 1, I went up to the smokeroom of the D.B.C. in O'Connell Street, and, as I surmised, I saw Skeffington there. He was sitting with his back to the west wall playing chess with Alderman Cole. I did not make my presence known, but stood behind Cole waiting for Skeffington to raise his eyes toward me. He had not heard from me since we parted in New York, and I was interested in seeing how he would react when he saw me. When he did look up, and saw me, his reaction was completely in character and exactly what I had anticipated. He did not move nor make any immediate utterance; a blush slowly mantled his face as he blinked blandly a couple of times, and then said crisply, "Tea or coffee, Byrne?"

On my return to the United States in the autumn of 1916, I wrote an article on the situation in Ireland. This article I offered to the big weeklies, but without actual success, although one of the editors of Collier's, whose name was Uzzell, told me that it had been rejected reluctantly after an editorial conference lasting more than two hours, and that while it had been rejected, the consensus of the editors was that "it was an historic document of first importance." Ultimately my article was accepted, but only in an emasculated form, by the Century Magazine, and published in the January, 1917, number, in which it appeared under the title, *The Irish Grievance,* with a two-page photograph of the artillery destruction in O'Connell Street, and adjoining quays, and a subtitle stating it was "The Case for the Anti-English Party." This article was almost unique in that I wrote it under my own name. It is here reproduced as it was originally written, and partly published; and the reader will note with more than casual interest, the diametric change that has taken place in the economic situations of the present two countries, Great Britain and Ireland.

CHAPTER TEN

The Irish Grievance

"Being convinced in our consciences that Home Rule would be disastrous to the material well-being of Ulster as well as of the whole of Ireland, subversive of our civil and religious freedom, destructive of our citizenship and perilous to the unity of the Empire,

"We whose names are underwritten, men of Ulster, loyal subjects of His Gracious Majesty King George V., humbly relying on the God of our fathers in days of stress and trial confidently trusted, do hereby pledge ourselves in solemn Covenant throughout this our time of threatened calamity to stand to one another in defending for ourselves and our children our cherished position of equal citizenship in the United Kingdom, and in using all means which may be found necessary to defeat the present conspiracy to set up a Home Rule Parliament in Ireland. And in the event of such a parliament being forced upon us, we further solemnly and mutually pledge ourselves to refuse to recognize its authority."

In the foregoing words, a bigoted and pampered minority in Northern Ireland gloatingly declared in 1914 its intransigent opposition to any form of Home Rule for Ireland. In Ireland there are four provinces of thirty-two counties. Ulster, comprising nine counties, is one of these provinces. Five of the nine counties in Ulster are predominantly nationalist; the remaining four have a majority of unionists. The unionists in these four counties do not like Home Rule; do not want it—will have none of it.

For 116 years the great majority of Irishmen have struggled in and out of season to regain even that measure of their liberty of which they were despoiled by the Act of Union—an act the passage of which was procured by the exercise of such bribery and corruption as would suffuse the cheeks of a Tweed with shame.

Twenty-eight counties in Ireland have clamored for Home Rule, have often fought and bled for it. Four counties do not want it. Not merely do they not want it for themselves but, being a grossly arrogant and bigoted minority, they are determined to thwart the heart-wish of the majority of their fellow-countrymen. Home Rule, they declare, would be disastrous not alone to Ulster but to the whole of Ireland; and so they bind themselves in the solemn Covenant given above to use all necessary means to defeat the conspiracy to set up a "destructive" and "perilous" Home Rule Parliament in Ireland.

Here is the proximate cause of the rebellion in Ireland; its remote causes drag a lengthening chain through dismal centuries.

The Covenanters of Ulster, banded and vivified by Sir Edward Carson early in 1912, and acting under his leadership, were then the only body of armed men in existence in Ireland. For more than a year after that time they continued to drill and to procure arms, mainly, be it noted, from Germany. They waxed in numbers and in strength, and their arrogance grew proportionately; and always they acted with what amounted to the covert connivance of the British War Office, which made no real effort to prevent the Ulstermen from acquiring arms, and enacted no special legislation to restrict them.

In November, 1913, Irish Nationalists, spurred into activity by the Ulster menace to the attainment of their ideals, founded the Irish Volunteers, who pledged themselves "to secure and maintain the rights and liberties common to all the people of Ireland." The Irish Volunteers, as Sir Roger Casement stated in his speech from the dock, had no quarrel with the Ulster Covenanters as such, "but against the men who misused and misdirected the courage, sincerity and local patriotism of the men of the North of Ireland."

Promptly on the formation of the Irish Volunteers the British government displayed its exquisite capacity for discriminate impartiality by issuing the Arms Proclamation of December, 1913. The Covenanters had had more than a year in which to secure arms without hindrance, and the aim of the proclamation was not to deprive them of the arms they had already secured, but to prevent the arming of any rival organization.

Despite this benevolent aim on the part of the British Government; despite the vigilance of gunboats patrolling the east, south, and west coasts of Ireland, the Irish Volunteers succeeded in smuggling small-arms into the country in considerable quantities, and, again be it noted, these arms were delivered for cash by English firms.

But the smuggling on the part of the Volunteers was always attended with real risk. Several attempts at landing arms were frustrated; quantities of arms and ammunition were seized, and many arrests made. Always there was the possibility of an open clash between the people and the forces of the Crown, a clash which came at last on July 26, 1914, in the famous gun-running incident at Howth, which ended that evening in the massacre by the military at Bachelor's Walk, Dublin, in which two women, a boy and a man were killed, and many people injured.

Meanwhile, the Home Rule bill was plodding its weary way through the House of Parliament, and, when finally it was about to pass that House for the third consecutive time, the opposition to it from the Orange minority in Ireland—backed by British unionists—grew in intensity. The strongest Government in modern times, as was then the British Government, stood dismayed at the bitter and concentrated hostility to the enactment of Home Rule. The Home Rule issue developed into a thunderbolt which threatened to split the very shield of Britannia. The "Curragh revolt" under General Gough, in which he was supported by both French and Roberts, revealed a military conspiracy which had its root in the War Office and ramified to the rank and file, and made it clear to the Government that it could not rely on its own military forces to suppress armed opposition by the Covenanters to the establishment of a Home Rule parliament in Ireland. The full extent of this conspiracy has not yet become known, but it is certain that it was an important factor in the development of the European problem. It reached even to the Throne of England, as was disclosed about November, 1915, by Mr. John Dillon, M.P., who stated publicly in Armagh that King George ultimately signed the Home Rule bill "in spite of threats," and that "many men in the House of Commons thought for several days that the army might come down, turn them out of the House, and lock the doors" to defeat Home Rule!

In introducing the Home Rule bill in 1912, Prime Minister Asquith, in the peroration to his speech—amid the howls and heckling of prominent members of the Opposition, some of whom are his coadjutors in the present Coalition Cabinet—said, "Have you any answer to the demand of Ireland beyond the naked veto of an irreconcileable minority, and the promise of a freer and more copious outflow to Ireland of Imperial doles? There are at this moment between twenty and thirty self governing Legislatures under the allegiance of the Crown. They have solved, under every diversity of conditions, economic, racial, and religious, the problem of reconciling local autonomy with Imperial unity. Are we going to break up the Empire by adding one more? The claim comes this time, not from remote, outlying quarters, but from a people close to our own doors, associated to us by every tie of kindred, of interest, of social and industrial intercourse, who have borne and are bearing their share, and a noble share it has been, in the building up and holding together of the greatest Empire in history."

It may be well briefly to recapitulate here a few facts: After more than a century of strenuous effort by Irish Nationalists to wring some measure of redress by constitutional means from Great Britain, it became obvious that so long as the permanent veto remained vested in the House of Lords, so long would the achievement of such redress be impossible. A succession of Home Rule and other bills, calculated to ameliorate conditions in Ireland, had foundered through the decades on the adamantine rock of hereditary landlordism and plutocracy composing the upper chamber of the British Parliament. To make the passage of a Home Rule bill possible, it was necessary to wrest the veto from this House of Landlords, and this radical change in the British Constitution was accomplished finally by Lloyd George the Panurgic.

Between that time and the year 1914 the Liberal Government appealed three several times to the electorate of Great Britain on the Home Rule issue, and were three times successful. In defiance of this fact, the "irreconcilable minority" succeeded in shaking the foundations of the country, and in violating its parliamentary institutions. The Liberal government, a colossus clayfooted and weak-kneed, lacked the moral courage to do its plain duty, and the ultimate admission of the Home Rule Bill even to the limbo of the Statute Book was secured only on a public statement by Asquith that the "coercion of Ulster was unthinkable," and his promise that an amending measure would be passed.

Such was the situation at the outbreak of the European war. Home Rule for Ireland, with certain trimmings and amendments, was an accomplished fact—not in College Green, but on the Statute Book. John Redmond, after a lifetime of struggle, after years of dog-like fidelity to a Liberal party which had sometimes fed, sometimes whipped him, was hypnotized by a bauble which appeared so nearly within his grasp. Had he insisted, as he could and should have insisted, on the Home Rule Act becoming immediately operative; had he even returned with his followers to Ireland to take counsel with his fellow-countrymen as to his line of action, all might have been well. Redmond's position then was stronger than it had ever been before; stronger than it ever will be again, having at his back in Ireland the serried ranks of 100,000 Volunteers. What did he do? Laboring under a hypnotic trance, and in a fine frenzy at the violation of the rights of a small nation by Germany, he decided on his own initiative to waive the more urgent rights of the Small Nation which had entrusted him with their keeping; he pledged the economic and military support of Ireland in a war that was none of Ireland's making, and within a few days of the beginning of hostilities he opened negotiations with the British War Office about delivering the Irish Volunteers without even deigning to consult the Volunteer Executive Committee on his action. The result of this and similar efforts on the part of Redmond to cause the Irish Volunteers to break their pledges and become an Imperial organization was that the original Executive of the Volunteers turned the Redmondite whipperins off the Committee, and locked and guarded the doors of the Volunteer offices against them.

From this time forward the story of Ireland is one of aggravated oppressions and intimidation. The Defence of the Realm Act was used as an arbitrary engine of terrorism. Houses, public and private, were broken into by minions of the police and military, in many cases without any shadow of warrant or authority. The offices of almost all the periodicals which took a national stand were raided; the machines and type smashed, and publication suppressed. Many men, chiefly those connected with the Volunteer movement, were imprisoned or deported without any charge being brought against them. Others, who had no connection with the Volunteers or with any armed body in Ireland, but who sympathized in a general way with the national spirit and movement,

were similarly treated. Among these was my friend, Sheehy Skeffington, who was sentenced to twelve months imprisonment with
hard labor for making an anti-recruiting speech at Beresford
Place, Dublin. He, with the inspired courage of his convictions,
never served the sentence, for he immediately went on a hunger
and thirst strike and was liberated in a moribund condition under
the Cat and Mouse Act after seven days' imprisonment. Defying
all the conditions of his release, he came to this country in August,
1915, and stayed with me in Long Island City. While here he
made his presence felt both by his pen and on the platform. But
of Skeffington more anon.

The outstanding grievance under which Ireland was forced to
fret was the economic grievance. If it was true, as Asquith stated
in his speech in 1912 already referred to, that Ireland, "a poor
country, mainly agricultural, is, for financial reasons, yoked with
a rich country, mainly industrial, and the standard scale of financial provision suitable to England has been necessarily, and almost automatically, applied to Ireland"; how much more intolerable were the imperial burdens heaped on her by way of
huge increases in taxation resulting from the war—burdens from
which all the self-governing colonies and dominions of the British
Empire are entirely free? That the imposition of these burdens
on a country wholly unable to support them is the result of the
Act of Union, under which the finances of Ireland were amalga-
mated with those of Great Britain, was and is the strongest argument for repeal of that Union.

So far as Ireland is concerned she is overtaxed not merely rela-
tively with Great Britain but absolutely. To continue to drag
Ireland at the scut of Britannia's war chariot; to force Ireland to
sit in and take a hand in the most extravagant war gamble the
world has ever known; to compel her to keep up her end and put
up her stake *pari passu* with a bloatedly rich country like England, would not merely impoverish her absolutely, but would
bleed her to death.

And I beg the reader to realize that this is no mere rhetoric.
Already before the war the Emerald Isle was undergoing a grad-
ual process of etiolation. Not merely in point of finance was Ireland decadent, but in point of population. In regard to all the
States of Europe, whether sovereign or subject, one fact stands
out in bold relief—they all show an increase in population. In

the case of Ireland alone does the ghastly truth stand forth that she has been denuded of 50 per cent of her population in two generations. Just before the famine in 1847 the population of Ireland was more than eight millions; today it is only four millions, and yet there are those who prate glibly of the prosperity of Ireland.

The depopulation of Ireland is due, not to any fortuitous circumstances, nor to inexorable laws of fate; it is due to British misrule and to British oppression, and to the cold-blooded indifference of British governments to the interests of the great majority of the Irish people. Asquith called Ireland an agricultural country; how far Ireland is an agricultural country may best be gauged from the fact that in the year 1913 Ireland *imported* grain, flour, meals, and feeding stuffs to the value of $67,000,000. Under the benign influence and governing wisdom of England, Ireland, instead of being either an agricultural or an industrial country, may be designated more accurately as a cattle ranch, a turf bog, and an infirmary for the aged.

Up to the Fall of 1915 England had always sedulously encouraged and promoted emigration from Ireland. When the British government last year determined to introduce conscription into Great Britain, Irish emigration was forbidden. Why? Because although the British government was avowedly afraid to force conscription on Ireland, yet it calculated on pressing some Irish recruits into the army by putting on the small farmers and laborers of Ireland the economic thumbscrews of want and hunger. Let us see how the thumbscrew is applied.

In Ireland, as in Great Britain, not merely is there the imposition of a direct Imperial taxation, but there is the more crushing indirect taxation due to enormous increases in the prices of the necessaries of life, and commodities of all kinds. The Irish worker has to pay 100 per cent more for his beer and for his tea than he paid immediately before the war. For his tobacco he pays 75 per cent more; for his meat, flour, and vegetables, from 75 to 100 per cent more, and for his sugar about 200 per cent more. As I have said these increases are common to Great Britain and Ireland, but the cardinal feature of the situation is, that whereas the British tradesman or laborer is financially better off than he was before the war, owing to a more than proportionate increase in wages, the poor Irishman has to meet the extra cost of living without any increase in his earning capacity. In Great Britain untold millions are being spent for industrial and munition work; in Ireland hardly a penny. In these circumstances the Irishman is faced with three alternatives:

He may stay at home with his family and enjoy, in common with his wife and children, the privilege of slowly starving to death.

He may join the army and so secure for his family the tempting allowances promised by the military authorities, or,

He may go to Great Britain to sell his labor at the high rates prevailing there, but in this case he will be held to have taken up his residence in Great Britain and will be promptly conscripted.

More than twenty years ago a Royal Commission, appointed by the British Government to investigate the financial relations between Great Britain and Ireland, found and reported that Ireland had been overtaxed since the Act of Union to the extent of $15,000,000 a year. Notwithstanding that finding, no attempt was ever made to readjust the lop-sided relations, or to suit the burden for the back which had to bear it.

Is it any wonder that Irishmen, with their very existence at stake, should chafe under the mountains of injustice piled upon them?

In an able article published in September, 1915, in *Fianna*, Eoin MacNeill, Chairman of the Irish Volunteers, having analyzed the situation exhaustively, said in part:

"Apart from all questions of national right, Ireland cannot afford to pay one penny of Imperial taxation. To exact Imperial taxation from her is to use the power of the Empire to rob her—it is robbery with violence.

"We stand now at the parting of the ways. Within the next few months the entire governmental finance of Great Britain must be recast on a vastly larger scale than heretofore. If the new taxation scheme is made to include Ireland, or to be capable of extension to Ireland, it will hold out for Ireland no prospect but economic ruin. Against that prospect Ireland will have to make no half-hearted or indecisive stand. She must be prepared, first by a clear demand for right, and afterwards by resistance, active or passive to save herself from the last stages of impoverishment, depopulation, and national servitude."

It would be impossible to lay too much stress on the financial grievance of Ireland. Other causes for discontent there were a-plenty, but this cause was the most oppressive and the most readily calculable. Heaped as it was, like "Pelion upon Ossa," it becomes clear that the country which would bear such ills without vigorous protest would need to be peopled by slaves "lacking gall to make oppression bitter."

To redress the wrongs of Ireland and to preserve her inde-feasible rights was the sole purpose for which the Irish Volunteers organized, drilled, and armed. Neither they nor their spokesman, Eoin MacNeill, were imbued at any time with a feeling of ani-mosity towards their Ulster brethren. Against the people of Great Britain they held no bitterness in their hearts, and, most important of all, they labored under no illusions as far as Ger-many or things German were concerned. I remember once being told by a good old Irish patriot priest, Father Eugene Sheehy, one of the few surviving founders of the Clan na Gael, and well known in the United States, that he had said one time on a public platform in this country that if the devil himself were to offer his help in freeing Ireland from the tyranny of England, he would accept the offer. Be that as it may, I want to emphasize the fact that the great majority of the Irish Volunteers had no desire to exchange one diabolic vassalage for another; and that Pro-Germanism, in the commonly accepted meaning of the term, did not exist amongst them. To illustrate this, I quote a passage written by Eoin MacNeill in his own paper, *The Irish Volunteer,* in September, 1915:

"If most Irishmen are not absolutely and recklessly Pro-German or Pro-Turkish, it is not the fault of English domina-tion up to date. Our country has been depopulated, our people degraded, our industries destroyed. An incredible plunder, amounting to thousands of millions sterling, has been extorted from us. We have been set at each other's throats. If Hell itself were to turn against English policy, as it is known to us, we might be pardoned for taking the side of Hell. Those Irishmen who surrender to the prospect that the world must remain at the mercy of militarism, may be-lieve that Ireland, like Deirdre, has no choice except between two masters, and such people, if experience has forbidden them to be Pro-English, will naturally at present be Pro-German. But there is a saner belief abroad in Ireland, and a sounder purpose; and we may thank God that Ireland, amid this present orgy of militarism, is shaping her resolve to be no master's bondmaid and no empire's gateway."

MacNeill is a man of extraordinary erudition and ability. He is informed with a crystal soul. I know the man for many years and hold him in the highest esteem. I know that he had no Pro-German leanings. I know that his single purpose in his public activities was for the welfare of Ireland. In and out of season, in print and on the platform, he has always been consistent. His only object was to defend the rights of Ireland—to stem the swelling tide of British oppression. He was Chairman of the Irish Volunteers; he knew their strength and also their weakness. He realized that in a showdown of actual strength Ireland would never be able to make a successful stand against the superior numbers and resources of England, and, on that account, his consistent policy was to refrain from taking the initiative in armed conflict with Great Britain.

Last March there was a public meeting in the Mansion House, Dublin, convened to protest against the threatened deportation of three organizers of the Irish Volunteers. The meeting was an overflow one. Feeling ran high, and there was much fiery oratory. I remember hearing an earnest little curate from the West of Ireland calling on the people to prevent the outrageous deportations by force, and promising the blessing of God on the undertaking. MacNeill spoke that night, and, as he explained to me subsequently, his main object was to counteract the pernicious effect produced by the flamboyant orators who preceded him. In a deliberate speech, which was none the less impassioned because it was deliberate, he pointed out that the military authorities in Ireland were about to deport officers of the Irish Volunteers without even the formality of charging them with any crime; that any charge which could be adduced against these men could be brought against himself in far greater measure; that if it was the set purpose of the military authorities to persecute the Volunteers, to disarm and disband them, then, "let General Friend, or whatever other officer is in command, come into the open and attack us. If they do this; come they man to man, or two to one, or four to one, or twenty to one, and we will meet them. We will not shirk the fight."

Here was a clear enunciation of his policy and of the policy of the great bulk of the Volunteers. To be alert; to arm and drill; to increase their strength and to conserve it; to develop a sturdy discipline so that whatever plan might be adopted, whether active or passive, should be carried out in concert, but not to play the enemy's game by being drawn into the open.

But there were some with whom this Fabian policy of Mac-Neill's did not find favor. There were some in Ireland, principally in Dublin, who for a long time were open and avowed advocates of the insurgent policy of immediate action. Let me repeat the words *open* and *avowed;* for, notwithstanding the professed ignorance of the British government; of the Lord Lieutenant of Ireland; of Mr. Birrell, the Chief Secretary for Ireland; of General Friend, Commander of the Forces in Ireland; and of John Redmond, Leader of the Irish Parliamentary Party, concerning the real situation in Ireland and the imminence of an uprising, it is a fact that there was almost nothing secret in either the sayings or the doings of the rebel leaders. For months they have urged their views openly and in print. Not only did they make no secret of their intentions, but, as I will show presently, they outlined even the very methods they intended to adopt and which ultimately they did employ.

The head and front of this group was James Connolly. I met Connolly for the first time towards the end of March in the headquarters of the Irish Citizen Army, Liberty Hall. He was about forty years of age, of stocky build, obviously a hard worker, earnest, bullet-headed, and determined to the degree of obstinacy. He spoke with a pronounced accent which might be North of Ireland, but seemed to me like Scotch. A short time previously the Countess Markiewicz had declared his chief characteristic was unflinching tenacity to an idea, and that was my opinion of the man. My visit to Liberty Hall was made a few days after the military had raided the offices of several Nationalist publications and had suppressed them. At the time, Connolly feared they would next turn their attention to the *Worker's Republic,* which he edited, and which was printed in an annex to the Hall. To forestall this, he had sent out a hurried call to the Citizen Army to protect their headquarters and their paper. His call met with a quick and willing response and for more than a week Liberty Hall was guarded day and night. In going through the entrance, along the hall and up the stairway, I passed through two lines of men garbed in the uniform of the Citizen Army, and standing guard with rifles and fixed bayonets. I was introduced by a mutual friend to Connolly and two others in his inner sanctum. Of the five of us in that little room four were shot within the next few weeks.

I knew that Connolly was making every effort to force an immediate issue; and I knew also that within the Executive ring of the Volunteers there was another ring which sympathized with Connolly's views and supported them covertly. One of the members of this ring was P. H. Pearse, Head Master of Saint Enda's College, Rathfarnham, where he had for months been preaching to the boys that this generation of Irishmen ought to consider itself disgraced because it was the only generation in history that had not struck a blow for freedom. It is a fact—an amazing one, no doubt—that Eoin MacNeill, the Chairman of the Irish Volunteers, was unaware of the full extent of the activities of this inner ring. From time to time his attention had been drawn to some matters which, for the moment, need not be detailed. It is true that these incidents might have caused him to exercise more vigilance, and to exert his personal authority in greater measure, but the multiplicity of his responsibilities and activities forced him to delegate secondary administrative details to his associates on the Executive. Certain resolutions were passed, and passed unanimously, by the Executive, which, had they been observed, would have prevented the outbreak. One of these resolutions forbade the issuance of any order, whether merely local or general, without that order being countersigned by MacNeill. These resolutions were not observed, and when the Minute Books of the Executive again see the light of day (for they are at present in safe keeping) it will be found as I have said.

With Connolly as their chief figure and dominant personality, the advocates of immediate action had for their motto: "England's difficulty is Ireland's opportunity." Their aim was the very excellent one of achieving the absolute independence of Ireland; their method was to strike a quick, decisive blow, and they argued that even if they should fall short in their aim they would succeed, at any rate, in lifting the Irish question to an international plane—on a level with that of Belgium. That Germany would lend a helping hand, some of them, especially Connolly, felt certain; but even he, when closely questioned, could give no reasonable grounds for his confidence on this score; neither could he name definitely what form he thought the expected aid would take. Another miscalculation which I know was made by some of the leaders, and conveyed by them to the rank and file acting under them, was that if they held the field for three days they would be regarded as belligerents and treated as such. But as to the motives of Connolly and of those who thought with him, let them speak for themselves. In the *Worker's Republic* of Nov. 20, 1915, there appeared a front page article commemorating the Manchester Martyrs, Allen, Larkin, and O'Brien, eulogizing their action and holding it forth as an example:

"This week our anniversary is not of thinkers but of doers; of men who when a duty was to be done did not stop to think, but, violating every rule of prudence, sanity, and caution, obeyed the highest dictates of wisdom and achieved immortality. Allen, Larkin, and O'Brien died that the right of their small Nationality to independence might be attested by their blood—died that some day an Irish Republic might live."

In another article in the same number entitled "Why an Irish Republic is Unthinkable" is the following passage:

"An Irish Republic is unthinkable because it was for the establishment of an Irish Republic that Irishmen lived and died during the last hundred years! Because the 'clutching hand' of Britannia is squeezing the life-blood out of Ireland! Because an Irishman has no right to die in Ireland now, as he had no right to live in Ireland some years ago! Because we never had such a chance of realizing the hopes of Emmet and of Tone!"

And then, in order to show how much "secrecy" there was about their contemplated method of action, let us turn to another page of the same number and look at an article headed:

STREET FIGHTING
Its Terrible Danger to Regular Troops.

This article is a reprint of extracts from the *Soldier's Pocket Book*, by the late Sir Garnet Wolseley. I give only a few phrases referring to house-fighting that were italicized in the *Worker's Republic:*

> "If the roofs cannot be used, openings must be made with crowbars from one house to the other in the uppermost story, whereas if the columns are pushed through the streets without obtaining possession of the houses on each side, the losses are sure to be very great, and the operation has a demoralizing effect upon the men."

That even thus early divided counsels prevailed may be gleaned from an article which appeared the following week in another paper called *"The Spark."* Under the caption "Courage Under Control" we read:

> "No rash act must precipitate a conflict. The duty of Ireland is to preserve its neutrality inviolate. The act of the Martyred Three and their comrades has been held up as the true model for militant Irishmen at all times and in all places. It has no such lesson. The military lesson it teaches is the possibilities of careful organization. It was no unpremeditated act. It was the fruit of sound planning. It showed what men may do who dare—shows also how men who dare can restrain themselves until the right hour strikes."

In the *Irish Volunteer* for Aug. 7, 1915, an article had appeared under the heading "Disposition of a Small Force on the Defensive." This article proves that in regard even to the *method* of fighting to be adopted there were differences of opinion, for the plan here discussed is one of operations in the open country. Again I give only a couple of extracts that were italicized in the original:

> "The first requirement of a defensive position should be concealment, and not a field of fire at long distances. Sacrifice the field of fire so long as you get cover from view. Trenches are very effective if you get a field of fire of about 100 yards. The upshot of the whole matter is that a force of men with firearms, well hidden behind a fence, with a level field of ordinary size in front, is formidably posted. In Ireland these conditions could be reproduced times without number."

As further proof of the strict "secrecy" which cloaked the designs and plans of the insurgents, let me turn to the *Worker's Republic* for April 1, 1916. I quote a couple of extracts from an article entitled "Windy People":

"A man should never threaten physical force unless he means to use it. The existence of armed men in Ireland is a threat. They have not armed for defence. They have no country, no liberties to guard; nothing but the half-established right to possess guns. Each man's gun represents the value of his life-lease. Each man's life is worthy of preservation to such degree as he is willing to use it for Ireland. The Swiss, the Greeks, the Swedes have armed for defence. Each has a country to guard. Each of these peoples is free. We must take our land from the stranger before we can defend it. Since we have armed, we must be preparing for attack.

"Ireland is cursed with an abundance of logicians. They have demonstrated, proved to the last hair in Solomon's beard, the madness of the suggestion that Ireland should find an opportunity in England's difficulty. Their logical predecessors existed in the days of Tone and Emmet, and Mitchel, and flourished exceedingly in the days of the Fenians. They proved, to the satisfaction of their logical devotees, the madness of these patriots; proved their madness not a curse from Heaven but a madness entered into deliberately, through Celtic perverseness. The memories of the great Madmen are sacred in Ireland now. Even our latter-day logicians sing the praises of the men whom their logical predecessors considered fit for strait-jackets. Logic in Ireland! Let an Irish slave acquire a few shreds of philosophical tissue, and the fool will hie him to the church-yard to rake up and dishonor the bones of noble men; men with great hearts and minds, manly men who hated as heartily as they loved. Logic in Ireland! Eulogize dead patriots, the leaders of forlorn hopes, and condemn, and logically annihilate the living men who would seize the greatest opportunity that has come to Ireland in a century."

Another article in the same paper bearing the caption: "The Irish People Must Free Ireland," by J.J.B. I give in extenso.

"In recent articles in the Republic I advocated immediate action. At the time I wrote these articles I was aware of the different agencies working for (and against) Ireland at home

and abroad. I knew, as all the world knows, that Roger Casement is Ireland's Ambassador in Berlin to-day just as Wolfe
Tone and Robert Emmet were Ireland's ambassadors in the
courts of England's enemy in 1798 and 1803. The letter from
the Irish Brigade in Germany does not in any way alter my
views.

"I recognize the assistance which a friendly power at war
with England can give us. Indirectly, we have already received
much assistance. England is on her knees bleeding from many
old and new wounds! Ireland is the only sore spot in the
British Empire which would appear to have "healed up."
We may receive direct assistance from our friends—we may
not. The best laid plans are those that turn out the best!
Things do not always happen as we would like them to happen. Ireland was disappointed before.

"A Nation's redemption is too precious a thing to be left
to chance. The salvation of a Nation like the salvation of
one's soul is a matter which cannot be accomplished by external forces. In both cases external forces may play a big
part, but when all is said and done the success or failure of
the whole business depends on the person or Nation engaged
in the transaction. *The people of Ireland alone can save Ireland's soul.* And if I were as sure of defeat as I am confident
of victory I would still advise the people of Ireland to strike
a blow at the British Empire to prove to the world our love
for one Small Nationality.

"To make sure that no matter how England wriggles out
of her present difficulties Ireland takes her place among the
Nations of the earth we must make ourselves felt—*we must
fight.* That England will wriggle out of the war before she is
gone too far I firmly believe. That she is in a bad way at
present we all know.

"*If the war ends before Ireland makes a move to regain her
Independence Ireland will have very little claim to repre-
sentation at the Peace Conference.*

"The great war for small Nationalities, to my mind, as far
as Ireland is concerned, *is no more than an opportunity* for
Irishmen to regain their Independence. *This war is not a war
for Ireland's Independence, but if we are wise we will make
the Independence of Ireland an absolute issue in it!* Apart
from the war altogether, however, we have a duty to perform.
We must banish the British from our soil—not even in the
expectation of a German invasion of this country should we
forego the pleasure of getting rid of the reptiles of England.

From the competent military "authority" down (or up, if you like,) to the prostitute-auxiliary of the "G" division—all must go. *The present time is the only time.*

"In some sketches dealing with 'Private Pat McGinty, V.C.' which were published in *Honesty* some time ago, I wrote: 'Nothing short of the extermination of the Irish people or the downfall of the British Empire will change England's attitude towards Ireland.' *A good push from Ireland now will overthrow the British Government in Ireland, and secure our recognition as an Independent state after the war.*"

In these you have a complete and cogent statement of the insurgents' case. Adverse criticisms are met and answered, in fact they are anticipated. Here they state clearly what they want and why they want it; already they had often discussed plans for getting what they wanted. Many a time I have heard it said that the rebels must have overlooked the possibility of artillery being brought into action against them. To show that this point had not escaped them, I cull a paragraph from an article written by Thomas MacDonagh under the heading "Terms, Commonsense, and a Story." This appeared in the *Irish Volunteer* for April 1, 1916, the same date as the preceding two quotations, more than three weeks before the rising:

> "Encourage discussions of practical questions among your men. Do not let theory run away with them. If some wiseacre still wags his goatee at you about your lack of artillery, give him command of an imaginary battery placed wherever he likes in your neighborhood, and get him to shoot your men where you post them. Get him to advance with his artillery through the hedges or even over the roads against you. If he wants to go up in the air as an aviator, let him go. He will never from there see your men, even when they move about. This is Ireland, and your hedge-bound fields are neither plains nor deserts."

The reader, after a perusal of these excerpts, can now see the real situation as it existed in Ireland in the last week of March, 1916. It is clear that the camel's back was loaded to such an extent that it only required the imposition of a straw to break it; or, to use another figure of speech, the pyre was ready for the torch, and the torch was near at hand.

A few days afterwards, on April 10, some copies of a document which had just come into the possession of one of the rebel leaders were given me. In its original form the document purported to be a verbatim and unpunctuated copy of a secret-cipher order stolen from the castle. It contained details of precautionary measures which had been "sanctioned by the Irish Office on the recommendation of the General Officer Commanding the Forces in Ireland," and it recommended the wholesale arrest of all the leaders of the various Irish organizations, including "All members of the Sinn Fein National Council; the Central Executive Irish Sinn Fein Volunteers; County Board Irish Sinn Fein Volunteers; Coisde Gnotha Committee Gaelic League," and further recommended the occupation of all office buildings and headquarters, and the isolation of various other premises, including the Archbishop's Palace, Drumcondra. Copies of this document were sent to all the persons interested, and to many of the Irish hierarchy. The contents of this cipher order first became known by the public when it was read at a meeting of the Dublin Corporation by Alderman Tom Kelly, on Spy Wednesday. The following day the military authorities denounced the document as an absolute fabrication, but the military authorities did not tell the truth. To the appearance of this document at such a time, more than to any other cause, was due the partial failure of MacNeill to keep his war-dogs on the leash.

On Monday, April 17, I went to Woodtown Park, Rathfarnham, the residence of Eoin MacNeill, and learned that he was in attendance at a prolonged Executive session in the Volunteer headquarters. On my way back to Dublin I met MacNeill and had a brief talk with him. He told me that matters had been looking bad; that there had been a long and stormy meeting of the Executive Committee; that calmer counsels had prevailed in the end, and that he was satisfied the worst of the storm had blown over. That evening I crossed over to London to attend to one or two things, and returned to Dublin on Good Friday morning.

At midnight on Good Friday an automobile drew up outside MacNeill's residence. Three members of the Volunteer Executive stepped out of the car and aroused their Chairman from his bed to tell him that all preparations had been made for the rising to take place on the following Sunday. They urged MacNeill to fall in line, and boldly told him that if he was not prepared to do so, he should step aside and let matters take their course. Things had progressed to such an extent, they stated, that he was now powerless to prevent an outbreak, and if he could not see his way to give his active support and cooperation, he could withdraw from the movement and remain aloof.

This was the first time that the real character of the operations conducted in secret by men who were bound to him by every tie of allegiance became known to MacNeill, so, having listened to the representations of his three junior officers until two o'clock in the morning, and being now thoroughly on his mettle, he drove over to the residence of P. H. Pearse to find out at first hand what had been done. Pearse admitted the truth of the statements made to MacNeill by his midnight visitors, and took his stand with them at that time. But later in that day there was another prolonged and exciting session of the Executive, and when it was over, Mac-Neill was again hopeful that he would be able to ward off the impending blow. He published an official notice in the Sunday press canceling all arrangements for the parades in Dublin on that Easter Sunday, and sent special delegates to various parts of Ireland to prevent contingents from the outlying, and less easily accessible districts, from setting out for the Capital. De Valera was one of the delegates; another was James MacNeill, a brother of the Chairman, who got out of a sick bed and traveled in his own automobile all night from Dublin to Cork, disseminating the news of the order of cancellation as he went. As a result of these eleventh-hour efforts, the parade in Dublin on Easter Sunday— the day originally fixed for the rising—was attended by only a very small portion of those who had been called upon. Notwithstanding this, the rebel leaders in Dublin, although they had been deprived of almost all support, in a spirit of reckless, magnificent daring started the insurrection on Monday with a bare handful of followers.

Most of the events of the ensuing week are known all over the world, but there are a couple of incidents to which I will refer briefly. The first is the case of Eoin MacNeill.

On Tuesday, April 25, the insurrectionists had taken up their various strategic positions, and had occupied several public buildings in the city, but very little blood had been shed. That day MacNeill tendered his good offices to General Maxwell, Commander of the Forces in Ireland, to stop the development of the outbreak and prevent further bloodshed. Maxwell replied inviting MacNeill to a parley, and from that parley MacNeill never returned. He was promptly arrested; locked in close confinement; tried after some weeks by secret Court Martial and sentenced to penal servitude for life. Not one of the twelve counts on which he was tried and found guilty connected him in any way with the rebellion or with treasonable conduct. Each of the twelve counts could have been brought against him two years before that time. He was charged solely on his written and spoken record as Chairman of the Irish Volunteers, and on his activities in that capacity. The Irish Volunteers were a legal organization, just as the Covenanters of the North were a legal body. MacNeill was acting within his legal rights at least as closely as Sir Edward Carson had acted within his, but Carson is at present a free man and a power not alone in Ireland but in Great Britain, while Eoin MacNeill is breaking stones in Dartmoor under a life sentence of penal servitude. Just one more example of the discriminate impartiality of perfidious Albion.

About six o'clock in the evening of Tuesday, April 25, Sheehy Skeffington was returning home. As he was crossing Portobello Bridge he was arrested unarmed and unresisting. Later that evening he was marched out as a hostage with a military raiding party, the subaltern in command of this party being under orders to shoot Skeffington if a single rebel shot were fired. The following morning by the order of Captain Bowen-Colthurst, Skeffington, with two others, was lined up in the barrack yard and murdered in cold blood. He was murdered without any form of a trial. He was refused spiritual assistance. He was not allowed to send a message to his wife—who was wholly ignorant of his predicament—and, worst of all, he was not only murdered but tortured to death. Two hours after the firing party had done their dirty work Skeffington was seen to be alive and writhing on the ground in the barrack yard, and a second firing squad was ordered out to dispatch him where he lay. Colthurst was tried by Court Martial and found guilty of murder (a signal triumph for the plucky determination of Skeffington's widow, who, almost single-handed, had worked up the case for the prosecution) but held to be insane; one more example of the Sassenach's keen sense of discriminate impartiality.

I met Skeffington for the first time about twenty years ago in University College, Dublin, and grew to know him intimately. I would call him a pacifist, but to do that would be to classify him, and you could not classify Skeffington. Certainly, so far as the rising in Dublin is concerned, he was a pacifist in this sense that he deprecated militancy and bore no arms, and only a few days before his death I heard him reiterate a statement he had often made, that he would rather be shot than shoot at anyone. All his life he was a close observer of men and affairs, and an enthusiastic student of politics—international as well as domestic. Always he kept his ear to the ground, and often he heard the murmur of the dim shadows nestling in the lap of the gods. That he knew the situation in Ireland is shown in a letter written by him on April 7 to the *New Statesman,* in which he said in part:

"The situation in Ireland is extremely grave. Thanks to the silence of the daily Press, the military authorities are pursuing their Prussian plans in Ireland unobserved by the British public; and, when the explosion which they have provoked occurs, they will endeavor to delude the British public as to where the responsibility lies. If General Friend and his subordinate militarists proceed either to disarm the Volunteers or to raid the Labor Press, it can only be because they want bloodshed—because they want to provoke another '98, and to get an excuse for a machine gun massacre. Irish pacifists who have watched the situation closely are convinced that this is precisely what the militarists do want. The younger English officers in Dublin make no secret of their eagerness to 'have a whack at the Sinn Feiners'; they would much rather fight them than the Germans."

On the Tuesday Skeffington was arrested he had promulgated a notice calling public spirited civilians, both men and women, to a meeting in the Westmoreland Chambers with a view to prevent "such spasmodic looting" as had taken place. Mrs. Skeffington parted from her husband in the Westmoreland building that evening; she never saw him again. Of her subsequent crosses I will say no more here, but I pay a tribute to her fortitude and magnificent courage in prosecuting her fight for her husband's vindication. Alone she fought against a host of mighty and subtle influences, which were working—and are still at work—to prevent the exposure of this case in all its horrible details.

CHAPTER ELEVEN

Continuation of "Irish Grievance"

O N THE OUTBREAK of the rising in Ireland the military authorities were placed in the position for which they had yearned so long in vain. The British government threw Ireland to the military wolves, with Sir John Maxwell leading the pack. Every vestige of civil law was obliterated. The only law in Ireland was martial law, and, where the drastic stringency of martial law was found to be too lenient, recourse was had to that octopean monster, the Defence of the Realm Act, under which every outrage became legal.

But it is not my intention to dwell on the subject of outrages. The whole government of Ireland during the past three centuries has been one long outrage, and the conduct of the military authorities during the rising was only in line with what their conduct has always been. The reader will observe that I put the blame on the military authorities, not on the rank and file. The non-commissioned officers and men behaved as well as, and better than, might have been expected, and in many cases they carried out the brutal orders of their superiors with unfeigned reluctance. Besides, there were at least two regiments in Ireland which refused to obey orders to operate against the insurgents; one was an Irish regiment—mainly composed of young Englishmen of the middle class—stationed at the Curragh, and the other was a Canadian regiment encamped near Longford.

World-wide publicity has been given to the murders of Sheehy Skeffington, MacIntyre, and Dixon, but these cases were only samples. Monsignor M'Alpine, P.P., V.G., stated before the Connemara Executive, United Irish League, that a peer had told him that if the terms of reference at the Sheehy Skeffington inquiry were wider, it would have had to investigate thirty-nine deaths. Military murders were committed all over Dublin, but no investigation of these has been ordered, nor is any contemplated. In fact the details of the Skeffington case became known only through the singularly upright conduct of Sir Francis Vane, who was put in command of Portobello Barracks a day or two after Skeffington had been murdered there. Sir Francis insisted on making in person a report of the circumstances to Lord Kitchener, and, like a gentleman and a soldier, he was not afraid to express his sympathy to Mrs. Skeffington in her trouble. A few weeks subsequently the British War Office rewarded him by relieving him of his commission in the army.

There is one outrage, however, to which I must refer, not because it was unprecedented in Irish history, but because of its enormity, and because it is being perpetrated to the present day. I refer to the outrage of the wholesale deportation from Ireland of thousands of men and many women.

It is one thing to try a man, whether by Court Martial or before any other tribunal, and sentence him either to death or to imprisonment; but it is another thing to swoop down on thousands of men and carry them off from their homes and families, without any charge being preferred and without any attempt being made to show that they were guilty of any crime. The wholesale "plantations" in Ireland in the Elizabethan and Cromwellian periods were not a whit worse than this. To bear men away from families depending on them to the unspeakable internment camps in England and Wales; to confine them amid surroundings bitterly hostile, and to refuse any kind of compensation either to them or to their dependents, is an outrage not merely against the unfortunate Irish victims, but against the universal concepts of liberty and justice.

Apart from any other consideration, it is astonishing that the British government does not perceive the folly and futility of such inhuman persecution. The dragon's teeth are being sown all over the country to bring forth a bountiful harvest of men and women with bitter memories rooted in their hearts. I saw an instance of this one evening during the second week after the rising as I stood on the stoop of a house on the North Circular Road in Dublin, the city being then under strict martial law. A crowd of about two hundred small boys, not one of whom looked more than thirteen years of age, came marching around a corner and down the road opposite where I stood; they were carrying republican flags, and singing lustily and defiantly "A Nation Once Again." Thus the old fires of antagonism and hatred, some of which had been almost smothered in the preceding ten years, are being rekindled and fanned all over the country.

To bring about such a result as this was one of the objects of the leaders of the rising. Apart from absolute success, they knew that their action would elevate the Irish question into one of international importance, and they believed they would breathe new life into the almost moribund spirit of Irish nationality.

A month after the outbreak there was published in Dublin, and for a few hours sold on the streets, a copy of Thomas Mac-Donagh's speech from the dock. The publication, however, was promptly suppressed by the military, and the printers were prosecuted. From independent sources I know that this document, although incomplete, is substantially a correct version of what the unfortunate patriot did say, and it is a revelation of his lofty and detached idealism. I quote *in extenso:*

Gentlemen of the Court Martial:

I choose to think you have but done your duty, according to your lights, in sentencing me to death. I thank you for your courtesy. It would not be seemly for me to go to my doom without trying to express, however inadequately, my sense of the high honor I enjoy in being one of those predestined to die in this generation for the cause of Irish Freedom. You will, perhaps, understand this sentiment, for it is one to which an imperial poet of a bygone age bore immortal testimony: " 'Tis sweet and glorious to die for one's country." You would all be proud to die for Britain, your imperial patron, and I am happy to die for Ireland, my glorious Fatherland.

A MEMBER OF THE COURT—You speak of Britain as our imperial patron.

THE PRISONER—Yes, for some of you are Irishmen.

A MEMBER OF THE COURT—And what of your imperial patron; what of Germany?

THE PRISONER—Not if Germany had violated and despoiled my country and persisted in withholding her birthright of Freedom.

THE PRESIDENT—Better not interrupt the prisoner. (*The prisoner bowed.*)

THE PRISONER—There is not much left to say. The proclamation of the Irish Republic has been adduced in evidence against me as one of the signatories. You think it already a dead and buried letter, but it lives, it lives. From minds alight with Ireland's vivid intellect it sprung, in hearts aflame with Ireland's mighty love it was conceived.

Such documents do not die.

The British occupation of Ireland has never for more than one hundred years been compelled to confront in the field of fight a rising so formidable as that which overwhelming forces have for the moment succeeded in quelling. This rising did not result from accidental circumstances. It came in due recurrent season as the necessary outcome of forces that are ever at work. The fierce pulsation of resurgent pride that disclaims servitude may one day cease to throb in the heart of Ireland—but the heart of Ireland will that day be dead. While Ireland lives, the brains and brawn of her manhood will strive to destroy the last vestige of British rule in her territory. In this ceaseless struggle there will be, as there has been, and must be, an alternate ebb and flow. But let England make no mistake. The generous high-bred youth of Ireland will never fail to answer the call we pass on to them—will never fail to blaze forth in the red rage of war to win their country's Freedom. Other and tamer methods they will leave to other and tamer men; but they must do or die. It will be said that our movement was doomed to failure. It has proved so. Yet it might have been otherwise. There is always a chance of success for brave men who challenge fortune. That we had such a chance none knows so well as your statesmen and military experts. The mass of the people of Ireland will doubtless lull their consciences to sleep for another generation by the exploded fable that Ireland cannot successfully fight England. We do not profess to represent the mass of the people of Ireland. We stand for the intellect and the soul of Ireland. To Ireland's soul and intellect the inert mass, drugged and degenerate by ages of servitude, must, in the distant day of resurrection, render homage and free service—receiving in return the vivifying impress of a free people. Gentlemen, you have sentenced me to death, and I accept your sentence with joy and pride, since it is for Ireland I am to die. I go to join the goodly company of the men who died for Ireland, the least of whom was worthier far than I can claim to be, and that noble band are, themselves, but a small section of the great unnumbered army of martyrs, whose captain is the

Christ who died on Calvary. Of every white-robed knight in all that goodly company we are the spiritual kin. The forms of heroes flit before my vision, and there is one the star of whose destiny sways my own, there is one the keynote of whose nature chimes harmoniously with the swan-song of my soul—it is the great Florentine, whose weapon was not the sword, but prayer and preaching. The seed he sowed fructifies to this day in God's Church. Take me away, and let my blood bedew the sacred soil of Ireland. I die in the certainty that once more the seed will fructify.

When MacDonagh, while admitting the movement had failed, said, "Yet it might have been otherwise," he had in mind the opinion that if different methods had been adopted by the insurgent leaders a greater measure of success might have been achieved. Two distinct plans had been considered: the first plan was to take to the open country and carry on a purely defensive campaign behind artificial and natural trenches. In favor of this it was argued that the ditches and hedges which abound would be almost impregnable. Lord Kitchener himself, it was pointed out, had publicly stated that the best defenses against modern artillery were not those fortifications "of which until lately the engineers were so proud," but trenches dug deep in the soil.

Connolly opposed this plan. He urged the occupation of the city of Dublin, and an attempt to seize the principal government and public buildings, arguing that a swift stroke at the heart of the enemy position would be the more effective strategy. That Connolly's counsel prevailed ultimately was due mainly to the two circumstances that the great bulk of the Irish Volunteers were opposed to taking the initiative in having recourse to arms, and that both the Volunteers and Connolly's Citizen Army were wanting in organization, in munitions, and in commissariat.

As a strategical move the occupation of the city of Dublin was worse than foolish. The total number of insurrectionists in Dublin was at no time greater than seven hundred, yet they took up their stand in a city in which the great majority of the citizens were unsympathetic, if not hostile. The city of Dublin was a position wholly indefensible. Half a dozen British warships could have demolished the entire city in a day. A few pieces of artillery of small calibre actually did demolish the chief rebel strongholds in a couple of hours.

But in the fact that the British forces did not hesitate to employ artillery against a handful of men who had no artillery—not even a machine gun—there is much food for reflection. The destruction of Louvain and Ypres by the Germans was denounced universally, and nowhere more forcibly than in England. Yet the military forces of England did not pause for a minute to use exactly the same vile methods of wholesale destruction in Dublin, under the pretext of "military necessity." Operating against a few hundred men and boys, untrained, unorganized, and unequipped—a few isolated groups who could have been starved out of their positions in a week—they had resort to shell fire and incendiary bombs, laying waste vast reaches of the city tenanted by peaceful inhabitants.

Much has been heard of the fate of the Cathedral of Rheims, and the plea made by the Germans in defense of their bombardment that the towers of the Cathedral were used as observation posts. In this connection it is interesting to note that one of the first places seized by the British forces in Dublin as an observation post was the spire of Haddington Road Church. A party of the Sherwood Foresters demanded the keys of the spire from the man in charge. He explained he would have to get permission from Bishop Donnelly, whose residence adjoined the Church, whereupon the soldiers aimed their rifles at his head and forced him to lead the way to the belfry. Within five minutes after reaching the belfry two of the Sherwood Foresters were dead, being shot by machine-gun fire trained on them by a detachment of the same Foresters at Beggars' Bush barracks!

Of the general good conduct of the insurgents I need not say much. Public testimony to it was borne by Premier Asquith in the House of Commons. To Asquith's testimony I will add that of one other man, Colonel R. K. Brereton, J.P., of Ladywell, Athlone, who was a prisoner in the hands of the rebels at the Four Courts, Dublin, from Easter Monday till the following Friday, when the position was surrendered. Speaking afterwards of his experiences, Colonel Brereton said: "They [the rebels] had possession of the restaurant in the Court stocked with spirits and champagne and other wines, yet there was no sign of drinking. I was informed that they were all total abstainers. They treated their prisoners with the utmost courtesy and consideration, in fact they proved by their conduct what they were—men of education, incapable of acts of brutality, though, alas, misguided and fed up with lies and false expectations. The officers with whom I came in contact were Captain Daly, Captain Fahy, Lieutenant M'Guinness, Lieutenant Duggan, and their Sergeant-major. To all of them I owe a debt of gratitude for their generous treatment of me and my fellow-prisoners."

Looting, of course, took place, but most of it was done by the British army. I do not say this lightly, for I know of several cases where valuables were missing in houses after they had been rummaged by military search parties. The insurgents could not loot even if they desired, for they were closely confined to their several positions until their final surrender. Some looting was done by women and boys of the poorest classes in Dublin. It was such spasmodic attempts that poor Sheehy Skeffington endeavored to check by calling on public-spirited citizens of both sexes to police the streets. But the amount of looting done by these, and in fact by the military, was negligible. To the poor of Dublin it seemed a shame that when a shop was threatened with complete destruction by fire some of the goods should not be snatched from the burning. To them it was not a question of conscience, it was simply one of salvage. To their minds it seemed as if they had a *right* to save all they could from going up in smoke. An interesting example of their mental and moral attitude in this regard is shown in the story of a poor old woman who wheeled a perambulator to a shop doomed to destruction. The store was in North Earl Street, and she left her baby-carriage outside while she went in to forage. After a while she emerged with an armful of underclothing, boots and such like, which she deposited in the perambulator. Seeing that the little vehicle had room for more she went back into the shop to do some more picking. Coming out a second time with another bundle, she saw that her baby-carriage and contents had vanished. "Glory be to God," she was heard to ejaculate, "would y'ever think there wuz such thievin' villains in the world?"

In the Hardinge inquiry into the Sinn Fein rebellion two points were developed which were interesting commentaries on the ignorance professed by the civil and military authorities in Ireland concerning the possibility of a rising, and on the actual numbers and strength of the insurgents in Dublin.

Although the leaders in the insurrection had for months proclaimed from the house tops, as it were, not alone their intentions but the line of action they would follow, General Friend, who had been Commander of the Forces at the time of the trouble, in his testimony before the Commission, referred to the outbreak as having occurred "on the spur of the moment, with no warning, and, as far as I could see, not foreseen by anybody." The Right Honorable J. H. Campbell, K.C., Attorney General for Ireland, stated that he had received "no official communication of any sort, kind, or description, intimating the possibility of any trouble." Major Price, Intelligence Officer at the Irish Military Headquarters, testifying before the same Commission, read a translation of an intercepted Irish letter, dated April 14, 1916—ten days before the rising—giving an account of the parade of Irish Volunteers in College Green, Dublin, on Saint Patrick's day, and pointing "to some outbreak during the summer of 1916." This letter had been written from Saint Mary's College, Rathmines, and copies of it had been sent by the major to the Chief Secretary, the Under Secretary, and the Lord Lieutenant, with the expression of his opinion that "It is an extremely bad letter." The Chief Secretary, Mr. Birrell, wrote in reply, "The whole letter is rubbish." The Under Secretary wrote, "The outbreak in summer I look upon as vague talk," and the Lord Lieutenant, Wimborne, simply initialed it.

Colonel Johnstone, Chief Commissioner of the Dublin Metropolitan Police, testified that the Irish Volunteers in Dublin numbered 2,225, with 825 rifles; the Citizen army 100, with 125 rifles; the Ancient Order of Hibernians (American Alliance), 140, with 25 rifles! When it is remembered that the big majority of the Irish Volunteers held aloof from the rebellion, one can easily weigh the exigency of the "military necessity" alleged by the British military authorities as an excuse for the reduction of the chief business center of the capital of Ireland to a heap of ashes, together with the permanent establishment of a reign of terror all over the country.

It is useless at the moment to discuss the wisdom of the leaders of the so-called Sinn Fein rebellion in forcing an issue. The fact is an accomplished one and must be taken as such. Certainly, the immediate results, owing in great measure to the diabolical mishandling of the situation by Great Britain, were favorable to Ireland. The Irish Parliamentary Party was thrust into an advantageous position, but, under the inept leadership of John Redmond, the opportunity was thrown away. English opinion about the Irish question suffered a complete modification in the weeks following the rising. This change of sentiment was noticeable even in quarters where rancorous hostility had previously been displayed. To give an idea of the change, I quote an extract from an editorial in the *Daily Sketch* of June 13: "Had not the Ulster Unionists threatened rebellion, armed for it, and thus set the fashion for the Sinn Feiners of Dublin, Home Rule would now be in operation, and the Irish problem would have ceased to exist. Ireland is a nation. This is a fact which only those who admire Prussia's treatment of Poland and Belgium can dispute. And she is an ally of ours in this war. Had we done the sensible thing, and started the working of Home Rule in August, 1914, there would have been no complications between that nation and ours. There would have been no disorders—or, if there had been, the Parliament of College Green would have suppressed them with more severity than we have the right to use."

For a time after the suppression of the rebellion Great Britain recognized the international importance—the diplomatic necessity—of settling the Irish question. The enormous weight of hostile American opinion was superimposed as an intolerable burden on the back of John Bull, a back already laden to the breaking point. Citizens of this country, I say deliberately, do not realize the immense importance which was, and is, attached by the British government to American opinion, and this applies to more things than the troubles of Ireland.

But after a while, English sentiment underwent another change in a different direction. The proposals put forward by the coalition government for the immediate application of the Home Rule Act were gradually whittled down to nothing. The old forces slowly but surely crept into the ascendant, exerting all their strength and using the same old wily means to betray the Irish people, and in this they were helped by the apathy which speedily overtook the feeling of indignation in the United States.

At the present time the situation in Ireland is worse than it ever was. The country is under the iron rule of martial law and the Defence of the Realm Act. Ireland is completely isolated. Not a letter nor a cable can issue from it except under the strictest censorship. Not an Irish man or woman can leave the country or revisit it for any purpose without a written permit from the

British government, which can be obtained only with the greatest
difficulty and may be arbitrarily refused.

Apart from the added, and grossly unjust, impositions under
which Ireland labors as a result of huge increases in both direct
and indirect taxation, levied on account of the war, the economic
position of Ireland is altogether bad. It is clearly impossible to
develop this argument fully here, but I will refer briefly to a
couple of points.

No country can be prosperous unless it is supported by either
industries or agriculture. To forestall the possibility of quibbling
objections, I restate the truism in this way: If a country is not
agricultural, it must have some other source of income.

Outside of shipbuilding and the manufacture of liquors, Ireland possesses almost no industries. The liquor trade, in itself a
bad one, has been almost destroyed as a result of the war, and is
threatened with total extinction. Shipbuilding is flourishing, but
only in one center, that of Harland and Wolff's, Belfast, which
gives employment to about 26,000 people. The industries of Ireland have been smothered by the studied policy of Great Britain.
English capital controls everything everywhere, and English capital has seen to it in the past that Ireland should not be allowed
to compete with Great Britain. That is a matter of history. Here
is an example: In Ireland, in Queens County and in Kilkenny,
there are valuable coal mines; but the freightage on coal from
these mines to Galway, Belfast, or Dublin is about 100 per cent
more than the freightage from Wales to these places, and the
explanation for this is that British capital controls the Irish rail-
roads, as well as the British mines.

It is a common error to suppose that Ireland is an agricultural
country. Ireland is nothing of the kind. In the year 1913, Ireland,
with a total population of four million people, imported grain,
flour, meals, and feeding stuffs to the value of $67,000,000. The
iniquitous land laws imposed by Great Britain upon Ireland,
with their consequent rackrents, make it impossible for the Irish
farmer to cope with colonial and foreign (such as Argentine and
Egyptian) competition.

Since the passage of the Free Trade laws early in the nineteenth
century, Ireland has been gradually developing into a cattle
ranch, and the country has suffered from a depopulation absolutely unparalleled. This is not an argument for protection.
The case of Ireland is an isolated one, and the economic position

of Ireland could have been adjusted, and is still readily capable of adjustment, by an equitable solution of the land question. There is no necessity to repeal the Free Trade laws, but, since it is perfectly obvious that the Irish farmer cannot compete with oversea producers on account of the exorbitant rents he has to meet, the situation should be faced boldly and the scale of rents should be regulated to make such competition possible. Otherwise, the Irish farmer will be forced gradually more and more to confine his activities to the rearing of fat cattle and the production of fresh dairy products, and Ireland will tend more and more to become a stock farm and an infirmary for the aged and incapable.

There is one more vital question affecting the immediate future of Ireland—the question of conscription. Should Great Britain attempt to force conscription on Ireland, she will have stooped to the nadir of infamy. Neither in fact nor in theory, neither morally nor legally, has England any right to use compulsion on Irishmen to fight in a war in the origin of which they had no hand, act, or part. British officials, according to figures recently promulgated by Lord Lieutenant Wimborne, claim that nearly 200,000 Irishmen have joined the colors, and these figures, if even approximately true, provide an illuminating comparison with the recruiting in any of the self-governing colonies. Leaving aside the unfortunate fact that thousands of Irishmen already have been forced into the war by economic and social pressure, Britain's Parliament has no more right to force conscription on Ireland than it would have to force it on Canada or on South Africa.

It is true that the salvation of a nation depends greatly on the efforts of its own people, but, with the deportation from Ireland of thousands of her active men and women as a result of the recent rebellion, she has been deprived of the heroic effort and articulate voice of her most devoted children. In these circumstances Ireland needs support. She needs support, whether it be in the attainment of Home Rule, or in the attainment of any other measure calculated to adjust her grievance. Such support may not be active—it may not even be financial. But Ireland is no longer "A Forgotten Small Nation." That she *has* a grievance is now a matter of world-wide knowledge, and nowhere in the world should her grievance meet with more eager sympathy than in the mighty and liberty-loving United States of America.

CHAPTER TWELVE

Appeal to End Civil War in Ireland

ON THE FOREGOING article I do not, at this time, purpose making more than a few appropriate comments. Where I said in the article that "I was introduced by a common friend to Connolly and two others in the inner sanctum," the "common friend" I referred to was Sheehy Skeffington; and the two others in the "inner sanctum" were Joseph Plunkett and Sean MacDiarmada, who, along with Connolly, made up three of the seven signers of the "Declaration of the Irish Republic." A perusal of the Declaration will reveal its close affinity to our own Declaration of Independence.

Amplifying my statement in the article that "on April 10, some copies of a document which had just come into the possession of one of the rebel leaders were given to me," I say now that the person who actually gave me the copies of this secret-cipher document was Sheehy Skeffington. Skeffington and I then went to see Connolly, who told me he was "most anxious" that the secret-cipher document be given the widest publicity; and Skeffington was no less desirous of having a copy of the document put in the hands of two Members of Parliament, John Dillon and Larry Ginnell. I wrote to Marshall, the New York Times correspondent in London, giving him a brief of things to come, and from Marshall I received, on April 15, 1916, the following telegram:

PORTARLINGTON AP15

LONDON
J.F. BYRNE   LA BERGERIE PORTARLINGTON QUEENS CO.

LETTER RECEIVED HAVE HEARD OF POSSIBLE DEVELOPMENTS

YOU SPEAK OF PLEASE COMMUNICATE FURTHER AS OCCASION
REQUIRES

MARSHALL

On Monday evening, April 17, I told Connolly and Skeffington that I was going over to London that night, and would bring with me some copies of the secret-cipher transcript. Both of them expressed alarm at my temerity, pointing out that mere possession of the document might send me to jail, or worse. To this I replied only that I'd take a chance. Skeff and I left Connolly and we walked around to the D.B.C. to have a tea, with pastry—Skeffington adored pastry, but only if it was good. As he and I were entering the D.B.C. there were the usual newsboys calling out their familiar cry that sounded like "Haggle or Mail"—meaning "Herald or Mail." The Herald was a more-or-less liberal paper, but the Evening Mail was strictly Tory. The newsboys, however, were quite impartial, they didn't care which they sold, so long as they got their ha'penny for it. As for me, I bought an Evening Mail.

Having tea'd with Skeff, I parted with him in the D.B.C., he recognizing the validity of my objection to his accompanying me to the ship at the North Wall. I had with me a small suitcase, for, as I intended staying only a few days in London, I traveled extremely light. The lock of my suitcase was insecure, so I had a strap buckled around it, and, attired in a suit and overcoat that had just been tailor-made for me in Dublin, I walked along the quays to the boat. As I was stepping on the deck from the little gangplank, a rather flustered officer in the uniform of a lieutenant-colonel approached me diffidently and said, "You're with General Friend's party,'are you not?" I said, "No, I am not."

This beginning to my trip certainly was not too auspicious, for I had chosen to cross over to England on the very night and in the very ship that the British commanding officer in Ireland, Major General L. B. Friend, had chosen to go on a leave of absence in England. I realized, instantly, that I was likely to be a marked man, and that I could not take the chance of being caught with copies of the secret-cipher. These copies of the cipher document were printed on thin flimsy paper, each sheet being about eight by five inches, and my problem was where to hide them. I felt sure my suitcase would be investigated; and, above all, I could not possibly take the risk of having them found on my person.

So, what to do? I went down immediately and left my suitcase, having my name and address on it, in a sleeping bunk; then I went to the lavatory for a moment and returned to the suitcase. There were only a few items in it, socks, shirts, pajamas, handkerchiefs, brushes, shaving materials, a guide to London and little else. I took out the guide and went up to the saloon where I sat reading it for an hour as I smoked a few cigarettes and drank a couple of bottles of stout. Then I went down; put the guide in my suitcase; undressed; and went naked to bed and soon to sleep under a couple of the ship's rugs. About 6:30 in the morning I awoke, put on my pajamas, washed, dressed myself, and put back my pajamas in my case, all the while noting, with considerable interest, the various evidences I found that my clothes and suitcase had been thoroughly searched.*

That Tuesday afternoon I reached London and immediately called the Times office and was told that Marshall was at home ill, but that I could go there to see him; I said I would. Then I went to the House of Commons and had a talk with Larry Ginnell. I gave Ginnell one copy of the document and told him that whether it was or was not authentic, the knowledge of its existence was seeping through the country and was having a big effect in precipitating matters.

After my talk with Ginnell, I sought John Dillon, and while I was waiting for him I decided not to mention anything about the cipher-script, or even to discuss the situation in Ireland. To these decisions I was moved by the realization that Dillon was completely out of touch with the ponderable forces in Ireland, and that nothing he could do would have any effect—one way or the other; and I felt he would be only embarrassed by any information I would give him. Moreover, I decided to ask Dillon to help me get a permit to go back to the United States. In view of what I foresaw, it would prove, I believed, beneficial for me to have made formal overtures for this permit before, instead of after, the approaching storm. Dillon was very courteous and friendly to me, and acted immediately, and successfully, on my request, as may be seen in the accompanying letter from him to me written the following day on the stationery of the House of Commons.

* I put the four copies inside the pages of the Evening Mail, which I left casually on the floor by my cot, feeling confident that no one would think of looking in such a pro-British newspaper for allegedly subversive material.

19 April 1916

My dear Mr. Byrne

I have spoken to Mr. Birrell—and I have no doubt your case will be all right.

You must of course make application in the usual way—any Magistrate or Policeman in Ireland will direct you how that can be done.

Yours Sincerely
John Dillon

That same evening, Tuesday, I went to see Marshall and had a chat with him. I found him a tall, thin, ill, and elderly man, and very pleasant and courteous to me. As the London correspondent for the New York Times, I assumed he must be well-informed on many things; but among these things an elementary knowledge of Irish affairs, or even of things connected with Irish affairs, was not included. And this ignorance of things Irish was not a characteristic which at that time differentiated Marshall from any of the other London correspondents of American newspapers. More than three months elapsed after my visit to Marshall in London before I was able to return to the United States, and to this day I do not know whether he cabled to the New York Times any account of what I told him, or of the secret-cipher document I left with him.

It was no coincidence that on the day after my visit to Ginnell, a sensation was caused in Dublin when, during a discussion of the police rate at a meeting of the Dublin Corporation, Alderman T. Kelly read the cipher document, which was then publicly promulgated for the first time. Kelly said he had been given the document by Mr. Little, editor of *New Ireland*.

It is curious—indeed, in view of the actual circumstances, a grotesque and ironic fact—that the one incident of the rising which embarrassed the British government more than any other was the murder of Sheehy Skeffington by Captain Bowen-Colthurst; and the reason for this was the universally accepted notion that Skeffington was purely and simply a pacifist. In my article it may be observed that I wrote of Skeffington at that time:

"I would call him a pacifist, but to do that would be to classify him, and you could not classify Skeffington. Certainly, so far as the rising in Dublin is concerned, he was a pacifist in this sense, that he deprecated militancy and bore no arms."

When I wrote these words they were, and still are, objectively and subjectively true; but it is also true that they require amplification, and by way of doing just that, I believe that the time has come when I can say that Sheehy Skeffington, acting according to his lights as a patriotic Irishman, had been engaged, as far back as August 1914, in activities for which he, as a British subject, could have been tried for his life. On this matter I shall add only two remarks now. First, what I say is not founded on hearsay or assumption, but on personal knowledge—a knowledge I possessed from the time of the beginning by Skeffington of the activities to which I refer. Second, in writing what I have just written, I am acting only in accordance with Sheehy Skeffington's expressed wish to me that some day I would give, or bequeath, testimony to this effect.

The one thing really pitiable in Skeffington's death at the hands of a cowardly murderer was that he would have joyously faced a firing squad if he had been tried and found guilty by the British occupation forces in Ireland. Nothing would have given him more spiritual exaltation than to stand in utter defiance before a British military tribunal; and, since he knew that he was fated to die anyhow, the actual manner of his murder was for him a sublime tragedy.

How embarrassed the British government was by Skeffington's murder was demonstrated a couple of weeks afterwards when Lloyd George invited Mrs. Skeffington to London and, during a conference with her, was profuse in his expressions of regret for the "incident" and of his sympathy with her in her "spiritual" loss. That, he went on to say, was something for which he knew no atonement could be offered, but he did actually put in front of her a blank cheque which he pleaded with her to fill out for any amount she might care to accept as recompense for her material loss. Mrs. Skeffington refused to accept any money from the British government.

About the middle of May it was announced in the Dublin press that the trial of John MacNeill would be open to a limited number of the public. I applied at once to military headquarters for permission to report the trial for the New York Times, but within forty-eight hours the military command reversed its plans for the trial, deciding to hold it *in camera,* and I received the following letter from the commanding general, John Aloysius Byrne.

HEADQUARTERS, IRISH COMMAND,
PARKGATE, DUBLIN

20th May, 1916.

Sir,

In reply to your letter of 17 instant I regret to inform you that the only persons to be admitted to the trial of John McNeill are those who are officially connected with the case.

Yours faithfully,
J Byrne
Brig.-Genl.
D.A.G.

J.F. Byrne, Esq.,
Crown Hotel, Dublin.

When I got back to the United States in the late summer of 1916, I launched at once a campaign with influential persons in this country to endeavor to effect the early release of John Mac-Neill from jail. This is another story; and about it I will say no more now than to observe that it wasn't so very long before John MacNeill was released.

Before coming back to the United States, and after my return, I urged Mrs. Skeffington to come here to put her case before the American people; for I felt certain that she would not go home empty-handed. Finally, around the end of 1916, she did come with her young son Owen, and during January and February 1917 she gave lectures in various parts of this country at which contributions were offered; and in this connection the appearance in that January of my article in the Century Magazine helped not a little. Early in 1917, she returned to Ireland, and on the night before she left here, I went out to acquaintances of hers in New Jersey to fetch her son Owen back to New York. Owen was then around eight years old—I wonder now if he remembers the incident.

In the fall of 1922, Mrs. Skeffington arrived once more in New York, but this time alone. Just then the "throuble" was at its height in Ireland with the members of families everywhere in the land divided in allegiance, separated one from another by chasms of hatred. For hours I talked to her about this condition, and I remember saying to her, "I hadn't even begun to realize how terrible the state of affairs is over there till you came; and now that you are here I can sense an actual exudation of hatred for certain people from every pore in your body." And she admitted freely that in sensing this I was quite correct.

I suggested then that maybe something might be done to help, even if very little, to pour a few drops of oil on the troubled waters, and finally she agreed with, and encouraged, my idea that an appeal to all Irishmen should be made to stop their demoralizing fratricidal struggle. To this end I had a talk with Bradford Merrill, publisher of the Hearst papers, and he was all for my idea and suggested that I get a few prominent Irishmen in the country to sign the appeal. This I set out to do; and on a description of my odyssey in this labor I could use up a lot of words; but I won't—I'll be brief. I will only say that for my labor and time in this effort I neither asked, nor would I have accepted any remuneration whatever.

On Sunday, October 29, 1922, my appeal was published in a two-column article on the first page of the New York American. Here is a reproduction of my preamble and appeal, both of these constituting another of the very few articles I have ever written over my own name. To the appeal were added the signatures of ten prominent Irish sympathizers, James A. O'Gorman, Morgan J. O'Brien, Richard Campbell, Alfred J. Talley, John Pulleyn, Thomas J. Maloney, Thomas F. Woodlock, Lawrence Godkin, E. J. Doheny, and Frank P. Walsh. The preamble and appeal:

Editor, New York American:

Being in the profound belief that the time has come for making a supreme effort to re-establish peace in the twenty-six southern counties of Ireland, I am moved to make this appeal to my fellow citizens of the United States who are interested in the promotion of peace for its own sake or for the welfare of Ireland.

As a native of Dublin and a graduate of the old Royal, now the National University, I have many life-long friends in both camps, and I have enjoyed since nearly twenty-five years ago the friendship of many of my illustrious countrymen who have moved all too soon to their final resting place in the melancholy Hall of Erin's Fame.

Example being better than precept, there is nothing that would have a more salutary effect on the contending parties in Ireland than a demonstration by the Irish sympathizers in this country of their ability to combine for the achievement of a common object. The object I have in view is the

declaration of a truce in Ireland and an immediate conference between Free State and Republican leaders.

I ask you, sir, to realize that I am not now holding any
brief for the protagonists of the Irish Republic. I will go
further and say that, on grounds of utility and expediency,
there was no more reason for refusing the Free State treaty
than there would be for refusing a lift to Los Angeles because
the car wasn't going to the Golden Gate.

On the other hand, it behooved those who did accept the
Free State treaty to use ordinary caution in avoiding the pit-
falls which the light of experience should have shown gaping
in their path. For instance, is it not a measure of question-
able wisdom for the Free State Government to hand over,
in times like these, as was done on October 15, the power of
inflicting the death penalty to a military committee including "one member certified as possessing knowledge and experience at law"—possibly a shyster tout?

Denouncing this proposal in the Dail, Labor Chairman
Johnson warned against transferring the authority of Parliament to an undisciplined army. "You have not got in your
army today," said Mr. Johnson, "that perfect discipline and
control which will prevent a fearful disaster coming upon the
country's good name."

And, later, Dr. McCartan, in an effort which he explained
was intended to counteract the "monstrous proposals" of the
Government, asked leave to introduce in the Dail a motion
declaring for an "immediate truce" lasting not less than fourteen days to save the country from "economic disaster."

The condition of Ireland is bad, but it is not ameliorated
by recrimination and abuse, especially when slung from this
side of the Atlantic.

Other nations have had their civil wars—and have waged
them with scant civility. If Irishmen do kill one another they
do so only in what has come to be regarded as fair fight, and
loose accusations of murder hurled against either side are
slanders born of an invincible and corroding ignorance.

In an editorial on the funeral of the redoubtable Michael
Collins, the Dublin Freeman's Journal said:

"For the honor of Irish human nature be it recorded, too,
that hundreds of those comrades whom he had lost joined
in the honor paid to the dead leader. Perhaps out of the
feeling that this action represents may spring a new hope."

There is the hope that is fluttering timidly in the hearts of millions and for the realization of which they offer up their prayers in secret.

Speaking a few weeks ago in Ireland on the political situation in his native land, John McCormack is quoted, again by the Freeman, as "expressing an earnest hope for termination of the bitterness and tragedy which prevail, and for a speedy settlement which will bring peace and prosperity to the country he loves so well."

There it is again, the "earnest hope," the hope of all of us.

The hills and roadsides of Ireland are bespattered by the blood of Irishmen spilt by brother Irishmen. This is, unfortunately, no mere figure of speech. It is a deplorable condition illustrated most vividly in the recent death of young Brian MacNeill while fighting in a Republican army against a Free State army in which two of his brothers are soldiers, and against a Free State government in which his own father is Minister of Education.

Can anyone imagine a condition more calculated to gratify an hereditary enemy?

For this reason, therefore, and in the name of peace and of the salvation of Ireland, I call for a countrywide endorsement, or approval, of the annexed message already signed by many eminent Americans, sincere friends of Ireland.

                                                        J. F. BYRNE

                          *   *   *

To the Government of the Irish Free State and to the Responsible Leaders Among the Republicans in Ireland:

In the name of peace, and of the salvation of Ireland, and of all the dead patriots who, like Griffith, Collins, Burgess, MacNeill, Boland and the rest, have made their last sacrifice in upholding their convictions, we urge you with all the earnestness that in us lies forthwith to put aside your arms and to confer immediately one with another in order to arrive at an honorable agreement.

And we express our belief that in the present circumstances the matter and form of that agreement will not be of nearly so much importance as its achievement.

To this end we pledge our support, and we avow our readiness to stand by you during your deliberations in an attitude of cordial sympathy.

On the Sunday of the publication of this appeal there were rumblings of dissent and disapprobation in certain quarters in

the United States, and, indeed, Mrs. Skeffington herself saw fit to write disparagingly about it, giving no hint in what she wrote that she herself had approved of the idea. However, I don't now, nor did I then, blame her for her inconsistent disparagement— the good lady was distraught.

Coincidences as a rule are strange, and not the least strange of them is the fact that on the very same day, October 29, 1922, Pope Pius addressed an appeal to the factions in Italy to stop fighting. Practically all big newspapers in this country carried a reference to the Pope's appeal, and on the front page of the New York American on Monday, October 30, there appeared in a story about Italy this paragraph:

"Pope Pius has addressed an apostolic letter to the Italian Bishops in which he deprecates 'the fratricidal struggle afflicting our beloved country.'"

In his appeal the Pontiff said in part:

"Italian citizens, in the name of our universal brotherhood may we all unite in love toward our Italian land so blessed by God, and in the name of that noble brotherhood which in the religion of Christ united Italy's sons in one single family, the Pope calls out to you all, like St. Stephen in the acts of the Apostles, 'Stop, oh men, be brothers—why do you molest each other?'"

CHAPTER THIRTEEN

I Visit James Joyce in Paris, 1927

DURING THE PAST couple of decades, I have sometimes felt inclined to deplore the mediocrity of the biographical work done on James Joyce, and also the literary and critical evaluations of his works. But my misgivings on these points have been allayed by two reflections. The first of these reflections is this: Of the great number of persons who have achieved, for one reason or another, a niche in the temple of fame, how many do we really know anything about? How many of them have had biographers with any aptitude or ability for biographing? It is my conviction that of even those who have had the best biographical work done on them we really know almost nothing. This conviction of mine derives, in some degree, from the fact that I knew James Joyce so well that I wouldn't recognize him from the pen pictures of his biographers.

The second of my reflections derives from the fact that at no time since I knew him, and that was from the time he was 11 years old, did Joyce care what the vast majority of people said or wrote about him. There were a few persons—an extremely small few—who could have been excepted from this generalization. "The friends thou hast and their adoption tried," says Polonius, "grapple them to thy soul with hoops of steel." Joyce could and did grapple tenaciously—but he did not grapple many.

In June 1933, Joyce told me that Mr. Gorman was going, for the second time, to do a biography of him; whereupon I commented, "Wouldn't you think of giving the job to somebody else? You know what kind of biography his first effort was." And Joyce said simply, "But there isn't anybody else that I know of, do you?" I admitted, "No, I don't. But I think it would be better not to have the biography done at all, than have somebody turn out a poor job." Joyce's response to this remark of mine was laconic and in character: "Ah, sure I don't care what they write."

Well, the biographer in question did not produce his opus until 1940, and I never had an opportunity to discuss it with Joyce. What with the world being in such turmoil, I never saw him again.

In the back of this second "biography," there was a kind of postscript page captioned "acknowledgments." On this page the author "tenders acknowledgments for material, hints and suggestions" to a great number of persons, among them one named J. Francis Byrne. It would seem as if he must have meant me; but if so it is puzzling, because he was "tendering his acknowledgments" to me for nothing. I never spoke or wrote to Mr. Gorman about Joyce in my life. And to this statement I add that I have never until now spoken or written a word to anybody about Joyce for publication.

But in this paragraph of "Acknowledgments" there was something even more puzzling. The author says: "To James Joyce himself I am indebted for his patience in answering questions, his calm unconcern for my deductions and assumptions." Now there is a statement which is self-contradictory. As for the first part of this statement regarding Joyce's "patience" in the given circumstances, I don't believe it. And as for the second part, why should the author express indebtedness to Joyce for his "calm unconcern for my deductions and assumptions"?

I do not intend to dilate on the subject of this biography, but there are a few things in it that I would like to animadvert upon for the record. For instance, this author says of Joyce that "he had no mercy for easy 'writing,' grammatical slips or loose ends." But in this very book he quotes what he describes as "odd scraps, phrases and hints set down" by Joyce as they "reveal so clearly the widely-searching antennae of the creator for precisions and motives." And among these illustrations of "precisions," he has one relating to "Byrne" which describes his "aquiline nose." Now I know that Joyce nodded, Homerically, now and then in regard to spelling. But I do not think Joyce used many words without knowing what they meant; and I do think he probably knew the meaning of the words "aquiline nose." My nose is not and never was aquiline, a fact which the author of the biography should have observed for himself on the occasions when I was imparting to him the "material hints and suggestions" for which he so graciously "tendered" to me his "acknowledgments."

Regarding Joyce the author says, "We have the spectacle of the young man assiduously analyzing the works of his contemporaries * * * and pouncing upon their lapses with an unholy glee." I doubt very much whether the biographer appreciated the full import of the accuracy of this observation.

Let me digress here for a little while. I sat in the same class with Joyce in Room No. 3 in Belvedere College, from 1894 to 1895. The large windows of this classroom gave south; and in the southwest corner there was the teacher's dais. At the west and east walls there were folding doors, opening respectively to the preparatory and middle grade classrooms. At the northeast corner in the north wall was the door to the corridor outside. In the room there were two rows of desks; four desks to the row, with a passageway between the rows. Each desk could accommodate four pupils. Joyce always sat near the window in the front desk of the left row, facing the teacher, and immediately under the dais. I sat always in the back desk of the right row, just one seat space from the door; that space next the door was occupied during that year by Joe Culhane; Joe's brother, Frank, sat in the back desk of the left row. I don't know about Joe, but Frank has been dead since 1927. He was Taxing Master in Dublin City and had been married to Maggie Sheehy, one of the four daughters of David Sheehy, the M.P. One of these daughters is referred to by Joyce in the *Portrait of the Artist*. The eldest daughter, Hannah, married Skeffington; Mary became the wife of Tom Kettle, and Kathleen wedded Cruise O'Brien.

In this class there were about thirty boys, all of them good lads, and some of them really intelligent. There were two brothers, Keogh, who were obviously great chums. They lived over Rathmines way. The younger of these two brothers was one of the best and best-looking boys I ever knew—I think he was the youngest and he was certainly one of the brightest, in the class. He was small, but well-built and strong; with large blue eyes and curly golden hair. Towards the end of that school year this little fellow took sick and died. We were all very sad about it; at least I know I was. Joyce was a little boy, bright, well-looking, and apparently delicate. But he really wasn't delicate; he was virile enough physically. He was a bright boy, always the good scholar, and he was favored by all the teachers, especially Dempsey, the English teacher, who, as I recall now over the intervening years, resembled Justice Holmes.

In some respects Joyce was precocious; in others he was, and remained, rather strangely simple. Dempsey liked him a great deal, but I think he liked the little fellow for his own sake, just as much as for his proficiency in English. Each Monday we were supposed to bring in an English composition, and of course all of us—well, very nearly all—complied. A few of the "composers" would be asked by Dempsey to read their lucubrations, and among these James Joyce was one of the most frequently called upon. Joyce was a good reader, and the while he read, Dempsey would literally wriggle and chuckle with delight. Generally, the class, too, liked Joyce's efforts, but there were occasions when the floridity of his stuff made you feel as if you were in the hot-house out in the Botanic Gardens.

Joyce had a fine sense of humor, but his definitely favorite mirth rouser was when anyone pulled a boner. Always he sat in an elfin crouch waiting and hoping for a blunder. For instance, that day when the word "pedestrian" came up and Dempsey asked the class, "What is a pedestrian?" One kid's arm shot up like a semaphore.

"Well, Reuben, what is a pedestrian?"

"A pedestrian is a Roman soldier, Sir."

Joyce's spontaneous shout—well, you couldn't describe it as a laugh—was more like a howl of agony, as if his little frame were being torn apart.

And now I have arrived at the point I wanted to make: A boner remained always the great outstanding source of mirth for Joyce. I know that if he ever read the biography I am talking about it afforded him ample scope for many such howls. And this, mind you, would not be wholly the author's fault. I say deliberately that it would have been at any time quite within Joyce's sense of propriety to refrain from pointing out an error not merely in "deductions and assumptions," but in actual matters of fact.

There is one passage in this book that doesn't belong even in a waste basket. I wonder what the author's source for this passage was? Could it have been the ill-begotten offspring of his "deductions and assumptions"? The author is narrating incidents immediately prior to Joyce's departure with Nora from Dublin. Here is this tidbit:

> "There were a few farewells to be made. These were easy for Joyce sensed the lack of faith in his acquaintances and comrades and this, as always, heightened his arrogance and steeled his determination. John Eglinton was sure that he would come back begging to Dublin; J. Francis Byrne was certain that he would become a drunkard; Cosgrave, the 'lecherous lynx,' prophesied that he would develop into a nymphomaniac; Skeffington, the bearded, knickerbockered, stout reformer of society, averred that he had made the mistake of his life in the comrade he had chosen. All of them appeared to think that he was an obstinate creature with no sense of values. . . ."

From what corrupt source this passage first crawled I don't know. Regarding it I have this to say: Of Cosgrave, I say that he knew the meaning of the word "nymphomaniac," which, obviously, the author does not. For Skeffington, whom I knew well, I say the passage lies; and for myself, I say it is calumnious.

More than a fortnight before they left Dublin, Joyce spent a long evening with me in my home at 100 Phibsboro Road. There he unfolded the ideas that were in his mind; and he asked me for my advice. Specifically, he told me he would like to take Nora away with him; and he wanted to know whether he ought to ask her, and whether I thought she would go with him if he did. I knew what he meant, so I looked at him earnestly, and I said to him, "Are you very fond of Nora?" "Yes, I am," he told me simply.

"Do you love Nora?" I pressed him.

"Honestly, Byrne, there's not another girl in the world I could ever love as I do Nora."

And I said then to James Joyce, "Don't wait, and don't hesitate. Ask Nora, and if she agrees to go away with you, take her."

After Joyce and Nora left Dublin in 1904, I did not see Nora again until I visited them in Paris in 1927. Looking back on that visit, I can review it in fond memory. There was a scarcely perceptible trace of apprehension regarding the children; but on the whole it was a happy home. Joyce was enthusiastically putting the finishing touches to his *Work in Progress* which was appearing

monthly in Transition since April of that year. He gave me copies
of Transition covering April to November, and I still have them.
Yes, we had an enjoyable reunion; everyday Joyce and I discussed
the *Work in Progress* for hours, and he would ask me to read
aloud passages he would indicate from his manuscript. This gave
him a kind of thrill, because—well, I was a good reader, and I
wasn't so long away from my pure Dublin accent as I am now.

> 2, Square Robiac
> 192, Rue De Grenelle
> Paris

Dear Mrs. Byrne: I am very glad to meet my old friend
Byrne after so many years and it is most kind of you to allow
him to stay a few days. I hope you will not be annoyed if we
press him to stay over the weekend as the weather is very fine
and he ought to see a number of things here before he leaves.
The change too will do him good. He will go back on Monday or Tuesday unless you should wish him to return earlier.

> With kind regards
> Sincerely yours
> James Joyce

10.XI.27

On one of these days in Paris, Nora came with me alone on a
shopping trip. I wanted to buy a few souvenirs, and she very kindly
suggested that maybe she ought to come with me to protect me
from being gypped. She and I spent an enjoyable afternoon, and
we talked freely. She told me about Jim—his family life, his work,
and about the children. She said to me, "There's only one fly in
the amber of my happiness."

"And what is that?" I asked, although, indeed, I had intui-
tively guessed.

"Don't you know what it is?"

"Yes, Nora. I think I do. But have you ever talked to Jim about
it?"

"No, I haven't—not in so many words."

"Would you have any objection to my broaching the subject
to him?"

"Certainly not," Nora assured me. "On the contrary, I told you,
thinking you might."

"Nora," I averred with conviction, "whatever may have been
the case in years gone by, I am certain that now Jim would not

have the slightest objection to doing what you want. I'll ask him about it this very night."*

I did—and he assented warmly. And Nora was glad because the fly in the amber of her happiness would soon be removed.

It is a noteworthy fact that a general survey of the "literature" on Joyce shows a great number of the authors of this "literature" to be mentally biased, bigoted, or in some cases, just plain potty. And some good examples of this last named category may be found among the commentators on, and explicators of, *Finnegans Wake*. But leaving this group, and also the subject of *Finnegans Wake,* on which I will remain silent, I return to the bigots.

Before I do, I want to amplify something that I have already stated about myself. I have stated that I have been an unbeliever since I was 10 years old. Confining myself here to the general subject of religion as my "universe of discourse," I restate simply that there is not a line long enough to plumb the profundity of my unbelief. On this subject, too, "the rest is silence."

About the biography under discussion I have said nothing for more than 10 years, except that on its production I wrote to the publishers protesting the inclusion of my name among the "Acknowledgments." I didn't make any effort to pursue the matter because I thought that the book would soon achieve its deserved reward of eternal rest in limbus. But in 1949, its cadaver was resuscitated; it is stalking around in a fresh collar and shirt, and with a new noserag sticking out of its breast pocket.

"Indeed," this reanimated corpse still chirps "there does not appear to have been one boy of Joyce's years at Belvedere introspective or analytical enough to penetrate beyond the Jesuit conception of life and culture." Imagine, if you can, the gall of an ignorant guy prating about the boys of fifty-five years ago in Belvedere College; and imagine, too, the extent to which the mind of this mental pigmy himself has "penetrated beyond the Jesuit conception of life and culture."

Reflecting with his customary sapience on Joyce's disqualification as a postulant teacher by the Board of Education in Rome because of the "inadequacy of his Dublin degree," Mr. Gorman

* The "fly in the amber" to which Nora Joyce referred, was that they had not been married officially.

ignorates that this official decision "deserves a very high place indeed in the annals of Comic Opera Culture." Certainly it does. But when Mr. Gorman holds up to ridicule the Board of Education in Rome for its official decision, he is plainly not aware that the official decision of the Board of Education in New York would also have disqualified Joyce because of the "inadequacy of his Dublin degree."

Another of Mr. Gorman's "deductions and assumptions" is the one arising from the tale he tells about Joyce cooking stews, rice and chocolate in a second-hand pot which "he never cleaned out. The mingled gout must have been indescribable. Murger would have appreciated this."

When he indulges in an orgy of "deductions and assumptions" Mr. Gorman believes in going the whole hog or nothing. He is thus able to make the "assumption" that the gentleman associated with *Scenes de la Vie de Boheme,* dead since 1861, would have appreciated his, Mr. Gorman's, "deduction" that Joyce's pot stank because of his, Mr. Gorman's, "assumption" that it was never cleaned out.

Or could it be that Joyce, with "his calm unconcern," actually did tell Mr. Gorman that he, Joyce, "never cleaned out" the "second-hand pot," and, having imparted this insignificant information, could it be that he went on to confess to Mr. Gorman the really significant tidbit that he, James Augustine Joyce, had found himself at a loss for words to describe the resultant "mingled gout"—which is a euphemism for stink?

"Deductions and assumptions" this man calls his ravings, and he expresses his indebtedness to Joyce for the latter's "calm unconcern" about them. It is to howl!

And no doubt Joyce did lots of howling: at the reference, for instance, to those Dublin companions of his who, "of course, scoffed in the *natural Irish fashion";* and at Mr. Gorman's prattle about the awesome bogie of *"plump-paunched* priests and their frightening admonitions at hushed Retreats," and at the description of Joyce's "conscious struggle to shake off the incubus that had striven to crush him to conformity at Belvedere and University College."

What a blatant bigot a fellow can prove himself to be in his literary eructations after a surfeit of unassimilated and undigested "biographic" pabulum. Observe how biliously he can drool and dribble about the "scornful and malicious Dublin circle" that encompassed Joyce; and about "that gossiping, backbiting, scandalmongering free-and-easy, whiskey-and-porter-drinking community." And then, by way of bolstering and corroborating what he is pleased to call a "deduction" or "assumption," he adduces in evidence the unidentified testimony of "more than one commentator" who "has pointed out that the young university men of Joyce's youth were all brought up in a rigorously classical atmosphere, that they were forced into assiduous application to classical studies * * * and devoured Aristotle as later generations of young men devoured Mr. Edgar Wallace." What an Ireland! What a fate! What a "Hell Open to Christians!" By day, and maybe by night, they are a besotted whiskey-and-porter-drinking community, and, at dinner every evening, they "devour" a Plato Aristotelian soup topped off by a broiled rumpsteak of equine ass!

This all reminds me of the fervent ejaculation of a dear old lady in London who a great many years ago was admonishing her family that there was at least one thing they ought to be grateful for. Said she: "Let us thank God we're not like the poor Irish—hopping about from tree to tree!"

CHAPTER FOURTEEN

Joyce with Me in No. 7 Eccles Street

IN THE GARDEN of the house in which I resided thirty years ago in Long Island City, I once observed a tomcat staring steadily upward into the branches of a tree. As the cat stared, the tip of his tail moved in a barely discernible oscillation; otherwise the cat was motionless. My curiosity being sharply aroused, I watched the cat almost as steadily as he himself was staring; and as I watched, I saw drop down from the tree a fluttering fully-grown sparrow—right into the open mouth of the cat. I had often heard of such a thing happening; but I had never before—nor have I ever since—seen it occur.

Of course, the plausible explanation for this phenomenon is that the cat hypnotized the bird, and that the bird was fascinated.

Glancing through Stuart Gilbert's *James Joyce's Ulysses*, it has occurred to me that Mr. Gilbert, like the sparrow whose fall may or may not have been marked, was fascinated with or by something in Joyce's book. What was that something? It was the address, which he and Joyce mention so frequently, of Mr. Bloom's home, his "omphalos," at No. 7 Eccles Street. Concerning No. 7 Eccles Street, Mr. Gilbert writes in part:

"The importance and influence of numbers have been recognised by many schools of mystics, the most important of which was probably the Pythagorean. 'Since of all things numbers are the first,' Aristotle tells us, 'in numbers they (the Pythagoreans) thought they perceived many analogies to things that exist * * * they supposed the elements of numbers to be the elements of all things.' Numbers play an important part in *Ulysses*. As Mr. Bloom remarks, 'Do anything you like with figures juggling,' and the number of his house in Eccles Street (to which I shall refer later) is a 'mystic number.' "

In his chapter on "Ithaca," Mr. Gilbert keeps his promise to elaborate on "the number of his house in Eccles Street":

"Mr. Bloom and Stephen advance 'at normal walking pace'— for everything in this episode is normal all-too-normal— towards Eccles Street, the street with a Greek sounding name, the street of meeting, within sound of the tolling hours of Saint George's Church, the only church in Dublin with a Greek inscription (referred to in *Work in Progress* as 'St George-le-Greek'). And the number in Eccles Street of Mr. Bloom's house is *seven,* the sacred number *par excellence* of the East, of the Homeric world."

And in a footnote on this passage, Mr. Gilbert proceeds to say:

"*Seven* was held to be a number of peculiar virtue by Chaldaeans, Phoenicians, Egyptians and Greeks alike. Thus the Chaldaean towers had seven storeys, Anou seven messengers, Hell seven gates, Sinbad made seven voyages, the Nile has seven mouths, etc. 'We find in the Odyssey,' M. Bérardob serves, 'an alternation of septenary and quinary rhythms, and this system of enumeration is, like the Homeric toponymy, Graeco-semitic.' 'The number seven,' according to Hartmann, 'is the scale of nature, it is represented in all departments of nature from the sun whose light is broken by a dewdrop into the seven colours of the rainbow, down to the snowflake crystallizing in six points round the invisible centre.' 'Seven,' as John Eglinton observed, 'is dear to the mystic mind.' "

This house—this "omphalos"—at No. 7 Eccles Street was my last fixed abode in the City of Dublin. I resided there with my two cousins, Mary and Cicely Fleming—just the three of us—from 1908 to April, 1910. Mary Fleming, as always, was tenant of record, and her name as such, with the erroneous appellation "Mrs.," may be found in Thom's Dublin Directory for 1909 and 1910. During the time we resided in No. 7 Eccles Street, we did not have many visitors. But of course there were some, as well

as quite a few persons who came there to me for "grinding," and
the visitor who came to see me the most often was James Joyce
during the two trips he made to Dublin in 1909. In December
of that year, I mentioned to Joyce the possibility of my going to
the United States, but my determination to emigrate did not
crystallize until February, 1910. I then made somewhat reluctant
haste to arrange for the disposal of the furniture and effects in
No. 7 Eccles Street. We decided to auction off all the stuff, except
as much as would be needed by my cousins in an apartment they
rented in April; and in that month the auction was held in No.
7 Eccles Street, the auctioneer being Mr. Denis Carton, who was
head of the firm of Carton Bros. of Little Green, Dublin, a firm
that is still hale and hearty.

I have two photographs of No. 7 Eccles Street taken in 1947,
and, judging from them, the exterior of the house seems to be
practically unchanged. The house is now subdivided into flats,
but in my time it was a one-family residence. There was a yard
in the rear as wide as the house and about twenty feet deep. In
this yard there was a supplementary toilet to the left as you went
out; and a garden, which in my time was fairly good, extended
behind the yard about two hundred feet to a coachway called
Stable Lane. I have no idea what the garden is like now—it is
more than forty years since I last saw it. Our garden was presided
over, very efficiently, by my beautiful thoroughbred collie, "Boy."
He had been given to me three years before by Denis Carton and
had grown up into a tawny, lionlike beauty. There were in the
garden fruit-bearing shrubs and trees, the latter including pear,
plum, and apple trees, two of these last-named bore large, succulent "cathead" apples. I didn't have to worry over the little
orchard being robbed—Boy attended to that.

Joyce paid a surprise visit early in August, 1909. I did not see
him this first time he called, because I was down in Wicklow.
But having heard from Mary of his visit, I hurried home and was
there to greet him when he called again. This time he brought
with him in beaming pride his 4-year old son, Giorgio.

The back parlor on the ground floor was the dining-room, used
as such mainly when there were visitors, and from its window
there was a full view of the yard and garden. Looking out that
August afternoon Joyce and Giorgio could see the fruit on the
trees, especially the apples which were already well advanced,

and which when fully ripe would be ten to twelve inches in circumference. I asked Joyce and the boy to come out into the garden. Giorgio was all for it, but Joyce was not so eager because out there in the garden, for all to see, stood Boy, with head erect, in majestic splendor—a magnificent beast fully aware of his kingship in his own domain. So Joyce demurred.

Of course, I had well known his nervousness where dogs were concerned; and I never blamed him for that, since allergy to dogs is very common, and sometimes justified, because there are certain people dogs just don't like. On this occasion I was sure that it wasn't himself he was thinking about so much as of Giorgio. The little fellow was looking out to the garden, and the very sight of the dog attracted him. He pleaded eagerly to be taken out. Joyce wanted above all things to gratify his child. He turned to me and asked, "Would it be safe?" "Jim," I said, "that dog out there is a real dog—not a cur. I know him and he knows me. If I bring you and Giorgio out into the garden and make him aware you are friends of mine, he would not alone never molest you, he would give his life to defend you. Remember he is *my* dog." And then, in perfect confidence, Joyce came out after me with his little son to the garden. And Giorgio and Boy rambled the garden together just like pals.

Joyce had good reason to remember No. 7 Eccles Street, for it was to that house one subsequent afternoon that he came, in a state of utter perturbation, to see me. He told me of something that had just occurred to him in Dublin. Of this "something" I will not say any more than that it was not related to either his literary work or his business efforts. I had always known that Joyce was highly emotional, but I had never before this afternoon seen anything to approach the frightening condition that convulsed him. He wept and groaned and gesticulated in futile impotence as he sobbed out to me the thing that had occurred. Never in my life have I seen a human being more shattered, and the sorrow I felt for him then and my sympathy were enough to obliterate forever some unpleasant memories. I spoke to him and succeeded in quieting him; and gradually he emerged *de profundis.* He stayed for dinner and supper and spent the night in my house. The following morning he was up early, fully out of the gloom, and after breakfast he went off, humming as he went.

In the late afternoon of that same day he returned, and with almost childlike pleasure he opened a little jewel box to show me a trinket he had bought for Nora. It consisted of five matched pieces of ivory, each about half an inch in diameter; they were strung on a gold chain and made a beautiful and uncommon token. "It's beautiful," I said, "you got one ivory for each year you've been with her." "I never thought of that" he admitted frankly, "but it's a splendid idea; and I'll add one to it every year."

One night after supper with us, Joyce asked me to go for a walk with him. He was soon to return to Trieste, and he wanted to renew acquaintance with old scenes in Dublin. I readily agreed to go with him; and as it was already late I went upstairs to put on an older suit than the one I was wearing. We walked Dublin that night and early morning, coming back to my residence by O'Connell Street; Britain (now Parnell) Street; George's Street to Belvedere; and then Denmark Street to the corner of Frederick Street, opposite Findlater's Church. At this corner, outside a drug store, there was a penny-in-the-slot weighing machine, on which Joyce suggested we weigh ourselves. Then we sauntered over to No. 7 Eccles Street where we arrived about three in the morning. Nonchalantly I put my hand in the back pocket of my trousers for the hall door key, but the key wasn't there. It was upstairs in my trousers in my bedroom. It wasn't by any means the first time I found myself on the outside of a hall door to my residence without the instrument of ingress; so I wasn't a bit dismayed. There was no one in the house except my two cousins, whose bedroom was on the top back floor. I couldn't think of rousing them with the clattering kitchen bell; so I simply climbed over the railing to the right of the hall door, dropped down to the front area, and went in to the basement of the house by the unlocked side door. Boy, of course, was inside waiting to welcome me. If it had been an unknown intruder, Boy would have been there to "greet" him, too.

This incident is described in Joyce's *Ulysses*, where Joyce gives accurately the "length—five feet nine inches and a half," of the body of the man (meaning me) who climbed over the railings, and also accurately the "body's known weight of eleven stone and four pounds," which was the weight revealed only a few minutes earlier by the penny-in-the-slot machine.

Joyce narrates in minute detail our arrival at the hall door of
number 7 Eccles Street; my belated discovery that I had forgotten
my key; my dropping over the railing to enter by the area door,
and my reappearance as I opened the hall door. This kind of
writing is hazardous and slippery; and Joyce slipped. One of
the slips is where he says of the missing key, "It was in the corresponding pocket of the trousers which he had worn on the day
but one preceding." In this sentence Joyce over-reached himself,
because if my key was in the pocket of the trousers I had not
worn since "the day but one preceding," how could I have let
myself into the house at any time on the day before?

And in the six words "premeditatedly (respectively) and inadvertently, keyless couple," the words "premeditatedly" and
"inadvertently" are incorrectly used in connection with "keyless
couple." For as far as Joyce was concerned, the absence of the
key was not due either to his premeditation or his inadvertence;
and neither was its absence due to my premeditation, nor to my
inadvertence—because, as Joyce himself has just remarked, "He
remembered that he had reminded himself twice not to forget."

And to the question "What were then the alternatives before
the . . . keyless couple?" The answer is:

"To enter or not to enter. To knock or not to knock."

"To knock or not to knock" was undoubtedly one alternative;
but "To enter or not to enter" obviously was not. In fact it never
entered the mind of either of us not to enter the house.

One of the most interesting features in Joyce's treatment of this
story is the series of questions propounded:

> "What action did Bloom make on their arrival at their des-
> tination?"
> "Bloom's decision?"
> "Did he fall?"
> "Did he rise uninjured by concussion?"
> "What discrete succession of images did Stephen meanwhile
> perceive?"
> "Did the man reappear elsewhere?"
> "Did Stephen obey his sign?"
> "What in water did Bloom, waterlover, drawer of water,
> watercarrier, returning to the range, admire?"

And observe the lacuna that immediately precedes the unamplified question:

"What reason did Stephen give for declining Bloom's offer?"

Let us glance now at the paragraph answering the question "Did he fall?" Not alone is the action described here in detail, but the events are dissociated and referred back to preceding dates memorable in the Joyceean era. Here is the paragraph:

> "By his body's known weight of eleven stone and four pounds in avoirdupois measure, as certified by the graduated machine for periodical selfweighing in the premises of Francis Froedman, pharmaceutical chemist of 19 Frederick street, north, on the last feast of the Ascension, to wit, the twelfth day of May of the bissextile year one thousand nine hundred and four of the christian era (jewish era five thousand six hundred and sixtyfour, mohammedan era one thousand three hundred and twentytwo), golden number 5, epact 13, solar cycle 9, dominical letters C B, Roman indication 2, Julian period 6617, MXMIV."

On the foregoing paragraph I offer only light comment. Joyce's narrative here is powerfully effective. The event he describes was to him a striking "epiphany," to use his own word, and of it he gives a striking description. It is a pity that this particular paragraph, in which Joyce wanted to express himself with explicit precison, should be marred by two errors which, however trivial, are still a blemish. One of the errors I refer to is in "MXMIV"; and the other is in the word "indication." This word should be "indiction." It refers to the fifteen-year period established by Constantine the Great in 313 A.D.

All of these data about the Mohammedan and Jewish eras; golden number, epact, solar cycle, dominical letters, and Julian period, together with many others, were given in 1904 and are still given—without explanation—in the United States Nautical Almanac.

Commenting on this incident, Mr. Gilbert has this to say:

> "Mr. Bloom finds he has forgotten his latchkey (Freudians please note!) and is doubly annoyed 'because he had forgotten and because he remembered that he had reminded himself twice not to forget.' He enters, as Odysseus revisited

his palace, like a menial, by the service door and with the aid of ruse."

I agree fully with Mr. Gilbert's apostrophization, "Freudians please note!" But to what, or rather to whom, should the Freudians devote their attention?

Mr. Gilbert says that the man "enters, as Odysseus * * * like a menial, by the service door and with the aid of ruse." The door in the area was not a service door; there were no steps leading down to it, and messengers were not supposed either to throw their goods into the area, or drop down themselves with them over the railings. In the actual circumstances, no menial would have entered the house the way I did. Only the master of the house would have dared to do it, and there was no "ruse."

I hope no person will be foolish enough to assume from what I have written that I mean to imply Joyce portrayed me in the character of Mr. Bloom. Such an assumption would be contrary, not alone to my intention, but to the fact. One may consider the totality of Mr. Bloom as a concoction dished up by a skillful chef. After partaking of this concoction some more or less initiated tasters have declared their recognition of one or other of the ingredients, and have given names to them. But happily, no one has named either the constituents of the concoction or its essence, and it is most unlikely that anyone ever will. This is as James Joyce wanted it to be, although he himself sailed more than once pretty close to the wind.

In this babbling seventeenth chapter, there are a few trivia, which, to me, are specially interesting, because the scene of the babbling was my residence. While it may be freely admitted that Joyce did nod once in a blue moon, yet it must be borne in mind that he, was on the whole meticulously accurate. Note, for example, his reference to the "dwarf wall" under the area railings at No. 7 Eccles Street, and also his description of the "semicircular glass fanlight," and then see how his descriptions tally with the photographs of the house.

So when in this chapter several blunders appear, these blunders have a significance in that they are not Joyceean in character.

Take, for example, that stuff about the "existence of a number computed to a relative degree of accuracy to be of such magnitude and of so many places, e.g., the 9th power of the 9th power of 9, that, the result having been obtained, 33 closely printed volumes of 1000 pages each of innumerable quires and reams of India paper would have to be requisitioned in order to contain the complete tale of its printed integers. * * *" This as stated is just nonsense. And consider also the reference to the "thousands of degrees below freezing point or the absolute zero of Fahrenheit." And then there are also the curiously similar minor errors towards the end of this chapter in one of which reference is made to Bloom's "cicatrice in the left infracostal region . . . resulting from a sting inflicted 2 weeks and 3 days previously (23 May 1904) by a bee." Between May 23d and June 16th the elapsed time is 3 weeks and 3 days. In the other error reference is made "to the birth on 29 December 1893 of second (and only male) issue, deceased 9 January 1895, aged 11 days."

Examine also that paragraph in which Joyce speculates on his own and Bloom's ages, and "What relation existed between their ages?" Prescinding from minor errors in this paragraph, I comment solely on the miscalculation arising in the following excerpt: "Bloom, being 1190 years alive having been born in the year 714, would have surpassed by 221 years the maximum antediluvian age of Methusalah, 969 years, while, if Stephen would continue to live until he would attain that age in the year 3072 A.D., Bloom would have been obliged to have been alive 83,300 years, having been obliged to have been born in the year 81,396 B.C." The egregious error here arises from the fact that someone did not know how to multiply 1190 by 17. The figure 1190 was multiplied by 7 to produce 8,330, and then instead of multiplying the 1190 by 10, and adding the product 11,900 to 8,330 for a total of 20,230, the calculator erroneously multiplied the 8,330 by 10 to produce the absurdly wrong total of 83,300.

In that paragraph wherein are detailed the contents of "the first drawer unlocked" there is this item: "the transliterated name and address of the addresser of the 3 letters in reversed alphabetic boustrephodontic punctuated quadrilinear cryptogram (vowels suppressed) N.IGS./WI.UU.OX/W.OKS.MH/Y.IM". That the long word "boustrephodontic" is misspelled is of no consequence; but Mr. Gilbert's reference to this cryptogram is odd. He says of it in a footnote: "The second word, a secret name, is 'reserved'; the clue to this reservation may be found in the

Black Mass of *Circe*." Here one could charitably suppose that Mr. Gilbert's use of the word "reserved" was a slip of the pen, but when he goes on to amplify his remark by reference to "this reservation"; and when he says vaguely where the "clue may be found," he is clearly floundering.

Let me put aside Gilbert for a moment, and take a brief look at the output of another writer who has promulgated a book on Joyce. This writer acknowledges his indebtedness to Mr. James T. Farrell for his "comments on my interpretation," which he declares to have been "most stimulating." Perhaps they were too stimulating; maybe they went to his head. Anyway, there is abundant evidence of something or other in this work of "interpretation" of James Joyce, but you need look scarcely any further for it than the title the author has given to one of his chapters. This title is "The Cursed Jesuit." See how James Joyce and his works are interpreted and lit up by the blinding brilliance of these three words lifted out of context. Anyway, something was interpreted; something was lit up—could it have been the author?

In this book, too, there is a reference to: "Lyster, Thomas W. librarian—obsequious, tiptoeing around, eagerly but stupidly following discussion." Lyster was a gentleman and a scholar; and, incidentally, a Quaker. He was polite and soft-spoken, and, far from being stupid, he was mentally quick as a flash. He was highly educated and cultured, and to all the heterogeneous readers of the National Library he was a paragon of courtesy. In *Ulysses* Joyce uses the word "obsequious" three times; but never in connection with Thomas Lyster. It has remained for this most stimulated interpreter to refer to Lyster as "obsequious."

Commenting on the paragraph in this chapter referring to "the 9th power of the 9th power of 9," this author's sententious platitude is: "Surely a beautiful *reductio ad absurdum* of mathematical enquiry."

"Other indications of cosmic relativity abound in this chapter," says this author, and continues, "We have an extended mathematical disquisition on the relationship of Stephen's and Bloom's ages, toying with proportions and projecting them until we must have Stephen live until 3072 A.D. and Bloom born in 81,396 B.C." Prompted, no doubt, by the most stimulating comments of Mr. James T. Farrell, this author penetratingly observes: "Here is a case of Parallax with a vengeance."

Another excellent instance of mental bias and bigotry was shown in a review of *Stephen Hero* done by Francis Hackett for The New York Times of Jan. 18, 1945. In his review Mr. Hackett wrote, "One of the foils in this book is so reported from life that he is not MacCann but Sheehy-Skeffington, who did indeed die because of obstinacy, as Stephen Hero said he would."

In this sentence Mr. Hackett reveals his slovenly reading; for it was not Stephen Hero who said Sheehy-Skeffington would die of obstinacy—it was Cranly who said this.

And later in the review Mr. Hackett has this to say about the Jesuits and what Stephen did to them: "The Jesuits, of course, he devours without salt." And Mr. Hackett closes this same review with the following words: "The Jesuits tried to smooth his way and his intransigence by offering him a little job. But no one could sit on that geyser."

Mr. Gorman tells us that Joyce was forced by the Jesuits to "devour" Aristotle; and then Mr. Hackett came along to tell us, as a fitting sequel, that Joyce "devours, of course, the Jesuits without salt." Now, a fellow who could be crammed, and who then could gorge himself, like that, must have felt some disturbance in his metabolic processes of ingestion, digestion and egestion; and it is not so astonishing after all, that he should turn from a super-cannibal into a geyser—spewing something or other with approximately regular periodicity, and with accompanying rumbling noises which the muddy-brained Mr. Hackett may have been able to construe into a sound like FEE FA FI FO FUM.

Returning to my main thesis: In the ninth chapter in Joyce's *Ulysses* there is the following passage:

"to a son he speaks, the son of his soul, the prince, young Hamlet; and to the son of his body Hammett Shakespeare, who has died in Stratford that his namesake may live forever."

And in the fourteenth chapter, it is told that "young Stephen. . . said also how at the end of the second month a human soul was infused. . . ." To the subject matter of these passages, and especially to the general, if somewhat disguised, disquisition on embryology in the second of the two chapters named, Mr. Gilbert devotes much comment.

"A hint of the direction in which we must look to find the hidden trend of the long soliloquies of the Jew, Mr. Bloom, and his spiritual son, Stephen Dedalus, may be found in their frequent references to the East, its occult sciences and the oriental sources of all religion."

And in this connection he quotes from Hartmann: "Physical parents cannot be the progenitors of the spiritual germ of the child, that germ is the product of a previous spiritual evolution"; and later on he quotes from "a curious esoteric tract named *Venus Magique* (Chamuel, Editeur. Paris, 1897): 'Dans le neuvième mois, l'esprit entre dans sa nouvelle résidence élémentaire; il y connait par une profonde contemplation le Mot indestructible.' "

That it should not have occurred to Mr. Gilbert to refer to Saint Thomas Aquinas on these matters is not surprising; but it is noteworthy that Joyce seems not to have known what the Angelic Doctor had to say. For, indeed, Aquinas has quite a lot to say on this subject, as for instance, in *Summa* pars prima Q.76, Art.3. But nowhere is Saint Thomas more definite than in *Gent. 2, CLXXXIX* where he says:

"Anima igitur vegetabilis, quae primo inest, cum embryo vivit vita plantae, corrumpitur, et succedit anima perfectior, quae est nutritiva et sensitiva simul, et tunc embryo vivit vita animalis; hac autem corrupta, succedit anima rationalis ab extrinseco immissa, licet praecedentes fuerint virtute seminis."

The importance (from a fundamentally jurisprudential point of view) of this passage is accentuated by the fact that, since Leo XIII, Aquinas has been formally ratified as spokesman for the Catholic Church. If one approaches to an examination of this passage with a mind divested of preconceptions or prejudices, one can appreciate that it is vastly significant both in what it says and in what it, specifically, does not say. But the first salient reflection that arises from its examination is that Saint Thomas must have devoted a lot of time to the coordination of his thoughts in this matter; and that it was with cautious circumspection he proceeded to pen his carefully-worded dictum.

Aquinas says explictly and specifically that the embryo lives a plant life, and that it afterwards lives an animal life; and he states, that when the "anima perfectior, quae est nutritiva et sensitiva simul" becomes "corrupta," then "succedit anima rationalis *ab extrinseco immissa*." But it is to be noted that Saint Thomas does not say *when* the "anima rationalis succedit," and it is no less to be noted that the Saint does *not* say that after the "anima rationalis succedit," the embryo "tunc vivit vita rationalis." Let no one say or think that this was due to inadvertence on the Saint's part—Aquinas was never inadvertent.

For the sake of clarity, permit me to repeat: Seeing that Aquinas had already stated that the embryo, while it is informed with a vegetable soul, lives a vegetable life; and that, subsequently, while it is informed with an animal soul, it lives an animal life, why did he *not* state that subsequently, while it is informed with a rational soul, it lives the rational life? It should be needless for me to say that, so far as I am concerned, the question is rhetorical.

But what is it that appears to be the most important truth that Saint Thomas desired to establish in his dictum? This truth is contained in his assertion that the rational soul of the human being is "ab extrinseco immissa." He wants to make it clear that the rational soul does not derive its origin from human parentage. That the vegetable, and animal souls "may" (his word is licet) so derive he allows, but he asserts categorically that the rational soul *does not*. In another place in the same chapter he is more specific when he says, "Sed actio Dei producit animam humanam, quam virtus seminis producere non potest." And thus Saint Thomas takes his besom and sweeps into the discard the notion of the human "spiritual father."

Digressing here for a moment, let me observe that I have always held Saint Thomas in affectionate regard. When I was very young—say in University College, Stephen's Green—I often daydreamed of how delightful it would be to walk out with him over the Dublin and Wicklow mountains and maybe talk as we went, or maybe not utter a word. But if I ever had talked to him, I would have pleaded with him to be less of a hero-worshiper of Aristotle. Of course, when he refers, as he invariably does, to Aristotle as "philosophus," as if no other "philosopher" had yet existed, he was partially correct. But Thomas himself had now arrived; and he must have realized this. Thomas was perfectly well able to walk or run as he pleased—and he did not need a crutch; and he should not have used one.

When he was 5 years of age, Aquinas was sent to the renowned monastery of the Benedictine monks of Monte Cassino (you remember Monte Cassino, and how the eyes of the world were focused on it a few years ago). After he had been in the monastery about seven years, its Abbot wrote to his father, the Count of Aquino, that "a boy of such talents should not be left in obscurity." So Thomas was sent, about the year 1239, to the University of Naples. Here, we read, he had two preceptors, one Pietro Martine and one Petrus Hibernus, and we are told that he, having soon outstripped Martine in grammar, was put under the tutelage of Petrus Hibernus, whose name is translated as "Peter of Ireland." I wonder if this translation is correct. I have not been able to trace this Peter of Ireland or find out much about him, but I would like to know if he was really an Irishman; for he is the man to whom credit is given for training the young Aquinas in logic and the natural sciences.

We are told also that on Dec. 6, 1273, a little while before Thomas died, "he laid aside his pen and would write no more. That day he experienced an unusually long ecstasy, during Mass. What was revealed to him we can only imagine from his reply to Father Reginald, who urged him to continue his writings: 'I can do no more. Such secrets have been revealed to me that all I have written now appears to be of little value.'" (Modica, Prümmer) I have always had the feeling that I knew sympathetically just how Thomas felt. As a parting observation on this subject of Saint Thomas and his works, I wonder why no Concordance has been compiled. The nearest thing to this is a little "Lexichon" done by Schuetz, but this work is only a trifle. Surely the Vatican must have one for its own reference?

Reverting again to Mr. Gilbert: He might have turned out a better job if he had the "assistance" from James Joyce for which he acknowledges his "indebtedness," but Joyce's attitude towards Mr. Gilbert and his "biographer" was unquestionably one of indifference. In effect what he did was to put a hillock of material in front of them and say: "Here; take it and do what you please with it—make bacon of it, if you like." In such circumstances, Mr. Gilbert, unlike the "biographer," preserved a modicum of praiseworthy restraint; he did not run amuck with scandalous "deductions and assumptions."

On occasions, Mr. Gilbert is naive. In one of his notes he says, "Lynch is one of Stephen's oldest friends. It was with him that Stephen held the remarkable dialogue on aesthetics (recorded in the *Portrait*) from which I have so often had occasion to quote." In an editorial note in *Stephen Hero,* Theodore Spencer observed: "In the manuscript Stephen does, to be sure, discuss his aesthetic theory with a friend. But it is interesting to note that the friend is Cranly, not Lynch; that the conversation comes long after the main theory is expounded in the public essay, and that Stephen is personally disappointed in Cranly's failure to be interested in the argument." I am not concerned here with the question whether Stephen's conversation was with Lynch or with Cranly, meaning me, for that is of no importance. But what is significant is the fact that Mr. Gilbert writes: "Lynch is one of Stephen's oldest friends." Plainly, he is not aware of the significance of the anathema Stephen uttered on Lynch during the celebration of the "Black Mass."

STEPHEN

(Points.) Exit Judas. Et laqueo se suspendit.

In another place Mr. Gilbert opines: "In the cause of Bushe's frustration we have one of the *few** instances in *Ulysses* of a mystery unexplained." Is Mr. Gilbert still of this opinion?

The last observation I have to make regarding Mr. Gilbert's book has to do with something which has always deeply pained me. I am speaking about his cheap sneer directed against the memory of young Robert Emmet, who at 23 years of age, was standing in the dock in the Criminal Court in Green Street, Dublin. He had been betrayed by Plunkett, the friend of his family, and he had just been found guilty of being a rebel, after a trial in which he refused to make any defense or call any witnesses.

Shortly after I came to the United States I became a friend of Joseph I. C. Clarke, himself an exiled Fenian, who introduced me to Dr. Thomas Addis Emmet, Robert's grandnephew, famous physician, Irish patriot, and author of many books including the damning record of *Ireland Under English Rule.* For and with

---

* Italics mine.

Dr. Emmet I had the great pleasure of doing some literary work in 1913. I have before me an autographed presentation copy of Clarke's play *Robert Emmet;* and in the preface to this play Mr. Clarke writes in part:

> "The prose form has been chosen in the present work for many reasons. Chief among them is that no maker of verse could rise to loftier heights than Emmet himself in the prose of that marvellous speech in the dock which has become a classic of the language. Its great periods and its arrowy sentences may not be rashly broken to suit the needs of verse. It sets high the mark for all that can be written about Robert Emmet, his purpose, his love, and his doom."

After Emmet had been found guilty, and as he still stood in the dock, the infamous trial judge, Lord Norbury, said to him:

> "Prisoner, you speak of facts in evidence as calumnies. Speak, if you can in mitigation of your crime."

And Emmet spoke:

> "Was I to suffer only death, after being adjudged guilty, I should bow in silence to the fate that awaits me; but the sentence of the law which delivers over my body to the executioner consigns my character to obloquy. The man dies, but his memory lives. That mine may not forfeit all claim to the respect of my country, I seize this opportunity to vindicate myself against some of the charges alleged against me. (Pauses) I am charged with being an emissary of France; it is false. I am no emissary. I did not wish to deliver up my country to a foreign power. Connection with France was indeed intended; but only as far as mutual interest would sanction or require. The preliminary to this assistance was a guarantee to Ireland similar to that which Franklin obtained for America. (Murmurs in court) Were the French to come as invaders or enemies, uninvited by the wishes of the people, I would meet them with all the destructive fury of war. I would animate my countrymen to immolate them in their boats before they had contaminated the soil of my country. If they succeeded in landing, I would dispute every inch of ground, burn every blade of grass, and the last entrenchment

of liberty would be my grave. (Murmurs) My object and that of the provisional government was to effect a total separation of Great Britain and Ireland *** But I have toiled for the destruction of that government which upholds its dominion by impiety against the Most High; which treats a hapless people as beasts of the field; which sets man at his brother's throat in religion's name; which reigns amid the cries of the widows and orphans it has made."

And then Robert concluded in this fervid peroration:

"I have but a few more words to say. I am going to my cold and silent grave; my lamp of life is nearly extinguished. I have parted with every thing that was dear to me in this life and for my country's cause—with the idol of my soul, the object of my affections. My race is run. The grave opens to receive me and I sink into its bosom. I have but one request to make at my departure from this world—*it is the charity of its silence.* Let no man write my epitaph; for as no man who knows my motives dare now vindicate them let not prejudice or ignorance asperse them. Let them rest in obscurity and in peace; let my memory be left in oblivion, and my tomb remain uninscribed, until other times and other men can do justice to my character. When my country takes her place among the nations of the earth, then, and *not till then,* let my epitaph be written. I have done."

Young Robert Emmet went to a scaffold erected in full view of the public, outside Newgate Jail, Dublin, and on this scaffold he was hanged, drawn and quartered. And it is at the memory of this young man that Mr. Gilbert, with a strangely perverted sense of humor or irony or sarcasm, chooses to shoot an arrow that had its tip dipped in a sneer.

Here is the passage in Joyce's *Ulysses* which evoked Mr. Gilbert's delicacy.

"Seabloom, greaseabloom viewed last words. Softly. *When my country takes her place among.*

Prrprr.

Must be the bur.

Fff. Oo. Rrpr.

Nations of the earth. No-one behind. She's passed.
Then and not till then. Tram. Kran, kran, kran. Good oppor.
Coming. Krandlkrankran. I'm sure it's the burgund. Yes.
One, two. *Let my epitaph be.* Kraaaaaaaa.
Written. I have.
Pprrpffrrppffff.
Done."

And here is Mr. Gilbert's delicacy:

"The ambiguous prophecy of Teiresias is recalled by a mention of Robert Emmet, the text of whose 'last words' is cited
at the close of the episode of the *Sirens*. '*When my country
takes her place among the nations of the earth, then and not
till then, let my epitaph be written: I Have Done.*' The equiv-
ocation of that utterance lies, of course, in the fact that, assuming that Emmet had the normal desire for prolongation
of life, he was, in reality, impetrating a long postponement of
Ireland's freedom—a double-edged postulate like the oracle's
Ibis redibis nunquam in bello peribis, and akin to the strange
rigmarole, about a wayfarer who takes an oar for a winnow-
ing fan and death that shall come from the sea, which the
Theban seer rendered to Odysseus."

The one thing—the only thing—that Robert "impetrated" from
the world was "the charity of its silence."

Was Mr. Gilbert too stingy to afford even that?

I have never written nor spoken a word for publication about
Emmet; and I feel sure that thousands of others, respecting, as
I did, Emmet's impetration, have for that reason maintained
reticence. But now that his own stipulation has been met—now
that "My country takes her place among the nations of the earth,"
I feel there is no longer need for silence, and I look forward also
to the composition by an able and sympathetic writer of a fitting
epitaph for Robert.

To me the memory of Robert Emmet has always been a most
cherished one; and despite the futility of his effort I have always
regarded him as being among the very noblest of men. Indeed,
it is noteworthy that in this connection so many of the men who
have struggled and died for Ireland were amongst the noblest.

Robert Emmet was the grand-uncle of Dr. Thomas Addis

Emmet; and when I met Dr. Emmet in 1913, I told him that my paternal grandfather was acquainted with and associated with Robert. My grandfather's headstone in Glasnevin Cemetery shows that he was born in 1781 and died in 1851. He was, therefore, three years younger than Robert Emmet; and he was 22 years of age when Robert was hanged, drawn and quartered at the age of 25.

My grandfather was present at the trial of Robert Emmet and witnessed his devilish execution; and there was a tradition which, when I was very young, was passed on to me from two sources. This tradition was that nearing the end of Robert's trial, Robert managed to convey to my grandfather a small package with "For Sarah *Only*" written on it; and that grandfather took this little package with its last message to Sarah Curran, who opened it in his presence, and, seeing its contents, wept bitterly as she murmured, "Merciful God—my poor love!"

I told this story of my grandfather to Dr. Emmet who, when I had finished, surprised me by saying, "I heard about that when I was a child—that some young man brought Sarah a package from Robert just before his murder, and my recollection is that the name of the young man was Fari Byrne."

"That is the name," I said, "my grandfather was called by his close friends."

"Well, young man," said Dr. Emmet, "I am very glad Joe Clarke introduced us. This world is surely a small place after all. But did you ever hear what was in the package?"

"My grandfather never told that."

CHAPTER FIFTEEN

Midnight in the Hell Fire Club

ONE OF MY greatest pleasures in Ireland was in rambling through the country, but especially in the Dublin mountains and all over the County Wicklow. On these expeditions, even when I was setting out alone, Joyce was not anxious to join me, and his reluctance to do so was because he knew my big purpose on such occasions was the pleasure of a walk, and not the pleasure of a talk. Joyce loved to meander with me about Dublin City and its outskirts; but the enjoyment he found in doing this consisted not in the walk, but in the talk—the accompanying conversation, or discussion, or argument, or exposition, or, indeed, occasional monologue. He loved those peripatetic discussions not a whit more than I did; and there were three other companions in Dublin with whom I was wont to enjoy ambulatory conversations in and around the city, these being Francis Skeffington, Paddy Merriman, and Jim O'Toole. But all three of these often joined me on my long expeditions through the country, and the reason for this was that they could find pleasure in the walk even if there was little serious talk. Indeed, with Jim O'Toole alone I often walked through Wicklow for the length of a day, without either of us feeling an urge to say a word.

In July 1899, the year after my solo trip to Vinegar Hill, I was accompanied by Merriman, Skeffington, O'Toole, and Paddy Doherty, on a walk from Dublin City to Glendalough and back; and, prompted by some strange motive which I had ample cause to regret, I started out on that walk in an ill-fitting pair of wafer-soled cycling shoes. The five of us met in Dublin at four o'clock on a Saturday morning, and we reached Glendalough, via Dundrum, Stepaside, Knockfada, Roundwood and Annamoe, at one o'clock. There we went into a little hotel, the one nearest at that time to Kevin's Bed; and having signed the register, we ordered a dinner of roast chicken and peas, boiled bacon and cabbage, tea and apple pie, which we were told would be ready for us in an hour and a half. My four companions went directly to the ledge over Kevin's Bed, from which they clambered down into the Bed. I didn't go over to Kevin's Bed with the group because I had often been in it. Besides I had some more pressing business on hand. I found a secluded spot on the river where I tended my aching feet, on both of which I drained blisters almost as big as eggs.

After dinner we set out on our return journey, reaching Laragh about half past four; and there Paddy Merriman and Doherty decided to take a car to Rathdrum, and proceed by train to Dublin. Skeffington, Jim O'Toole and I immediately began the big trek back to Dublin by way of Glenmacanuisge and Glencree. Fifty years ago, from a couple of miles north of Laragh till you came to Loch Bray, a mile south of Glencree, there was not a house or shanty for about twenty-four miles of the old military road, which hithered and thithered with commendable contempt for any such mathematical axiom as the one about a straight line being the shortest distance between two points.

That evening, on the road from Laragh to Glencree, I suffered. I did not feel the least bit sick; but my feet pained excruciatingly, and I was afflicted with an insatiable thirst of a kind that I never experienced before or since. Along the side of the road there was water to be found in plenty—some, not all of it, fresh and good. At one pool we all stooped to swill, and Skeffington admonished face- tiously, "Jim, look out for the microbes." With his mouth in the pool, Jim was keeping a wary eye on the black water beetles scur- rying in the brown water, but he lifted his face just long enough to retort with comforting reassurance, "They're too big to be microbes." As for me, while I had heard Skeff, I didn't deign to answer. I was engaged in holding my face in the water with my mouth wide open, unable to contain any more water, and yet parching in the agony of a horrible thirst that I could do nothing to relieve.

At two o'clock the next morning, we reached Terenure Road where we parted from Skeff, who turned off to go to his home in Ranelagh; Jim and I trudged through Harold's Cross to Dame

Street, where we parted at about three o'clock, Jim to go to his
home on Summer Hill, and I to Essex Street, after limping 70
miles.

On a few of my trips I invited Father Dinneen, the Irish lexi-
cographer to join our little party; and he always seemed delighted
to be asked. When he came with us, the walks were not long in
point of mileage, because the sogarth was not very robust, and he
would always be wearing his tall hat and his long impeding coat,
with the added and wholly decorative encumbrance of a fat umbrella. On one occasion when he was with us we walked from Rathfarnham through Glendhu, and then over the crests of the mountains till we arrived at the top of the Skalp, where we came upon a
farmhouse at which I stopped to ask whether they would kindly
prepare for us a light tea. "Bring in your friends," they told me,
"and we'll have tea ready for you in two shakes of a lamb's tail."
I brought in Merriman, Skeff, Jim O'Toole, and Father Dinneen,
and introduced myself and them to the person who was obviously
the lady of the house; and when I mentioned Father Dinneen's
name, all the members of the family were plainly pleased at having him in their midst.

In a few minutes, the five of us were enjoying one of the most
bountiful teas we had ever partaken. There were lashins of home-
made bread, with boiled eggs, butter, hot pancakes, cake, jams,
marmalade and tea—six pots of it. After tea we sat around the
kitchen to chat with the family before leaving. As we were about
to go, I went over to the lady of the house who was sitting beside
her husband, and asked her gingerly to tell me how much we
owed for the "tea." Instantly her jaw, and her husband's jaw,
literally dropped in open-mouthed astonishment. "Tell me now,"
said the lady in an aggrieved tone, "sure it must be jokin', y'are."
And I, very much abashed, said, "Well, yes—if you like to put it
that way you can say I'm just jokin'—but all the same we would
like to give you something in just the same spirit that prompts
your splendid hospitality." "I know, I know, young man; but
we're all only delighted to have you and your friends and especially Father Dinneen here to tea, and we hope it won't be
long before you'll all come again."

At another time, around the summer of 1901, I formed a party
to make an overnight visit to the ruins of the old Hell Fire Club

on the summit of Mount Pelier. This was a big party of about ten; and along with my usual companions, Merriman, Skeff and Jim O'Toole, it included Tom Kettle, Alphy O'Farrelly, and I think the two Sheehy boys. The Hell Fire Club house had been the notorious resort where the profligate scions of the aristocrats and plutocrats of the eighteenth century foregathered in their infamous bacchanalian orgies, and on account of the atrocious conduct there the place had acquired a black reputation as "hanted." In order to spur the ghosts of the place into action, I suggested we bring along with us a naggin or two o' the craythur, a bottle of port, and a couple of decks of cards. We all set out for the "Club" on a summer evening and reached it about ten o'clock that night. Having gathered a lot of wood, we lit a huge fire in the large room; and then, although near suffocation from smoke, we made a great show of spreading cards around the place, pouring some of the "sperrits" and port into glasses for those of us who would take a sip, and we played pranks around and through the house till long past the witching hour of midnight, in a futile effort to tempt the reputed ghostly denizens of the place to manifest themselves. Failing to make the ghosts walk, in the literal sense, the party broke up around two o'clock into three groups, one of which started back to the city; while the other two groups started out, one for the top of the Three-Rock Mountain, and the other for the summit of the Two-Rock, to watch the sun rise. And, as it happened, it was a glorious sight from the Two-Rock; the sun arising in magnificent splendor and revealing in sharp outline the cone of Snowdon away in Wales at the far side of the Irish Sea.

Of the numerous walks I loved I shall mention just one more which was my favorite. This walk began at Bray, from where you went to Kilmacanogue; then up to the top of the big Sugarloaf; and then to the Long Hill, or Knockfada, and along that to Douce Mountain, from which you returned via Glencree to Dublin. At a point a couple of miles from Roundwood you ascended Douce Mountain, nearly four hundred feet higher than the Big Sugarloaf, and as you reached the summit of Douce you came, at a certain place, with astounding and startling suddenness on the breath-taking beauty of Lugela and Lough Tay, set there like a jewel of unique splendor. Nothing that I have ever seen has surpassed this sudden revelation of sheer beauty; and often, as I looked at Lugela, the thought has occurred to me that any human being who suffers from the urge to depict in line or color the beauty of nature, must have something wrong with him; he must be unable really *to see* the beauty that is there, for otherwise he would tear up, destroy and burn his deplorable travesties of natural beauty; and in saying this I am not talking of amateurs. I am referring to the accepted best of such productions.

From what I have already written, it is understandable why James Joyce did not care for a long and strenuous walk; he was unequal to it and he engaged little in any form of exercise or games. Once in a while he did play handball—after a fashion, and somewhat in the manner of an unathletic girl. To a person who did not know him it might have seemed amusing that when in the course of play the ball came unexpectedly toward him, Joyce would lift up both hands as if to shoo it away, but to me who knew him this was not amusing, for I realised it was due to Joyce's weak vision.

Joyce was a good runner. I mean by this that his style was good and he was fleet for short distances. If he had trained he would have shown up well in the hundred-yard or hundred-meter class. Joyce was also a good swimmer; and during the summer months in the late 90's he frequented the Bull Wall, at the southwest side, where he swam or sat sunning on the rocks, attired, like all the boys and young men at that place, in nothing at all. Owing to the circumstance that I had been twice unconscious from immersion, once in Heronford when I was four, and again in Ardnaree when I was six, I did not like being in water beyond my depth. And although I did subsequently learn to float and swim I was no adept; and this made me admire natatory skill in others.

I remember one afternoon watching with almost envious admiration a youth effecting the courageous and skillful rescue of a sturdy man who was attempting suicide in Anna Liffey, just a few yards west of Butt Bridge. This young rescuer had left his bicycle, with his coat thrown on it, on the footpath beside the Liffey wall; and I stood there admiring the way he lugged his reluctant and recalcitrant freight to the foot of a flight of steps, where he, the freight, was lifted out of the water and attended to by a few men, including a bobby. The young rescuer, seeing that his charge was apparently in good hands, ran nimbly up the steps and came to retrieve his coat and bicycle; and then, having put his coat on over his dripping shirt, he immediately jumped on his bicycle, turned into Hawkins Street, and sped away without a word to anyone. This young man had done a deed which was triply courageous: first in jumping into the Liffey at a time and place where the current was swift and treacherous, second in tackling a would-be suicide, and third in plunging into a stretch of water which, at that time, was just a cesspool. Indeed, when he came up out of it with his face smeared with filth, and black muck dripping from his clothes, I was scarcely able to recognise him as the customarily spruce, well-groomed, and debonaire Oliver St. John Gogarty.

CHAPTER SIXTEEN

I Lecture on Spinoza

IN THE AUTUMN of 1902, I was invited to join a chess club which had been formed among patrons of the Dublin Bread Company restaurant (DBC) in the splendid new building erected by that company on O'Connell Street—a building, by the way, which was occupied by the rebels in the 1916 uprising, and was utterly demolished by the British during their infamous and wholly unnecessary artillery bombardment of Dublin City. In this new Sackville Chess Club I quickly became a top chess player; and during several years won as many first-prize gold medals. In a few months, this new chess club proved by far the strongest in the Dublin area, winning the Armstrong Cup, and retaining it year after year, against the best competition from many other clubs, including the Dublin University (Trinity College) Chess Club; the Dublin Chess Club; the Blackrock Chess Club; the Clontarf Chess Club, and occasionally others. The teams of the clubs competing for the Armstrong Cup consisted of eight players and almost invariably I played first board for the Sackville. The best club in point of playing ability among our opposition was the old-established Dublin Chess Club. But the club which the members of the Sackville Club liked best to meet was the Dublin University Club, particularly during the period when "Tony" Trail was Provost. Harry Thrift, a Fellow of Trinity and professor of mathematics, usually played first board for this club. Harry had acquired a reputation as a player, and he undoubtedly was a good, and a gentlemanly, player. I enjoyed having him for an opponent.

I have said that the Sackvillians enjoyed most the encounters with the Trinity Club, and the reason for this was earthy. Tony Trail played somewhere about fourth board; and he liked to take his time. And Tony didn't play silent chess. He was voluble in comment and muttered chessy banalities in the gruff voice of an elderly gaffer, for which he could easily be mistaken. Tony never finished his game at a sitting, but his opponent on the Sackville team wouldn't be annoyed about that, because Tony, being the Provost of Trinity, could not be expected to leave the college for the continuation play. Tony would then invite his opponent to continue the game on a subsequent night in the Provost's house; and the opponent was told to bring as many of his friends as he cared to. I went one night to one of these continuation plays, and the cause of the popularity of the Trinity team was not far to seek. Tony and his opponent sat down to their unfinished game in a setting of medieval splendor, amid jars, bottles, flagons and cruiskeens of all kinds of spirituous liquors and liqueurs that had been exhumed from the vast and ancient and cobwebby cellars of Trinity.

There was another player in these Armstrong Cup chess matches I liked to meet; he was a blond, blue-eyed, medium sized man, a few years my senior, who played first board for the Clontarf Chess Club. This young man's name was Baker; and like Thrift, he was not alone a good, but a gentlemanly, player, and although there were many Jews in Dublin who played and seemed thoroughly to enjoy chess, Baker was alone among them in being a really first-rate player. This poor fellow was very delicate, yet always cheerful—even though living in the valley of the shadow, as, of course, he knew well. And it was not long before he finally lost his fight against tuberculosis.

As an indication of the standard of chess played in Dublin, I can relate a couple of facts. One afternoon in the Sackville Chess Club, I was sitting alone and unoccupied, when a middle-aged, stout and florid gentleman with a large blue patch over one eye approached me and asked me in Teutonic accent whether I would care to play a game of chess with him. I said I would and we did. And as the game progressed, I noticed to my astonishment that a big crowd of kibitzers gathered around our table. After we had played a while the game developed into what was, I knew, a winning position for me; and at this point I was amazed when my opponent suddenly stretched out his arm, swept all the pieces off the chessboard, and said, "It's yours—will you play another?" We played again; and this time, before the game was finished he said, "It's a draw—have another?" I refused to play a third, because I had to go away; and when I got up to leave, several members of the club clustered round me clapping me on the back, saying, "Well done, Byrne, you gave him quite a shock." "But who is he, I never saw him before?" I asked. "Didn't you know? He's Teichmann."

Teichmann was at that time a prominent international chess master, who usually came out somewhere about fourth in the international tournaments. The Sackville Club had been in correspondence with him about giving some exhibitions in Dublin, and when he arrived he was met by Porterfield Rynd who escorted him to the club where, without my being aware of what was afoot, he sicked him on to me. Rynd was very fond of a little practical joke. He himself was a really good player; and he knew, though I was not a student of chess, that I was a player who had a winning chance against anyone. Another chess master who came to Dublin for exhibition purposes was an Englishman named Lee. He also played in international tournaments, but usually did not do so well as Teichmann. With Lee I played a few solo games; and I felt quite sure that if I were to play a match with him I could beat him, but I also felt doubly sure that I never would play a serious match with him—or anyone else. The strange thing about Lee is that I remember him so vividly. If I were an artist, I could sketch him exactly as he appeared to me then. He looked to be in his middle fifties, about my own size, with long pasty face, grey eyes, sparse and thin greying hair brushed back from his forehead, large, but not protruding ears, thin grey moustache, a quiet manner, and soft, but slightly raucous, voice, this quality in it being probably due to his continuous pipe smoking combined with his love for snuff. He wore a high collar, large cravat, frock coat, striped trousers and spats. And as I played with him and thought about him I marveled how in the name of heaven he was able to make both ends meet as an itinerant professional chess player. And the more I thought about Lee, or Teichmann for that matter, the less I wanted to play any professional chess player in those simultaneous exhibitions. In play either against

Teichmann or Lee, I won a brilliancy prize; but instead of feeling elated over this, I felt sad. These fellows, I realized, were eking out a precarious existence dragging the devil by the tail, and I felt no glory in adding my poundage to his satanic majesty.

A third professional who visited Dublin in my time for exhibition purposes was the famous Blackburne. His exhibition in the Sackville Chess Club consisted of playing blindfolded against about eight players simultaneously. I was an emcee that night—relaying moves, and helping Rynd, who was a long-time personal friend of Blackburne's, to prepare vast quantities of whiskey punch to slake the eager thirst of the aged, daddy-Christmas-looking chess master. And, inspired no doubt by his spirituous quaffing, Blackburne won a smashing victory.

En passant, and in reference to blindfold chess, I have read the statement that while chess is encouraged in Russia by being taught in schools, yet blindfold play is prohibited by law. Authority for this statement, as given by Chernev in *Curious Chess Facts,* is the late world champion chess player Alekhine in his *Auf dem Wege zur Weltmeisterschaft.* This categorical statement that blindfold chess is forbidden in Russia seems incredible and is probably inaccurate. Possibly the thing forbidden is simultaneous blindfold exhibitions.

However, in regard to the Russian people and chess, it is rather strange, and perhaps indicative, that the game enjoys a widespread popularity comparable to baseball in America. Some chess tournaments in Russia have had nearly a million competitors, a large proportion being women. The average standard of play there is well above the average outside of Russia; this fact being exemplified in the results of two exhibitions given, one in Leningrad and one in Moscow, by the great Capablanca. Playing a total of sixty players in these two exhibitions, Capablanca won seventeen, drew eighteen, and lost twenty-five. Whereas when he played a total of one hundred and thirteen players in Manchester, Paris, Bayreuth and Leipzig, Capablanca won one hundred, drew twelve, and lost only one.

This term "blindfold" is misleading to many; so let it be understood at once that a blindfold player is not actually blindfolded—he just plays without seeing either the chessmen or the chessboard. I could play quite well blindfold—as a matter of fact better than I could over the board—and I did in Dublin play quite a lot of chess this way. I have played blindfold chess with a player seated in one corner of a room while I played bridge in another corner. Nevertheless I did not care for blindfold play, the reason for this being that blindfold play, by its very nature, meant serious play, and I was rarely eager to play chess seriously. However, when I wanted to make an exhaustive analysis of a chess position (problems didn't interest me) I would always prefer to do it blindfold—a fact which, unfortunately, influenced my subsequent handling of another unrelated matter.

In the Sackville Chess Club there were several Jews, but not one of them was in a class higher than our third, which meant odds of a knight. With one of these Jews I became friendly and dined often in his home. He was a small, dark, middle-aged, black-bearded man, whose name was Zaks; and he ran a little junkshop off Redmond's Hill. He was a Russian Jew, trained to be a rabbi. He was intelligent, widely and diversely read, and he enjoyed nothing in life more than an argument. Mr. Zaks was active in a local Jewish literary club where one night, at his request, I read a short essay on Spinoza. For that Jewish thinker I had great admiration, although I always deplored his falling under the influence of the mathematically-minded Descartes. In this matter Spinoza might better have been guided by the opinion of that great philosopher of his own race, Maimonides, who had but little respect for mathematicians in the field of philosophy. Descartes did not belong in the realm of philosophy, but I have neither space nor time, nor the inclination, to elaborate on this point. However, I will say that as far as mathematics and philosophy are concerned no man can be a philosopher who can accept unquestioningly a fundamental mathematical "truism" such as the proposition, "One and one make two." It is a philosophical absurdity.

When Descartes enunciated his dictum "Cogito, ergo sum," and then proceeded to derive from that dictum his criterion of truth, his mind was in a mechanistic fog. Having arrived at what he conceived to be the ultimate basic fact, Descartes states that fact tersely as "Cogito"—"I reason"; and from this fact that "I reason," he states, it is an *evident* conclusion that "Ergo sum"—"I am." He then goes on to argue that the indissoluble link which binds "Ergo sum" to "cogito" is *evidence;* and this quality of "evidence," he declares, is the criterion of truth—the criterion by which any statement connecting any two or more concepts must be assayed before such statement is accepted as valid.

Man may say during his whole life, "I think," but during one-third of his life his "thinking" is "dreaming," and during the remaining two-thirds of his life this "thinking" may or may not be erroneous, but it is often self-contradictory; and, so far as the attainment of ultimate truth is concerned, there is no way by which man can determine whether at any given time he is "thinking" or "dreaming." When Descartes was six years old, Shakespeare's *Hamlet* appeared, and in it the sable-vested Prince of Denmark, whose life was "sicklied o'er with the pale cast of thought," ponders on the advisability of "To be, or not to be," and reflects cautiously:

> To die, to sleep;
> To sleep: perchance to dream: Ay, there's the rub;
> For in that sleep of death what dreams may come
> When we have shuffled off this mortal coil,
> Must give us pause.

However, with Descartes' naivete in arriving at and accepting as the ultimate truth the nebulous and inchoate "Cogito—ergo sum," and in declaring "evidence" to be the criterion of truth, I am not now concerned. I am concerned with a more important point, which is this: Let us suppose that Descartes' criterion really worked. Let us suppose that in refilling the human mental basket he was able to put back none but "perfect" apples. Did Descartes really believe that these perfect apples would remain perfect, and continue unchanged toward one another, unaffected by one another, in the ceaselessly digestive human mental basket? That such a notion should ever enter any man's head at any time is peculiar; but that it should have entered the head of Descartes in the period of Galileo surpasses understanding.

Spinoza did not believe in miracles, and for that I admire him, but I would have admired him more if the reason for not believing in them had been based not on mathematically mechanistic ground, but on some such ground as equity and justice.

In the paper I read before the Jewish literary group, I spoke of that hideous incident in the life of Spinoza, when the rabbis pronounced against him—he was 24 then—their notorious writ of excommunication, dated sixth of Ap. 5416, July 27, 1656. The writ, which is in Spanish, is still in the Synagogue Archives. After a preamble, in which the rabbis referred to "horrendas heresias que practicava e ensinava" and to the "ynormas obras que obrava," the writ continues:

"After the judgment of the Angels, and with that of the saints, we excommunicate, expel, curse, and *damn* Baruch de Espinoza with the consent of God, Blessed be He, and with the consent of all the Holy Congregation, in front of the Holy Scrolls with the six-hundred-and-thirteen precepts which are written therein, with the excommunication with which Joshua banned Jericho, with the curse with which Elisha cursed the boys and with all the curses which are written in the Law (Pentateuch).

"Cursed be he by day and cursed be he by night; cursed be he when he lieth down, and cursed be he when he riseth up, cursed be he when he goeth out, and cursed be he when he cometh in. The Lord will not pardon him; the anger and wrath of the Lord will rage against this man, and bring upon him all the curses which are written in the Book of the Law; and the Lord will destroy his name from under the Heavens; and the Lord will separate him to his hurt from all the tribes of Israel with all the curses of the firmament which are written in the Book of the Law. But you who cleave unto the Lord your God, you are all alive this day.

"We command that none shall communicate with him orally or in writing, or show him any favor, or stay with him under the same roof, or within four ells of him, or read anything composed or written by him."

As I proceeded with the reading of the writ, I could see that my audience, made up mostly of young Jewish men, began to shift uneasily in their seats, and the shifting and squirming became more evident as I continued to read with slow, clear enunciation. It seemed to me, as I read, that some of my listeners were under the delusion that it was I myself who was cursing Spinoza. And when I had finished reading the writ, and also my paper, I was puzzled by an ominous silence. At this point, Mr. Zaks stood up beside me on the platform, and thanked me in a few complimentary words, for my paper. And then he said, addressing me, but in reality talking to and for the audience. "Mr. Byrne, when you were reading that writ of excommunication pronounced by the rabbis against our great Spinoza, you were surprised, I think, at the behavior of your audience. But maybe it will explain something to you when I say that I strongly doubt whether more than two or three of your listeners had ever before heard this writ of excommunication. To the great majority of them, I feel sure, it must have come as a stunning surprise." Mr. Zaks then proposed the customary vote of thanks to "the lecturer," which was promptly seconded, and passed by acclamation.

I stood up immediately to acknowledge the vote of thanks, and I explained that in discussing the excommunication of Spinoza I had two points in view, both of which I had intended to be implicit rather than explicit. The first of these two points, I said, was one which I did not desire to discuss, but which I raised for for the consideration of my audience. This point was whether Spinoza, as a result of his excommunication and in view of the fact that he never recanted, did or did not, ipso facto, cease to be a Jew. In this connection, I suggested, it would be highly desirable for the Jews themselves to formulate an authoritative definition of the word "Jew." I concluded by saying that the second of my two points was to advert to man's inhumanity to man; an inhumanity that often reveals itself in its most virulent form in man's relationship with his own people—"The near in blood the nearer bloody." And the deplorable circumstance about this condition is that it appears to exist universally in all human societies. That the rabbis cursed Spinoza was a lamentable fact; but, compared with the curses uttered in fifty-three verses of the twenty-eighth chapter of Deuteronomy in the Old Testament of the Bible—which is acclaimed as the bulwark of Christianity—the rabbis' maledictions of Spinoza were not so malevolent.

*　　*　　*

About 1905, there was a most interesting group of visitors to the D.B.C. smokeroom, which was the habitat of the Sackville Chess Club. This group was headed by the famous Japanese jiu jitsu wrestler, Yukio Tani, who had an engagement in the local Theatre Royal situated only a few hundred yards away. In the afternoons he and his associates came to the smokeroom where they sat chatting, smoking, and sipping coffee. I had gone on the very first night of his show to see Yukio at the theatre, where he tackled and threw one after another of his assorted opponents.

When I saw Yukio sitting there so quietly and unobtrusively in the D.B.C., I could not help going over to talk to him. By way of breaking the ice, I asked him whether he or any of his companions would care to play chess or checkers, and assured him they were entirely welcome to the club facilities. Yukio was, of course, the acme of politeness, and pointing to an empty chair beside him, he asked me to sit down and take coffee with them, and I did so. Yukio understood and spoke English a little and I found no impediment to our conversation on this score, because one of his group was able to act as interpreter when the occasion required. I told Yukio how much I admired his skill as a wrestler; and I expressed my surprise that he, in the street clothes he was wearing, did not look different from anybody else. I said to him that if a stranger to both of us were to see the two of us sitting there, he would probably choose me as being the stronger of the two, because I was slightly bigger and heavier. Yukio smiled, and held out his hand to feel mine, then he felt my arms, chest, thighs and legs, and said, "I think you be stronger than me—but you don't know how to make your strength work. You not trained." And then he put his hand up to feel my throat, and said, "Suppose I want choke you—what you do with your throat to not let me?" I admitted there wasn't anything I could do—with my throat—to prevent being choked or to protect my carotids. Yukio then told me to feel his neck, which I did, and found it, in relaxation, just the same as my own; then he told me to grip it and try to choke him, or to compress the arteries or veins in it. I gripped his neck, and the impression I had was as if I were trying to squeeze my fingers into a thick, closely-wound silk hawser.

Among the members of the Sackville Chess Club and frequenters of the smokeroom, Porterfield Rynd was, as he had been in the Dame Street D.B.C., one of the best known. Rynd was a highly talented man and an able barrister. He seemed always to be in the pink of condition, never appeared to worry about anything; never was affluent, and never seemed to care a straw about that. He loved games—but particularly chess, at which he would play hour after hour while prominent solicitors sat waiting for him to finish and give them an "opinion." Rynd was an ardent supporter of the Baconian "theory," and he was never happier than when arguing about it with someone sitting beside him, while he played chess with someone else sitting opposite. He was thoroughly informed on the pros and cons of the Baconian subject, and often tried to wheedle me into a discussion of it, but I wasn't interested. However, on one occasion he asked me how did I interpret the Earl of Kent's hot retort to King Lear,

> "Do;
> Kill thy physician, and the fee bestow
> Upon thy foul disease."

I said that Kent was simply telling the senile reprobate that he, Kent, was trying, like a physician, to cure him of his "foul disease," and that he, Kent, would be quite satisfied to accept death as his fee if Lear would only give the same fee to his "disease." Rynd said my interpretation of Kent's defiance was not what Shakespeare intended. This passage, Rynd argued, furnished a point in favor of the Baconians, in that it must have been written by a person acquainted with legal terms. Kent's retort meant, according to Rynd, that if Lear killed him, Kent, Lear would thereby bestow the "fee simple"—or permanent tenure—to his "foul disease."

At another time Rynd tried unsuccessfully to interest me in the secret meaning of the word "Honorificabilitudinitatibus," which, he declared, also furnished an argument in support of the Baconians. Points like these, I told him, did not interest me. For instance, I suggested, you might argue forever on the meaning of "He jests at scars that never felt a wound." It is simply a case of "You pays your money—and you takes your choice."

Among the members of the Sackville Club there were a few whom I knew well and whose friendship I enjoyed; such as F. J. C. Skeffington, murdered in Portobello Barracks during the 1916 revolt; Eoin MacNeill, subsequently Chairman of the Irish Volunteers, and Arthur Griffith, the tenacious and devoted leader who won for his earthly reward the crown of martyrdom. Here and now I will say nothing futher on this subject than that there were some fine men in those days in the Sackville Chess Club.

*　　*　　*

In *Ulysses* there are several references to the Phoenix Park murders of May 6, 1882. In the seventh chapter Myles Crawford, editor of the Freeman's Journal, is made to say erroneously, "That was in eighty one, sixth of May, time of the invincibles, murder in the Phoenix Park, before you were born." Although I was but two years old when these murders were perpetrated, they had for me a personal interest—an interest which was heightened by my experiences in connection with the house on Cork Hill.

In *Ulysses* Myles Crawford eulogises the ingenuity of Ignatius Gallaher for getting a scoop to the New York World.

"Look at here, he said, turning. The *New York World* cabled for a special. Remember that time?
Professor MacHugh nodded.
—*New York World,* the editor said, excitedly pushing back his straw hat, Where it took place. Tim Kelly or Kavanagh I mean, Joe Brady and the rest of them. Where Skin-the-goat drove the car. Whole route, see?"

The coverage of the news of the Phoenix Park murders was extraordinarily extensive in Jay Gould's New York World. On Sunday, May 7, the day after the murder, there were more than three columns on its front page; and on Monday, May 8, virtually the whole front page was given to Ireland. As exemplifying the reaction of the New York World to the news, I quote an excerpt from its editorial on May 7.

"It is sufficiently notorious throughout the world that the murder of a landlord or of a British agent in Ireland cannot be punished through the ordinary processes of British law. Did not England educate the Irish people for centuries to believe that English law recognized no criminality in the oppression and murder of Irishmen? Is such teaching forgotten by people in a score of years or in a hundred years? * * *

"These murders . . . will assuredly be taken to mean that England must choose whether she will go on, as she has for centuries gone on, to govern Ireland by force, or whether she will make up her mind to leave Ireland free . . . to govern herself absolutely at a day not distant as an independent nation."

But a column written by L. J. Jennings, and published on the front page of the World on May 7, is especially interesting in its juxtaposition of news and comment about the Irish and the Jews —the two oppressed peoples who, after centuries of effort, have finally and almost simultaneously achieved at least a semblance of their national aspirations. Referring to the Gladstonian policy of "conciliation," as shown in his appointment of Lord Cavendish and Thomas Burke to their high posts in Ireland, Jennings wrote:

"It is possible that for a time Ireland will become more tranquil, the people being almost tired of outrage and disorder, but the demand for Home Rule will be very soon revived in its true form—that is total separation from England."

And in the very same column Jennings proceeds to say:

"I have further news from Mr. Lawrence Oliphant. Two members of the Mansion House Committee have been at Lemberg assisting him in the transportation of the Jewish emigrants. Owing to defective arrangements for their reception in America, considerable delay has taken place and renewed persecutions have swelled the number of refugees collected at Brody to between three and four thousand. It seems likely that the Austrian Government will be compelled to place guards along the frontiers to prevent a further influx.

"Meantime the whole of southern Russia is possessed with an enthusiasm for emigration to the Holy Land which is rapidly spreading through Poland (sic). Deputations are arriving every day from all parts of Russia to confer with Mr. Oliphant, but as the Russian Government prohibits the collection of money although hundreds of thousands of rubles are ready, it is not safe to place them anywhere. The government also takes care that no rich Hebrew shall leave the country. Consequently great practical difficulties attend this remarkable exodus.

"The last news is a discouraging report. The Sultan is opposed to any further emigration to the Holy Land."

Also on its front page the New York World of May 7, carried a story under the caption of:

"The Tale of a Hebrew Refugee."

"Irion Natka, a tongueless Hebrew refugee from Russia, who arrived at Castle Garden by the steamer *Greece* yesterday, wrote an account of his sufferings on a slate. Almost a month before leaving Russia, he said, he was dragged from his bed by a mob

of men who hanged him to a tree. . . . The people then cut off
the end of his tongue and let him go. . . . The Russian Society
in this country will send him to Philadelphia where work will be
obtained for him."

The New York Tribune for May 7, 1882, reveals two very interesting interviews on the Phoenix Park murders; but before I
quote these I would like to quote the following news item, dated
London, May 6, also printed by the Tribune:

"A dispatch to the Times from Berlin says: 'Secretary Freling-
huysen's dispatch to Mr. Hoffman in regard to the treatment of
Russian Jews has produced a most favorable impression in Liberal
circles. The United States is hailed as having taken the place of
England as the champion of the downtrodden and oppressed.' "

Regarding the two interviews in the Tribune on the Phoenix
Park murders, one of them was carried under the modest caption,
with one-eighth inch letters:

"Views of Lord Randolph Churchill."

"A Tribune reporter called upon Lord Randolph Churchill
last evening at the house of his father-in-law, Leonard W. Jerome,
to ask his opinion as to the political significance of the assassina-
tion and its probable effect upon English politics. Lord Randolph
received the reporter cordially in the diningroom, where he was
taking his after-dinner cigar with Mr. Jerome * * *

" 'Do you think the ultimate effect will be injurious to the
Government?'

" 'Isn't this Ireland's answer to Gladstone's new policy? It is
the first tangible result of conciliation and concession. That is
what the Tories will say, and they will be able to use it effectually
against the Government. What else, they will ask, could be expected as the result of appointing Lord Cavendish, a man with no
qualifications for the position, simply to *appease* his brother,
Lord Hartington, and to lead him to suppose that he would be
able to control the Government's Irish policy? For that was the
only reason for appointing Lord Cavendish—to prevent the de-
fection of Lord Hartington from the Liberal party.'

" 'Do you think it possible that Mr. Parnell or any other of the
Land League leaders had any connection with this murder?'

" 'No, I don't think it possible that Mr. Parnell or the Land
League were at all connected with the deed. It has always been

doubtful how much power Mr. Parnell had in Ireland after all. It has been impossible to tell whether he could prevent the outrages committed in the interests of the Land League. There is no doubt that the outrages of the last few years have strengthened and helped the League; but whether or not the leaders could prevent them, or wished to, even, it has been impossible to decide.'

" 'Do you think the Coercion Act was a failure and that repression was the wrong policy to pursue?'

" 'No, I do not. Repression, I think, was the only course for the Government to pursue.' "

The second interview, also carried under a modest caption with one-eighth inch letters, was:

"Oscar Wilde's sentiments."

"A Tribune reporter met Oscar Wilde about midnight sauntering down Broadway with a friend. Both wore long overcoats, flung open wide, and wide-brimmed felt hats, nearly covering their long hair.

" 'What, Thomas Burke assassinated!' was Mr. Wilde's exclamation; 'the friend of my father, and who has often dined at our house! And Lord Cavendish, too! I do not see why they would wish to assassinate mediocrity, for he was just an easygoing, pleasant, mediocre gentleman, whom no one could have a grudge against. Such, too, was Mr. Burke. He had filled many official positions, but none that brought him in contact with the Irish people. The assassinations were undoubtedly the result of intoxication at what the Irish thought a complete victory.

" 'They turned liberty into license. But when Liberty comes with hands dabbled in blood, it is hard to shake hands with her, eh?'

" 'Hear, hear,' said Mr. Wilde's friend.

" 'But then we forget how much England is to blame,' said Mr. Wilde; 'she is merely reaping the fruit of seven centuries of injustice. There must be trouble ahead. I presume martial law will be proclaimed, and the Conservative party must come into power again, though I do not care to see it there. Of course, we must not blame the whole Irish nation for the acts of a few men. . . .' "

CHAPTER SEVENTEEN

Country Life in Wicklow

IT WAS MY good fortune in Ireland that from the time a yard made me a coat I had always the choice of several country farms where I could spend my holidays and vacations. My father had been a farmer for most of his life; he had owned, or rented, three farms in the County Wicklow, one each in Knockfada, Knockadreith, and Cronroe. This last named, which was about equidistant from Rathnew and Ashford, was by far his best property, but somewhere around 1875 it was completely wiped out by a fire, the origin of which was the same as the reputed origin of the great Chicago fire. It was this event that made my father decide to sell out all his property in Wicklow, and come up to Dublin where he hoped to follow in the footsteps of his elder brother Simon, who had made himself a rich man in the dairy and general provisions business. Although my father died when I was three years and ten months old, I remember him well. But I do not remember him well enough, nor did I ever learn enough about him, to explain why he was so widely known, and so generally liked—his principal friends, of course, being mostly farmers. It was due to this that there were so many places where, as my father's youngest child, I was welcome. In these families I was not regarded as a visitor—it was more as if I were one of themselves.

Two summers, when I was four and five years old, I spent in Heronford, County Dublin, in the farmhouse of a family named Owens. This farm was about a mile from Shankill, and the house was situated on the side of a small hill about a furlong off the main road. To reach it from the road you had to turn into a bohareen along which you went down a slight declivity for about seventy-five yards. At this point you came to a ford in a river, where you could drive across your horse and car, or your ass and car. To the right, at this spot, there were flat-topped stepping-stones over which you could cross the river without getting too wet. It should be borne in mind that I am speaking of this ford and stepping-stones from the viewpoint of a five year old boy. I have never been in the place since.

During my first summer vacation in this place I suffered two misadventures, the first of which was a bit laughable, while the second was not so funny. The river of which I speak skirted the Owens farm and I was attracted to it irresistibly. One day, after I had been sitting for quite a while on a little grassy mound by the river's edge, I became conscious of itchiness; and on investigation I found that my whole body was crawling with little swift-moving insects. I hurried up to the farmhouse where I was taken in hand by an old lady whom I used to call Granny. She had me take off all my clothes; and gave me a thorough tub bath with lots of soap, and uttered a one-word diagnosis of my trouble—"pismires"! It was the first time I had ever heard the word; and I didn't like it. In fact, it was a toss-up which I liked least—the word itself, or the things it meant; but one little truth I learned from this experience was that you should avoid sitting on little dome-shaped grassy mounds near river banks—especially if you are clad in petticoats. About a week after my person had been so thoroughly investigated by the pismires, I was down again by the river one late sunny afternoon. I wasn't allowed there any more unless someone was with me; and as the only person available was "Granny," the duty of keeping an eye on me devolved on her. So on this evening Granny was sitting knitting on a three-legged stool which I had carried down for her to the river bank. As Granny knitted diligently, I wandered maybe fifty yards downstream where I came to a sharp bend in the river at which spot there was a deep pool. When I was near this bend, I heard a splash in the river and as I looked I saw emerge from the far side of it a slick-haired dog with bright, beady, startled eyes and with a fish that must have been nearly a foot long in his mouth, the tail of the fish sticking out at one side, and the head at the other. I shouted out, "Bad doggie, you shouldn't do that—let the fish go." But the doggie dived under the water, fish and all, in the direction of the bank overhanging the deep pool. I ran to the bank to chastise the doggie, but I couldn't see down under it. At this spot there was the withered trunk of an old tree which had formerly grown out over the river, and there was a white branch of this tree sticking out a yard or so beyond the river bank and on a level with it. I climbed a couple of feet up the tree to this branch, and walked out on it over the river, balancing myself by holding a higher branch of the tree. As I stepped farther out and tried to look in under the river bank where the doggie had apparently disappeared, the branch on which I stood snapped suddenly, and with a yell I plunged into the sluggish pool about five feet deep. I remember splashing violently in the pool, and yelling; but after that I remember no more. When I next became aware of things I was in the farmhouse lying on my cot; and just above me was the face of Granny, and I heard her murmur fervently, "Oh, thank God!" And around the cot, stood farmer Owens and his two grown up sons, Greg and Tom; and two of his daughters. In a little while a car drove up in the dusk to the yard, and a man hurried in to stand beside me in my cot, and as he came, I heard voices telling the doctor how glad they were he was there, and they were so happy "the poor little fellow has come to."

I never learned exactly what happened; nobody seemed to want to talk much about it. But I was told that Granny had heard me cry out to the "bad doggie," and that she was nearing me when she saw me plummet into the river. Her shouts for help were heard by a husky young laborer, whose name I was never told; this young fellow, who happened to be doing some work at the other side of the river, heard her yells, and being told by her what had occurred jumped into the pool, pulled me out, and rushed me to the farmyard where they put me over a barrel. As for the "bad doggie," the reader will, of course, have already guessed it was an otter.

In the following August, 1885, I was again in Heronford; and on a Sunday in that month a married daughter of farmer Owens was spending the day at her father's farm with her husband, whose name, I think was Tynan. In the forenoon Tynan and Tom Owens mounted towards the crest of the little hill above the house, and they allowed me, being almost a big boy now and no longer in petticoats, to go along with them. Tynan was carrying a loaded single-barrel gun in the hope of bagging a rabbit. We stalked through several fields, but without any luck, I mean from Tynan's point of view, not the rabbit's. So the two men decided to go down home to the farmhouse. Just as they had so decided, an intrepid crow flew so invitingly near overhead that Tynan was unable to resist the challenge, and whipping up his gun to his shoulder he fired at the crow. At least that's what he aimed to do, but all he did was pull the trigger—the gun didn't go off, it hung fire. Disgusted, he put the gun under his arm with its muzzle sticking out in front, and I romped down the hill about thirty yards ahead of the two men. Suddenly there was a blast; the gun had gone off, and I had a substantial part of the charge of number three shot in my thighs and legs. A doctor was sent for, but he advised my being brought up to Dublin for treatment; so farmer Owens and one of his daughters drove up with me to Dublin in a high-wheeled speedy trap with a fast-trotting young horse. When we arrived in Essex Street, they went straight to Mary and not to my mother, because they didn't want to frighten her. Mary got into the trap and we all went immediately to Dr. Barton, who, having examined me, said that the pellets were all too deeply embedded for easy extraction, and that we should wait and see. This "treatment" worked out all right for my twenty-three punctures all healed without giving me any trouble. Nevertheless, this incident finished my visits to Heronford; from that time onward my holidays and vacations were all spent on farms in Wicklow.

In that county there were several farms where I sometimes stayed, and in all of which I was welcome. These included the Neale place at Bonalee, Ashford; the Brian farm at Ticlash, near the meeting of the waters and only a couple of miles from Avondale, the seat of Charles Stuart Parnell, and the small Fogarty farm at Carrigmore. The Fogartys I visited for the first time when I was six years old, and the family at that time consisted of Michael Fogarty; his wife Hannah; his brother Matt, who facially was the image of Abraham Lincoln; three daughters, Mary Ann, Bridget, and Hannah; and two sons, Michael and Willie. Willie was the youngest of the children, but he was eleven years older than I, yet he became and remained one of my fastest and most loyal friends. About a year after my first visit to this farm, Hannah, the mother, died; and it was not until 1898 that another death or separation occurred in this family, and then it was the gaffer himself who passed along at the age of sixty-eight. Although I was only eighteen years of age at the time, the family entrusted to me the task of negotiating for a tombstone in Dublin, and this I did to the satisfaction of all concerned. The price I paid for a Gothic Cross of Carrara marble, with granite pediment, and sunken leaded lettering, the stone standing about six feet and a half in height, was twelve pounds fifteen shillings, and this sum included cost of shipping the stone down from Dublin and erecting it in Glenealy cemetery. On this headstone I had a Gaelic inscription cut near its base. I selected a quotation from the Book of Wisdom in an Irish Bible; and the English equivalent for it was: "The souls of the just are in the hands of God, and the torments of death shall not touch them." I knew that the old gaffer liked that quotation, so I had it carved on his headstone in Irish.

In the Fogarty farmhouse I was really never a visitor. I was to them the youngest member of the family, who because of circumstances had to be away most of the time. And I was accepted on a similar level by all the neighbors. When I was on the farm I did everything that a young and active son of a farmer would be expected to do. I harrowed, tilled, ploughed, spread dung, planted, sowed, thinned, reaped (in my early years with reaping hook and scythe) mowed, when later on a mowing machine was bought. This machine was a two-horse, two-seated affair, one seat being for the driver and the other for the sheafer. Always I operated this machine single-handed, sitting in the sheafer's seat and driving at the same time.

When I was a small boy I always got a kind of thrill at the sight of four or five men following one after another in perfect rhythmic motion as they went along with one knee on the ground, reaping in a cornfield. The sight of men with sythes following one after another in similar motion was also pleasing, but not nearly so much as the men with reaping hooks, making their cuts and waving the corn gently with one hand as they proceeded on padded knee from cut to cut with the other.

We made hay and pitched it; we bound, stooked and stacked wheat and oats which we later threshed with a flail. And when the threshing was on the hens in the barnyard watched like so many hawks the field mice that dropped occasionally from the stack as the sheaves were thrown down. The hens gobbled the mice instanter, sometimes catching them in air before they reached the ground.

I helped to milk, churn, clean out cowhouses, stables and fowl houses, and frequently acted as midwife for mare, cow, or sow. This last-named "blessed event" was always a source of wonderment—how it was that the great sow, moving clumsily like a wounded leviathan, did not crush her brood to death; and how the opalescent-skinned little bonavs made with unerring instinct for their new fountains of nourishment; and how these same little toddlers, when they had regaled and wanted to relieve themselves, would, again with unerring instinct, refrain from doing so till they had by fumbling and tumbling on rubber-like legs reached beyond the edge of the litter. Another phenomenon connected with this event was always to me a source of mild astonishment; and by way of introduction to this subject let me say that when I was very young, I came across an anthology of poetry in a bookcase near the balcony window in the Dublin National Library. This anthology was in several large blue leather-bound books; and browsing through it, I suddenly looked, as "stout Cortez" must have looked "when with eagle eyes he stared at the Pacific," at a poem bearing the title, "Ode Written to a Fart Let in the House of Commons." This ode didn't make enough impression for me to remember either the author or the date of publication, but I guess the latter was early eighteenth century. Well, the point I am getting to is that the gentleman, or lady, who wrote that ode could never have been present at the accouchement of a sow. For never was there an involuntary·sulphurated gaseous expulsion in the windy House of Commons, nor even in the august and possibly more gusty House of Lords, that could come near being as worthy of commemoration in verse as one of the prolonged ventricose expirations of a sow in labor.

The Fogartys had a contract for the upkeep of about six miles of road in their vicinity, and this entailed the digging for and spreading of sand, which was used chiefly on footpaths and taken mostly from the Potters River, and the furnishing every year of about four hundred cubic yards of broken stones to be spread where needed on the roads. For this purpose they had opened a

quarry at what they called the cat-rock in their "lower field," and
at the quarry we bored deep holes with jumper and sledge and
dripping water; then drying them out and loading them with
blasting powder, inserting fuse, tamping, igniting fuse, and running like blazes for safety. Then back to the quarry where we dis-
lodged huge boulders with crowbars, sledged at these till they
were small enough for hand hammers, and then sat, wearing gog-
gles hour after hour on an improvised straw mat, beating at the
hard granite rocks till they were small enough for carting off to
the various depositories alongside the roads. This was all hard
work, but I found the hardest part of it was shovelling the broken
stones from the huge pile at the quarry into carts. Shovelling
stones that are resting on a hard surface like concrete is easy, but
shovelling stones from a soft earth surface is a tough job. And we
had to do this twice; first at the quarry, and then later on from
the numerous temporary piles of stones at the side of the roads.

But for this kind of work there were compensations; as, for
instance, going to markets and fairs, which I always enjoyed.
The nearest fair to Carrigmore was Rathdrum, four Irish miles
away, and next Wicklow, and Arklow, about five and eleven Irish
miles, respectively. Getting to a fair meant that you arrived there
just as the morn had begun to peep over the eastern hills; and
in order to get there at this time, you might, if you had cattle to
drive, have to start out the night before.

And then at the fair: "What are y'askin for the baste? Eh—
musha don't ye hope ye may get it!" This bantering, it seemed,
might go on forever; but then a likely buyer whom you could spot
instantly, if you were experienced, would put the same question;
and when you said "I want fifteen pounds for her," he would say;
"What was that ye said—if ye make it ten, I might be talkin t' ye;
now if I was to say eleven, what would ye say?" And you'd say: "I
won't take a farthin less nor fourteen." At this, or similar junc-
ture, a bystander would break in, unasked but most certainly not
unwelcome, to enquire "What's betune yez—just a matther iv a
couple iv pounds! Here, split the differ."

"I'll do no sich thing," declares the coy purchaser, who already
has made up his mind to buy. "He's askin fourteen pounds for a
baste that never got a dacint feed in its life. But, begorra, maybe
if it was fed, it might look like a rale cow. I'll take a chance, I'll

gie ye twelve pound ten." "Here now, says the mediator to the seller, "You come down ten bob, and then let the two of yez split the differ." At this point he puts the end of his stick in cowdung, holds it poised, ready to "brand" the animal as sold, and then he says his last verse: "Here now, don't be stubborn, split the differ I tell ye, *don't break me word.*" And as a rule they didn't break his word.

It must be borne in mind that I have narrated a rite common at fairs half a century and more ago; whether this rite is still customary I do not know, but whether it is or not, let no one scoff at this ritual of the mediator in the buying and selling of a cow. Vastly larger and more important human differences might be favorably reconciled, if the services of a mediator were available, and if the parties in dispute would see a light and agree to "split the differ."

I loved almost every minute of my time on the little Fogarty farm, with its thatched dwelling house containing four rooms and two attic rooms. Some of the outhouses were roofed with zinc, but of course the dairy adjoining the living house was not so desecrated. One of the things I learned that gave me the greatest satisfaction was how to thatch. Always the gaffer, with Bill assisting him and me helping Bill, had done this; and in the year before he died he had put in two acres of wheat so as to have wheat straw to thatch the dwelling house. But old Mick died—and the job was still to be done—so in the following year Bill and I did it. And in regard to thatching, I can say that if Father Darlington had tried his hand at it, he would certainly have been justified in stroking down his long chin with his right hand and declaring to all and sundry, " 'Pon my word, ladies and gentlemen, there is quite an art in thatching a roof."

One hot day immediately after dinner Mick Fogarty went into the dairy to get himself a mug of buttermilk, and as he was putting the ladle into the churn he saw the body of a three-month old chicken floating in it. Buttermilk in those days was correctly named, and chickens, whenever they were given the slightest chance, would perch on the rim of a churn to peck the morsels of butter from it, or from the surface of the buttermilk if they could crane down to it. This chicken had overreached herself; so Mick took the body up and threw it violently toward a small dunghill at the far side of the haggard. I followed after the body; picked it up, and saw that its lifeless eyes and beak were thickly clogged. I took the body into the kitchen where I wiped it carefully, and with a straw I picked the thick buttermilk from its mouth. Of course the whole family wondered volubly what I was up to, and when I told them I was going to see whether I could revive the chicken, they all thought it was a great joke and they laughed and laughed—all except Bill. To make this story brief: having dried the chicken with cloths, I placed her body on a piece of thick flannel on a chair by the side of the kitchen fire, and I sat on a low form manipulating the wings and chest in what I thought were the desired movements for artificial respiration, and I worked thus unremittingly on the lifeless body from about half past twelve o'clock till "tea-time" at four—with never a sign of life from the chicken. Of course when they came in to tea the whole family, except Bill, again laughed and laughed as they saw what I was doing, and because I refused to take a rest and come to tea. But Bill having rapidly devoured his cup of tea and a hunk of apple cake, came to kneel beside me as I persisted doggedly in my effort. And as I worked, and while Bill and I were peering intently at the chicken, we both saw just the trace of a flicker of its left eyelid—and I knew I had won. Bill jumped up with an excited "Gosh!" and shouted out to the family "teaing" in the lower room, "It's comin to life." And slowly, very slowly, as I worked on it for another hour, the chicken did come to life.

This experience of mine had a sequel, which I tell briefly. On a July Sunday afternoon several years later, I was at Booterstown station, when I saw some men carry the naked body of a man, who had just drowned while bathing, and lay it on the platform where they put his shirt, coat, and trousers over, but not on, the body to cover it. I walked down to the group and was told the man's body had been immersed for a "half an hour or so." I said, "This man looks dead, but maybe he's not—maybe we could revive him. Let's all try." And, to my surprise, they all agreed to try. I got one of the group, a sturdy fellow, to kneel forward with his back horizontal, and using the back as an improvised barrel we lifted the body over it to empty the lungs of water. Then for the sake of warmth we put on the man's trousers, and I began to perform the accepted movements for artificial respiration, the while asking some of the group to fetch three or four rugs from wherever they could get them. In about twenty minutes several rugs were provided, which were put under the body, and over it as much as feasible. Meanwhile, I had asked a couple of likely-looking fellows to watch what I was doing so as to be able to relieve me, and both of them were only too eager to do just exactly what I wanted them to do. We worked thus in relays without ever a thought of giving up, from three o'clock till nearly six o'clock; and then we were rewarded by seeing the slight twitching of the "dead" man's eyelids, and the scarcely perceptible thoracic movement indicating the resumption of normal breathing.

Often my days began before 3 A.M., when I would get up and creep out of a window with a loaded double-barrel gun. Underneath my window there was always a dog waiting hopefully, and when I touched ground he would simper and whine softly in a mild paroxysm of joy. Then before setting out on our hunt we would go over to the little vegetable-and-apple garden where I, guided only by the sense of touch, would fill my pockets with pea-pods. I wonder how many boys have known the delight of munching young green peas taken from dewy pods picked blindly from their vine in the "darkest hour" of the morning!

On rainy days work was usually put aside and all the males would equip themselves with fishing poles, lines, little hooks, and worms, and try their luck in the freshet in the "big" (Potters') river. But the fish were few and small; and only rarely was one hooked big enough not to throw back; and occasionally you would pull up your line to find an unwanted eel wriggling in a knot round your hook.

Every day after the milking had been done we all sat down to a supper graced usually by a huge apple cake; and then Matt, Mick, and Will would saunter over to Russel's farmhouse where they would play cards with the sons, Matt, Mick and Tom, and sometimes the gaffer Paddy, till maybe the unearthly hour of 9:30 P.M. Sometimes I played, but I didn't like the game, which usually was "forty-five for a ha'penny." In this game you robbed with the king, if the ace wasn't out. It seemed to me there never was a new deck; it was always short of a couple of cards, and those that remained were worn, scarred and thick, and everyone knew each card from its back. They played always at the kitchen table, candles being used whenever light was needed. Matt, or the gaffer, sat sideways on the end of the adjoining settle-bed, and the others sat on a bench before the table, while Tom invariably ensconced himself on the table itself.

On Saturday evenings, before clean-up time, a few neighboring farmers always came over after supper to hold a confab about the doings of Mick McQuade and his henchman, Terry Gerahty, as narrated weekly by the little Dublin Colonel in the pages of *The Shamrock*. Sundays the jaunting car was got out, chiefly for the benefit of the daughters and the gaffer and his brother, and they were all driven over by Bill to first Mass in Barndarrig parish church. Sometimes I went with them, but much oftener I walked to "hear" Mass in the chapel of ease up on Kilbride hill. At this little church most of the males heard Mass on one knee outside the church, the younger ones chattering and throwing gravel at one another, while the oldsters chorused, "Whisht, stop it, ye varmints." It was in the front yard of this church that I had my first striking lesson in practical aerodynamics when I saw a hawk remain poised absolutely motionless in the air a few hundred feet away over the valley. It must have been a full three minutes before it showed any sign of motion, and then it dived suddenly earthward like a meteor from the sky. I knew that the hawk was poised for a kill, and I was disappointed in my hope that it might be "attacked" and forced to ignominious flight by a flotilla of swallows. Often the swallows did this, but on this occasion they didn't.

One Sunday morning in the late '80s, Father Maloney, the parish priest, chilled the marrow in many of his parishioners in Barndarrig by the simple tale of an adventure that had befallen him on a night in the preceding week. The priest was responding to a sick call and was being driven in a vis-à-vis trap by his coachman and general handy-man, and as they were proceeding along the "Green Lane" skirting Colonel Acton's deerpark, the horse and trap, with Father Maloney and the man still seated safely in it, were literally "translated" into the deerpark. Not a trace of the pony's harness was broken, and, knowing so intimately the spot where this occurred, I can say that the incident seemed inexplicable. It must be remembered that the road was separated from the deerpark by a deep, wide moat, built for the one special purpose of preventing full grown deer from getting out of the park.

Yet it was over and across this very moat that Father Maloney, his man, horse, and trap were lifted right into the deerpark; and, as I have said, without any harm being done to either the men, horse or trap. In the dark of the night Father Maloney's man made his way to the gamekeeper's lodge, and the gamekeeper let them out by a gate nearly half a mile away.

I had lots of experiences of the occult in Wicklow. I remember one morning about one o'clock, Bill Fogarty, who was then courting his future wife Lizzie Waldron, and I were coming down the hill from Waldron's farmhouse in Ballycapple. It was clear and quiet, when from away across the valley we heard a cry—long and loud and mournful. We both stopped instantly without saying a word. Then in perhaps two minutes, the cry was repeated; and we both uttered, but not seriously, of course, the word *Banshee.* As we still stood to listen the cry was repeated, but that was all; although we waited a long time, we did not hear it again. We resumed our rapid walk homeward and while we walked we talked about the direction the sound came from, and the distance of its origin, and I said to Bill that it seemed to me the cry originated right over Grant's farmhouse on the side of Grant's hill. That morning we were having breakfast shortly after five, when the youngest son of the Grant family came in to tell us that his grandmother had died about an hour after midnight.

On an autumn evening when I was in my late teens I was walking from Ticlash to Carrigmore and, coming down beautiful Kilcandra hill, I met Bill Keegan who was out rabbiting. Bill was a big young man about 6 feet 3 inches in height, and then in his late twenties. His farm adjoined the Fogarty farm; and his farmhouse was in Kilmanogue, almost within a stone's throw of Kilmanogue old church and graveyard. By the time we had come down to the little road turning to the left to the Keegan farmhouse, it had begun to rain heavily, so Bill asked me to come over to their house to shelter for a while. We both turned in to the narrow roadway and walked towards the Keegan house. On the right side of this road there was a high shrubby ditch, at the far side of which was a field of almost ripe oats. As we plodded along quickly, there was the distinct and unmistakable sound of horses whinnying and snorting behind the hedge in the oatfield. "Bill," I said, "your horses are loose in the oats, if we don't turn them out, they'll have played the devil with your crop by the morning." To my amazement, Bill didn't answer—that is, not directly. All he did was step out more briskly, and then he said to me, "Hurry up." We had gone down the road maybe forty yards when there was a frightful screech from the oatfield, and then Bill said to me, "Come on John, get going." And he himself was certainly practicing what he preached. We had proceeded to maybe within sixty yards of the house when our ears were smitten by another screech, this one being directly behind us; immediately upon the utterance of this second screech, Bill charged with all the fury of a stricken bull for the house. I followed after him in bewilderment, more than in consternation, and just as we got to the farmhouse door, a third screech, louder, more menacing, and nearer—right on top of us in fact—split our ears, and Bill threw himself at the farmhouse door in such an abandoned effort to get into the house, that he tore the door off its hinges, and it landed on the kitchen floor, with Bill lying like a corpse on top of it—he had fainted from terror!

I had often before this time heard about the notorious, unearthly "three shrieks" that always seemed to originate somewhere in the neighborhood of the entrance to the Acton estate near the foot of Kilcandra hill; but until that night with Bill Keegan I had never heard them. What they were, by whom or what uttered, and what they signified, I do not know. All I do know is that there were strange and unexplainable noises and happenings not alone in the County Wicklow, but even in Dublin City itself, as I narrate elsewhere in this book.

His sister and I tended Bill Keegan in his faint in the customary manner but he did not come out of it for a quarter of an hour; and when he did his face was livid and his body was limp. I pitied him, of course, but my pity was mixed with annoyance and surprise. Frankly, I could not understand why such a big and powerful fellow should permit himself to be so terrorized. That these infernal screeches were heard and had been heard for years, I now accepted unquestioningly. That they derived from something sinister, or something with malicious intent, I felt inclined to believe; but, on the other hand, although the screeches had been going on for maybe scores of years, no one, it seemed, had ever actually come to harm from or by them.

At about half past ten that night Bill had recovered sufficiently to be able to go to bed, and then, as I wanted to go down to Fogarty's I started to say goodnight to him. When I did so, he sat up in his bed and implored me not to go out. He was so frighteningly earnest, and so mentally disturbed, that I agreed to stay longer, maybe for the night. I left him then in his room, with his sister sitting by his bedside, and in about ten minutes she came out and told us he had fallen asleep. I then prepared to go home to Fogarty's, and, over the fervid protestation of the two sisters, I left the house, with my trusty ash plant in my hand. When I got out into the open the night was clear, with a moon nearly full and bright, and the rain had ceased an hour before. Instead of taking a short cut round the back of the Keegan house to Fogarty's "White Meadow," I retraced my steps of a couple of hours before until I came to a gate opening into the field of oats. I vaulted this gate, and walked round the whole field on the headland; and as the field was only about three acres in extent, no large animal could have escaped my observation; but I could see no trace of damage, nor any sign that horses or asses or cattle had been in the field. I revaulted the gate, walked the narrow laneway to Kilcandra hill, went down to the left past Molly Locke's turn, and continued for about five hundred and fifty yards to Fogarty's gate. Although it was now approaching the witching hour of midnight, I encountered nothing out of the ordinary. The feeling always aroused in me by any occult mani-festation, such as the one on that night, was a mixture of disgust and indignation. I was not afraid; on the contrary, I wanted to investigate, and, if I had been given a chance I would have loved to fight it, meaning by "it" the thing that was the origin of the manifestation. The attitude of the Irish country people in these matters was one of acceptance; but generally they were awed, in many cases cowed, by them. And this was true whether of Catholics, or Protestants, or any religion. Bill Keegan, for example, was the Protestant son of a Protestant family, and a splendid family they were, but he reacted exactly as would most other men of his time and neighborhood.

I will not here discuss the possible explanations for these phe-nomena, but I do think that some of them—although definitely not all of them—were perhaps superinduced by auto-suggestion.

In this connection I may remark that I do not recall ever hearing of a drunk experiencing an occult manifestation. I have known many habitual drunks who came toddling and staggering home at all hours, and who never experienced anything out of the way, and never saw anything more ghostly than a pair of coupled nanny goats.

In July 1894 I had an experience which might be called mysterious, or occult, or, at any rate, inexplicable on known natural grounds. The time of this experience was the evening of the hay-drawing on the Douglas farm in Kilnamanagh and the place where it happened was in the Douglas house. Let me explain, first, that in my childhood I had often heard Emily Pentland tell of a mysterious experiment which interested the Allingham family and many of their guests. This experiment involved three persons; one of whom was put sitting in a chair, with the other two standing one at each side of the sitter, and each of the standers having the tips of two fingers—not more—under an elbow of the sitter. I cannot say that I remember the precise conditions under which this experiment was supposed to be conducted, but I do remember the most important condition was that all three persons participating in the experiment, the sitter and the two standers, should simultaneously take a deep breath, which all three should exhale at the same time. This breath-taking and exhalation was to be repeated, and then all three were to take a third deep breath which all three were to hold; and while holding their breath the standers were supposed to be able to lift, by the tips of their fingers, the sitter out of the chair.

Emily Pentland told us that while some persons in the Allingham entourage had asserted they had seen the experiment performed successfully elsewhere, yet the experiments in the Allingham house never were successful. As for me, I had tried it many times but always without success.

This July evening in the Douglas farmhouse, I thought I'd make another try, so I enlisted Bill Fogarty's aid and we both decided we should be the standers, and that we'd try to find a sitter, preferably a big heavy fellow. But when we approached the biggest and heaviest fellows and told them what we wanted to do, not one of them would sit—they weren't having any of that stuff "not damn well likely!" After four or five of the big, husky, but leery, ones had refused, we asked smiling Paddy Kavanagh to sit for the experiment—and Paddy consented. But when it came to the simultaneous breath-taking, the experiment was a complete washout, because Paddy simply could not help laughing—this being at least partly due, as I suspected at the time, to Paddy's effort to disguise his nervousness.

Bill and I had reluctantly decided to abandon the experiment, when who should walk into the kitchen but Matt Russell, who was no flyweight. Matt hadn't been able to be at the haydrawing, but he came over to spend the evening, and immediately he came in, Bill and I buttonholed him, and explained what we wanted—and Matt consented.

The three of us—Matt, and Bill, and I—made four efforts to perform the experiment, but at each effort we failed in the breath-taking synchronization. On the fifth effort, however, we succeeded in reaching the end of the third inhalation, and at this point Bill and I found ourselves, to our own astonishment and mystification, holding 215-pound Matt Russell, by the tips of two of our fingers, high up above his chair. As we held him thus, Matt remained in the crouched position of a person sitting, or, as I distinctly remember thinking at that moment, in the attitude of an athlete who is midway in the making of a long jump. We lifted Matt to a height where our fingers that were sustaining him, under his bent arms near his elbows, were well above our eyes; and we held him thus for about fifteen seconds, when we began to feel the weight increase rapidly, and we lowered him to the chair.

If you were to ask me what did it feel like to lift Matt at that time, I think I can best describe the feeling by saying that it seemed as if Matt were no longer in air, but in some much denser medium, a medium nearly, but not quite, as dense as water. Another way of describing my sensation and Bill's too, at the time, would be to say that it seemed, for the fifteen seconds or so, that the influence of gravity had almost ceased to act on Matt. On comparing our sensations, Bill and I agreed that we had felt some weight on our finger tips, a weight equivalent perhaps to a small chicken.

This "successful" experiment with Matt Russell produced a peculiar and increasingly unpleasant aftermath in my life. For ever since that time a strange dream has recurred frequently; it is a feeling of levitation, in which I am able by force of will to proceed, for a while, without touching the ground, but never for a long time—only it seems for a minute or two. This dream is always vivid, and in it, as I levitate, I am always astounded that no one out of the numbers who see me defying gravity pays the slightest attention to my extraordinary motion. Always in my dream it seems to me that my ability to move above the ground is due to an exercise of will power, which, on awakening, as I invariably do immediately after the dream, I find a little exhausting.

Only a day or two after the preceding paragraph was written, the dream once again recurred; this latest occasion—and, I hope, the last—being in the early morning of Labor Day, 1949. On that morning I had this dream of levitation more vividly and in far greater detail than ever before. The scene of my dream this time was the hall and first flight of eleven steps in number 20 East Essex Street. In this dream I found myself, as always, in the crouched position of an athlete doing his damndest to stretch his long jump, and in this position I was able, by the exercise of a supernatural will power, to avoid touching the ground as I moved a few feet in the air above the hall and above the steps as I ascended. And on this occasion I had, for the first time in my life, an astonished and admiring witness—this witness being Joe Culhane, the boy who sat beside me in No. 3 classroom in Belvedere College. From this dream on that morning I awoke feeling quite unwell, being near exhaustion, and very chilled. That is why I express the fervent hope that this latest recurrence of my levitation dream has been the last.

Pertaining to the notion of the occult, or of auto-suggestion, or maybe, hypnosis, is a simple story I heard as a boy from gaffer Fogarty. He said that when he was a boy of about twelve years old, he saw one day, after a fair in Rathdrum, a ring of people on the fairgreen surrounding three roving jugglers and entertainers; the three being ostensibly father, mother, and a young lad, their son. When the trio had exhausted their bag of tricks, the father asked the assembled audience would they like to know what the weather was going to be during the next few days; if they would, he said, he would send the lad up to find out. Of course the ring of spectators were all for knowing about the future weather, and when the man passed the hat, they contributed generously. The collection having been made, the man took a cotton ball out of his pocket, and holding the end of the thread in his fingers, he tossed the ball away up until it disappeared from sight.

Then pointing to the thread suspended from the sky, he said to the boy: "Here, you, climb up and see what kind of weather we're going to have." To the amazement of the surrounding circle of gazers, the boy clambered rapidly, hand over hand, up the cotton thread until he disappeared into the sky. The man and wife continued their palaver for a while, and then the man said to the woman, "I wonder what's keeping sonny up there. Maybe he's lost, you'd better go up and look for him." And this the woman proceeded to do, as she, unlike the boy, climbed up slowly, hand over hand, till she, too, disappeared in the heavens. The man chattered idly for a couple of minutes and then he began to worry about his son and wife, neither of whom had reappeared. "I don't know what's become of them" he wailed, "maybe they've both got lost. I'll have to go up and see."

So up he went, climbing even faster than the boy; and as he ascended he took the cotton thread up with him, and he disappeared from view. The spellbound circle of spectators stood for maybe ten minutes craning their necks, and then a farmer who was driving into town asked what was up. He was told excitedly, "Three people are up—up there." "Up where," he says. And still the crowd pointed to the sky. "What d'ye mane—three people gone up there—gone up where—are y'all gone mad!"

Then a few of the crowd came to him and told him about the three ascensionists, and what they had been doing—and described them. "My God," said the farmer, blessing himself, "tis only too thrue—ye're all turned into lunatics. Why I met the three o' them —man, woman and boy—only five or six minutes ago walking on the road towards Greenan."

Let me give a couple of annotations to this story: Gaffer Fogarty died in 1898, and the age on his headstone was sixty-eight. He must have been born, therefore, around 1830; and if he was twelve, as he thought, when the incident took place, it must have been about 1842. It was as we sat around the kitchen fire in his own house that the gaffer told us the story, and that was a few years before he died. The gaffer said he himself was present and saw the incident; it was not the story of what some one else had seen. I knew old Mick Fogarty well, and I knew that when he told the story he believed that what he told was true. And I know, too, that at the time he told it, neither he nor I nor anyone present as he told it, had ever heard of the Indian rope-ladder trick.

A couple of weeks after that night of the three screeches, Bill
Keegan's sister was married, and the morning of her wedding she
had to be led, like a blind woman, in the church. The day before
her wedding she had been stung between her eyes by a bee; and
both her eyes had swollen so badly that she was unable to open
either.

At a haydrawing shortly afterwards on the Keegan farm one
Saturday that summer, all the workers in the haggard were both-
ered by bees. Bill told us that there had been for some years a
bees' nest in a tree growing a few yards away by the side of a
small brook; formerly, he said, they did not give much trouble,
but this year they had become a real pest, and one of them, he
was sure, must have been responsible for the temporary blindness
of his sister. He said he had bought sulphur to smoke them out,
that he was sorry he hadn't done it before the haydrawing, but
he would do it that very evening.

I said to him that if he had made up his mind to get rid of the
bees, he should try to salvage the honey.

"But how can I do that?" he asked.

"If you are really determined to destroy the bees," I replied,
"I'll take the honey out of the nest. For the bees' sake, I wouldn't
like to do it, but if the bees must go I think the honey should
be saved."

When the hay was in and the rick finished, they all feasted at
a sumptuous supper; and evening had already come before Bill
Keegan and Bill Fogarty and I went round to look at the tree. It
was, if I remember rightly, an ash—great, tall and old—that had
many of its roots in the bed of the brook running by the back of
the farmhouse. Standing on the bank of the brook opposite the
tree I could see the bees flying in and out of an oval-shaped opening about eight inches by six, and about ten feet up on the side
of the trunk. I went back to the haggard and returned with an
eight-foot ladder which I set up, with its foot in the brook, against
the side of the tree.

"What are you going to do—you're not thinking of going up
there without netting on you, are you?"

"Bill, I've been stung by bees and wasps scores of times, and
never yet have they left a mark on me. Bee stings don't bother me
—they hurt, of course, the same as they do anyone else, I presume,
but that's nothing—I can bear it."

I then went up the ladder to investigate, and I put my right hand and arm into the hole in the tree. In the hollow tree trunk I felt high vertical slabs of honeycomb separated one from another by perhaps three quarters of an inch. There was no doubt about it; there was honey—go leor. So I came down at once. I had been stung, of course, lots of stings, but I had hardly felt them. I told Bill Keegan I wanted a couple of clean pails, so we went to the dairy where we got two large shiny, cylindrical pails, the kind they used for milking. We went back to the tree where, having re-ascended the ladder, I hung the pails securely on two branches, one at either side of the hole. Then because it had impeded my arm movement, I rolled up my right shirt sleeve securely to my oxter, and started to tear out the combs. When I began doing this the bees really set out to give battle to their foe. I was stung—stung everywhere, from face to foot, and the mass impact of the universal stinging did hurt. So painful was it that before I had finished I got down off the ladder, lay flat in the brook, with all my clothes on, and rolled in it. Then I climbed up the ladder again, and in a trice I had removed all the comb I could. Both pails were packed full, away above their brims, and then I brought them down one at a time. Bill Keegan insisted on my taking at least one pail of the honeycomb, and Bill Fogarty and I started homewards. When we got in the house I went to the lower room where I took off all my clothes and Bill Fogarty and I picked a regular stubble of bee stings out of my body; and I want it to be noted here that I felt none the worse for the experience. In fact, I felt fine. About nine o'clock I went to bed, it being then eighteen hours since I had got up that morning, and I fell asleep right away.

In about fifteen minutes I awoke in the hot August night shivering. My teeth began to clatter violently and I quickly developed nausea. I called Bill, and he, seeing I was very ill, said he would send one of his hired men in on my bike to Wicklow to call Dr. Byrne; but I managed to mumble to Bill that I knew what was wrong with me, and that no doctor could arrive in time to do me any good, but Bill sent for Byrne, anyway.

Immediately on getting the attack that night, I sensed the cause of my illness. Bee stings, by twos and threes, or more, I had often got, and suffered from them not at all. But I realized now that the cumulative effect of the bee sting acid injected simultaneously by many hundreds of bees had caused acute poisoning and could easily be deadly. This acid is usually identified with—but is not quite the same as—formic acid.

Having diagnosed, to my own profound astonishment, the nature of my trouble, I told Bill just to "stand by" for we would have to handle this thing ourselves. I asked him for some warm water, and the package of bread soda. Into the water I put two heaping dessertspoonfuls of the soda, and swallowed it as fast as my rat-a-tat jaws would allow me. I had in a few minutes grown much worse, and by now the little room was shaking from my ague and the violent shivering of my body. I asked Bill to heap blankets on me, and to put jars of boiling water at my feet and alongside me in the bed; and then I asked him to give me a real stiff tumbler of punch without lemon. Bill told me afterwards that as soon as I had swallowed the punch I became delirious and remained so for maybe quarter of an hour. Then I came to earth again, and seeing Bill standing over me I realized for the second time my condition, and asked him for another similar dose of the warm water and bread soda. Bill brought me both, but I was too weak to help myself so he mixed the stuff and held the drink to my mouth; and in about ten minutes I asked Bill to give me another punch like the first one I had taken. After that I simply lay motionless in bed, but I did not relapse into delirium, nor did I go to sleep.

Shortly after eleven o'clock that night, Dr. Byrne arrived from Wicklow, and he, having taken my pulse and temperature, the latter being 107, called Bill outside the door into the kitchen for a minute, and I didn't know till I was well that he had then advised Bill to "send for the priest." Byrne then came back with Bill into the room, and said to me that he wanted me to take a couple of pills. I lay motionless and unresponsive, but although weak—indeed too weak to talk—I knew that I was already much better than I had been and that I was going to be all right. When I did not answer, Byrne asked Bill to help me sit up to take his pills because he didn't want to risk my choking on one or both of them if he were to put them in my mouth as I was lying down. As Bill attempted to raise me, I managed to make him understand that I wanted to know what was in the pills. Bill asked Byrne, and he replied instantly and with assurance, "quinine." Upon hearing which word, I shook my head and uttered as vigorously as I was able an emphatic "No."

In all the years I have lived it has fallen to me a few times to owe my life to someone's devoted ministering; but only once has that someone been a male, and that male was Bill Fogarty. Perhaps the most amazing thing about this whole incident is the fact that by noon of the following day, Sunday, I felt as fit as a fiddle and there was not a mark on my body.

That Sunday evening there was a big "party" in the Keegan house, attended by all the male help at the haydrawing on the preceding day; and there were also invited about a dozen girls, most of whom I met then for the first time. I am not going to try to write a pen-picture of the occasion, which was declared by those present to be the most pleasant and memorable in their lives— surpassing by far in sheer merriment, the widely celebrated and loudly sung "gaiety at Phil the Fluther's Ball" or the much-vaunted time "that was had by all at the christening of McSorley's two iligant twins." But seriously and modestly speaking, it really was a pleasant affair. Of provender and liquid refreshments there was far more than go leor—with plenty of wine for the ladies, or for the few men who would occasionally deign to take a sip of it. There was singing, to which I contributed a little; and there was, of course, to the tune of piper and fiddler, much dancing, to which I contributed not at all. Coming daylight on Monday morning, the party was about to break up; and there was talk of "Auld Lang Syne"; then someone suggested a "toast," and asked me to propose one. I did propose a toast to "our host and hostesses," and also "to the ladies," but they wanted something more, something I could not give because I knew none. The guests, especially the ladies, were insistent, so I managed to slip away for a few minutes, and strolling outside the house in the beauty of the country and the night, I concocted a few lines roughly suitable for a "general toast." Then I came back to the noise and merriment, and being again pressed to give the party a toast, I filled from a decanter of port, not a beaker, but a dandy; and holding it up, with its "beaded bubbles winking at the brim" I gave:

> Let us drink—to the drains—
> One and all!

Our wine grows as
Sweet as red roses
When honeyed words fall.
Naught shall we know, but of things
That are gladsome and true—
A bouquet of violets and pansies
Ungarnished with rue.
Let each drink to that
Which each to his heart holds most dear;
I drink to the love of my soul—
A cuisle mo croidhe!

*   *   *

About the turn of the century, I made the men around Carrig-more a little more handball-minded than they had been; showing them by example that the mere fact of a fellow having put in a hard twelve-hour day was no adequate reason for lolling around in the evening in the ditches or on the side of the hill chatting about nothing. At that time there was a very passable handball alley about two miles away right beside Galvin's Mill at Ballina-meesda bridge, and once in a while we played in it on Sunday, but we didn't like doing this because there were plenty of fellows from that immediate neighborhood who had more right to play there than we had. So we contented ourselves with playing hand-ball up against the door and wall of the Fogarty car barn.

One Saturday night in the summer of 1899, I arrived in Fo-garty's after a quick walk down from Dublin. When the usual stirabout supper, with jorums of milk and buttermilk, was over, and the rosary and litany said, it was the invariable rule for the male members of the household to disperse each by himself far from the house for astronomical observation. On this night I was surprised as I was going out by the front door to hear Bill say to me, "John, I want you to do me a little favor—I've a reason for asking you—promise?"

"Certainly, Bill, what is it?"

"It's just this—wherever you go, don't go by the crossroad."

"That's surely a funny request, Bill. All right, I won't."

Next morning Bill and I were up, as usual, at daybreak, and he said to me, "John, come out, I want to show you something."

He brought me over to what they called the crossroad (it was really a fork in the road), and there, on the site of what had been for perhaps a century an abandoned quarry, stood a perfectly splendid ball alley. It was a large alley, about forty-five feet deep by thirty-five feet wide. Construction of it had involved blasting, excavation, and removal of about five hundred tons of rock and earth, mostly from the side of Russel's hill, right up against which stood the back "wall" constructed entirely of lumber, planks, and wire netting, with a short wing wall of same material at either side. The work had all been done in the evenings of a month; and the local boys, farmers' sons, and laborers, had all lent a willing hand to the job and had chipped in to defray the cost of the material. Bill Fogarty was, of course, the leading spirit in the project, but he was ably and enthusiastically aided by his brother Mick; by Matt and Mick Russel; Bob, Pat and Tom Douglas; Con Brian's three sons, Matt, Bob, and Jack; Bill Keegan; by the brothers Tom and Jack Brian, who worked here and there; and another pair of brothers, Paddy and Jack Kavanagh, who did the same. When I stood in that ball alley on that Sunday morning, I felt that indirectly I had been paid one of the greatest compliments I could ever hope to receive.

A couple of amusing incidents occurred in this ball alley, neither of which had anything to do with handball. About two Sundays after it had been completed, I was stalking around the road in front of it, mounted on a pair of stilts, with the pegs for my feet six feet from the ground; I had made the stilts myself out of a pair of young unseasoned birch poles. The stilts were not strapped nor fastened to me; the poles were more than eleven feet high, and I grasped them with my arms near their tops. As I walked around with a beehive hat on my head, taking three-yard strides, I saw a couple of gentlemen coming towards me from the "Pass." They had evidently got off the Dublin train at Glenealy about an hour earlier; and as they drew nearer I recognized them as Henry C. McWeeny, brother of pathologist Edmond, and Joseph Gibney, both of them professors of mathematics in University College, and both, of course, knew me well. When they had come in front of the ball alley, Gibney asked some of the "boys" to direct them to the "Beehive." The "boys," not knowing perhaps what he asked, were unable to direct him, so I strode over to the two professors and told them how to get to the "Beehive," a little wayside inn owned by one McCoy, and situated at the crossroads about two and a half miles away on the Wicklow road. As I spoke to the two professors they both, of course, stared up at me, and neither of them knew me from Adam.

It was, perhaps, on the evening of the following Sunday that as I was standing around the alley on my stilts I had a sudden notion to chalk up a line of verse near the top of the plank wall. On my stilts, with the top of my right stilt against the wall, I was easily able to reach up more than twelve feet, and write in large chalk lettering the words:

"Lasciate ogni speranza voi ch'entrate."

You may consider my surprise, when, early the following morning, I saw written in chalk under my line, but still a full ten feet from the ground, the following bit of doggerel:

"Whoever wrote this wrote it well;
For the same is written on the gates of Hell."

It was only a bit of trite doggerel, of course, but on this occasion it hit the nail right on the head—for that is exactly where Dante read the words.

The Fogartys were good judges of cattle, and their small herd of cows, usually seven or eight, was always good stock. Somewhere about this time of the construction of the alley, the cows broke into the "upper field" in which there was oats in stooks on one side, and potatoes and mangolds on the other. One of the farmhands went after the cows to chase them out, but he was too impetuous, lashing about with a long whip. As he lashed out at one splendid three-year old red cow, she snatched friskily at a small potato, one about an inch and a half in diameter, and the potato lodged in her throat. I don't want to dwell on the long drawn out tragedy of that evening and night. No one seemed to know what to do for the cow; but a Mr. Cod, a well to do farmer with his place off the main road to Rathdrum, was sent for, and he "treated" the cow. I know that one of the treatments he administered was to stick a more or less flexible tube down the beast's throat. I felt reasonably sure when I saw him do this that he didn't know or indeed care what passage he was sticking the tube into, so long as it went down somewhere.

To cut this story short: I saw—anyone could see—that the animal was dying, so I pleaded with the Fogartys to put her out of pain by killing her in the regular way, and incidentally, save at least the best part of her meat for food. Would they do this? No, they wouldn't, and they didn't. The cow died in agony some hours later, and the beautiful young animal was buried next day in "the field beyant the road."

The cow had been buried in a dugout about six feet deep, and two tons of rocks were imbedded in the mound on top, and in the earth around it. Yet about three nights afterwards it seemed as if all the dogs in the country for miles around foregathered by common concert at the spot, and in a fury of animal rapacity, clawed at the mound, rocks and all, until they completely exposed and ravenously devoured the rotting carcass. It was about midnight when we were all awakened by the howling, whining, and barking; and the infernal din grew rapidly more hellish as more and more dogs joined the bacchanalian feast. About two o'clock in the morning I got up and dressed, loaded the double-barrelled muzzle loader, and stepped out alone into the early morning. No one would come with me, nor was there any dog to welcome me as I emerged from the house, because even the Fogarty dogs had gone "native." It was a clear starry night, but the moon was waning thin and visibility was low as I made my way cautiously to the western gate where I turned to the right for about one hundred yards. At this place I mounted to the top of the road ditch, and right before me in the field, about forty yards away, was the seething maelstrom of a canine hell. For a couple of minutes I stood on the ditch, my ears racked and shocked by the infernal noises of the frenzied dogs. I wondered could I do anything about it; but I realized as I fingered the trigger of my pathetically ineffective muzzle loader, that this hell was a dog's hell, and that it was a hell of a good place to stay out of. I went back to bed.

This horrible occurrence made me determined that when I returned to Dublin I would try to learn what should have been done, or rather what should be done were a similar accident to happen again. It was with this purpose in mind that I asked Mr. Lyster, the librarian in the National Library, for some book treating on the subject, and the book he got for me was the very book that made James Joyce detonate with mirth when he read in it the printed words "Diseases of the Ox."

In one of the years around the turn of the century, there was a peculiarly interesting arboreal phenomenon observable in Wicklow, and I presume, in the rest of the country. I refer to the appearance of laurel berries in extraordinary profusion. I was told at the time that this phenomenon recurs in cycles of about ten years, although I never observed it but once. To give some idea of what I mean by "profusion," let me say that I climbed a laurel tree and, without moving from one branch, I filled two bushel-sized wicker baskets with great, luscious, and delectably edible black and near-black berries the size of large cherries. The laurel tree in which I gathered these berries was one of a small grove growing back of a four-foot stone wall bordering the northern wood at Deputy's Pass, and about three hundred yards up the old mountain road from the little bridge over the Potter's River. And while on this subject of berries, I'd like to comment on the annual profusion of froghans, perhaps the most delicately tasty of all berries, in the very wood I am talking about. Of course, froghans were available elsewhere in fairly wide distribution, and it was amazing to me that so few persons seemed to care for them enough to take the trouble to gather them or even to care for them enough to pay one-and-six for a two-gallon can of them gathered by a "gypsy" or by an enterprising "tramp."

About three miles north of Deputy's Pass rises one of the most sublimely shaped and pinnacled mountains in the world. It is not really a mountain, for it is only a little over one thousand feet high, and its name is Carrick MacReilly. But the slopes of this glorious hill are, or at least were a half century ago, garbed in a thick and richly variegated coat of the most luxurious, sweetest, deepest, and softest heather. John Keats would have loved it; for it is quite evident the poor fellow didn't know anything about what real heather could be like.

To his "Devon maid," his "tight little fairy," he says,

> "But oh, on the heather to lie together,
> With both our hearts a-beating!"

And in the next breath he continues,

> "And we will sigh in the daisy's eye,
> And kiss on a grass-green pillow."

No, poor John didn't know anything about heather. If he had known, and had lain in, the heather on Carrick MacReilly he would never have dreamt of himself and his girl friend sighing in the eye of a daisy. When you lay on the side of Carrick MacReilly, you lay in a heather bed uninfested with daisies—a heather bed compared with which a feather bed is but as the spiked plank an Indian fakir lies on for torture.

In August 1896, I climbed Lugnaquilla for the first time. That summer Mary had given me a second-hand solid tire "safety," bought for thirty-five bob by a friend of hers, "a rale expert in machinery." So "expert" was he that he never noticed the top bar had been broken, and then welded and enameled by a botch; and off this contraption I later got one of the worst spills of my life. But before this happened, I rode over on it one morning at daybreak from Fogarty's to Drumgoff, where I left the bike in an outhouse of an inn at the crossroads. I walked south along the military road, past the old barracks and overtook a mountain-man on horseback. Rider and horse were barely moving along the road, for he was slowly driving about six hundred sheep in front of him. As I overtook the man, I saw that his sheepdog was moving lazily, with pendant tail, closely behind the horse. Of course, the man hailed me and we got to talking, and after a while he asked me where I was going. I told him I was going to the top of Lugnaquilla, at which he chuckled, and said to me, "D'ye know where it is?" "Yes, in a general way," I said, motioning my arm, "I know it's away out there." "Come up the road a bit here with me," he said, "and I'll show it ti ye."

As I walked along the borderless road, I noticed that some of the sheep had one brand while others had another. I asked him about this; and he explained that there were two different flocks belonging to two different owners, and that one of the owners had his land on the east side of the road, and the other on the west. Seeing that the two flocks were commingled, I asked him how he could possibly separate them. He didn't answer me directly, but he grinned and uttered sharply a couple of words to his apparently moribund dog. The dog responded as if electrified, and in a jiffy the two flocks were rounded up, each on the correct side of the road.

A few minutes later we had ascended to a curve in the road, and the man pointed out to me a convex-topped mountain away behind the similar convexities of lower and nearer mountains.

"D'ye see that cairn over there on that far mountain—well that's Lugnaquilla; and that's where ye say ye want to go."

"Thanks," I said to him, "that's splendid. I'll make a beeline for that cairn."

And as I left him I was surprised at his surprise at my aiming to go there; and with my ashplant in hand, I was at the cairn about three hours later. On the way I had a strange experience. I was walking on the top of the broad convex summit of the mountain above Kelly's Lake, where, noticing that the ground was so soft that it seemed almost to throb, I tried inserting my stick into it, and found that I could, with little pressure, drive it to the handle into the mountain top.

From the cairn on Lugnaquilla I scanned the country round through a sixteen-power telescope I had picked up for two bob at a rummage sale a few weeks earlier on Wood Quay. Having put in a couple of hours picking out objects and landmarks through the telescope, I sat down at the foot of the cairn, took out of my pockets a pen, notepaper, a little bottle of ink in a leather case, and wrote a letter to Norah. When I had finished the letter I looked up and around me and there was nothing to be seen. A thick mist or cloud had crept stealthily over the mountain and so dense was it that visibility was zero, and this unexpected experience, unprecedented in my life, was eerie.

I could prattle about Wicklow till the cows come home, but I have to cut it short and get to the business in hand; so I will only mention the names of such places as Avoca, with the old copper and lead mines; Glenmalur, at the foot of Lugnaquilla, and famed for Fiach MacHugh O'Byrne's victory; Glendalough, my mother's birthplace; "Divil's Glin"; Ardnaree, Jack's Hole, and Brittas, with the sublime sandbanks; and Douce mountain on the summit of which you come with startling suddenness on the ineffably beautiful view of Lough Tay.

There is, however, another incident about which I would like to say a word. On August 15th, 1898, the foundation stone for a monument to Wolfe Tone was laid at the Grafton Street entrance to Stephen's Green; the occasion being in celebration of the abortive rebellion of 1798. For several weeks prior to that day I had been in Wicklow, and as the day drew near I toyed with the notion of going up to Dublin for the event. Practically everybody else was going—by train, car or bicycle; and, of course, as Mary Fleming would say, "Ye might as well be out o' the world as out o' the fashion."

Came Saturday, the 13th of August, and what did I do? I rode on shank's mare from Fogarty's to Lugnaquilla, starting out at three in the morning, and arriving back at ten o'clock that night. Next day, Sunday, everyone was making appointments to meet me on the following day somewhere in "The City," for they were all quite certain I would ride on my brand-new Rudge-Whitworth bicycle over "the rocky road to Dublin." That Sunday evening some of the Carrigmore folk went up to Dublin, and early next morning more of them followed, all of them being still confident that I'd ride up there on my two-wheeled charger in my usual time of an hour and fifty-five minutes.

I did get my bicycle out of the car-barn, with, I thought, the idea of going to Dublin. But as I was about to start, something made me start in the opposite direction, and two hours and forty minutes later I was riding into the lovely and historic little old town of Enniscorthy.

Why did I go to Enniscorthy? I went to Enniscorthy because it nestled at the foot of Vinegar Hill, a scrubby elevation 389 feet high, and about 5 furlongs away. This hill was the scene of the one striking, but disappointing, victory over the English in the Rebellion of 1798. And on that hill I sat during the whole afternoon of August the 15th, 1898, dreaming dreams of one hundred years before—dreams that were mingled with more than one grim memory of whispered family traditions.

Late in the evening of that day I started back from Vinegar Hill; and passing through Ferns on my way home I got a puncture. Since I had no means of mending the puncture, and, of course, I wouldn't ride on the rim of my new bike, I had to face the prospect of walking that night nearly forty miles to Carrigmore. But I didn't care a button about this; on the contrary I was almost glad to have to walk, for it gave me an opportunity to continue my dream more appropriately as I led my bicycle northward in the night.

And as I walked I felt almost gay, because the northern heavens were illuminated by one of the most glorious auroras I have ever seen. For many hours the sky seemed vibrant with the incessant illumination and the brilliant, searchlight flashes, and multicolored radiance of one of nature's most beautiful and most mysterious phenomena; and the appearance that night of this aurora was in my youthful imagination doubly auspicious.

CHAPTER EIGHTEEN

Introduction to "A Parable in Gold"

IN 1926 I HAD an interview with the late Mr. E. W. Fairchild, President of the Fairchild Publications in New York City, and as a result I became financial editor of the Daily News Record, for which paper I wrote under the pen-name J. F. Renby, a simple anagram of my own name. For a long time E. W. pressed me to do a daily column for the paper, but it was not until January, 1929, that I yielded to his importunity and began writing a daily column—a stint I continued till March, 1933. For about a year and a half my column was headed "Wall Street Comment," but in August, 1930, I changed its title to "Money Matters—Mostly," and it so remained until the column was ultimately disembodied. I do not intend to dilate here on my experiences with the Daily News Record, but I do say that the business organization of which that paper was a part was then extremely successful and financially prosperous, and its success and stability were due largely to the personality of its chief, E. W., and also, and perhaps to a degree not generally recognized, to the individuality of his brother L. E. Fairchild.

When I first met E. W. Fairchild he was tall, thin, ascetic-looking, quiet-voiced, unusually well-dressed and groomed, gentlemanly and hard-working. He was self-opinionated, but this did not prevent him from listening to, or even from printing, the opinions of others with which he was not in agreement. However, as the old saying has it, "Circumstances alter cases."

I have said that E.W. was a hard worker, but he would not have thought so—he would have thought of himself as being a hard player at a game he loved. But, call it work or play, E.W. did a lot of it, aided by his extremely capable secretary Miss Mac-

Intosh. Indeed, the amount of work he put into the dictation of inter- and intra-office notes was tremendous. I, myself, still retain all he ever sent to me—and they make quite a heap. All these communications were typed without editing by his secretary as they came semi-literately from his mouth.

Here is a little word picture of the man, E.W. For some time after I joined the organization it was my practice, at his suggestion, to have a chat with him first thing each morning after I came to the office. On one of these mornings, I brought up a subject in which I thought he might be interested, that the Daily News Record, owing to something that had been rather wildly written in it by one of its contributors, was taboo in the banking house of J. P. Morgan & Co. I had become well-acquainted with the famous Morgan partner, "Tom" Lamont, and I knew that I had only to broach the matter to Mr. Lamont to have him remove the Morgan taboo. All the while I was speaking to E.W. about this matter, I noticed that he did not look at me directly even once; he sat immobile except for a little flicking movement by his fingers on his desk, and then, when I had finished what I wanted to say, he remarked in a low voice, but still without looking at me, "Who is this J. P. Morgan & Co.?"

And all I said in reply was "H'm!"

In the very first columns I wrote in January, 1929, I inveighed against the malignant mushroom growth of the so-called "investment trusts," as then constituted and uncontrolled; and one morning, I think it was the fifth, after I began to run my column, I met L. E. Fairchild, E.W.'s brother, on the stairs, and he told me gayfully, "I read this morning what you had to say about investment trusts, so I called up my broker and told him to sell out all the holdings I had in them."

But only a few months after that, as I was having my usual little chat with E.W. he pointed to my column of that morning in which I had written something that could not be construed as complimentary about two "investment trusts" that had just been launched, with the picturesque names of "Blue Ridge" and "Shenandoah." Pointing his finger at the place in my column where my animadversion was printed, E.W. said, as if enquiring, in a soft, low voice, but without looking at me, "These are our good friends Goldman Sachs & Company?"

And all I said in reply was "H'm!"

It was a strange quirk of fate that made me begin to write a financial and economic column in, above all years, the year 1929. I can't say that I liked writing it, because I always hated to write —anything. But I did find a certain attraction in the chore; and judging by reader interest, I did pretty well. In 1929, the Daily News Record had a circulation of only about ten thousand, but a tabulation of its subscribers would almost have been a Who's Who in the Business and Financial Worlds in America. Soon I became aware that a considerable proportion of these subscribers were regular readers of my stuff, and that of course was gratifying.

Yes, the year 1929 was a hectic and dramatic year in finance, and in the short space of a few hours toward the close of its tenth month, there must have been hundreds of thousands of persons in this country who found themselves reduced from a condition of comparative riches to actual rags. On Monday, October 28, 1929, an incident occurred which, I think, is of interest. On that Monday I came up from the Wall Street district and entering my office at about 5 P.M. I found a note on my desk saying that E.W. wanted to see me as soon as I came in. I went immediately to E.W.'s desk, where I found him sitting with three men who were strangers to me; they were not members of the staff, but all three were "important persons." Briefly and gravely E.W. introduced us, and then at once came to the point which concerned everyone deeply, and he asked me directly, "What do you make of it. It was a terrible session down there wasn't it—but the general opinion here," and as he said this he turned to look at the three men sitting around his desk, "is that the worst is over. Now, Renby, what do you think?"

And I said to him, "Well, E.W., I'm going over to my desk to write my stint, and I'll be back here in three minutes to show you the first two paragraphs of what I write. That will answer your question and tell you what I think. Is that satisfactory?"

"Yes, surely, we'll all be glad to hear what you have to say."

In a few minutes I was back at E.W.'s desk and handed him the first two paragraphs of my column. The first paragraph was a factual comment on that day's session in Wall Street; and the second paragraph was ominously prophetic. E.W. read the first paragraph in a low voice, but loud enough for the three I.P.'s to hear, and then he slowly but solemnly intoned the second paragraph, which I quote here exactly as it was written on Monday afternoon, October 28, 1929, for publication in the Daily News Record the following day, Tuesday, October 29.

"There was a bad break—a very bad break—in stock prices yesterday. Readers of this column will know we are no alarmist but we must describe the break in stocks yesterday as a very bad break, and, what is much worse than that—it was a menacing break that foreboded further immediate evil. It is altogether within the range of probability that today, Tuesday, October 29, 1929, may be hereafter remembered as one of the darkest of the "black" days in the history of the Stock Exchange. We have hesitated a long time before making up our minds definitely to write the preceding sentence. We can say, too, in all sincerity, that we devoutly hope we are wrong. But there is no gainsaying the fact that at the present moment things are extremely precarious."

When E.W. had finished intoning this paragraph, there wasn't a word said by anyone. E.W. remained silent; and so did the three men sitting round the desk. Having waited for a minute or so I said to E.W., "What you have just read is what I think; and I'd like it to go in the paper just that way." And E.W. agreed. "Oh certainly, of course."

And that was the way it appeared in my column in the Daily News Record for October 29, 1929, and if anyone can show me an equally precise and dramatic example of stock market interpretation and forecasting, I would like to see it!

All through the early morning of that Tuesday, and until some time after the opening of trading on the New York Stock Exchanges, the telephones to various desks in the Daily News Record were ringing with enquiries from shocked readers asking, "Who is this guy, this croaker, Renby!" They all talked as if they believed that what I had written in my column was a kind of wizardly incantation uttered for the purpose of debilitating the stock markets.

*   *   *

From time to time, when discussing international affairs in my column, I had often written of the money concept, and I had as often commented on the well-nigh universal delusion regarding international debts. In a column late in 1932 I wrote in part:

> " 'Great is the truth—and it WILL prevail!' Thus spake the hoary old proverb; and never did hoary old proverb utter greater untruth.
>
> "President Hoover has invited Governor President-elect Roosevelt to 'advise with him' in Washington on the subject of those 'international debts' so-called.
>
> " 'Already,' says Mr. Hoover, 'two American experts have met with the technical experts of other governments to prepare tentative agenda for the world economic conference which will be held during the course of the coming winter. While this conference will be begun during my administration, it is certain that it will not complete its labors until you have assumed office.'
>
> "And what is this pow-wow of the world famous 'economists' and 'statesmen' to be about? It is to be about the subject of war debts.
>
> "And that, my friends, reminds me of the famous 'Council' of the church which gravely deliberated the question whether women have souls.
>
> "What is the REAL truth in this matter to which all minds seem to be closed?
>
> "The real truth is that no free and independent and sovereign STATE CAN OWE MONEY TO ANOTHER.
>
> "And, per contra, if there be any two nationals who claim that they do or can owe each other money—then these two nationals ARE NOT FREE AND INDEPENDENT AND SOVEREIGN STATES.
>
> "That is axiomatic—THAT IS THE SIMPLE TRUTH. But when, think you, is it going to PREVAIL?
>
> "For years I have enunciated this axiom in this column, but —SO FAR—I have been but as the voice crying in the wilderness."

To elucidate and expound this thesis regarding international debts, I had written in 1930 a long article in fictional form, with the title, *A Parable in Gold*. This article was submitted to some popular publications, including "Cosmopolitan" but without a nibble. I then rewrote and cut down my article to about 3,800 words. In August, 1932, I submitted it to "Collier's" and on September 1, 1932, I received from W. L. Chenery, Editor of "Collier's" the following letter:

September 1st, 1932

Dear Mr. Renby:—

I have read with great interest your article "A Parable in Gold."

The point you make that we lent goods and that the debts are recorded in money makes, I think, a very sound distinction. We have, however, already published editorials stressing the same point and in our issue of August 27th we published an article by Winston Churchill dealing in more general terms with the world distribution of gold.

I think your article is vividly presented and am sorry that it is not possible for us to publish it.

Very truly yours,
W. L. Chenery
Editor.

As a matter of fact, when talking shortly afterwards to Mr. Chenery, he gave me to understand by implication that he wanted to print my *Parable* but was overruled.

In November, 1932, I sent a copy of my *Parable in Gold* to Franklin D. Roosevelt, who was then Governor of New York, and President-elect of the United States, and I got E. W. Fairchild's son, Mr. L. W. Fairchild, who was then managing editor of the Daily News Record, and is now President of the Fairchild Publications, to write a letter covering my communication to F.D.R. Following is my letter to Mr. Roosevelt:

November 18th, 1932

His Excellency,
Franklin D. Roosevelt,
Governor of New York.
Dear Sir:

There is not very much that I can add to the accompanying gracious letter written by my chief, Mr. Louis W. Fairchild. My one purpose in writing my "PARABLE" is to convey a simple truth to our befuddled citizens, as well as to the rest of the world, which, in this matter, is only more befuddled than we are our-selves.

What I aim to do is to move men so that they will be able to view money, and money matters, not from their own individual viewpoints, but from the totally different *national* viewpoint of the *community as a whole.* And I want to tell you, Sir, that I realise the tremendous—the almost insuperable—difficulty of just that very task.

My story has been submitted to only two publications, *Collier's,* and *Liberty,* both of which held it for long periods before return-ing it with suitable expressions of "appreciation" and "regret." I have been reliably informed that in both cases there was a divergence of editorial opinion, and that the story was ultimately rejected because the prevailing opinion held that "it looked too much like a stick of dynamite."

Enclosed you will find three of my recent columns of "MONEY MATTERS—MOSTLY," these being self-explanatory. I am also enclosing a letter which has just this moment come to me from Chicago; it being typical of many others that have reached me from business executives in 27 states of the Union; and it shows that the American business man is *not* offended at being told the truth, and is NOT AFRAID to have it explained to him.

In connection with my story, which, of course, I am submitting primarily for your personal study, may I with all respect and sincerity request that you test the reaction to it of the female mind? This request I make because I have found that of the men and women who have read it, the women were my most ap-preciative and enthusiastic supporters.

If the truth in my "PARABLE" is revealed to you, maybe you might help me—NOT DIRECTLY, OF COURSE,—to have it put before the people in a suitable national medium? And of these there are very few.

You may hold the story as long as you please, but I would like to have it ultimately come back to me, together with the Chicago note.

With profound respect, Sir, and cordial good wishes, I am,

Sincerely yours,

J. F. Byrne

For nearly four weeks I awaited a reply to my letter, but got none. Then on December 15, 1932, I wrote again to F.D.R., asking for some kind of an acknowledgment, and I added:

"That you should entirely *ignore* this matter I cannot bring myself to believe. It would be very serious for me; because I persuaded Mr. Fairchild to write you in my behalf and it may mean that I may be out of a job . . . after December 31st, next. . ."

On Christmas Day, 1932, the following dispatch was sent out from Cleveland by the AP and widely circulated in numerous newspapers, and I reproduced it in my column on December 27.

" 'Technicians will arise in the science of politics because much of what is called knowledge in political science is cockeyed,' in the opinion of Professor Raymond Moley, of Columbia University.

"Professor Moley, who was one of the advisers to President-elect Roosevelt during the election campaign, observed Christmas at the home of his mother, Mrs. Agnes Fairchild Moley, in suburban Berea.

" 'Political technicians,' declared the professor, 'haven't been called on much in the past, but, as I see it, that is not the fault of the political leaders. I haven't yet found a politician who would *ignore* reasonable and reasonably proffered information and advice.' "

Instantly I recognised this AP dispatch as being a message to me from Professor Moley, the key word in it being the word "Ignore." And this message gave me a modicum of reassurance, although I could not help thinking how strange was the method employed for sending it to me.

And five days later, another message came to me; this being a personal one from Guernsey T. Cross, Secretary to Governor Franklin D. Roosevelt, who wrote as follows:

December 30, 1932

Dear Mr. Byrne:

I regret I have been unable to locate the material to which you refer in your letter of December 15th. No doubt it has been received but I know you will appreciate the volume of mail which comes to this office each day and I fear it has been temporarily mislaid.

Very truly yours,
Guernsey T. Cross

About 4:30 P.M. on Tuesday afternoon January 17, 1933, having learned that Professor Moley was in Columbia University, I called him up on the phone. I told him my name, and that I would like to have a talk with him. He said, "I'm leaving New York tonight," and I said, "I know that, and I'd like to see you before you go."

"Oh, you would, would you?"

"Yes, I would."

"Where are you now?"

"I'm calling from my office."

"Well, can you come up here by 7:30?"

"Yes, professor, I'll be there at 7:30."

"Yes, at six o'clock."

"Very well, professor, I'll see you at six o'clock."

"Yes, 5:30—you know how to get up here."

"Certainly."

"Well, you get off at 116th Street station, and it's just a short walk to Barnard."

When I arrived at Barnard, I was led by an attendant down the corridor to the right, where we came to a door on the right of the corridor. When this door was opened I saw Mr. Moley sitting in a smallish room with a couple of other men whom I fancied I recognized from photos I had seen rather frequently in the paper. I stood at the door, and Professor Moley invited me to come in and take a seat, but I declined, saying to him, "Professor, I'd rather talk to you alone."

"Oh, you would, would you, very well. I'll find somewhere."

And at that he led me back along the corridor to a bench where he and I sat talking for half an hour. I told the professor that I had got his "message" sent out over the AP wires on Christmas Day, but Mr. Moley was noncommittal—and he would not even admit that he had ever heard of me. To my direct questions he would make no direct reply, but frequently resorted to an equivocal "Maybe," and you could not tell whether he meant this expression to be one word or two.

I spoke to him at length about my *Parable in Gold,* and I told him of the insurmountable difficulty I would encounter in trying to have it published.

"Perhaps," I said, "you might be able to find some way or some one, to convince some reputable publisher of a really representative magazine or newspaper that it should be printed."

"Have you got this *Parable* with you?" the professor asked me.

"Yes, I have."

"Well, give it to me and we'll see what we can do about it."

I put my hand in my pocket and took out a copy of my *Parable* which I handed to Professor Moley.

On February 3, 1932, sixteen days after my interview with Professor Moley, a letter, written at the stated behest of Franklin D. Roosevelt by his famous secretary, Louis McH. Howe, arrived at the Daily News Record office. Here is the letter.

FRANKLIN D. ROOSEVELT
HYDE PARK, DUTCHESS COUNTY
NEW YORK

February 2nd, 1933

Mr. Louis W. Fairchild,
8 East 13th Street,
New York, N. Y.

My dear Mr. Fairchild:

Mr. Roosevelt has asked me to apologize for the delay in writing you about your interesting letter of November 18th, and the article which you enclosed on behalf of Mr. Byrne. In accordance with Mr. Roosevelt's request, the manuscript was referred to Professor Raymond F. Moley, of Columbia University, who is, as you doubtless know, one of Mr. Roosevelt's consultants on economic matters.

Mr. Roosevelt asks me to act for him in thanking Mr. Byrne both for his thought in conveying this to his personal attention, and for his letter telling him of his past history.

Professor Moley has now returned the manuscript, after making his personal notations, and I am therefore returning it, in accordance with Mr. Byrne's request, and at the same time sending the samples of his work, as well as the letters which were attached.

Very sincerely yours,
Louis McH. Howe
Secretary to Mr. Roosevelt.

Toward the end of February, 1933, in a telephone conversation with Professor Moley's secretary, the late Celeste Jedel, I said to her that since the professor did not seem to be doing anything, or at least getting anywhere, in the matter of the publication of my *Parable,* I would like her to ask Professor Moley to return it to me. And Miss Jedel said to me immediately, "But Mr. Byrne, your story has been incorporated in material which is being prepared for the Governor."

"Do you mean Mr. Roosevelt, the President-elect?" I asked her. And she replied, "Yes."

One afternoon a few days later the telephone at my desk in the Daily News Record office rang, and when I took it up a male voice asked, "Is this Mr. J. F. Byrne?"

"Yes, I am."

"I have been asked by Colonel McHenry Howe to tell you he would like to have a word with you."

"Certainly, where should I come to see him?"

"The Colonel suggests that you come to the Roosevelt house this afternoon or evening, or, if you prefer, you could see him tomorrow morning in the Democratic headquarters here."

"Kindly tell the Colonel I'll see him either this evening or tomorrow morning."

And on the following morning, March 3, 1933, I had a brief, but decidedly pleasant, chat with the famous devoted Colonel at the Democratic headquarters. We talked casually about various things including the sudden death, reported that morning, of Senator Walsh. And then Colonel Howe said, "About that article of yours, we are very glad to have it, and are grateful to you for sending it to us. We expect to make full use of it in a couple of weeks. The Governor wishes me to tell you this. If you had come to see me at the house last evening I would have introduced you to him."

I did not tell Colonel Howe that I had anticipated such a contingency, and had purposefully evaded it.

Exactly two weeks after my visit to the Colonel, I received an acknowledgment of a little material I sent him pertaining to the thesis of my *Parable*. He wrote:

THE WHITE HOUSE

WASHINGTON

March 16, 1933

My dear Mr. Byrne:

I have received your letter and thank you for bringing the enclosed clipping to my attention.

Sincerely yours,

Louis McH. Howe

Secretary to the President

And then, around this time, there were reports of strange happenings; one of these had to do with the book "Looking Forward," published by the John Day Company, and the author of record being Franklin D. Roosevelt. In the month of March, 1933, several hundred copies of "Looking Forward" were sent out all over the country for review, and then, in scarcely more than twenty-four hours, these copies were all recalled by telegram, with a request that they be returned unopened.

Many will remember that at this time, no matter where you went in Washington, from almost every window and stand, a little red-covered book glared at you and seemed to shriek at you, like a shrewish schoolmarm to her kindergarten class, to come in out of the wet and learn "The ABC of War Debts."

As I sat in the waiting room outside the President's office in the White House that morning, I fancied I could discern a trace of gloom on the faces of some of the many Senators who were seated by me and were talking about the disaster to the dirigible "Akron" which occurred in the early hours of that day; and I observed, with astonishment, that at least two Senators were perusing the Congressional Record.

Over by the door leading to the President's office there was a switchboard at which sat a busy, but bubbling, young lady; and I was once more astonished to hear this young telephone operator ejaculating quite audibly over and over again, "Oh, if I only had a New York Telephone Directory." When she had so ejaculated seven or eight times, a man who was passing near heard her and said, "Do you really want a New York Telephone Directory?" and she said, "Oh, I do. I wish I had one." And the man said to her, "We have several of them in my office. I'll send you one." To me the fact that a switchboard operator sitting just outside the door to the office of the President of the United States on the thirty-first day after his inauguration, should have to reiterate her yearning for a New York Telephone Directory was something that would have tickled the renowned team of Gilbert & Sullivan.

After waiting perhaps twenty minutes, I was ushered to a small office in which Louis Howe was seated at a desk, and to the side of this desk there was seated a youngish man, perhaps in his middle thirties. He seemed to me like a secret service agent, but I don't know anything about him, for Colonel Howe did not introduce us. Only one month had elapsed since I had seen Colonel Howe in New York, and I was amazed at the change which seemed to have come over him in this little while. Obviously, he was a sick man; tired and apparently disillusioned. Indeed, one could easily imagine that he was a kind of indigo-hued mummy that had become partially reanimated. When he spoke to me, I felt chilled, for the warmth with which he had greeted me in Democratic headquarters was gone; and plainly he was distrait and anxious to get this meeting over. He told me that my *Parable in Gold* had been found unsuitable to the Presidential purposes and expressed regret for my disappointment. Up to that moment during my short interview with Colonel Howe, I had said scarcely a word. The simple truth is that—odd as it may seem—I felt genuinely sorry for him, and still respect his memory.

Whereupon, I bade goodbye to Colonel Howe and left the White House after my first and last visit. And I felt better when I got out into the open air—even of Washington, D. C.

For a considerable time after my interview with Louis Howe in the White House I tried without success to see Professor Moley. However, after some three weeks, I caught up with the professor in Columbia.

"Where is the manuscript of my *Parable in Gold?*" I asked him.

"Your manuscript is in the Washington Archives."

At this point I had some words with Professor Moley, and I remarked to him that as an aftermath of the affair I was out of a job.

"Well," said Professor Moley, and the manner of his saying it cauterized my memory, "I can't do anything about that."

Having shot this dart, Professor Moley was pulled aside by one of a bevy of young girls, four or five of whom came to me, asking me to be seated with them in an anteroom. I took it that these young ladies, whose names I did not get, were pupils of Professor Moley, and to me they were, one and all, sympathetic and consoling, saying almost in unison that they were sure everything would turn out all right. Well, they were a group of nice kids; and I want even at this late date to let them know I cordially appreciated their sympathy.

In May, 1933, a few weeks after my last interview with Professor Moley, I sailed for Cobh on the Manhattan. I had become quite ill, and I knew I needed a long rest to pull myself together. After the ocean voyage and a few weeks of quiet in Leix, I felt able to go to Paris to visit James Joyce, in whose apartment I stayed for a week. Joyce and his charming wife Nora did their utmost to make my visit a pleasant and memorable one—as indeed it was. I told Joyce casually about my experience in regard to my *Parable*, and he begged me to read it. I did read it for him, and I was surprised at the interest he took in it. When I came to the part where I speak of the United States wanting not its oil but its barrels, James Joyce gave one of his, at that time, rare howls of laughter, and tears of merriment came into his poor eyes. When I had finished reading my *Parable,* he again surprised me by commenting that it reminded him of Swift and Newman. I did not say anything to this because I knew that he was probably more recently familiar than I with the works of both the men he mentioned. But I did think it was a rather strange blend—Swift and Newman. And that night, and on some subsequent occasions, Joyce cautioned a few of his friends facetiously as we all sat down to eat either in his apartment or in a restaurant, "Be careful—don't knock against Byrne. He has a stick of dynamite in his pocket." It certainly struck me as curious that Joyce, like some others who had read it, should think of my *Parable* as being a "stick of dynamite." For myself, I never thought of it as anything of the kind.

Joyce was most anxious to have the *Parable* published, and he gave me introductions to several persons he thought might be in a position to help achieve this. Among these persons were J. Kingsley Martin, The Editor, New Statesman, and John W. Duranty, I.F.S. High Commissioner. He told me that "Transition" would run it; but this I declined, and I made up my mind that if I could not have it published in the United States, I would not have it published at all. But although I never used any of Joyce's introductions I was none the less grateful to him for the warmth and friendly intent with which he gave them to me.

Having recuperated in Ireland till late in the autumn of 1934, I felt able to return to New York. I then got in touch again with Miss Celeste Jedel, who at the time was on the editorial staff of the now defunct "Today."

In response to my question as to what had become of my manuscript of *A Parable in Gold,* Miss Jedel wrote to me on the stationery of the "Office of the Editor," that my *Parable* was "in our files." A week or so later she returned the manuscript to me, and I had further correspondence with her which continued for some months.

Some years later, Miss Celeste Jedel, a lovely and brilliant young lady, became a confirmed invalid, and in New York City on the night of October 31, 1948, she, poor child, suffered the tragedy of being burned to death in her bed.

Many years ago, my friend Charlie Ronayne made a comment on my Parable that was both complimentary and comprehensive. Having read it for the fourth time, he remarked slowly and deliberately, "John, this piece of yours is a Klondike of Intellectuality." In view of the fact that Charlie had been Assistant General of the Carmelite Order, President of the Irish College in Rome, Professor of Canon Law in the Gregorian University, and Legal Adviser to the Vatican, I think it may be granted that he was to some degree qualified to express a weighty opinion.

It may be stated with certainty that if my Parable had been promulgated twenty years ago, this nation would never have had the "Lend-Lease" monstrosity foisted upon it. And, in this connection, be it remembered that the United States Government has been, and still is, persistently dunning the Soviet Government for payment of loans totaling more than eleven billions of dollars. As recently as December 26, 1952 a U.P. dispatch from Washington, D.C., said that:

"Russia and its Communist satellites have balked at repaying more than $12,000,000,000 in American debts, a survey revealed today, and there is little the United States can do about it."

May I ask this question of the reader or of the United States Government: Suppose the Soviet Government should decide to do all in its power to pay at present these eleven billions of dollars to the United States Government, where and how would the Soviet Government get the dollars?

Regarding the general concept of money, it seems that mental haziness is still prevalent, as exemplified in the customary prattle about National Income. It should be obvious—but plainly it is not—that, in terms of money, the aggregate of the National Incomes of all the nations on earth is precisely the aggregate of their National Expenditures.

Yes, the world seems still in the dark regarding most of the fundamental and even rudimentary notions of economics, but I think I see far off on the horizon an appearance of approaching illumination. I am referring to Henry Ford 2nd who recently proposed this four-point program.

1. "A new law without loopholes encouraging the most rapid possible elimination of all tariffs."
2. "Abandon completely the quota system" of imports.
3. "Abandon the buy American act" limiting government buying of foreign goods.
4. "A workable law for simplifying the customs procedures," thus lifting "a virtually impenetrable barrier of red tape."

I reproduce here verbatim the manuscript that Miss Jedel returned to me.

CHAPTER NINETEEN

"A Parable in Gold"

by J. F. RENBY

AN 'INTERNATIONAL DEBT' is the figment of an undeveloped mentality; it is a delusion and an impossibility; it is a contradiction in terms; it is a thing which is not, never was, and never can be."

The speaker was Frank Thornton, and his declaration was in reply to an amazing scheme which had just been propounded to him by his brother Jack.

"I know how you must feel about this whole business, Jack, but I've got to speak as I think. What I have just said I mean exactly. If I could express myself more forcibly or more unequivocally, I should do so. Free and independent nations cannot owe money to one another, and all obligations between them can be discharged only in goods or services.

"More than two years ago," Frank went on, "you passed completely out of the picture. Where you went to or where you hid yourself, whether you went away on a long exploration or whether you simply locked yourself in a laboratory for all that time—nobody knows. And now at last you return—or emerge—to explain to me that you have spent all that time in a concentrated effort to do something for the benefit of your country and for humanity in general. You say the task you set yourself was to procure sufficient gold to discharge the sum-total of all these international debts—and you assure me that you have achieved this task.

"You ask me to believe you," continued Frank, "and you say you can give me ample proof. Of course I believe you, Jack; sure I know you are telling what you believe to be the truth; and in view of the fact that you are an expert, not merely in mining engineering, but in metallurgy and chemistry as well, I am quite willing to concede that you should know what you are talking about.

"But the point is that, so far as international debts are concerned, it doesn't matter a straw whether you have or have not achieved this task. For, if you mean by 'international debt' an obligation in money, then an international debt between two sovereign and independent nations is, as I have already flatly told you, a contradiction in terms.

"To you, as an individual, this gold discovery may be vastly important and beneficial; but for our country and for the world the discovery might prove anything but a blessing. Yours was a noble conception, brother, and for that reason I am sorry for your disappointment. But this scheme of yours would be all wrong. Not alone would the cure be worse than the disease—but it wouldn't be a cure at all. On the contrary it would be a most serious aggravation of our present ills."

"But let me try to get this straightened out," Jack protested. "In the matter of these international debts you have on one hand the European nations declaring that they cannot pay them, and on the other hand you have the United States declaring that they must be paid. And altogether, the condition that has arisen as a result of these debts is one that can be described without exaggeration as the most serious menace to international amity and to the economic solidarity of the world. Am I right?"

"Perfectly right," Frank acknowledged simply.

"And now then, Frank, how in the name of heaven can you defend your attitude? For here am I both able and willing to pay for all these debts in full and unconditionally—and in gold; and yet you, having conceded the gravity of the international situation, advise me to do nothing. Is that really your position?"

"That's my position, Jack."

"Well, I give it up; what is the answer? For, so far as I can see, the position you have taken is paradoxical, contradictory and absurd. Europe owes these billions of dollars to the United States; and I want to pay this money for Europe to the United States—and still you advise me to do nothing. In fact, you declare I *can* do nothing. Your advice is an enigma to me. I don't understand it. Can you explain?"

"Yes, I can explain this apparent enigma—fully. In fact, if you will only view the whole matter in the light of common sense, you will see that there is no enigma at all.

"If this scheme of yours were to be carried out, the result would be disastrous and possibly catastrophic; and our whole financial structure would be rocked in an economic earthquake. To predict the full extent of this cataclysm would not be possible, chiefly because of the human element involved; and the human element is not a constant.

"This scheme, Jack, is intended by you to be an act of supreme beneficence to these United States and to Europe. But instead of being that, it would—if carried out—be a malignant cancer on the whole social organism. You propose to pay these debts to the United States by dumping an additional thirty—or forty—thousand tons of unneeded, and even unwanted, gold into the United States Treasury. I do not know how this proposal of yours would be received by the European nations involved in this great international debt catharsis; but in view of the fact that all of them, except France, complain incessantly and bitterly of what they call the present maldistribution of gold, and are clamoring for a redistribution of the metal, one may presume that they would be violently hostile to your proposal.

"But let us get away from that point; for after all, it doesn't matter to the United States what the opinion of any or all of our debtor nations might be on this subject. The one important thing for you and me to consider here and now is how the United States would be affected. For it may well be doubted whether the addition of an extra thirty or forty thousand tons of gold to the United States Treasury would make the new aggregate worth as much as the present comparatively modest total of seven or eight thousand tons."

Here Jack interrupted his brother.

"How can you possibly say that, Frank? I've been trying to follow you so far; and although I don't see this matter from your point of view, still there may be something in what you say. But in regard to this last point of yours about the present total of gold in this country being worth as much as—or maybe more than—the new total would be after all those international debts had been paid—well, that point, I think, is wholly ridiculous. But perhaps you intended an overstatement?"

"I intended no overstatement, Jack, as you will soon perceive for yourself. Consider a $20 gold piece. How is its value determined? Obviously, by its purchasing power—by which, of course, is meant the amount of such things as wheat, cotton, corn eggs, meat, butter, milk, clothes, and the rest, that you can get for it. Do you agree?"

"Yes, I do."

"Well, with your additional thousands of tons of gold cluttering up the United States Treasury, it is a reasonable assumption that you would not then be able to buy as much meat, cotton, corn, and all the rest, for *ten* $20 gold pieces as you can now get for *one* such piece. Even the very fact that this huge amount of additional gold had been pulled, so to speak, out of a hat—with the contingent likelihood, which you yourself state to be a fact, that there was probably any amount more gold to be obtained from the same source—would deprive gold of practically all its erstwhile purchasing power.

"To illustrate this point, Jack, let us make a supposition. Let us suppose that this whole country, from the Atlantic to the Pacific and from Canada to Mexico, should waken up some morning to find that a strange phenomenon had taken place during the night. Suppose that while the country slept there had descended from heaven, not a snowfall, but a goldfall—a fall of gold that covered the earth everywhere in city and country to a depth of six inches. Can you imagine the picture?"

"Yes, yes. Go on."

"Six hundred pounds of gold lie on every square foot of the land, which is stifled and smothered beneath this golden fleece of death. Buildings, dwellings, barns, and vehicles of all kinds are demolished beneath hundreds and thousands of tons of the hideous metal. Of traffic there is practically none—with permanent ways choked and electrified systems clogged and short-circuited. Boats and ships are sunk in river, lake and harbor by the sheer weight of the horrible filth. Everywhere, with vegetation destroyed, man and beast lie dying. With GOLD . . . GOLD . . . GOLD . . . twenty-trillion tons of gold, crushing and smashing the lovely face of our sacred land, and bringing nothing but death and destruction! ! ! !

"Well, Jack, if on the morning after that phenomenon had occurred, you were to go into the city or the country, and offer

to a shopkeeper or to a farmer a $20 gold piece for either a loaf
of bread or an egg—what do you think he'd like to do to you? Yes,
in these circumstances what would *any* man want to do to you if
you offered him a $20 gold piece for *anything?*"

"I can see the force of your argument now all right," admitted
Jack, "but I'm still up in the air in regard to those international
debts. It seems to me that what you have just said only makes the
whole matter more complicated than it was before."

"No, Jack, that is not so; for the matter was not complicated
before, and neither is it complicated now."

"But these debtor nations *did* contract these debts, didn't
they?" argued Jack.

"They certainly did," Frank admitted readily.

"And they did get millions of tons of goods, including munitions of war and all kinds of commodities—wheat, flour, cotton,
coal, oil, meat, lard, sugar and all the rest—through the whole
gamut of human supplies and necessaries. Isn't that so?"

"They most certainly did," Frank asserted.

"And didn't the citizens of these United States," Jack pursued,
as he warmed to his subject, "deprive themselves of a large
part of many of the necessaries of life in order to provide for the
needs of our present debtor nations?"

"Most assuredly, we did," Frank replied with vigor.

"Well then, Frank, these people—these nations—bought all
that stuff from us with money that they borrowed from us. And
isn't it now *only a matter of common honesty* that they should
repay the billions—the fifteen or twenty billions, or whatever it
is—of dollars that they borrowed from us and *which they con-
tracted to pay us?*"

"In asking that question, Jack, you have dissected to the very
heart of this subject. If you only have the courage to cut that
heart open and examine it for yourself, you will discover this
fundamental truth: These debtor nations do not owe, *and never
did owe us,* fifteen or twenty billions of dollars."

"What!" said Jack in manifest astonishment.

"No. First, because they *never borrowed* fifteen or twenty billions of dollars from us. Second, because we never lent them fifteen
or twenty billions of dollars. Indeed, it is a matter of plain fact
that in its whole history the United States HAS NEVER HAD
FIFTEEN OR TWENTY BILLIONS OF DOLLARS.

"The United States lent unstintedly both goods and services to these debtor nations, and the money value of those goods and services was fixed at the time and agreed to by both parties to the contracts. And ever since that time, the United States has been insisting on a return, not of the goods and services lent, but of the money value thereof.

"The United States," Frank continued, "does not want a return of an equivalent amount of the goods and services lent. In fact, we would spurn the services. As for the goods, *not alone do we not want them,* but we have erected a tariff barrier against them more effective than the Hindenburg line! ! No, we don't want a return of the goods lent. Everybody knows that. And everybody knows too that if we *were* to accept payment in goods for these international debts, we would be giving this country an absolutely fatal dose of unemployment poison.

"What we are demanding, then, is NOT the return of what we actually lent, but a return of the *measure* by which we estimated its *value.* And what we are demanding, and what we THINK we want, is the return of the money WHICH WE NEVER LENT, WHICH NEVER LEFT THE COUNTRY, AND WHICH IN SHORT NEVER EXISTED.

"Let us consider such commodities as oil or potatoes or the like, of which we lent huge quantities to our debtor nations. Now, if we want to measure a given quantity of oil, we express that *quantity* in terms of *barrels.* And if we want to measure the *value* of that quantity we express the value in terms of *dollars.* But when the oil was shipped to Europe, although we measured the *quantity* of it in terms of *barrels,* we did not actually ship it in barrels but in tankers. Isn't that so?"

Jack nodded agreement.

"And when that same oil was sent to Europe," Frank elaborated, "we measured the *value* of the oil in terms of *dollars.* Bear in mind that it was oil we sent, NOT THE DOLLARS. Isn't that again so?"

"Yes, it is."

"Very well, then, Jack. And now I want you to give your closest attention to this point:

"We say to our debtor nations: 'We don't want you to give us back our *oil* but we *do* want you to give us back our *dollars.* We admit of course that WE NEVER GAVE YOU THE DOLLARS, but we did give you the *oil*. Since we *don't* want a return of the *oil*, we must insist in having the *dollars* in terms of which we measured the *value* of it.'

"In making that demand," Frank continued earnestly, "we are acting and thinking just as foolishly as if we were to say to our debtor nations: 'We don't want you to give us back our *oil* but we *do* want you to give us back our BARRELS. It is true, of course, that *we never gave you the barrels,* but we *did* give you the *oil*. Since we *don't* want a return of the *oil*, we must insist on having the *barrels* in terms of which we measured the quantity of the oil we lent you. And furthermore, WE DON'T WANT BARRELS MADE BY YOU—WE WANT BARRELS THAT HAVE BEEN MADE RIGHT HERE IN THE UNITED STATES, AND EVERY BARREL MUST BEAR AN UNITED STATES GOVERNMENT STAMP!'

"Have I made myself clear?" Frank asked.

"Yes, perfectly clear—to the extent that I follow your argument, and feel that it compels assent. But for some reason I find myself reluctant to give that assent. As you present the facts, the conclusion seems inescapable. But I feel that there is—there must be—a fallacy somewhere in your argument."

"There is no fallacy in *my* argument, Jack. Where the fallacy *does* exist is in the crassly ignorant assumption that we can successfully and indefinitely apply the financial methods and book-keeping system of a peanut stand to the affairs of a mighty nation."

"And what about private debts as between citizens of various countries?" Jack enquired.

"One thing at a time, Jack. You brought up this matter of *international* debts. That's the only subject I am going to talk about *now*.

"Let us establish—and grasp clearly—the simple axiom that an international debt is an IMPOSSIBILITY. In order to grasp this fact clearly you must look at it NOT FROM YOUR OWN INDIVIDUAL VIEWPOINT, BUT FROM THE VIEWPOINT OF THE NATION. When we have grasped this fact, we will be able to discern its vast ramifications and implications in the whole domain of economics and especially in the fields of foreign trade and exchange. We will be able to abandon—once and for all

—the futile effort to make the concrete facts of our present-day life fit an antediluvian economic theory.

"In all FINANCIAL contracts as between independent nations there is a latent error. When the amount of money involved in these transactions is small—or comparatively small—this latent error remains obscured. International credits involving millions—or even hundreds of millions—of dollars can be 'adjusted' without doing undue violence to our present financial system. But when the 'money' involved in a so-called international debt is of such proportions as to be *many times the total currency* of this, the richest country on earth—well, then, the latent error is revealed as STARK IMBECILITY.

" 'In a multitude of counsellors,' says Bacon, 'there is much wisdom.' And I want to say right here, Jack, that Bacon never wrote himself down more of an ass than when he wrote that. For, at the present time, all over the world, a babel of financial and economic 'experts' and 'counsellors' are belching windy verbiage on the subject of 'money.' Yes, when men talk of money, and particularly BIG money, they pour forth an inexhaustible stream of words . . . words . . . words. But when men venture into the subject of 'international debts' they flounder like finless fishes in a quagmire of stultiloquence.

"Stark imbecility, Jack; that's what it is. Just think of the situation. Just look at it for a moment. Just consider the amazing spectacle of a creditor country demanding 'money' payments aggregating *several times our own total currency.*

"And then, to cap this astounding manifestation of infantilism, you have the obvious fact that if—by some feat of legerdemain or by the Black Art—this demand could be immediately met, *this country would not thereby profit* one whit. IN NO WAY WOULD WE—EITHER AS A NATION OR AS INDIVIDUALS—BE BETTER OFF. In fact, the condition that would result from this magical and supernatural repayment would be IDENTICAL with the condition that would arise if the United States Treasury were to print overnight an extra fifteen or twenty billions of dollar bills and dump them over the land.

"But here is another aspect of the matter. When the United States demands payment from our debtor nations *in dollars,* we must base that demand primarily on our conception that our foreign debtors have a *duty* to pay us in dollars. Now, where one *asserts* a duty, one must *concede a right*. If we assert that it is the duty of our foreign debtors to pay their debts to us in dollars, then we must concede that our foreign debtors have the *right* to acquire our dollars with which to pay these debts. But there is *No* foreign nation—there is NO OTHER NATION ON EARTH —that has the inherent and inalienable RIGHT to possess a SINGLE DOLLAR—NO, NOT A CENT—of OUR MONEY, except by and with OUR VOLITION AND COOPERATION.

"If the United States should desire to do so at any time, *we have the perfect right* to cut off all our trade connections with every other country, AND TO FUNCTION THEREAFTER AS A CLOSED SYSTEM. I'm not talking about the pros and cons of this question. I am only pointing out that we have the right to do this if we want to. If we were ever to do it, WHERE THEN, DO YOU SUPPOSE, ANY OF OUR DEBTOR NATIONS WOULD EVER BE ABLE TO GET A CENT OF OUR CURRENCY?

"And whatever may be said against this policy of complete isolation, it could be defended as being at least economically consistent and rational. But instead of this procedure, what is the policy that is being furthered by millions of our deluded citizens? It is the policy of trying to make this country operate only as a one-way system; namely, to send away as much of its goods as possible, and to take back as little of the other fellow's goods as possible.

"Total blindness and cerebral chaos, Jack; but there you are. THERE is the condition we are up against, and with which we have to cope."

"It is a somber picture, as you paint it, Frank. But to revert for a moment to the main subject. Do you think that if the world were to be thoroughly exorcised of this 'international debt' ghost, the quick return of prosperity would be assured?"

"Most emphatically no," Frank replied unhesitatingly. "This international debt fallacy is not only a figment of an undeveloped mentality. It is unfortunately much more—and much worse—than that. It is the symptom of an extremely serious malady which I might call PLUTOMANIA and which I would define as that form of dementia having to do with the expression of the concepts of 'wealth' and 'value' in terms of money.

"Everybody—everywhere—is talking of 'money' as being the great cure-all for the malady that afflicts our stricken country. Gold and money and international debts—these are the topics of the whole world. Yet there seems to be scarcely anyone, anywhere, who makes even an effort to grasp the connotation of such simple terms as *wealth, value, dollar,* and *government.* Mind you, your ordinary citizen is by no means the worst sinner in this respect. Not at all. It is the pseudo 'financial experts' and 'economists,' and bloated national and international bankers, who have erred and are still erring most flagrantly. It is among these last-named that you will find the most rabid plutomaniacs.

"And PLUTOMANIA is absolutely pandemic. No matter what form the government of a country takes—whether monarchist, socialist, fascist or communist—its people, in common with ourselves, will be found afflicted with this disease.

"As to the origin of this dreadful malady, it may be traced to the slavish subservience to the absurd and ludicrous mathematical RULE OF THREE. You know the kind of thing I refer to. Problems like this: if 10,000,000 bales of cotton are worth $500,-000,000, how much would 1,000,000,000 bales of cotton be worth? Or this one: if 1,000,000,000 bushels of wheat are worth $500,-000,000, how much would 100,000,000,000 bushels be worth?

"These problems are exactly on a par with the one we have already considered, namely: If a $20 gold piece will at present buy you 40 bushels of wheat or a suit of clothes, how many bushels of wheat or how many suits of clothes, could you buy with TWENTY TRILLION TONS OF GOLD?"

CHAPTER TWENTY

Introduction to "Throne of Chaos"

WHEN I WAS a student of elementary chemistry in the class conducted by P. Bertram Foy in Belvedere College, I was vastly interested in numerous chemical experiments in some of which Foy permitted his students to participate. Among these experiments the electrolysis of water, and the effect produced on it by, for instance, the metal sodium, were to me especially fascinating. At that time I conceived the possibility of certain developments of a totally cataclysmic character; and I had it in mind that some day I would write my conception in the form of a phantasy in science. Owing to procrastination, however, I did not actually start to do anything about this till it became clear to me, in the latter part of 1916, that the United States was heading, or was being headed, directly towards war. Anyone who remembers the presidential campaign in that year will recall the Wilson slogan, plastered on billboards all over the United States, "He Kept Us Out of War!" Largely due to the influence of that slogan, Wilson was elected; but immediately after his inauguration on March 4, 1917, he changed his mind about the advisability of a nation's being "too proud to fight," and thirty-two days after he entered on his second term the United States was in World War I—a development which, from the middle of 1916, anyone with normal mental vision could have foreseen was ineluctable. It was in these circumstances, and three years before Rutherford's nitrogen-hydrogen experiment, that I wrote my story, with two alternative titles, both Miltonic, "The Throne of Chaos," and "Sable-Vested Night," and this story I submitted in turn to dozens of publications in this country, including the Saturday Evening Post; Collier's; Harper's; Scribner's; Century, and the rest, only to receive a symphonic dirge of rejections. Finally, however, I received from Bob Davis, editor of The All Story Weekly, an offer of $40. for the piece, and an invitation to come to see him.

When I did go to see Davis, he "regretted" his "inability" to give me a better price for the story, and he ventured, "Judging by your manuscript, you must have submitted it to a number of others before you sent it to us," and I replied laconically, "That manuscript is the tenth copy I wrote, I sent the story out forty-one times, and got it back forty." And then Davis said: "Well I don't know what the editors must have been thinking about. If you don't mind me saying so, Byrne, my advice to you—if you want to make a big name for yourself, and bigger money—is write fiction." And my reply to Bob Davis was: "Fiction is definitely not my line. This piece of mine reads to you like fiction; but some day sooner or later—it will be grisly fact!"

Anyway Davis published the story in the All Story Magazine in which it appeared, with some minor errors and a couple of inconsequential omissions, on September 1, 1917. One of the errors that crept its way insidiously into the story as published was that the word "mortifer" in my manuscript was turned out "mortifier" in print—and I am not punning when I say that that error was to me mortifying. The story follows.

THE THRONE OF CHAOS

By

J.F.B.

Whether or no I am doing wisely in giving to the world a full and true account of the mysterious death of Fred Ryder may be open to question, but having given the subject the most careful consideration of which I am capable, and being sustained by the opinion of the dead man's wife, I am moved to reveal the stupendous facts of the immediate circumstances of the tragedy.

Fred Ryder was my brother-in-law and my closest friend. We had known each other from early boyhood, and, as the years sped, our friendship waxed to the full development of a complete understanding. Ten years ago he married my only sister, Alice, and the bond of their mutual love had been tightened by the advent of their two children—John, now eight years old, and Annie, six. My brother-in-law had an income from real estate sufficient to provide him with all the necessities and most of the luxuries of life. Alice, too, has an independent income of her own, so Fred was wholly free to devote all his time to the study of applied science, particularly chemistry, which was his pet subject.

Shortly after the birth of Annie the family went to reside in a house which had been built to Fred's specifications on a little estate he owned on the slope of Overlook Mountain in the Cats-kills. There was nothing remarkable about the house except in its prevailing feature of comfort, the work of housekeeping being reduced to a minimum by a host of electrical appliances installed by Fred. The power for these was supplied from an immense turbine on a mountain river a few hundred yards away which operated a powerful dynamo, and this also furnished electrical energy in Fred's laboratory which was located conveniently at the end of the garden in the rear of the house.

Situated as it was, the place, of course, was a little lonely, but the solitude appealed to Fred for it ensured freedom from inter-ruption in his work. My sister, however, felt the lack of human companionship, and it was this, I believe, which actuated her and her husband in giving me a pressing invitation to come and live with them, an invitation of which I was only too glad to avail myself.

I speak, therefore, with intimate knowledge when I say that the family life of my brother-in-law and sister—of all of us, in fact,—was one of almost unmitigated felicity. Up till that day, now nearly two months ago, when the dreadful blow fell, not a cloud bigger than a man's hand had appeared in that domestic heaven.

For a few months before the catastrophe we had observed that Fred became more and more absorbed in his work. Day after day he would spend all his time in the laboratory, remaining there until far into the night. My sister would have been alarmed at his complete absorption had I not reassured her. I knew Fred well, with the less intimate, more detached, but more observant knowledge of a life-long friend. I believed I saw in the abstracted eagerness of his manner that he was on the trail of some discovery. I did not pretend to him that I noticed anything unusual in his conduct, nor did I question him. Often before I had observed him in moods of exaltation only a little less lofty than the one in which he was now soaring, and I knew that at such times he hated interference. So now, although he told me nothing —indeed, he rarely even spoke to me—I was not surprised, for I was well aware that I was quite unable to follow him into the intricate recesses of science where he stepped with confidence.

And then suddenly his manner changed. One morning he came down to breakfast and was again to all of us the same unabstracted, normal, Fred as of old. He looked haggard and wan, but he was in high spirits as he joked and laughed about commonplace things. But though his manner was superficially the same, yet it seemed to me that there was a subtle, an indefinable, difference. To me he was more companionable than ever; to his wife and children he was even more tender than usual, with now and then an unwonted wistfulness in his affection. After breakfast he took John and Annie out with him to the garden, and Alice seized the opportunity to tell me she was very much worried about him. The night before, she said, he had left the laboratory and gone to bed much earlier than had been his custom of late. She could not tell the exact time, for she had been asleep, but she thought it was before eleven o'clock. At midnight he had wakened her by rising in a state of excitement which he endeavoured vainly to subdue, and as he dressed he had explained that there was an important phase of the work he was engaged on which he had overlooked, and that he could not rest until he had satisfied himself of the result of certain reactions. She did not see him again till nearly six in the morning, and then he had returned cold, fatigued, and dejected. He had come and put his arm around her, sitting beside her on the bed, and kissed her with profound—almost solemn—devotion. She had not asked him where he had been or what he had done; she had deemed the moment inopportune for that. She had simply urged him to come to bed and snatch a few hours of sleep to relieve his nervous emotion. He had gotten into bed, and although he could not sleep, he had grown gradually calmer, and when the first gong sounded for breakfast in the morning he had insisted on rising to join the family.

Looking out of the dining-room window which gave on the garden, we could now see Fred and the two children enjoying themselves in boisterous amusement round a bonfire he had built under the copper beeches near the laboratory. He had gathered a great heap of dead leaves and twigs, and set fire to it. As we watched, we were amused to see him enter his workshop and emerge a moment later with an armful of scientific instruments which he threw recklessly on the pile. Several times he re-entered the laboratory and came out again with his arms full of books, papers and instruments which he heaped upon the blaze to the shrieking glee of John and little Annie. I say we were amused, for, of course, we attached no special significance to his action; he having many times recently referred to the antiquity and inefficiency of his scientific outfit, and we were satisfied that he was simply cleaning house in preparation for a more modern equipment.

During the next six days Fred retained his accustomed manner; he was himself again. Only one thing did we notice that struck us as a little strange, which was that after the morning of the bonfire he never again entered the laboratory. Most of the day he spent in his smoking den, and, after dinner, in the evenings he would sit with me before the open fireplace in the dining-room, a baize-covered table between us, on which were a tantalus, a box of cigars, and a chessboard. Happy evenings they were to me, and I know they were happy, too, to Fred.

On the night of the sixth day, after he had checkmated me in the most brilliant game I had ever seen him play, he remarked casually to Alice and me that he thought he would take down his rifle and go out for a little moonlight hunting expedition. Alice did not oppose him, although I knew she always held such expeditions dangerous. As for me, I felt a bit chagrined that he did not ask me to go with him, but, feeling that he might want to be alone for a quiet meditation, I said nothing about it.

The following morning, as I was taking a pipe in the garden after breakfast, Peter, our chauffeur and coachman, brought me my letters. The superscription of one of these, I observed with a shock, was in Fred's handwriting. I felt immediately that something was wrong; many little things in Fred's conduct which I had only half observed, or to which I had attached no importance, came crowding on my memory. In anxious trepidation I tore open the letter, and this was what I read:

I know that the very receipt of this note from me will, to some extent, have prepared you for a shock. You may, indeed I know you *will,* believe me when I say that the only regret I have in doing what I am about to do is the grief it will bring to Alice and you. As for my children, they are too young yet to be affected, and there is none else for whom I care.

When you are reading this I will be dead. You will find my body lying beside the black pool over Echo Lake, near the summit of Indian Head Mountain. Break the news gently to my wife, and, when you have done this, give her the enclosed note.

All my affairs are in order. I have made you executor of my estate. You will find my will in the safe. I need not admonish you to take care of Alice and my children, you would do that in any case.

I enclose, also, two sealed copies of a memorandum—one for Alice, and one for you—in which I set forth the awful, the sublimely horrible experience which befel me, and which has driven me to self-destruction. These are not to be opened until a week after the inquest, when my fate will have been forgotten by the gossips. I leave to Alice's judgment and to yours the question of making known the contents.

Remember me always as your affectionate brother,

Fred.

There is no need to intrude on the grief-stricken privacy of my sister. Peter and I went to the place indicated in Fred's letter. It was a small pool of semi-stagnant water. I knew the spot well, and often I had admired the thick profusion of its broad fringe of sedge. As we approached it now we were mystified to observe that the pool had dried up and that all around it the sedge and grass had been burnt up and scorched for a distance of many yards. At another time this would have aroused in us the most profound astonishment, but our thoughts were diverted now by the sight of poor Fred's body lying weltering at the edge of the scorched zone. The head had been almost torn from the trunk by some disruptive force applied, apparently, within the mouth. But the extraordinary fact was that expert medical testimony at the subsequent inquest declared that the disruptive force had been produced by *no known human agency.*

I believe I have now told all the salient incidents in this case as they were observable to us who were so closely in touch with the central figure, and, having in mind the grave possibility, if not likelihood of error creeping into the record were I to continue the narration in my own words, I think it best to produce the memorandum left by Fred exactly as he wrote it, and let the dead man tell the facts:

> "............................... the fruit
> Of that forbidden tree whose mortal taste
> Brought death into the world, and all our Woe."

And it came to pass that I, too, did eat of the fruit of the forbidden tree—the Tree of Knowledge—and the veil was lifted from the mystery of this world's destiny, and I saw Death and Destruction. I have stumbled, or I have been led, into the hideous arcanum of nature, which is Chaos.

It is difficult for me, almost impossible, for I am but a mere man, to tell you my story. An experience which transcends all human experiences defies depiction. But I will try. I must, however, disclose only so much as will set up the truth of what I relate. I may not be too precise, for that would be to defeat the very object for which I am about to immolate myself.

For months past I have been engaged on many scientific problems, chiefly of a chemical nature. The exigency of the times led me to conceive the possibility of being able to provide for the safety of our magnificent United States by presenting her with a potent instrument of defense. The object I had in view was to produce an explosive substance which would be at the same time abundant, easy of production, altogether safe to handle, and available for all purposes.

You know that the prices of the ingredients of every known explosive have increased enormously since the outbreak of the European war. Some chemicals necessary to the manufacture of explosives hitherto commonplace are almost unobtainable, and others, being mineral derivatives, are monopolised by the countries in which these mineral deposits occur. But in any event, even in normal times, the manufacture or production of explosives is always costly.

The first object I had in mind was an explosive compound or mixture, the component parts of which would exist in superabundance, and the production of which would be cheap. My second object was safety,—both before and after explosion. It is a point generally overlooked in discussing the ethics of the use of poisonous gas, that all explosives in common use give off gases which are either highly deleterious or poisonous. In this sense, they are all dangerous *after* use. Before use, they are all dangerous because there is none of them proof against either the fool or the foolhardy. To overcome this I aimed at producing an explosive which would give off no poisonous gases, and which would respond neither to severe shock nor to direct inflammation.

Finally, I wanted to make an explosive in which I could regulate both the rate and the resultant force of the explosion, so as to make it usable for every purpose.

All explosions may be regarded as processes of quick combustion, in which the residual gases are hundreds of times greater in volume than the original explosive or combustible. The only difference between combustion and explosion is in the length of time occupied in the disintegration. When an explosive action has begun in any substance, the phenomenon is propagated throughout the whole mass of the substance by being reproduced from molecule to molecule. It is the rapidity with which this propagation proceeds that determines the nature of the consequent reaction, and it may vary from the rate of ordinary combustion to the inconceivably high velocity of detonation.

Roux and Sarrau were, I think, the first to differentiate between explosives, and to divide them into two classes. These they called explosions of the first order, or detonations; and explosives of the second order, to which ordinary explosions belong. The detonation of an explosive, such as nitroglycerine, guncotton, or picric acid, is obtained by exploding with fulminate of mercury, and in this case the explosive substance is disintegrated almost instantaneously. Ordinary explosions may be produced either by direct application of fire, or sufficient heat, or by a small quantity of gunpowder. It is this kind of explosion which takes place in firing a projectile from a rifle or cannon. In fact such an explosion is the only suitable one for the purpose because a detonating explosion would probably burst the breech.

The phenomenon of varying rates of combustion or disintegration may be observed sometimes in the same substance. You can, for instance, burn a stick of dynamite. You can also burn a bit of celluloid, but if you heat it and strike it with a hammer it will explode. Guncotton, however, affords about the best example: When wet and closely compressed, guncotton burns slowly; if loose and uncompressed it will flash off; if spun in threads it can be used as a quick fuse, and dry guncotton can be exploded by a fulminate.

Many mixtures and compounds which are capable of quick exothermal decomposition, or which, in other words, are capable of explosion, are less sensitive than those I have just mentioned, and require a very powerful initial impulse to cause them to explode. Some of these substances, such as ammonium nitrate, trinitronaphthalene, and potassium chlorate, were until recently regarded as non-explosive, because the method of exploding them had not been discovered. The explosiveness of potassium chlorate was, I think, first discovered at the fire which took place at the Kurtz works, St. Helens, in May, 1899, when 156,000 kilograms of the chlorate, which up till then had been regarded as a combustible merely, exploded with terrific force, bringing vast destruction, and death to unwitting bystanders.

I have given you a general idea of the proximate object of my research, but you will readily understand that the conception of this object was only secondary in point of time sequence to other problems to which I had already devoted my attention. I believed, too, that it was subsidiary to them in point of importance, but in that I have been disillusioned.

Many years ago, acting on the assumption of the universal applicability of the hypothesis of evolution, I had begun to study the chemical elements with a view to finding out the nature and course of the evolution taking place in these elements themselves. Collaterally with this there was another problem which I regarded as the main object of my investigations. It is not necessary, nor is it advisable, for me to do more than outline this problem. It was suggested to me a long time ago by an address delivered by Ramsay, and it had to do with the discovery or isolation of the primal or fundamental element in all matter. I do not know whether I have actually succeeded in doing this, for my experiments have come to an abrupt, a terrible ending; but a few days ago I did finally succeed in breaking up one of the most familiar elements into two more fundamental than itself, and it was this discovery which laid open for me, and for all of us, the path of absolute ruin. But I anticipate.

Meanwhile, I had synthesised a great number of unstable chemical compounds composed of elements readily obtainable. These, from their very nature, were, I knew, readily capable of disintegration. But I had hitherto failed to find a suitable impulse, or an impulse sufficiently strong to effect the disintegration of any of them with explosive violence.

When, however, I did finally succeed in breaking up the element of which I have spoken into two more fundamental than itself, I found that one of these two, which I have named MORTIFER, effected the result at which I had aimed on some of the compounds I had synthesised, and on further investigation I discovered that this was due to the extraordinary affinity of mortifer for the hydrogen element in those compounds. Its affinity for the hydrogen atom was so intense, so powerful, that the disruption of the whole mass took place with detonating violence.

Satisfied at last that I was on the right track, that I had practically achieved the object I had set out to achieve, I decided that night, not yet a week ago, to make this a pausing place in my labor.

For many weeks day and night had ceased to have any special meaning for me. For weeks I had prosecuted my research restlessly, relentlessly, snatching now and then an hour or two of fitful sleep. I had felt, I had known, I was on the right trail. As game is to the pointer, so had my quarry been to the distended nostrils of my intellectual being. As a weasel pursues the hapless rabbit, so had I followed fast and ever faster the elusive object of my chase, until at last I had caught up with it, grappled with it, and beaten it to subjection. I felt the fierce, primitive, passionate triumph of the hunter. But over and above all, I felt the intense pleasure which attends alone the fruitful exercise of the rational faculty.

Yes, tonight I would go to bed early. Although it was not yet eleven o'clock I had become quite drowsy, which was not to be wondered at, I reflected, considering the severe strain to which

I had been subjected for so long. So I wrote down rapidly a few notes in a manner unintelligible to anyone but myself. These I locked carefully in my bureau, and then, as a final precaution, I double-locked the door of my laboratory, and stepped out into the garden.

The night was chill and clear, and a million eyes of heaven peered down upon me with the calm serenity of infinite mystery, as if to chide me for the pride I had taken in wresting one little secret from reluctant nature. Chastened by this thought, I entered my house; went up straight to my room, and crept into bed beside my wife who was already asleep. For a moment I thought of waking her to tell her of my discovery, but she being so sound asleep, and I being so jaded in mind and body, I postponed that sweet pleasure till the morning.

And now, how can I who am no writer,—I who am ever conscious of the clumsy awkwardness of my literary expression—hope to tell you through the medium of the written word the infinite horror of the tragedy which befel me that night?

On going to bed I had fallen quietly asleep, but my mind could not detach itself from the problems on which it had labored so long and actively. I know that I dreamed long and weirdly, but I remember definitely only the final portion of my dream. I seemed to have marched· in a long night tediously over an arid desert until I came to the edge of a precipice, whose depth my vision could not penetrate. Still as I stood gazing out over the void, it seemed to me that I saw a little star shoot forth from its celestial setting and approach me, and as it came nearer it grew into a huge, blue ball of intense brilliancy, becoming bigger and bigger until at last it burst into a glorious spray of surpassing splendor, illuminating by its glittering refulgence the surrounding waste. In an instant I saw that I stood at the edge of the earth beyond which there was naught.

I awoke. Calmly I awoke, and my opening eyes met again the cold, mysterious scrutiny of the unlidded eyes of heaven. And as I looked, there came to me as if from an immeasurable distance a wail of infinite pathos,—such a wail as might arise from the souls of a myriad unconceived babies sighing for existence. Whence, and from what, the wail came I do not know. I heard it only for a moment, and then it was lost in the slow and churchyard tones of the great hall-clock striking the hour of midnight.

Suddenly I sat upright as if electrified; every nerve and muscle in my body racked and taut in a paroxysm of terror. I felt—I could almost *see*—the hideous specter of an infinite, black doom crowding in on me as if to overwhelm me. Choking with dread, I craned forward eagerly to clutch at something—anything; to take hold of an object fixed and tangible. For a thought—Oh God! what a thought—had seared itself into my soul and left me numb with horror!

Many a time before in a dreary vigil of the night had I been stricken with a vague, an indefinable, terror. This I remembered now; and I remembered, too, how the first glimpse of russet dawn had soothed my weary spirit, and with the remembrance I felt a little easier. The thought I had conceived, I argued, was monstrous, impossible. Such a thing could not be. Yet, I could not remain one moment longer abed. I felt I could not put off for a minute the absolute proof to myself that my thought was nothing but an hallucination.

I arose, therefore, at once. And as I did so my wife awoke, and, while I dressed, I explained to her, in as quiet a manner as I could assume that I wished to test the effect of a reaction which I had overlooked in my researches. My heart bled for her, my darling Alice, in pity for the extreme worry which I knew my ill-concealed excitement and unusual conduct would arouse in her, and I felt inexpressibly grateful to her for the implicit trust she had always placed in me, no matter how eccentric my actions might appear.

Fully dressed, I left the house, and, walking down the garden, the bracing, nipping air of early winter whipped me into renewed vigor. Collected now in mind, and refreshed in body, I entered the laboratory, turning on the switch as I closed the door carefully behind me. Taking up a test tube, I walked over to a water faucet and allowed a few drops to trickle into the tube. Coming under the full light of a Tungsten lamp, I dropped carefully an infinitesimal quantity of mortifer into the water in the tube, and the water flashed off almost instantaneously! Repeating the experiment, this time with a few drops of water of normal salinity, I introduced once more a particle of mortifer into the water, and the result was, as I had anticipated, not a flash but an explosion, which shattered the test tube in my trembling fingers!

To describe my sensations at this moment would be wholly impossible. There are no words in any language to describe them, for no man had yet conceived the infinite import of my experience. Rooted in sublime dismay, I stood there in horrid contemplation of the destiny of the world as revealed in the fragment of broken glass gripped tightly in the fingers of my outstretched hand.

I do not know whether I have yet made clear to you the reason for my perturbation. Remember I have told you that I had found that the substance mortifer had an extraordinary affinity for hydrogen. Its affinity for this element was so great as to disrupt with extreme violence the water molecule, made up, as it is, of two atoms of hydrogen with one of oxygen, and the violence of this disruption was such as to propagate its influence through the whole mass of the water. More than this, I knew from the inherent nature of the reaction that its violence was, within certain limits, commensurate with the salinity of the water on account of the sodium element in the salt. In short, I had achieved what I had set out to achieve. I had discovered an explosive, "abundant, easy of production, and of such a nature that I could regulate the force of the explosion,"—and that explosive was *WATER!*

How long I stood in contemplation I cannot tell, for the notions of time and of eternity had already blended into each other and become indistinguishable. But as *you* would measure time, I stood there as if petrified for probably only a few minutes. And then a faint ray of hope that this chalice might yet be removed from my unwilling lips pierced the blackness that encompassed me. It was possible, I thought, that though an explosive effect had been produced by mortifer on a small quantity of water, yet the reaction might not take place where the quantity of water was very great. Urged by this faint glimmer, I resolved to put the question immediately to the test of actual experiment.

Far up on the flank of Indian Head Mountain there was, I remembered, a pool of stagnant water formed by the rain in a cup of the hill. The pool was isolated, and, after the week of drought which we had just had, I knew that the earth all around it would be quite dry. Here, I decided, would be just the ideal place for the momentous experiment.

Taking a minute quantity of mortifer, I encased it carefully in a soluble capsule, making the capsule of such thickness that it would take about ten minutes to dissolve in cold water. Then donning a light overcoat and a cap, I locked the door of my laboratory and went out into the night. Walking as quickly as I could, running, even, where the ground permitted, I breasted the slope of the mountain, and, aided by the clear light of a crescent moon, arrived at last, panting, at the side of the pool. It was then two o'clock.

As I stood there for a moment with open mouth to take breath, I could both feel and hear in my throat the throbbing of my over-strained heart. Knowing that no living thing, save, perhaps, a few small animals, would be in the vicinity at that hour of the morning, I lost not a moment but took the capsule of mortifer from my pocket, and placed it carefully in the water at the edge of the pool. Then I walked to a knoll a few hundred yards away, from which I could have an unobstructed view of the pool should anything happen.

Nor had I long to wait before something did happen! From the spot where the pool lay there rose up into the highest heavens a column of blue flame of miraculous volume which almost scorched me with its intense heat, and all around me there were innumerable cracklings and minor explosions, and I felt my face and hands bedewed by a mist of reformed water vapor,—produced, as I knew, by the recombination of the dissociated hydrogen and oxygen elements set free by the initial flashing of the water in the pool. As I have said, the initial effect of the mortifer on the water was a flash; there was only wanting the presence of the sodium element to have produced an explosion.

Aghast with terror, I cried aloud in the night, and fell upon the ground in a transport of unutterable woe. Who was I, or what was I, that fate should have singled me out from the uncounted human beings of the earth to be the unfortunate recipient of a secret so titanic? Blind fool that I was! But a few hours before I had prided myself on "wresting one little secret from reluctant nature." But now I knew that I had been made the luckless victim of a monstrous confidence, thrust on me by a ruthless nature only too eager to impart it. Great God! I, who had believed myself to be a free agent in my investigations, had penetrated a forbidden mystery to my own undoing. I had discovered a substance of such hideous potentiality as to invest me with the attributes of a malignant god of Destruction!

Lying prone upon the ground, my mind grasped gradually more and more fully the vastness of the awful secret, until at last the full truth swept over me with cataclysmal effect. Only to step to the sea shore,—to cast a particle of mortifer on the moving waters,—and, in a moment, the earth would be a nebula. Like Lucifer of old, roaming with his legions through the trackless universe, so, too, could I, in imagination,

> " .... behold the throne
> Of Chaos, and his dark pavilion spread
> Wide on the wasteful Deep! With him enthroned
> Sat sable-vested Night, eldest of things
> The consort of his reign."

For some reason I now became tranquil. I do not know why or how this was so, but I think it was due to the sublime, if satanic, grandeur of my reflection. Rising up, I essayed to walk back to the pool, but the ground around it over a wide zone was still so hot that I could not come near it. This did not trouble me, however, for I could realize well enough what there would be to see, so I bent my steps toward home where I arrived about six o'clock in the morning.

As to the course of action I would follow, my mind was now fully determined. Plainly I could not live. It would be impossible for me to go my accustomed rounds as if nothing had occurred. Such a secret as weighed on me would, I knew, inevitably bear down upon me and crush me with its intolerable burden. This I felt sure of. I might, of course, for a time preserve my counsel absolutely within myself. But the time would surely come when I would be driven to madness, and, in that condition, what might not I do? And, even if I were able by superhuman force of will to preserve my sanity, how could I provide for the possibility of falling sick, or meeting with an accident, and, in subsequent delirium, blurting out the whole facts of my infernal discovery? No, there is no way out for me, but to die.

But before I should die, it was necessary for me to remove all vestiges of my researches. You remember that morning after breakfast when I brought the children out with me into the garden, and danced with them around a bonfire of my books, instruments, and papers. That was the first part of the holocaust offered up for the safety of the world,—a sacrifice that is now complete in my own immolation.

The philosophy, the fundamental knowledge of the world and of the destiny of the human race has been revealed to me. I see now that we are but the playthings of nature,—a picture puzzle,—a set of blocks, provided for her amusement. Already she has completed one design of which she has become aweary, and, like a wanton child, she is crying to have the blocks jumbled up again to begin another picture. The world is but as a drop of water which condenses in the air, falls to the earth, and, in the passage, becomes tenanted with countless organisms. Then the sun dries up the drop. The organisms are no more. And the eternal cycle goes on forever.

Sometimes I have felt tempted to use my knowledge for my own aggrandizement; to exercise my power, or rather, to use the threat to exercise it to impose my will upon the world. Compared with my power, what would be the strength of potentates, princes, kings, or emperors? At my nod wars would cease, or be enacted with ten thousand-fold ferocity. I had nothing to do but to prove, to demonstrate, the efficacy of my terrible secret, and, from a houseboat on the Hudson I could dictate my pleasure to the world. I could crush the human race in absolute bondage. To hell with the thought!

But this I believe, of this I am fully convinced, that somewhere, soon, someone else, if not many others, will stray along the path which leads to destruction. Man is afflicted with the curse of reason, and many men are using that reason in a manner and in a direction which will lead with certainty to ultimate total disaster. There are, I know, scores of chemists on the face of the earth who are engaged in just such a pursuit as I followed. It may be a year; it may be a century, but the day of wrath—that dreadful day—is fast approaching.

And now I go from you. Tonight I will go up into the mountain beside the pool where the final proof of my damnable experience was established. For a sentimental reason I would like to die there, and, besides, I want to give myself a last demonstration. I will take with me a small soluble capsule containing the last particle of mortifer now in existence. This I will put in my mouth as I sit beside the pool, and I will then fill my mouth from a flask of salt water.

That will be the end.

CHAPTER TWENTY-ONE

Chaocipher

IN A PRECEDING chapter I have referred to Rutherford's achievement in 1919 of splitting an atom for the first time. In the preceding year, 1918, I had discovered a method of doing something to the written word, in any language, which affected that written word so as to result in its chaotic disruption. In two respects my method for achieving the complete annihilation of order and design in written language is more noteworthy than the method for the disruption of the atom. First, because my method for splitting the word is so simple that it could be performed by any normal ten-year-old school child, and second, because, unlike any other process of explosion or disruption, my method of disrupting the written words is identical and simultaneous with the complete restoration of order and design in the same written words.

Down through the ages, it has been the aim and desire of human beings to be able, on occasion, to write their thoughts in such a way as to be wholly unintelligible to anyone except the person or persons to whom these thoughts were intended to be exclusively addressed. Of course, I could remark here with more truth than flippancy that a great many writers have found no difficulty in presenting their "thoughts" in gobbledegook language which nobody at all can understand, but with that kind of thing I am not concerned.

While it has always been the aim and the hope of many to be able at times to express themselves in indecipherable script, the inherent difficulty of doing just that had never yet been overcome; and, indeed, the impossibility of doing it has been universally declared by all students of the subject.

Edgar Allan Poe was a most ardent and, to take him at his own word, a very capable cryptanalyst, and in two of his works he gives utterance to his conviction that all cipher is decipherable. In his well-known story "The Gold Bug" he states, "it may well be doubted whether human ingenuity can construct an enigma of the kind which human ingenuity may not, by proper application, resolve" and in his less known essay on "Cryptography" he declares, "It may be roundly asserted that human ingenuity cannot concoct a cipher which human ingenuity cannot resolve"; and in this same essay he goes on to say that "The reader should bear in mind that the basis of the whole art of solution, as far as regards these matters, is found in the general principles of the formation of language itself, and thus is altogether independent of the particular laws which govern any cipher, or the construction of its key."

My reason for quoting Poe here in this way is because of all the writers on the subject, he has expressed himself the most succinctly. So far as the accuracy of his observations is concerned I will only remark that Poe was far less cautious than he should have been when he uttered that dictum beginning with, "It may be roundly asserted . . ."

When I discovered my method for the utter disruption of the written word, or, to express this differently, my method for writing a cipher which would, in fact, be absolutely indecipherable, I discovered something which was just as accessible to Poe as it was to me. The ancient Egyptians and Babylonians could have been completely familiar with the principle, a fact which is readily deducible from a treatise on mathematics written by Hero of Alexandria in the second century B.C. The point I am making is that during the past two thousand years and more anyone could have had access to my method for the chaotification of language. The first device, or machine, which I constructed, solely for the purpose of demonstrating a principle, was a little model, constructed in an empty cigar box which, when full, had contained fifty small Havana cigars. I made this model myself, and to say that it was a crude affair would be only to describe it accurately.

Let me state simply what I claim to have accomplished in this connection: First, I formulated a principle for the development of a cipher which would be materially and mathematically indecipherable, and, second, I built the little model, of which I have spoken, for the purpose of demonstrating this principle. With these two things, my device and my principle, any person, anywhere, writing any language, could by applying my principle and using my device transcribe his written words into a script which would be absolutely indecipherable by anyone except the persons for whom the message is intended; and be it remembered that while possession of my device together with knowledge of my principle, would enable any person to write a script which would be absolutely indecipherable by anyone except the person or persons for and to whom the script was written and addressed, yet possession of my device together with knowledge of the general principle involved, would not enable any person to decipher any messages whatever written by anyone else and not intended for him.

In all my efforts to locate backing for my idea and device, I have found it practically impossible to make people understand exactly the import of what I have just written in the preceding paragraph. For this reason, I repeat, that if every person on earth were in possession of my device and applied my principle, he or she could encipher a message, in any language, and this message would be absolutely indecipherable by anyone except the person for whom it was intended. Moreover, if every person on earth were to encipher the same message, say for instance, this paragraph of which this sentence is a part, no two of the resultant encipherments would be alike.

In June, 1919, I went to Washington to consult with the then famous attorney, Marcellus Bailey, with whom I had arranged an appointment. When I arrived at his office I was informed that he was at home ill, but that he would see me there. At his almost palatial residence I was ushered into the aged attorney's bedroom, and there, sitting on the side of his bed, I demonstrated my principle on my little cigar box device. Marcellus appeared intensely interested during my full three-hour demonstration and at the end of that time he said, "Well, Mr. Byrne, you certainly have succeeded in scrambling your eggs; but my advice to you now is not to enter the patent office with that little device, for, after all, it is scarcely more than a toy. When you go into the patent office, go into it with your better foot foremost. You say you intend to collaborate with an expert draftsman in producing the blueprints of a readily operable machine, and my professional opinion is that you ought to wait until you have your blueprints ready."

It was only comparatively recently that I realized how I missed my cue at that interview with Marcellus Bailey. He had told me that my little device was "scarcely more than a toy"—and what I should have done was to enter it in the patent office as just that; for in this way the device would have come into general use, and its ability in enabling anyone to write an indecipherable cipher would have soon become a universally recognized fact.

But what I did then was to spend six months working with a first-rate draftsman, and at the end of this time I wrote to Marcellus Bailey who replied to me in part as follows:

Marcellus Bailey,
Attorney at Law & Solicitor of Patents,
Washington, D.C.

———

501 F Street, N.W.

January 24, 1920

My dear Mr. Byrne:—

I am in receipt of your letter of the 20th instant and I congratulate you on having at last the finished drawings of the Cipher Machine developed from the device which you exhibited to me on June 10 last. It must have been some job . . ."

Marcellus had more to say in his letter, but the point he evidently desired most to emphasize at that time was in going on record as to the exact date upon which I exhibited my device to him.

I then approached several machine makers asking for an estimate of the cost of making my machine, and from not one of them could I get anything approaching a firm bid, everyone of them was vague, and the best I could get by way of an estimate was that it would not be less than $5,000 and might run to $20,000 or more; so my blueprints are still gradually returning into the dust which is the ultimate destination of all things, including ourselves.

It would be impracticable and fruitless here to give a detailed account of my experiences in connection with my efforts trying to "put across" my cipher idea, efforts which entailed my expenditure of thousands of dollars and countless unrewarded days of time. So I shall do no more than tell briefly, and with occasionally necessary reserve, a few of the outstanding facts and incidents.

But before proceeding further with my story, let me make it clear that my discovery was not fortuitous. During many years previous to it, I had often questioned casually the accuracy of the universal consensus regarding the impossibility of constructing an indecipherable cipher; but it was not until the autumn of 1918 that I gave serious thought to the subject. Reading at that time a detective story in a well-known magazine, I came to a reference to a cipher message which the detective hero had little difficulty in deciphering because, as he was made to comment laconically, "all such communications yield to methodic and scientific analysis"—instantly I felt, as it were, my mind bristling, and I asked myself the question: Is it really a fact that all ciphers must yield to methodic and scientific analysis? The expert cryptanalyst's answer to this question is a categorical "Yes"; and he bases his "Yes" as Poe did, on "the general principles of the formation of language itself."

In his essay on "Cryptography" Poe states that some months previously he had "ventured to assert" that he would be able to resolve any cipher "of the character specified." This challenge, Poe asserts, resulted in letters being "poured in" on him "from all parts of the country"; and he continues: "Out of, perhaps, one hundred ciphers altogether received, there was only one which we did not immediately succeed in resolving. This one we *demonstrated* [italics are Poe's] to be an imposition—that is to say, we fully proved it a jargon of random characters, having no meaning whatever."

The foregoing statement by Poe is one of the most surprising and self-revealing declarations ever uttered by anyone; and it also furnishes a most beautiful example of a "non sequitur." Poe says he "fully proved" the submitted "cipher" to be "a jargon of random characters." This, of course, I admit Poe could prove to his heart's content, but why, I ask, why in the name of common sense did he go on to assume from the fact that it was "a jargon of random characters," that it had "no meaning whatever"?

I grant freely that Poe was almost certainly correct in saying that the "cipher" he was referring to had "no meaning whatever." The important point here, however, is that Poe did not perceive the *non sequitur* of his deduction—that he did not perceive that if "human ingenuity" were to aim at concocting a cipher which "human ingenuity" would *not* be able to resolve, that cipher *would have to be* "a jargon of random characters."

Almost twenty years ago a pretentious book written by one Herbert Yardley, and bearing the title of *The American Black Chamber,* achieved considerable popularity and notoriety. In this book there is a chapter devoted to "A Word with the State Department" and in this chapter the author refers to the actual, or potential, existence of an indecipherable cipher which is such because the cipher has no repetitions to conceal. And then the author proceeds to ramble incoherently about the pride he would feel if he were able to give to the United States an impenetrable and permanent cipher which would preserve its secrecy forever. Just what Mr. Yardley was trying to say in this chapter remains obscure, but it is a fact that years before it was written I had given a demonstration to the War Department in Washington of my first crude cipher machine. The persons to whom I demonstrated my "machine" were Major Frank Moorman, of the General Staff, referred to in Chapter XI of Yardley's book, and Mr. W. F. Friedman, cryptanalyst; and this demonstration was given by me in July 1922, some nine years before Yardley's *American Black Chamber* was published.

It is interesting to note that in his book Yardley displays the same ignorance that Poe did—and that everyone else does—regarding the essential character of an indecipherable cipher; for, in reference to a demand made on him by Colonel Van Deman for the decipherment of a certain message, Yardley told the Colonel that he had worked on the message all night, and, basing his opinion on "Scientific Analysis," declared the document was not a cipher but a fraud and a fake, put together by someone who had picked out a jumble of letters on a typewriter.

Let us consider here what kind of cipher script could properly be described as a jargon of random characters. Suppose you were to get a revolving drum and put into it twenty-six marbles, similar in size and weight, but each one designating a different letter of the alphabet; and then suppose you were to dictate, letter by letter, a piece containing, say, one thousand words to someone who would take at random a marble out of the drum each time you called out a letter, and then replace that marble in the revolving drum before the next draw; and all the while write down every letter in the sequence as they were fortuitously drawn from the drum—what would the resultant script written by this haphazard method be like? Would it not best be described as a "jargon of random characters"? Yes, it would. But does it necessarily follow that this "jargon of random characters" has "no meaning whatever"? No, it does not.

If it be agreed that this script, resulting from the casual drawing of a marble from a rotating drum for each letter in a piece of plain text containing one thousand words, could best be described as a "jargon of random characters," may we not ask how the script, resulting from the casual drawing of marbles from a rotating drum for every letter in a piece of plain text containing one million words, or one quintillion words—or, indeed words ad infinitum—could best be described? Is it not obvious that this resultant script would continue to be—ad infinitum—a "jargon of random characters"?

It should be obvious to anyone, as it should have been clear to Major Yardley, that the only cipher which would be materially and mathematically indecipherable is one which would present no feature other than that of having been drawn inconsequentially from a rotating drum, or pecked haphazardly on a typewriter—a cipher which would be devoid of discernible order, or design, a cipher which would, in actual fact, possess no order or design, a cipher which could only be adequately described as "a jargon of random characters."

When I first set out to discover a system for concocting an indecipherable cipher, I had it clearly in mind that such a system would and should be universally available. I had no thought of devising a system which would be available, say, for the War Department, or for the Navy, or for the State Department. What I had in mind, I repeat, was a system available for everybody; and I fully believed—and am convinced—that the really big market for my system would be in the commercial, general correspondence, and literary fields. I aimed at supplying for one and all a method and a means for conveying his or her thoughts in such a way that he or she could be absolutely assured that only the intended recipient would be able to read them. I envisioned, for instance, the utilization of my method and machine by business men for business communications, and by brotherhoods and social and religious institutions. I believe that my method and machine would be an invaluable asset to big religious institutions as for example the Catholic Church with its world-wide ramifications. I had, and still have in mind the universal use of my machine and method by husband, wife, or lover. My machine would be on hire, as typewriting machines now are, in hotels, steamships, and, maybe even on trains and airliners, available for anyone anywhere and at any time. And I believe, too, that the time will come—and come soon—when my system will be used in the publication of pamphlets and books written in cipher which will be unreadable except by those who are specially initiated.

I have an acquaintance whose grandfather was a close friend and an admirer of Alexander Graham Bell. Towards the end of 1876, Bell demonstrated his crude telephone to the grandfather I am speaking about, and, having done so, asked him whether he would care to invest $3,000 in its commercialization. "Oh, no, Alec," the grandfather replied laughingly to Bell, "don't ask me to invest in a thing like that—why, man, it's just a toy! But let me tell you, Alec, that if you need the $3,000 for yourself, either as a loan or a gift, you can have the money with pleasure."

"It's just a toy!" That's what the grandfather said to Alec Bell; and that's what Marcellus Bailey said to me about my crude device. And the "toy" that was Alec Bell's brainchild grew up, and up, and up, till it is even now the fundamental base of the largest corporate organization on earth—The American Tel. and Tel.

In 1920 a friend of mine, a New York lawyer, who was also a friend and former law associate of Bainbridge Colby, suggested to me that I sound out the State Department in Washington on the availability to it of my cipher system. Colby was then Secretary of State; and I approached him by letter, enclosing a personal introduction to him written by our mutual friend. About three weeks later I received a surprising letter, written on the stationery of The Secretary of State, and here reproduced in part.

THE SECRETARY OF STATE
WASHINGTON
October 28, 1920.

My dear Sir:

The Secretary desires me to acknowledge the receipt of your letter of the twenty-sixth regarding a cipher machine concerning which you wrote to him on September thirtieth. . . .

The Department has examined with interest the plan which you submitted, but it does not feel that it can undertake to pass upon the value of an invention of this sort.

I am returning to you herewith the papers which you sent to the Department.

Yours very truly,
G. Howland Shaw
Executive Assistant.

In the following year, 1921, there was a new President in Washington, and also a new Secretary of State, the great Charles Evans Hughes. Years before that time I had been introduced to Mr. Hughes, and I held him, as I still hold his memory, in high esteem. So once again I decided to approach the State Department in regard to the availability of my cipher. But before doing this I thought it would be advisable to seek an opinion regarding my cipher system from a person qualified to give an opinion about it, so shortly after Harding's inauguration, I got in touch with Colonel Parker Hitt, who had authored a little booklet which had been published officially in Fort Leavenworth, Kansas, bearing the title, *Manual for the Solution of Military Ciphers.* During the succeeding months, I heard several times from Colonel Hitt anent my cipher system, and I knew from him that he was vastly interested in it. But it was not until August 3, 1921 that he wrote me a definitive and formal letter about my system. It would not now be wise for me to give this letter in full, but in it he wrote in part as follows:

HEADQUARTERS 2ND CORPS AREA
Governors Island, New York City.
August 3, 1921

My dear Mr. Byrne:

I am returning to you herewith the machine and the accompanying papers which you let me have in connection with it. It has been impossible for me to do any connected work with it for many weeks, on account of the pressure of official business and the various things which I have to take care of. I am now about to leave for Washington for permanent station and we might as well call it a day.

As to the principle of the machine, it is undoubtedly a most ingenious and effective device. . . .

. . . but I have attempted to formulate a plan for breaking down this system of yours and so far have not been able to do it successfully.

I feel that you could safely go ahead with the commercial exploitation of the machine with confidence in the practical indecipherability of the product.

I regret that I have not been able to handle this matter with the care and deliberation which I like to give these things, but I assure you of my interest in it and I want to thank you for having let me see it and for your courtesy in putting the cards on the table for me.

Yours sincerely,
Parker Hitt

When I read Colonel Hitt's letter, it was clear to me that he had not at all fully apprehended the principle of my "machine," as he called it. But I was glad, however, to know that he was aware of the fact that "commercial exploitation" of my system and machine was the object I had in view.

Having received this letter from Colonel Hitt, I immediately communicated with the State Department, being ignorantly hopeful that Secretary Hughes would give me some encouragement. But in a few days I got one more shock of disappointment in the form of the letter, here reproduced:

DEPARTMENT OF STATE
WASHINGTON
September 2, 1921

In reply refer to
  IB 119.25/360
    Mr. J. F. Byrne,
      70 Wilson Street,
        Brooklyn, New York.

Dear Sir:

Receipt is acknowledged of your letter of the 29th ultimo with regard to a cipher machine invented by you and which you desire to demonstrate to the Department.

In reply I beg to inform you that while the Department appreciates your courtesy in bringing this matter to its attention, the codes and ciphers now used are adequate to its needs.

I am, Sir,

Your obedient servant,
For the Secretary of State:
Harry P. Fletcher
Under Secretary

Be it remembered that the foregoing letter, a paragon of smugness, was written to me twenty-nine years ago by the State Department of these United States; and then compare this fact with the fact that Robert E. Sherwood was reported only a little more than a year ago in all our newspapers as declaring that high Government officials, including the late Harry Hopkins, believed that the State Department code was "very vulnerable" as far back as 1941. And on December 8, 1948, Under Secretary Robert A. Lovett, talking about the Chambers-Hiss affair at a Washington news conference, assured the news gatherers that the State Department's diplomatic "codes" had been made as secure against espionage as it was "humanly possible" to make them—and this "new security," Mr. Lovett explained, had been achieved during the last ten years by steadily improved peace and wartime procedures and devices. But at the same time Mr. Lovett was reported as "conceding" that "great aid" to spies in cracking the old codes could be found in documents involved in the Chambers-Hiss case.

Before the end of this chapter I will consider further the general subject of Mr. Lovett's remarks, but right now I want to get on with my story.

During many months after receipt of the foregoing letter I succeeded in achieving nothing, and then in the following year, 1922, I got in touch again with Colonel Hitt at the War College in Washington, and he wrote me in part:

THE WAR COLLEGE
WASHINGTON
7 March, 1922

My Dear Mr. Byrne,

. . . .

But, if you come to Washington or want to correspond with the right man here about your machine, I will be glad to put you in touch with Major Frank Moorman, General Staff, Room 2648, Munitions Building, who handles these matters (in connection with the Signal Corps) and who is a personal friend and cipher pupil of mine.

As for the last paragraph of your letter, I deeply appreciate your offer but turn it down in the interest of my own liberty of action. I am a free lance at this game and expect to remain one. For that reason, I am returning your letter in order that we may consider it as never written.

Yours truly,
Parker Hitt

In the week after receipt of this letter, I arrived once more with my first model in Washington, where I was met on March 17, 1922, by Colonel Hitt, who immediately escorted me in person to give me a glowing introduction to both Major Moorman, and Mr. W. F. Friedman, Cryptanalyst.

Nearly five months later I wrote to Major Moorman and received the following reply:

MILITARY INTELLIGENCE DIVISION
WAR DEPARTMENT
OFFICE OF THE CHIEF OF STAFF
WASHINGTON
August 26, 1922

Mr. J. F. Byrne,
    70 Wilson Street,
        Brooklyn, N.Y.

Dear Sir:—

I have for acknowledgement your letter of August 21st and wish to assure you that I have not forgotten the profitable hour we spent together. I am sending a letter to Mr. Friedman with request that he communicate with you with reference to your cipher device.

> Very sincerely yours,
> Frank Moorman
> Major, General Staff

And a few days afterwards I received by parcel post from Washington a package containing my cipher model smashed into smithereens.

When I was devising my cipher system, I worked neither with model nor with diagram. I solved my problem in a short period of delicious mental concentration and exhilaration. In fact, I worked out the problem blindfold, as I would have worked out a chess problem; and I entertained the erroneous belief that merely to narrate and describe my system to a serious and disinterested student of Cryptography, or to any person of unbiased intelligence, would be sufficient to evoke his assent to the validity of my claims in its regard. This is where I made a big mistake; and this is what I had in mind in a preceding chapter of this book when I referred to the harmful consequences which might ensue from indulging in blindfold chess play.

A result of this mistake was that when I constructed my cigar-box model in 1918, I had in mind only the construction of a model on which I could demonstrate a principle. My cousin Mary Fleming was charmed with the resultant "toy"—it looked so simple and colorful; and when I told her the purpose for which it was intended and explained its operation, she was entranced with the idea which she grasped quickly and clearly. And very earnestly she said to me, "That will surely bring you a Nobel

Prize." At that time all I replied was, "Well it certainly is a strange thing that, being so simple as it is, no one ever thought of it before." And since that time I have seen many a Nobel Prize awarded for lesser achievements.

After my experience with the War and State Departments, I felt that it was, and would remain, quite useless to attempt to get anywhere with any department of the United States Government. In this opinion I abided for a full fifteen years; and then, in a weak moment, I fell for an item which appeared in the newspapers in 1937. This item was to the effect that Rear Admiral Harold G. Bowen had requested a congressional appropriation "for the development of a system of Cryptography by which warships can transmit signals to another vessel in the fleet which cannot be deciphered (sic) by an enemy vessel."

On reading this news item, I decided to construct a working model on which I could do extended encipherments and decipherments, and on which I could with some freedom put my principle into operation. Working through the summer and fall of 1937, I made my model and prepared on and by it, a document which I intended for submission to the Navy Department—this document being composed as a concrete example of the *kind* of work which one could accomplish on my model. After some hard labor in producing the cipher, I found even harder labor ahead of me in trying to find a printer who would be able to turn out the kind of job I wanted. Finally I did locate a printer who was willing to tackle the work, and who did turn out an excellent job. He printed for me five hundred copies. And they cost me plenty— both in time and money.

On November 18, 1937, I wrote my first letter to the Navy Department, addressing it to Admiral Bowen, who has since retired, and has become Executive Director for the Thomas Alva Edison Foundation of which Charles F. Kettering is President. In my letter to Admiral Bowen I told him of my device and system, stressing their universal availability. I enclosed also some copies of my document, *Chaocipher—The Ultimate Elusion.*

I never had any reply from Admiral Bowen himself; but a couple of weeks later, on December 7, 1937, I had the following letter from a Captain J. M. Irish, who was Assistant to the Chief of the Bureau of Engineering.

ADDRESS BUREAU OF ENGINEERING, NAVY DEPARTMENT
AND REFER TO NO. S67/68 (11-18-W9)

NAVY DEPARTMENT
BUREAU OF ENGINEERING
WASHINGTON, D.C.

7, Dec. 1937

Sir:

Receipt of your letter of 18 November 1937 is acknowledged herewith.

This Bureau regrets very much that its limited personnel does not permit deciphering the material enclosed with your letter. However, the Bureau would be very pleased to examine fully a detailed description of your general system and of the mechanical means used for obtaining the cipher.

Your courtesy in according the Bureau an opportunity of examining your system is very much appreciated.

Very respectfully,

J. M. Irish
Assistant to Bureau

On the following January 15, I wrote a further explanatory letter, this one to Captain Irish, with another marked copy of my ten-page cipher booklet, entitled *Chaocipher—The Ultimate Elusion*. In this letter I said in part:

"I am also sending you another copy of my booklet, "Chaocipher—The Ultimate Elusion." You will observe that on this copy I have written in, over the corresponding cipher, the plain text of the first hundred lines. But since each of the first hundred lines, (covering pages 1, 2, 3, and 4), is identical in meaning with the other ninety-nine, I have written the plain text only over the top line on the first four pages."

The plain text of each of the 100 lines on pages 1, 2, 3, and 4 reads thus:

ALLGO OD,QU ICKBR OWNFO XESJU MPOVE RLAZY DOGTO SAVET HEIRP ARTY.

"On page 5 I have written in the plain text of the first eight lines of the Declaration of Independence; and on page 10 I have written in the plain text of the last line of the Declaration of Independence, together with the plain text of the first line of the Gettysburg Speech and the last line of the same.

"I am sending you also the full text of the Declaration of Independence and the Gettysburg Speech written exactly as enciphered. The text which I used, of both these historic documents, is as printed, paragraphed, and punctuated in the World Almanac. For punctuation marks I have used letter equivalents. These, of course, are purely arbitrary, and would be largely unnecessary —except where a very high degree of literary precision is desired.

"The punctuation marks I have employed, with their letter equivalents, are as follows:

Paragraph	Z	
Period	W	
Colon	V	
Comma	Q	
Semi-colon	U	(Also QQ, this latter being used only once—in 11th word in Line 112)
Hyphen	J	
Apostrophe	X	
Dash	H"	

My correspondence with the Navy Department continued for several months; and, by appointment, I went to Washington for a preliminary conference on April 4, 1938, and a few weeks later, on May 3, I returned again to Washington to give a demonstration of my device and principle—a demonstration which was not even begun before it ended abruptly.

At the proposed demonstration there were three Commanders —one a senior officer to preside; and two younger Commanders, whose names were Wagner and Tucker, as assayers. Wagner being a cipher "expert" while Tucker was an expert in radio and electronics. I can only say about this "conference" that it ended before it began with Commander Tucker sagely suggesting to me that I should take my device and system either to the War Department or to the State Department.

For the record, let me say that since 1920 I have consistently offered my cipher system to the various departments of the United States Government for a "nominal" remuneration (something like $1 a year), provided that I were allowed to develop the commercial exploitation of my system. In one of my first letters to the Navy Department in 1938, I made this point clear; and in a letter to me written on March 12, 1938, Captain Irish wrote:

"Referring to the questions raised in your letter, the Bureau is unable to state at this time whether or not, in event of adoption of your system, it would elect to purchase your invention or merely the right to use same for Governmental purposes leaving all other rights to you. It is probable, however, that the former course of action would be taken for reasons of secrecy."

In using these four words "for reasons of secrecy," Captain Irish made it clear that he did not grasp my claim regarding the universal availability and indecipherability of my system.

Let me return now to the subject of that Washington news conference on December 8, 1949. At that conference it was revealed that Whittaker Chambers had produced stolen documents, the theft of which, according to Assistant Secretary of State John E. Peurifoy, meant that "our codes were being read by foreign nations" during a long period. And at this conference Under Secretary Robert A. Lovett stated that he "knew the State Department's code work now is completely secure—both against code-solving and theft of its documents." And then a few seconds later at this same conference Mr. Lovett added that "the State Department has been told by cryptographic experts *its code work is as secure as any material of that nature can be.*"

When such statements or elucidations as the one made by Mr. Lovett are to be imparted to the public, why should such an onerous job be loaded on the back of a high official like Mr. Lovett? Where were the "cryptographic experts" who reportedly "told" the State Department about the security of its "codes," and why were not these "experts," or at least one of them called upon to give at first hand to the public the assurances on which Mr. Lovett based his claim about the "security" of the "codes"?

Finally, may I ask Mr. Lovett, or anyone now in the State Department—or in any other Government Department—who or what is a "cryptographic expert"? I have a clear notion of the connotation of the title "cryptanalytic expert"; but I never heard any such expert—save one—express the opinion, or even concede the possibility, that *any* indecipherable script could ever be concocted. And in this connection I express here my belief that the persons who were dubbed by Mr. Lovett "cryptographic experts" were, in fact, "cryptanalytic experts," who would themselves unhesitatingly express their conviction that there never was—and that there never will be—a "cryptographic expert." These "cryptanalytic experts" are precisely the kind of persons who would give the most positive assurance to the head officials in any Department that "its code work is as secure AS ANY MATERIAL OF THAT NATURE CAN BE."

The most fitting comment on the last preceding sentence is, "A word to the wise is sufficient."

But much more recently, and more dramatically, the spotlight of publicity was brilliantly directed to the subject of what Mr. Lovett called the security of this nation's "code work." In the days when, after his recall from Korea, General of the Army Douglas MacArthur was testifying before the Senate Committee in Washington, the gist of some messages that had been sent to him in cipher was submitted to the committee, but always with the explanation that this gist was a carefully paraphrased version of the original plain text of the cipher messages. And the explanation offered for submitting such paraphrased versions was that this was done to protect this government's cipher system from being "broken" or "cracked."

In this connection, referring to a document that had been sent on January 13, 1951, Secretary Marshall testified: "It's been declassified with the approval of the President, and in a manner that *we do not think discloses any cryptographic information and things of that sort.*"

At the time that General Marshall uttered that insipid, cautious, and hedging pronouncement, he was the top man of the Armed Forces of these United States; and the plain inference from his pronouncement is that the highest ranking government officials of this country not only admit, but assert, that their cipher systems are defective and vulnerable and decipherable. Indeed, this inference would have been justified even if General Marshall had not uttered that wobbly, "We do not think. . . ." For from this mere fact alone that it was found necessary to issue "precise instructions for paraphrasing" the plain texts, the deduction is inescapable that the highest officials in this country are fully aware of the insecurity of its "code work."

In this connection, I assert and claim that the publication of the plain text of a trillion documents enciphered by my cipher system would not be of the least use or assistance to anyone attempting to cryptanalyze the cipher product of my system.

Let me repeat here that any person on earth using a device similar to my own home-made contraption, could produce a cipher message which would be indecipherable by any other person except the one to whom the message is directed. And let me add that devices far more operable than my crude model could be mass-produced to sell at ten dollars each.

I reproduce, herewith, four cipher exhibits, together with their plain text equivalents—which are given verbatim et literatim. The first and longest of these exhibits is the one entitled *Chaocipher—The Ultimate Elusion*, which was prepared by me for presentation to the Navy Department. As a matter of fact, several more copies of this document are, or were, in the various departments of the United States Government. Although I have already given the general schema of this ten-page document, let me repeat that the first four pages are devoted to the encipherment of an identical line which reads:

ALLGO OD,QU ICKBR OWNFO XESJU MPOVE RLAZY DOGTO SAVET HEIRP ARTY.

There was really no need for the two punctuation marks, the comma and the period, represented respectively by a free Q and a free W. They are just an illustrative embellishment. On page 5 of this document, lines 101 to part of 105 are devoted to a few introductory words to the two great historic documents that follow: These being the "Declaration of Independence," which begins at the third letter in the ninth group on line 105, and ends at the fifth letter in the fourth group on line 227; and the "Gettysburg Speech," which begins at the first letter in the fifth group on line 227, and ends at the third letter in the third group on line 248. In both the cipher and plain texts of the Gettysburg speech, there was an error of omission at the fourth character in the eighth group of five letters in line 239. At this point 35 characters were left out, these being a comma followed by the words "but it can never forget what they did here."

The second exhibit reproduced is an encipherment of four short passages from the first three chapters of Caesar's *De Bello Gallico,* with the exact plain text in Latin; and the reader will note the frequency of the recurrence in the cipher script of both the letters W and K, notwithstanding that the letter W does not occur at all in Latin, and the letter K is extremely rare in that language.

The third exhibit reproduced here is one which speaks for itself, and will, I fancy, be of some interest to a certain person in Washington.

I call the fourth exhibit reproduced "A Glimpse of Chaos." This is the encipherment, with exact plain text, of a portion of the memorable speech made by General of the Army, Douglas MacArthur, before the joint session of Congress after his recall from Korea. This encipherment is distinguished from the other three in that it bears within itself full and complete instructions to an initiate for its decipherment.

In regard to the first of these four exhibits, I have already said that several copies of this document were submitted to Washington, together with an abortive demonstration. Moreover, a formal demonstration of my chaocipher system, together with a decipherment of this exhibit, were given by me to the American Tel. & Tel. Company through some top officials of the Bell Laboratories, these including Mr. Ralzemond D. Parker, a former Telegraph Development Director for that organization. I cannot, therefore, issue a categorical challenge to everyone to decipher this document.

But in regard to the other three exhibits, I do challenge any person or group of persons—including the Bell Laboratories and the American Tel. & Tel.—to decipher these documents.

Now seeing that in the case of documents two and three I give the *exact* plain text equivalents, verbatim et literatim, of their cipher text, I can envision the possibility that some wags or wiseacres may claim decipherment of these two documents by simply copying the plain texts as given. For this reason I issue a further and more specific challenge in regard to exhibit four, this challenge being as follows: In the last two lines of the cipher text of the number four exhibit, namely lines 34 and 35, a little over a dozen words, with punctuation marks, of the plain text as I have given it have been re-enciphered. Now, to the first person, or group of persons, who within three months after date of publication of this book succeeds in deciphering this number four exhibit, I shall give ($5,000) five thousand dollars—this sum to be paid by me out of the royalties accruing to me from *Silent Years* during the said three months. And if the royalties accruing to me during these three months do not amount to $5,000, I shall give all the royalties that shall accrue to me during that period.

To the first person, or persons who may send me identification of the re-enciphered words in lines 34 and 35 I shall give credit for having submitted prima facie evidence of being able to decipher the whole of the number four exhibit; and such person or persons can then at any time, within the given three month period, give proof of being able to decipher this whole number four exhibit. Let me make it explicit here that anyone who *really can* identify and decipher the dozen or so specified words, must, *ipso facto*, be able to decipher the whole of this exhibit, because it is all of a piece.

And to all "cryptanalytic and cryptographic experts," including the Major Yardleys, I give cordial invitation to accept the challenge I make here. This invitation is extended also to the members—both individually and as a group—of the American Cryptogram Association, and its local affiliate, The New York Cipher Society. And finally, I issue to the believers in the wonderful capabilities of electronic calculating machines, a warm invitation to take up my challenge. Perhaps the genial-looking Professor Norbert Wiener of the Massachusetts Institute of Technology would like to embark on these waters of chaos in the hope that his cybernetical pilot might, by the exercise of superhuman navigatory prowess, be able to steer him to some port.

One final plea I make to all my readers in regard to these dozen or so re-enciphered words in exhibit four: Please do not send me guesses—they will do you no good.

Chaociphering is not guesswork. There *never was*—and there *never will be*—anything requiring a higher degree of exactitude and truth. Often when I look at the crude model on which I have done my work I feel as our beloved Keats felt when he apostrophized "The Grecian Urn":

> "Thou shalt remain, in midst of other woe
>   Than ours, a friend to man to whom thou say'st
>   'Beauty is truth, truth beauty,'—that is all
>   Ye know on earth, and all ye need to know."

CHAOCIPHER—THE ULTIMATE ELUSION

Exhibit 1

```
    ALLGO OD,QU ICKBR OWNFO XESJU MPOVE RLAZY DOGTO SAVET HEIRP ARTY.
 1  CLYTZ PNZKL DDQGF BOOTY SNEPU AGKIU NKNCR INRCV KJNHT OAFQP DPNCV
 2  LTVFI COTSS LWYYI HBICF UTHXN UVKGI MVEZY WSTHE PIEWX NNGFT OGHSR
 3  TBZXT MVGLT JXCSQ XLNJT ENCSV LCWRT BENZL SUVYI DAXLA FATQS RNZOP
 4  HKYGQ JTOGY SDBNV DJOWH KECRM LYWIQ IFIKS CYJGC VXNSK YHRYV YEDSZ
 5  RIFFZ AQNHS OMJPO RWTJO IJIPK VHZGP WQKRX DMAUE FFXIA CFLCZ MAFZS
 6  JEOZI FKJCF METES YHZU  VLFFU RRHRI IFFDZ MTTOV KLZOV LPVPP GVGEW
 7  WEFRF YHKXO PKXRQ SZKLC ZKHZW XRJXL MVFGG FGYIF DAEIN IWPOM OUVRF
 8  BUZLA GDBCU AMFQL ACRWW TUGSM PPZBR FASRO YIRCA GVEYN SRTOQ TDLFJ
 9  RUTKF KASGV LVYYF VRAIY NIVJK IUWPF ZBVRU EOTEJ GLCGY SSNHH QTIQW
10  UKQAS XKGSP WHRYM TQSOQ BAMAP FQRLI IUGTI VBEBY BLYQY XFBIU LKGOE
11  CSWUH TBIZZ HLBND IWTQA MAZBM YMBEK CYKCA UGSKT IMDWR OWNRV FZVKR
12  EBVUJ EQIAE MOHTG FHFFI DIQQJ UAWDH LUYRE RERHL XWAMY RNONJ KDPTC
13  JDCJN BVEOU TWXOF GRXND KITNL OXSLZ WQRDE NPIAX LRVPR JFHRA JGVUC
14  SDJWW OIWEV AVMRR NLRJM IFDHH ADDQC BZWYK DVPAY BYUKI JGVUC ZTBPI
15  ACJHF XRALO VRLZU VANAB NZDZT PFQRI YCLLZ YILTW JBPAF LPOIO JAGCX
16  USRXC DCITE EKMJB HPPYO NYEGS ZWGUR IFIPW UMTLJ YVYNE ACGJX HUXFP
17  QPDLA BSYMU DOKYD WRXCJ UFPXC PBWYQ PHMTA XNROB ASQRZ YVJXO YMEQR
18  BIHGG PKRFD MWTOT MKBOL BRRNO CHWLQ DVNEE VXBNE GHJQQ RHUTY KPRAO
19  XSYEW VJZTU XDEWK WSWIE EHDSN RHRCV DUYOG NGVDP VGYBN ECJOK IVCUJ
20  DYVLO WBMGS TFTXU VOXGZ ZUIIR YXSAV EPRWP KQJMS RHUTY VGYBN CNMFP
21  GPHLK QQMBS LPMAC OZCNB RYAUO HNHBE CEOBF SMIZT KWXCE IOXZX EEIVJ
22  HGLQP QHMNF HXETY YPEAQ BUDWK NDXDZ BSLXX XCTLH CIWBI QHXHN YYFNH
23  NHYXA RKZMC RNZTO NKZKO SGNWF KJXRP QZIBR CPXCW FCCIM EKLBA BSHYA
24  EYGFQ DVTSD RQBSV UQVTK IETFA TNGHQ CBERO OAHBA MSXAK VKBSY
```

```
25  LRORO IXQEZ APHAF CFFQW OZJUL UZBEQ AGYIP ZPHAB QQRIX LHRMS LJTSD
26  HHCVA HUPWS FMHVH JTRHA FDJFW CLEWE KUMFJ INAYG KRSLH NJFXY THFPU
27  PHULQ IZGLQ IMGWB EAVTJ AAPUM PYEMG DMUAG MAMZO TIRTT OWFVN KCYAQ
28  GZRFG XMBAV IXJCW NLIEP ENPVK QTWPR UMWEG GJUNR QXTAT EBLDI
29  UEZTE XHZYV WGXSO JGQHZ VPPAW LFSHD USONO QORTC MRNCE SRVXQ QWLJV
30  ISRPS BHJDV YSROS REHBD DEBAW PDOGJ MXAVJ KETMA PTTKR HQZAN XNGLM
31  QWJDT CQCYO UEYYC DNCPS HDRPG VNEAL LJJMG HGAOQ GRRHN CARAI QUKXS
32  IFUTU TEQMB JAYYP XCUTT NGFPX NWFOZ YSETA LWPNL MCQNP PQCEL
33  ZMUEL JYAJC PMLNT GDWEL PNEQX SVMXU AMSJI ZWVZZ YNXTE FYBNO ESLMN
34  VFYNP QHMNM IDEIH ISTYQ QVDRN ZIBXA IKSXO MTJIB KESPN XIMTE KILQX OPONS
35  NZPWQ ZEPOY CYCXJ FACZA EBXXG MPQDH NQTPP WXKIM ASNMO LVCVT VKJVY
36  SESPC SSLSG PPQZW PBIJO CZIPA FAPFP GSMOG UFPME BYEAL EIOEH IGPFC
37  SYSOC EAGXA SVYZE DCJRJ TIYBD INAOM YBGLP BRXZA NBCHF DZTNJ TSTCK
38  UUTKM GSURU LBJCM NIQKC XBJIX OIZHT ACVDK ITWPH XZCPM UBDBI MMZQR
39  VCPUF YHIOW BSBKF ZGRBE YVGSQ YCNVT ORGVO FRYFJ JEHTB WYAKI QYSFM
40  LQYMR QOSGK CVVEL TCYSV LLYHS HMAZC XCQNK KTCBH ZNOMM PTKKW XCIBO
41  OIQKK ELZNC XVBRZ GGOKS CGPBP LARQL RTVYO XMZCW EYBIH OZMSW BWCVV
42  USEYC YDPVG BPCUG DVEVC GKCAU PYZIT DITNZ XVKPY JROJI DQHIN ZULJA
43  FDEVG HWYWX LIKKF IHIIZ AXOPI DHUWQ XNWLM YVDDH GOIAZ SCCQF DKALN
44  OOLCM ADUWY TLYVT QWQTG HENGO ORMJW ZOEWT QLJCF BUGAI EUMRT YOHDQ
45  VVOON ASBIN QWRPB FCGWZ KNVXG QTXJB IQZYO XCFKU SOTXN NYRNV FMLFE
46  AXDDA CDLRC VKOMS XIHQI TUNOM AXDMI SISFS MBYTL SAEEI PGCNH GYTTA
47  AEXFA UPOKM SBMNZ YUHEM ZLBQM ROIUH KECCE IXDAR VFAEV WDHPS CLSCB
48  ZRNTO WRSTD YOKCW NQUIS WEFIF LFFZQ BSDCS CBNRQ SZLXB BRICQ NAIRA
49  INRYO RGNZE GCYAW PMCQL CGBMX BBUBO NQOZZ OFNQR YMZWA CDMGX YVEWO
50  ABKCI OWTGT CTOOK MFRPG XADLN AAJSU BMTIQ VHOUZ TBCZA LEOPO
51  USDUN TZTJT YXUIG OZQFS VDDSR JWUFH FGIZS ORJTB IVSKB BHMPQ NXMWK
```

```
52 AGSNT KJWOX HALUV WEATS VAIIF ADOMO NFZOS FZAOS DINWI UNIAA WADIA
53 PGPPU RINGD CGFDG ZALDT NXPUQ EPQSU ZVKDO TXTBN MUQAS ZKIGH WQRQI
54 DWXAI TYXBQ QCJWF YGNZE FMABH SBFPX RCYGT EQOTR OFXXH XEJYD QLKIL
55 KRNXC HWYWL EYFHB TUZXZ JKVSC VOYKJ NRCLO OZARV LBSZG TYHGU JZHZV
56 WTWCP CJURA BTHXC NSUHC GQYEA LLUPI CHXEU STQXX VTPBN SSGFH XJKGA
57 MXEZP QSVYN ZQFVE MKKQU EMQJA ZQVST GBCZN VIMZK OTWVY AMIBJ ATZCJ
58 WMDTM ZJFMZ ZNCCD OVLZF ALKUV ABWMM QXEGF UCTNG CFZKU BACBI URQBZ
59 JUYYT JGBIJ LFUFI PPIUW JMSYK WUPMY DBJOP RCGAU OWGLU BCHIK DMTWK
60 WBSIA VNKOQ GSPYV NYUZY RBPHG ZXIRA GIGFN RGZFM WOCGL XMGDK RNQQB
61 XTVGN LEOWT SQJXC OXMKB BQXBC HLWRI BDKLZ CXZBE MNYUJ BAJLP BSGQD
62 SSAZB DBXTS WDJBS RBUJB ZXBPC ACTVN TWIOP FZDQC YCHMM FKHUS RNTKW
63 COTOX GXTBU KDRBC ZYZNC YXLCA KQMIM NPNJH OPAJN VBWWF SZKXD RGSNR
64 XNIEK GFHYJ LIORG OFSPJ HBHWD MIOCW OHZCD LYSSP XUZTK SMMCG EAUMT
65 MQRVY WLJFB VVJFN LIKIB USXXT HOKZO USRWR UHUEV JKTUZ UVJKJ MZJYU
66 HLWJA VTYTH RCXTI ZHDCM KTWFT JISPR CBNFT OXOFK QCRUB NGLZG XRPMT
67 PEDGQ DKKHQ AYWRK AQQXR SVEFE OAXQU LXYUB ZOPBK MKQLM MZABC THZKR
68 JAZJW DLNAA PMJHG WMXBM UPULD BRDJQ FFZYW KCENN EQZQL KEAKL AJMPT
69 IBWGB UATXC YUTKB NPWTO QRIGB NFTZF TIGSV WHEQG DECFG VHOFM AIIRP
70 NXQRE FBYCB EDDZM RVSIE DYYDI BVGRP SBTFF WLVGX GUZMK YSYVL LODQP
71 STZRN JTINY WRAWA NCJQS BLXNE MEHFB CIWHC ODUJF LXHLY KASTO VPPEV
72 UGBMC UVYXX HNBMZ MEYNE LCINY VBVVB VCMAJ DIIJM ZDWOU YLGFO VTXXG
73 CDYCG TQFTF KXSPI CISAG WAJBK ANRVK HGLMK JFDPE BJLGS IIYAH GPRAC
74 YCGTM QXEHV UFDJG YHPZD RQNJO COEBJ IFECA XXNBE AIDUK NBGTU OJGJV
75 LQFSV UTZAS CQDQB ZOATI TQEJV XLBBT WROYW YVPCZ ICFPE RFYHA UDTSC
76 DBCYC LYMRD QMFYT GVOJE AYVDY GDJBN NPWTO SYTTM QYGPG JZJXT
77 QZAPN PHRAQ XIORJ HZAZA CYQDQ FKEHG UTNFV TEUOQ KIIHE AFUAF WHOFS
78 HJBJN HFRBF XAZMI CUKWE GFQRT FNKYQ LJYES IAAFR RKCQN LFERD FKDKS
```

```
 79  MQUON OYXGH PITVG MOQDE GYGKU BXWNT TKNBF BPWQD IMTIV ZWWMO IOJZQ
 80  MOWLH YHDWQ JADWC JCZZT TYAUW UJRFK SLLXM VEUVH TWIUP XVRHK PCHSM
 81  WLPLO TBJON YVETM MFPGH VEJEP IFSTY NCLUY IVOYC SYDUO QXHYD GSYMB
 82  XGWBG NWDFY TLEEK DJUUJ XZRTC SZEJR FXLNQ QYLPN NWARU CLRHS BOMOE
 83  OAIQL IXYNS AVDAC EIBKU DKADM YPRMY TQAWH AVTXO OPBFY SZDYK BGSJD
 84  FCNLQ NWAOG NTOIV JZRVS IACOO KEYIN OZBNP KEGHF JFASY SDIFB NXNXF
 85  JPSAM RVBQG XNIZB MVGVU VNFMU FJXEL BZLTP IFIWB LBXPB QDXAW FRHBF
 86  QPDCM OXOSU MMERK QNMYF YKDOC BOXIY SPLGV PBLNG NKTAK YNGBX MIPOM
 87  RIDCL TCIBZ HFLDV RXBKF LRKMU CQHEY RAAVH XAYDH NNNUN JCINA RAEXP
 88  UAQRP RUDMO OHOOM EMGUP IEEIX AQTLU PETXI BQEPN IWBRE BNSEQ RDUGG
 89  TGWUR QRJRL XGRDP MJPDX TSDBG YYQDR DQYSZ GLXDR IDLYX FIVSQ WZVQG
 90  QRXLN LBLGT EGHVN ZXRFN HFQOW XIXBE ULILO MRXQO GJXRC JOUZH OTJAK
 91  DMFER TTWFO XVGVE UIBDG WUGTF HBNXM EZNHB COGDE BBOPZ ZWMTR YRSDX
 92  CUTFL PHZYV HTOTI JOPJP QTPMU ZJYLU FPULW LWQOI AMJRS RAWNQ THMOW
 93  LHUGS XSNKF LAUOT UMXYT OFRYZ IRIDT ESKKM OGJHL BBDOD RLSWZ RRGVA
 94  VOGEN KOOZX MGWQS TUGJS WSOEU CIOYT IZYSE WUWWL PXMFB RRRPV PHVAC
 95  KESYK WKPJI FOJEQ LZZOK RMBSG LQYMR GAPCT ZJGHG GRCLY XPHXY LBIKH
 96  NSOZO MTAOE YJCBY IXDVZ VFENU DIUTJ GGPTE REYHK QLDCR UMBKN RSXQT
 97  CVXTB WQXZK QOSIM ELPDR OVWTR PITOO NSRUF PGQVS YBQDK OLCBV NXBUC
 98  GZMMW IKOWW ZEOZF DWSLY UTGXP LMDUF ESIHP KUCXM MFQQM QIOPA LOFBF
 99  PWSDP SMDZL ZOWOB IVZFK NEUBS AAIZY XOKGP VQCHE QUHGV OFZZJ DNSTP
100  VWSYQ SSYNT HGBTW ZBKGL IDSAF ARCJB WJDOQ GGOQO DVRHK OBYTI KGNSS
101  NVCCP HCZQV AWFWI GHMMB TZPTG AIYZV PZDYR HJVJT BPTPJ ADLWD XOGUL
102  WVDGK FGETB BOHDT JVYTD IFHXH VPLUM SZBMA VKUDL ORYBW YQVIN UMUSC
103  HQQBD XIDWX DPZDW PDCHC BNOAT WYDCG OXBUB JVAGG OSQBB GVOCY YPIBA
104  QBLLB BBDCS LZEMS TUWJV WLZRO FVMXS LAITG BHPEK SIIEE LKULQ WRMPX
```

```
105  TUUXW AIHAC SMFKU GSKFZ JWBJZ RPZEA RIQLG ZUUHW JSHVI* AIYVI GOVDD
106  RNFIW XEKMG RKBSC WEKEX NXXQL JJKPD REZEI ZAMOO VHOEH CKCES WHKLD
107  AKDFL FDDPJ MSBLU FXUIN MDKID WCRVA WMXEE SIKVS ZTAOE POMRV LBAOU
108  LYMNQ FIZIL XCHYH HKEMO IMRCK NDXDM MZEPI DGFFQ BVLDY YBBQT
109  LBAOW LOZSD YZFQE CGTAT TDSEX FVKJA YVVNU XDYLG VXZPX OGLZR
110  BZNMX FFWNU CTFXK VFBSP UMKMJ SAEVB PKLBQ OYMJR RHSQK YYKIS
111  ZUOEE DCYRQ PHZJC DIRIK QFRLT OBPLD BOLWB VLJHJ XQJQG XMQEL
112  BIHKW FFWUP OKOOK HZMPR OKWET WJWRZ IDQYD NRJUY YFPUO ABMPG
113  LOFRS OEYMQ MHSLF GVGAH EOOGW JOJNM CCNDS RVVPK IHKTR SVOND
114  FASLV SVWCV OAQRT XCBJJ YMRKH ZOVAD BWJFH DRGJA QAQMC OJMZV
115  EPQJS CELSV VCCKB OYRTN WICAI ILULK JZYYQ YVTJX BJYOL RQIVC
116  VZDUJ KISDE QFIMN GRYMB JZKUW EMFHV KNDZB OBUDE MLSQT RPQVW
117  PCQZY EXMWI MOLSF PDZPQ XLBMK YFUOM FRWFL OIXDV TKCCS YXFTA
118  EYIHE SPUOH BNPSM UQOAG FVSAL RFLYO VMBTM RKBMP ISKUH ITGEQ YBORX
119  SPDIX EUYCN YCEXU JPMPP THBGQ HWBKD VUHCF NNYQY HGDGO VXLIS BKDCD
120  ZCZHW RWWRR OHNTZ GMQIU TSPHS ULCFT MUGLD NAQJM OLYKZ BKJXI SJQWX
121  DBPOO ESCJM ROFLJ BEDGI UVAJK OYSQJ EUNJL OBZER HWUTZ ZMBYS CNOXM
122  DOWJT UFHZZ HBWLG PDNMZ NNFPQ DVBNG TXXAC GHVDS UQXGG ODUVL XFTGL
123  OWRCJ PZSME NBJJF OMQMI IZEUZ GXDQR WBKZS YMCUW IVRWU PJXOT MVDLR
124  VNHMX VAQLH JHQLW QJYSM VUYGW ODMEH NUPWV NCEBM QRCGQ ICTDB CNDZV
125  JEHAJ HRIOP QXIHH SELSF RAXFN PIRCA SKNRB EXSEP WWNON HIOCV FILYA
126  PMDDT GCWOR SDAXB FMKIU ZMMKM KRIYQ NQFLG NDWTT EZUDQ AMZJF QCDAE
127  HBGNN PQNNJ WSDUD HUAWG VNWIK MJRHX NNMMN ZTHQK AFBMS OJPKW XRCNW
128  JKKBX OFRET EAMRP GAOMR CDOFK BQRAJ CSIBX QVBVD XESGN YPFJA WWNVG
129  EHZRL XNCAE RWAZZ GCQRN BQKPS NSPLO HLZEP BOIAW DYDDK WKNMH CDTWG
130  ZNEXA WPTZF PTGYP AVQTE FKZZV JHTTT ICXNA XVDDK ZZINP MLZHS DHSRE
```

* The Declaration of Independence begins with the "H" in "JSHVI."

```
131  XYRUW MBTXT HYVNG ZLXEL VTZDC QMVFL CBBYK BMESG HSOEP SKPKE WMEQW
132  COQNB URIIQ BNQOG AAXPE ITCWN ZJKXL EKTTQ LQEOS NDBQF MBYIV DIAKZ
133  FHMBX LQOLK MLNLZ QLAXE UQOWZ PDOXX ACNFR RUCIN YQDHJ BCTUD GBLAI
134  EPPKO DVITL XJSOC UZYHN KVEGP NJROY YDKIM OKSWL OPTOD ILTSV SFYXC
135  DNMTH QVWTU FETHE DTIWZ ADLAH KOMBR GEMAH GSCHA OCUZA OYQGB YWKMT
136  GWYAJ MAGYS KHOSA RGVWZ PODNM OZNGY MEYAK KIKMQ GFJIW EFAOK MDUYT
137  JWWAH YOIIX REKWJ BALQV AMTJS ZGDAF BIEXV BVUEC AUCRP PJKQY DPBUL
138  TZNWQ KRXDC EHROQ JLDGM MTWFK GFMYK VISOU XCVPP BUKBV ISXHF ZNVLI
139  YEMBH DOSGC ZSGDC VRZWR QWHSC XOXSQ MHSSH OEEUG LGNAB AWELV XCMXB
140  ADMYX DNMKW FWXZF RFLFO DTJCX AXUPG IMAHG KEQXI DULBU APBXH JEZXZ
141  HGDCT SOXXL ULFGI IKQGO YXDVP DGPRQ ECYAZ XQTFG JPYHH TLWNJ ICYTQ
142  QOXHZ DYFXO APZWU HSCWQ UGCYY JOAHB SVQYG NISSC GNBVD BFBWY ZLOYB
143  SSTXJ CEPKR JKYVW TUEFQ SFKJY YWNEG GXYYU KEXAE QWLWD       XIGYA
144  RLTYS NDFAL TTZNA UGFUF LIARF VXWFW ADAKK QICHV IMXQE LYQPZ MHKGF
145  NRQVN TOTHF QQVTH OYBUM QVGFB MDUOS QNZDK USKOQ YBZJA QBONF WJRUM
146  BMELC PLFEO UADYT JHDEU GFHEA TZIXH LBITH IWVVK WVLNJ CDUWN YRRAI
147  YUGCG UBLQU NJKZZ VOZZI IIAWQ PGSTK XKWOO YPQDU ZGUGY ECVTL KHVTS
148  TXQYM YMZHV QYSLT EHMFC GBQFF OXISR KVWJC JDWIN IXNSF XTCRP XSVSD
149  ISACT JNGYY IYZGO BBCFO RLEPY SQMWQ FBKTY NEXRY KSXUY DURWH ZNOSV
150  MNWUL STMXX ZIDBQ MAETF NLDHV CBRGD ERKZQ ZEFQJ SYCMK IVDOH ONJSX
151  NCUPN OORFX OKHOW FILBO RAUDD DJESF WXQQR EXSUZ OXXUA KWREW YPVFG
152  VUENV INHKW GENDP QWXSE EBMVZ CRJOW MUCRU VEYFH NOKGN IDYZP ZENEA
153  YOAYO LCYQB CKZTD QCIOV RAUCG ZUIVB JRJOW OTSTO OPKHO KQOEB OITOM
154  ATEPE ZWFJU GQKLH ZOZSR EEHIV OPKHO OTSTO LHJTR BIVAS TKCWT ZBIJP
155  NZNLD PJNJD ZSIOH JNIHQ YLFXA BHWRO KSTFX IPTQC AMOOJ BIYTU FGFPM
156  KSQDS GDZXO RWJJV DTOYU SBBPZ SNLFY JIVQW ALDDE PFFQH IDOZL BKVHJ
157  KXHBJ PAJPA HCRDF JEMUE ZVWQO TIKIE IRORC AUIWP KBLWH KDUYZ IRYCZ
```

```
158  NBANC  MAWCT  AQUVO  JETTG  WTTSN  LGFTT  JJJNA  JTDAT  AVAIG  VADQL  ABAJI
159  GQCAC  KZFFF  XKCMW  NZWWE  GPIKY  KPJSX  WTVYL  NCDDL  MFMOZ  HSGBF  CCATU
160  ISKLQ  PZZHC  AWMHX  ZBKXG  FYZBV  IUVRW  ZRPKJ  JQMLO  QXQSR  DFGYY  GFXAD
161  YCPCN  TWARE  SPVRE  BIHYH  KZVCR  WDLMK  KTXOX  OMBNK  UXIQV  GFLPG  RMDRK
162  YKOQE  QDPLJ  FXALE  PTALU  GQPRN  DBAZC  QXEUK  GRIIX  JBCHV  MZCTI  QBXWR
163  OQOKP  RDQSU  LPIYH  GXXLL  NDOCQ  VKUBN  LGNST  SHQYE  MTDGQ  MREVD  QEWEB
164  SGNQS  XVZJR  NHQGK  AQNSD  CMKDY  IKHDJ  QXKPT  WKBZG  ULOJA  UFDCO  TPYAB
165  DHZVM  UTCCC  AIGGR  LBKOI  MXDUT  DJSRS  MDPRR  OMMSU  YJVHI  FFZDA  IZHYK
166  PPUCS  YCFMO  EJSDL  IYFQE  KBBCF  VPNJU  BZVLO  EZSNV  VBTDR  XYSWZ  TXUVO
167  PRHCQ  BTLVJ  PHPFT  YEENN  SVEYU  NEPVS  WGHZZ  KMVMS  TZLBD  MVRTA  SFIKE
168  LDZAU  FLZIC  PAFNC  OHDNR  PUMTA  EFASX  CYTUY  OCTVJ  KZCFP  PWAAN  ZLVSB
169  NAWGT  PXTIK  SCZAD  NWYZT  IHMUF  UIPEW  JQPEL  SHAOW  NZGKX  NYFRQ  OCOQT
170  PTBTX  BMFLR  KYDKE  KCOVQ  NGBHH  PEYNW  KZYHR  FETXL  CQUHO  YQQIS  MKBLF
171  HMFPK  NUZTF  FEVCJ  IFSAF  IWNUX  XTLPB  PBJDN  MMSOZ  UVIJN  VIGFR  VGLBS
172  BVXVD  QSCGD  UAOHT  WTQKE  BOYDV  PHPPG  FCLWI  MUQML  AACAM  POROA  EJAUM
173  AOAOI  SNBHS  QKZMB  GJJTH  OHSDE  WFLBZ  YXPEN  WYFJF  WISTG  IDEDP  GBGMU
174  XYEHL  UNAER  XTBJV  DHPHD  UMIIE  QEJOB  TPTAP  TEYJR  KFLMC  JZPZA  UUFCY
175  PTCTM  UXBAV  HNSRN  IEEEQ  ZOHXJ  HHFCA  VVBDW  KTHRV  MYUUJ  KVEGN  TZYMY
176  ZEVLT  WWPQK  FYOXF  DXZGP  XOUQF  OYUTE  VVODS  PGJYF  LJMAN  CALYW  QACQQ
177  SQUSE  DTRFK  GYEVN  GPOGR  NZUHN  QODCF  PWURI  DILGP  MWPBZ  WLIWR  NOMYH
178  TFFZH  HGZDH  LQGIF  WEDOL  PPXJX  DAZVT  MPDYE  TDPTY  NUFUX  WUVLA  RZBJR
179  ITGPW  WKVAG  TWNWQ  MLOHB  LQSJF  WVVSR  XDTYV  CGNMK  SREOO  VZNXY  PJKPV
180  ESXNU  DEPQL  TFAPO  BYDFO  HBEBS  NGTFP  BJVFK  NYGBX  BZXMS  NWSLG
181  BXHQL  BAYOB  BWVIS  MEHWB  TAYTV  THNVX  KCITU  XAEHC  UKZOO  MVTXK  PLVNR
182  AENJU  IJAZR  XBBKV  CPMWK  NGFIQ  EQEIT  NQINH  QPOPG  XVEXQ  HHISC  LBMHS
183  TTQSH  IPCSG  MSCOD  OOCCA  FWYAB  RYXZN  WWSIC  JFBXN  CVMXY  MYGMM
184  DZGCN  HCFPI  BGHLQ  ZNEVM  WADER  DSTWA  LZGDI  CEAEC  IAVRD  WALQS  XZCGM
```

```
185  DTZWK  CRMOT  QFGNO  UMCAJ  SDTPK  RASVL  UXXTV  AQFKU  YYKVN  ULZQD  AFHDS
186  YQILZ  TJLFN  DIUVR  SQIGG  NGHIA  HPEAG  IQXAN  WTNMM  WICCN  HVMFN  PJMDD
187  INWWP  WLCLB  GNYCV  RUBAO  WZVYS  YWEXB  KKDXB  HABNP  LPCEL  RCEAV  VUSWO
188  JBHTG  YQHJB  NTYWQ  YXHVL  AUNMX  OCBPW  PCAEC  ZOANW  XDGGY  LUPHB  XXEDO
189  XALNK  ZWQPF  PICTD  AQBRH  TPHIR  IBFYF  BDCPW  IIWVE  GOYTL  PBMJP  MFJSC
190  LISAP  RFIAG  LCUWW  SCKRH  MRGZB  GYORE  YWUVM  EFKBW  SIGHL  VDARC  ORNFW
191  ZENKM  KNKQU  TLGRS  FUPIX  OILPP  NPQFU  QNCNS  VBQLF  GZFEJ  SLFHP  PFKYJ
192  KERHY  OQOYJ  VZCTT  JJESR  RDOAX  TEHDK  XOROR  SITEQ  CBBFY  KRZJX  FUEPT
193  NWDTC  MFNTH  QVRVP  SIXKR  CXVPM  ZXIHM  DMJQL  FRWYZ  VOXQL  DQGLD  BAMLR
194  KVTHZ  KHXCS  YUJDC  KWRQC  AIMBO  QBGSF  YKQIA  BJEPB  VTSMA  PMPRQ  ZCOOJ
195  LCYKO  MZXLP  ZLTRD  KMQPY  RMGUJ  EFUSM  DBJCL  ZLZEH  WJJPA  NKTSW  KUQHR
196  REIUO  HXSMD  CZDRN  JBPPE  TQORV  ZNNHG  GTXYB  DIWOD  GQZID  VURZZ  ZENTT
197  CWFZP  QVGYF  WBXXI  HYXKE  DNGPK  ANCAB  SQRYJ  QQHVA  KHJUL  OQZPK  LDIJO
198  ORXKZ  LQURZ  YZDYM  IPYBM  PHPGY  YHIUJ  TGMHL  ELBSE  THIUN  ETKLO  YFRVS
199  CBCUS  HEAPT  LNZMJ  UVWEZ  HDNNE  BXKVY  RLDUP  ANUCN  HXAGG  LPUAN  SVMUP
200  MJDBT  NGRJK  ZPPXC  IYMKJ  VUUYK  AUHMC  ENHFM  BJZYM  WHRZN  DMSBA  USASZ
201  HXVTZ  RZZXN  LVMYJ  AHMUG  RNSUQ  JDDXO  GWZUF  EEJPN  ALZRC  GOSDN  UPXQG
202  VXZXN  KROKU  NOETO  SXKWR  JLRHI  EYKJM  LSYYP  RVCBH  HKEIS  OTXIN  NOVQJ
203  IGGZZ  AWYHD  RCEBJ  JUITF  YRRWN  LLPWG  HQDTZ  NHHRW  LAFHB  BNXUN  IWZGS
204  FFJEL  XXAWD  SOVDH  DKAUY  CHPLL  IGNNU  KTQKU  BCMSJ  UVLOP  KBXFA  UWFJH
205  EDVLH  SNAVU  DIHJH  YEGVP  QLJDQ  LBUVK  LFJVI  OVIOV  ODBCM  XXTFO  OLGVV
206  HFPQR  DQCPD  PZGOB  ZMSTC  FTBXU  GDESR  YEPCG  IFRLA  OZROA  RZLRI  GAVVX
207  IGYKF  RHTLJ  LOCCS  TTWCI  XEZWK  MLMBF  XPCWF  IMXKU  LTUNE  KMQZU  MEATP
208  OBLAL  HVUIU  SQUQF  ZYKFS  JIXYA  SNULA  FACYX  RDZWD  GPBKB  XRKCS  QGRFT
209  LIPSL  GHIGX  YAYFG  SDHVQ  GFOFQ  DYSZO  OJRVP  COGNJ  VJVHQ  KXTDJ  JBZEX
210  LHINQ  IMCZX  BUTLX  ROLQM  QBLLN  ETTFJ  ZDECF  CLKYS  UCWWU  JTWNU  CCIHK
211  VGHSU  DZOAE  UUGXL  VAROJ  LYGBJ  GIDUW  CUJAK  SIGVL  YPNOY  JATNX  JRCCJ
```

```
212  DAPQP HGEXB UMSEA EPEGI TCOVM SGLIW FLDKK NXEND XGYDU OKYAX LMAQM
213  NBEDT OXASS YZPTF IBIUU UMDFO MWSWE IEDJL PUNOO MXEVY KNWWE PLKQR
214  AAICA ILRPT ESDRY NDENI YAHCE POXED QVHXK KRUDY MNLJA GZBWA EYNTM
215  LEMRP HWZQD COVEG ZVPXF AOQAW YYPZV WVULH HCYWF PYMER DCQZO LRXFC
216  UKKEW NOEUY IQRJU NAARY XNRWW FQCLY XLIPC UZHYB TGQKY CWJML GDUAL
217  ATITJ HMING DXRLY PHZXN ZJWON FFHGC QCWBB PVSLI SHHMW CUGYS
218  JBJIZ NBKPD WTSKI SAMHI XKFOZ KYZIG MPSVY DCBOO AIVPZ UUWBY QAJYW
219  GWDPD XOXXL SKPFM IPOOS JUGYC VVNPS NAKTO. VDWXS POLFE LCIFH ODUXA
220  IZQCN ESQBJ ETMYN PIBYX FOHMS MMUVJ KOMEL VLVVU EXSID BAOKN KAZKC
221  UHNIC MGCRP FAUBQ JCGOG DNGDD IPQWU MERFH GTBPD FLFLQ LLYVB TOTOX
222  MZCDN MIESE QFMSI XHEBI AYVSY LMSNH LSDJO FVIDK XNYPV ZACYW TOTOX
223  BIQKI JVYAY XHEBI AYVSY VRKNQ CRSLP SSXYI YQCHB KJRPD AFNAS TZKGN
224  EWWDN GTNZH FNRXP MVENL WUGVR SWUNK OXOCU JBOPO ZCTMC UQMAL IYBVF
225  RYHRB ATZBE TFIPA QSCTL JXEIL REYBH BPDIZ IAVEU SKSFK RQQUP IYPDE
226  NHVCH GXIFM GPICA YNYJO QHUSG ORFNG SCGOM PBXDV CWSAQ UOWTA DUJNT
227  JPUIS DCCCJ ENGJT QMKSD*‡GPEBA EIRKP ZATPW CFYKI BDHFK XYDRN UKNEW
228  BOCTW PPAFD NYUHF GMAYY NCLLF IQFVU MSTEX TKBEP HXZEQ NYZFO OTPCU
229  BUSWZ RONJC QVMOH LGKPM XWYPJ YETIN GHRRO LNIWG EDXGE PQMCC IZJNU
230  LJPNR YHIWP XVZZK KQEOC ACTCL RAPDO SPMRA JNGYG ANPUL NMPPG RVDRB
231  MLBWX SJSIE ZCBBB JMGSD YFRDC TGBDV KNMBP PQXVS NGJXI GWKKJ ARLZQ
232  XQHPO OHAWY KJYOH PBHWI FDAFH JJAFQ GSFBR XTYMJ EFJFS CBMQV IQIJX
233  LTPJO KFQTS VZKKM YFKKX CBBLR IOYNF TKKMO OFUDP PXCFC EVWUO ADGPB
234  NWBJJ NPNCW SOTTO IBBMN ZTKFM BMTWP RHJZG WFARD JCDCE KLLPY DUHMX
235  ANKKG NQPJQ NAAZD WVELQ NISRH KRLLR ZPPCQ DNHRZ OHXHJ MXKOL OBIXW
236  EBSFE ISOTJ MDBID VMHWR WOAKK QQZCJ ERRHO KNQVE GICDO CMOYE ZNASK
```

* The Declaration of Independence ends with the "D" in "QMKSD."

‡ Gettysburg Address begins immediately afterward.

```
237  SJTGN NCJJI CIEVR PEJKK UHIRM BTAXT TREXT IBKCS IDGAO KRHWX NPOGD
238  NMAKN SRTNJ DEAGO YTDCM MOUWP KZGCC FASXQ MMHPK PWYLL LPVHX IGOPF
239  YWCHS HERBY NYLYI TINMU GSJAS KITWE SSIIO EECIN YDGHU IYARA WPKJV
240  CAWIU EXDVM AUBXV TZFSK OWETO SXYNW SLYYS XWJUI YWUUY UUDNH CHEUF
241  FVWYD VLSYF NVOND DQVLJ RPACI PLKXE FSYIA UQABT DOSVC HDPKP UPIUV
242  XFQIE TXUWG RUPXM ZNZWD HSSPE FUGNU XQCIM LRPOP CRIMV KPFWI EUORK
243  XVSXK ONBZV LNAGB JLHZT WMNCR GRYNL FHECD JHGUS QWUIQ ZYRRP HATER
244  UPQDW ODTHW MOIDF HHCPF GJUKX VNZBK CJPDP TGDYW AUJGP XGAJF DZTYH
245  HZAYT PIVWN QCVJR ITRKE ZGJSP IAOXM HAUPA MPNKV VHTMH SOPFP VATIU
246  PFMUE QQDGS QPXQH TFGHD BIJJQ AZRND EMKVQ AKZGK ABHEJ EMFXQ ZRYOE
247  UYYJI UNCUL GVTQV MQUJQ PXTAW ZYLVR AZVFZ IQSEN MNPJD RPFSR MFXQU
248  OOSJA VAVIA RDIUY†NQBAK ANNBS FEXTI
```

CHAOCIPHER

EXHIBIT 1

Plain text (in groups of five letters) of Declaration of Independence and Lincoln's Gettysburg Speech, as enciphered in the document entitled "Chaocipher–the Ultimate Elusion."

```
105                                                    WHE   NINTH ECOUR
106  SEOFH UMANE VENTS QITBE COMES NECES SARYF ORONE PEOPL ETODI SSOLV
107  ETHEP OLITI CALBA NDSWH ICHHA VECON NECTE DTHEM WITHA NOTHE RQAND
108  TOASS UMEAM ONGTH EPOWE RSOFT HEEAR THTHE SEPAR ATEAN DEQUA LSTAT
109  IONTO WHICH THELA WSOFN ATURE ANDOF NATUR EXSGO DENTI TLETH EMQAD
110  ECENT RESPE CTTOT HEOPI NIONS OFMAN KINDR EQUIR ESTHA TTHEY SHOUL
111  DDECL ARETH ECAUS ESWHI CHIMP ELTHE MTOTH ESEPA RATIO NZWEH OLDTH
112  ESETR UTHST OBESE LFJEV IDENT QTHAT ALLME NAREC REATE DEQUA LQQTH
```

† Gettysburg Address ends with "I" in "RDIUY."

```
113  ATTHE YAREE NDOWE DBYTH EIRCR EATOR WITHC ERTAI NUNAL TENAB LERIG
114  HTSQT HATAM ONGTH ESEAR ELIFE LIBER TYAND THEPU RSUIT OFHAP PINES
115  SWTHA TTOSE CURET HESER IGHTS QGOVE RNMEN TSARE INSTI TUTED AMONG
116  MENQD ERIVI NGTHE IRJUS TPOWE RSFRO MTHEC ONSEN TOFTH EGOVE RNEDW
117  THATW HENEV ERANY FORMO FGOVE RNMEN TBECO MESDE STRUC TIVEO FTHES
118  EENDS QITIS THERI GHTOF THEPE OPLET OALTE RORTO ABOLI SHITQ ANDTO
119  INSTI TUTEN EWGOV ERNME NTQLA YINGI TSFOU NDATI ONONS UCHPR INCIP
120  LESAN DORGA NIZIN GITSP OWERS INSUC HFORM QASTO THEMS HALLS EEMMO
121  STLIK ELYTO EFFEC TTHEI RSAFE TYAND HAPPI NESSW PRUDE NCEQI NDEED
122  QWILL DICTA TETHA TGOVE RNMEN TSLON GESTA BLISH EDSHO ULDNO TBECH
123  ANGED FORLI GHTAN DTRAN SIENT CAUSE SQAND ACCOR DINGL YALLE XPERI
124  ENCEH ATHSH EWNTH ATMAN KINDA REMOR EDISP OSEDT OSUFF ERQWH ILEEV
125  ILSAR ESUFF ERABL EQTHA NTORI GHTTH EMSEL VESBY ABOLI SHING THEFO
126  RMSTO WHICH THEYA REACC USTOM EDWBU TWHEN ALONG TRAIN OFABU SESAN
127  DUSUR PATIO NSQPU RSUIN GINVA RIABL YTHES AMEOB JECTE VINCE SADES
128  IGNTO REDUC ETHEM UNDER ABSOL UTEDE SPOTI SMQIT ISTHE IRRIG HTQIT
129  ISTHE IRDUT YQTOT HROWO FFSUC HGOVE RNMEN TQAND TOPRO VIDEN EWGUA
130  RDSFO RTHEI RFUTU RESEC URITY WSUCH HASBE ENTHE PATIE NTSUF FERAN
131  CEOFT HESEC OLONI ESUAN DSUCH ISNOW THENE CESSI TYWHI CHCON STRAI
132  NSTHE MTOAL TERTH EIRFO RMERS YSTEM SOFGO VERNM ENTWT HEHIS TORYO
133  FTHEP RESEN TKING OFGRE ATBRI TAINI SAHIS TORYO FREPE ATEDI NJURI
134  ESAND USURP ATION SQALL HAVIN GINDI RECTO BJECT THEES TABLI SHMEN
135  TOFAN ABSOL UTETY RANNY OVERT HESES TATES WTOPR OVETH ISQLE TFACT
136  SBESU BMITT EDTOA CANDI DWORL DWZHE HASRE FUSED HISAS SENTT OLAWS
137  QTHEM OSTWH OLESO MEAND NECES SARYF ORTHE PUBLI CGOOD ZHEHA SFORB
138  IDDEN HISGO VERNO RSTOP ASSLA WSOFI MMEDI ATEAN DPRES SINGI MPORT
139  ANCEQ UNLES SSUSP ENDED INTHE IROPE RATIO NTILL HISAS SENTS HOULD
```

```
140  BEOBT AINED QANDW HENSO SUSPE NDEDQ HEHAS UTTER LYNEG LECTE DTOAT
141  TENDT OTHEM ZHEHA SREFU SEDTO PASSO THERL AWSFO RTHEA CCOMO DATIO
142  NOFLA RGEDI STRIC TSOFP EOPLE QUNLE SSTHO SEPEO PLEWO ULDRE LINQU
143  ISHTH ERIGH TOFRE PRESE NTATI ONINT HELEG ISLAT UREQA RIGHT INEST
144  IMABL ETOTH EMAND FORMI DABLE TOTYR ANTSO NLYZH EHASC ALLED TOGET
145  HERLE GISLA TIVEB ODIES ATPLA CESUN USUAL QUNCO MFORT ABLEQ ANDDI
146  STANT FROMT HEDEP OSITO RYOFT HEIRP UBLIC RECOR DSQFO RTHES OLEPU
147  RPOSE OFFAT IGUIN GTHEM INTOC OMPLI ANCEW ITHHI SMEAS URESZ HEHAS
148  DISSO LVEDR EPRES ENTAT IVEHO USESR EPEAT EDLYQ FOROP POSIN GWITH
149  MANLY FIRMN ESSHI SINVA SIONS ONTHE RIGHT SOFTH EPEOP LEZHE HASRE
150  FUSED FORAL ONGTI MEQAF TERSU CHDIS SOLUT IONSQ TOCAU SEOTH ERSTO
151  BEELE CTEDU WHERE BYTHE LEGIS LATIV EPOWE RSQIN CAPAB LEOFA NNIHI
152  LATIO NQHAV ERETU RNEDT OTHEP EOPLE ATLAR GEFOR THEIR EXERC ISEUT
153  HESTA TEREM AININ GINTH EMEAN TIMEE XPOSE DTOAL LTHED ANGER SOFIN
154  VASIO NFROM WITHO UTAND CONVU LSION SWITH INZHE HASEN DEAVO UREDT
155  OPHEV ENTTH EPOPU LATIO NOFTH ESEST ATESU FORTH ATPUR POSEO BSTRU
156  CTING THELA WSFOR NATUR ALIZA TIONO FFORE IGNER SUREF USING TOPAS
157  SOTHE RSTOE NCOUR AGETH EIRMI GRATI ONSHI THERQ ANDRA ISING THECO
158  NDITI ONSOF NEWAP PROPR IATIO NSOFL ANDSZ HEHAS OBSTR UCTED THEAD
159  MINIS TRATI ONOFJ USTIC EQBYR EFUSI NGHIS ASSEN TTOLA WSFOR ESTAB
160  LISHI NGJUD ICIAR YPOWE RSZHE HASMA DEJUD GESDE PENDE NTONH ISWIL
161  LALON EQFOR THETE NUREO FTHEI ROFFI CESQA NDTHE AMOUN TANDP AYMEN
162  TOFTH EIRSA LARIE SZHEH ASERE CTEDA MULTI TUDEO FNEWO FFICE SQAND
163  SENTH ITHER SWARM SOFOF FICER STOHA RASSO URPEO PLEQA NDEAT OUTTH
164  EIRSU BSTAN CEZHE HASKE PTAMO NGUSQ INTIM ESOFF EACEQ STAND INGAR
165  MIESQ WITHO UTTHE CONSE NTOFO URLEG ISLAT URESZ HEHAS AFFEC TEDTO
166  RENDE RTHEM ILITA RYIND EPEND ENTOF ANDSU PERIO RTOTH ECIVI LPOWE
```

```
167  RZHEH  ASCOM  BINED  WITHO  THERS  TOSUB  JECTU  STOAJ  URISD  ICTIO  NFORE
168  IGNTO  OURCO  NSTIT  UTION  ANDUN  ACKNO  WLEDG  EDBYO  URLAW  SUGIV  INGHI
169  SASSE  NTTOT  HEIRA  CTSOF  PRETE  NDEDL  EGISL  ATION  VFORQ  UARTE  RINGL
170  ARGEB  ODIES  OFARM  EDTRO  OPSAM  ONGUS  VFORP  ROTEC  TINGT  HEMBY  AMOCK
171  TRIAL  FROMP  UNISH  MENTF  ORANY  MURDE  RSWHI  CHTHE  YSHOU  LDCOM  MITON
172  THEIN  HABIT  ANTSO  FTHES  ESTAT  ESVFO  RCUTT  INGOF  FOURT  RADEW  ITHAL
173  LPART  SOFTH  EWORL  DVFOR  IMPOS  INGTA  XESON  USWIT  HOUTO  URCON  SENTV
174  FORDE  PRIVI  NGUSI  NMANY  CASES  OFTHE  RENEF  ITSOF  TRIAL  BYJUR  YVFOR
175  TRANS  PORTI  NGUSB  EYOND  SEAST  OBETR  IEDFO  RPRET  ENDED  OFFEN  CESVF
176  ORABO  LISHI  NGTHE  FREES  YSTEM  OFENG  LISHL  AWSIN  ANEIG  HBOUR  INGPR
177  OVINC  EQEST  ABLIS  HINGT  HEREI  NANAR  BITRA  RYGOV  ERNME  NTQAN  DENLA
178  RGING  ITSBO  UNDAR  IESSO  ASTOR  ENDER  ITATO  NCEAN  EXAMP  LEAND  FITIN
179  STRUM  ENTFO  RINTR  ODUCI  NGTHE  SAMEA  BSOLU  TERUL  EINTO  THESE  COLON
180  IESVF  ORTAK  INGAW  AYOUR  CHART  ERSQA  BOLIS  HINGO  URMOS  TVALU  ABLEL
181  AWSAN  DALTE  RINGF  UNDAM  ENTAL  LYTHE  FORMS  OFOUR  GOVER  NMENT  SVFOR
182  SUSPE  NDING  OUROW  NLEGI  SLATU  RESQA  NDDEC  LARIN  GTHEM  SELVE  SINVE
183  STEDW  ITHPO  WERTO  LEGIS  LATEF  ORUSI  NALLC  ASESW  HATSO  EVERZ  HEHAS
184  ABDIC  ATEDG  OVERN  MENTH  EREBY  DECLA  RINGU  SOUTO  FHISP  ROTEC  TIONA
185  NDWAG  INGWA  RAGAI  NSTUS  ZHEHA  SPLUN  DERED  OURSE  ASQRA  VAGED  OURCO
186  ASTSQ  BURNT  OURTO  WNSQA  NDDES  TROYE  DTHEL  IVESO  FOURP  EOPLE  ZHEIS
187  ATTHI  STIME  TRANS  PORTI  NGLAR  GEARM  IESOF  FOREI  GNMER  CENAR  IESTO
188  COMPL  ETETH  EWORK  SOFDE  ATHQD  ESOLA  TIONA  NDTYR  ANNYQ  ALREA  DYBEG
189  UNWIT  HCIRC  UMSTA  NCESO  FCRUE  LTYAN  DPERF  IDYSC  ARCEL  YPARA  LLELE
190  DINTH  EMOST  BARBA  ROUSA  GESQA  NDTOT  ALLYU  NWORT  HYTHE  HEADO  FACIV
191  ILIZE  DNATI  ONZHE  HASCO  NSTRA  INEDO  URFEL  LOWCI  TIZEN  STAKE  NCAPT
192  IVEON  THEHI  GHSEA  STOBE  ARARM  SAGAI  NSTTH  EIRCO  UNTRY  QTOBE  COMET
193  HEEXE  CUTIO  NERSO  FTHEI  RFRIE  NDSAN  DBRET  HRENQ  ORTOF  ALLTH  EMSEL
```

```
194  VESBY  THEIR  HANDS  ZHEHA  SEXCI  TEDDO  MESTI  CINSU  RRECT  IONSA  MONGS
195  TUSQA  NDHAS  ENDEA  VOURE  DTOBR  INGON  THEIN  HABIT  ANTSO  FOURF  RONTI
196  ERSQT  HEMER  CILES  SINDI  ANSAV  AGESQ  WHOSE  KNOWN  RULEO  FWARF  AREIS
197  ANUND  ISTIN  GUISH  EDDES  TRUCT  IONOF  ALLAG  ESQSE  XESAN  DCOND  ITION
198  SWINE  VERYS  TAGEO  FTHES  EOPPR  ESSIO  NSWEH  AVEPE  TITIO  NEDFO  RREDR
199  ESSIN  THEMO  STHUM  BLETE  RMSWO  URREP  EATED  PETIT  IONSH  AVEBE  ENANS
200  WERED  ONLYB  YREPE  ATEDI  NJURY  WAPRI  NCEQW  HOSEC  HARAC  TERIS  THUSM
201  ARKED  BYEVE  RYACT  WHICH  MAYDE  FINEA  TYRAN  TQISU  NFITT  OBETH  ERULE
202  ROFAF  REEPE  OPLEW  NORHA  VEWEB  EENWA  NTING  INATT  ENTIO  NSTOO  URBRI
203  TISHB  RETHR  ENWWE  HAVEW  ARNED  THEMF  ROMTI  METOT  IMEOF  ATTEM  PTSBY
204  THEIR  LEGIS  LATUR  ETOEX  TENDA  NUNWA  RRANT  ABLEJ  URISD  ICTIO  NOVER
205  USWWE  HAVER  EMIND  EDTHE  MOFTH  ECIRC  UMSTA  NCESO  FOURE  MIGRA  TIONA
206  NDSET  TLEME  NTHER  EWWEH  AVEAP  PEALE  DTOTH  EIRNA  TIVEJ  USTIC  EANDM
207  AGNAN  IMITY  QANDW  EHAVE  CONJU  REDTH  EMBYT  HETIE  SOFOU  RCOMM  ONKIN
208  DREDT  ODISA  VOWTH  ESEUS  URPAT  IONSQ  WHICH  WOULD  INEVI  TABLY  INTER
209  RUPTO  URCON  NECTI  ONSAN  DCORR  ESPON  DENCE  WTHEY  TOOHA  VEBEE  NDEAF
210  TOTHE  VOICE  OFJUS  TICEA  NDOFC  ONSAN  GUINI  TYWWE  MUSTQ  THERE  FOREQ
211  ACQUI  ESCEI  NTHEN  ECESS  ITYQW  HICHD  ENOUN  CESOU  RSEPA  RATIO  NQAND
212  HOLDT  HEMQA  SWEHO  LDTHE  RESTO  FMANK  INDQE  NEMIE  SINWA  RQINP  EACEF
213  RIEND  SZWEQ  THERE  FOREQ  PRESE  NTATI  VESOF  THEUN  ITEDS  TATES  TATES
214  OFAME  RICAQ  INGEN  ERALC  ONGRE  SSQAS  SEMBL  EDQAP  PEALI  NGTOT  HESUP
215  REMEJ  UDGEO  FTHEW  ORLDF  ORTHE  RECTI  TUDEO  FOURI  NTENT  IONSQ  DOQIN
216  THENA  MEQAN  DBYAU  THORI  TYOFT  HEGOO  DPEOP  LEOFT  HESEC  OLONI  ESQSO
217  LEMNL  YPUBL  ISHAN  DDECL  AREVT  HATTH  ESEUN  ITEDC  OLONI  ESARE  QANDO
218  FRIGH  TOUGH  TTOBE  FREEA  NDIND  EPEND  ENTST  ATESU  THATT  HEYAR  EABSO
219  LVEDF  ROMAL  LALLE  GIANC  ETOTH  EBRIT  ISHCR  OWNQA  NDTHA  TALLP  OLITI
220  CALCO  NNECT  IONBE  TWEEN  THEMA  NDTHE  STATE  OFGRE  ATBRI  TAINI  SANDO
```

```
222  TESQT HEYHA VEFUL LPOWE RTOLE VYWAR QCONC LUDEP EACEQ CONTR ACTAL
223  LIANC ESQES TABLI SHCOM MERCE QANDT ODOAL LOTHE RACTS ANDTH INGSW
224  HICHI NDEPE NDENT STATE SMAYO FRIGH TDOWA NDFOR THESU PPORT OFTHI
225  SDECL ARATI ONQWI THAFI RMREL IANCE ONTHE PROTE CTION OFDIV INEPR
226  OVIDE NCEQW EMUTU ALLYP LEDGE TOEAC HOTHE ROURL IVESQ OURFO RTUNE
227  SQAND OURSA CREDH ONORZ FOURS COREA NDSEV ENYEA RSAGO OURFA THERS
228  BROUG HTFOR THONT HISCO NTINE NTANE WNATI ONQCO NCEIV EDINL IBERT
229  YANDD EDICA TEDTO THEPR OPOSI TIONT HATAL LMENA RECRE ATEDE QUALZ
230  NOWWE AREEN GAGED INAGR EATCI VILWA RQTES TINGW HETHE RTHAT NATIO
231  NORAN YNATI ONSOC ONCEI VEDAN DSODE DICAT EDCAN LONGE NDURE WWEAR
232  EMETO NAGRE ATBAT TLEFI ELDOF THATW ARWWE HAVEC OMETO DEDIC ATEAP
233  ORTIO NOFTH ATFIE LDQAS AFINA LREST INGJP LACEO FTHOS EWHOH EREGA
234  VETHE IRLIV ESTHA TTHAT NATIO NMIGH TLIVE WITIS ALTOG ETHER FITTI
235  NGAND PROPE RTHAT WESHO ULDDO THISZ BUTQI NALAR GERSE NSEQW ECANN
236  OTDED ICATE HWECA NNOTC ONSEC RATEH WECAN NOTHA LLOWH THISG ROUND
237  WTHEB RAVEM ENQLI VINGA NDDEA DQWHO STRUG GLEDH EREQH AVECO NSECR
238  ATEDI TFARA BOVEO URPOO RPOWE RTOAD DORDE TRACT WTHEW ORLDW ILLLI
239  TTLEN OTEQN ORLON GREME MBERQ WHATW ESAYH EREWI TISFO RUSTH ELIVI
240  NGQRA THERQ TOBED EDICA TEDHE RETOT HEUNF INISH EDWOR KWHIC HTHEY
241  WHOFO UGHTH EREHA VETHU SFARS ONOBL YADVA NCEDW ITISR ATHER FORUS
242  TOBEH EREDE DICAT EDTOT HEGRE ATTAS KREMA INING BEFOR EUSHT HATFR
243  OMTHE SEHON OREDD EADWE TAKEI NCREA SEDDE VOTIO NTOTH ATCAU SEFOR
244  WHICH THEYG AVETH ELAST FULLM EASUR EOFDE VOTIO NHTHA TWEHE REHIG
245  HLYRE SOLVE THATT HESED EADSH ALLNO THAVE DIEDI NVAIN HTHAT THISN
246  ATION QUNDE RGODQ SHALL HAVEA NEWBI RTHOF FREED OMHAN DTHAT GOVER
247  NMENT OFTHE PEOPL EQBYT HEPEO PLEQF ORTHE PEOPL ESHAL LNOTP ERISH
248  FROMT HEEAR THZ
```

CHAOCIPHER

EXHIBIT 2

EXCERPT FROM DE BELLO GALLICO IN CHAOCIPHER

```
TLXWF WYHBI COJSP URTJM FDKTJ BFAEF GBRJO SISVK RGRPK OKXZQ BXHSY
NZRXD YXZDX BDAGA LVCYG CMXEQ ISZIT MNICJ QHQXJ JUMSA GESXW FJUAK
JWURE KMUIX YMFAJ CVURV AECLA KDWJB HBSJD WRQOP HUHPF GDONU PWDIY
VDRSE SXPNR NSZMC XIYSO XBZPD SKBFS QXSYP DEGSJ USNXB JMVVW AVDPZ
ILECG XBKKN FKVOX QSCNK HDYQR YNNHN HQPJW XVUGW DGUWN DOIIU
HKWWJ MXXEG XITIK KTAXW LZRBF QFVEI VMMRX OBIFN PQDMP YUARZ ELHDK
DSCEK ACMDZ ZBGSU FMZRC LQUSI CSRVS FHHKH HPVIB CCNZJ HCRTO ZUOCC
LWDWI EWBGF YJPQN NHTNN IBTLY WZAQS DHBOR BHKBH FBBZH ZHQXU BURTI
EYELG DOFLB SVOEM GBFUC DLJDD RGGIO JVGJT ZXSRQ DGIKW IDKZP XFDCZ
WODHB WMRCV KJQRZ FRJGF CTCLY XTIMN IXCKO KWXKD RQMHL QWUAC SYWXE
VFSUG XNBCU ZJVKL SDLUP YVVIV HDZSY AXDAX LTPRP TCWQD XECKJ OQAEK
SKWNA TLVZU WZUDQ AHZCR OYYMC ENWQM YMJDH KAORT NPOAW NASLV HGOUS
WHLRF ROBQI SVRMT DOQPG BLITU PZXBV PDWVX UOBRE DOLFA CGKRK KGMBY
HDGOD KQRAZ HNULW BEJQK FSPXJ SXJQB OHYSR JXNCN IASEX DXUJY HJHLU
PIQTV PCWWJ IJQPP EKKTG CPVUA LISGU HVUMX XDIVX MMYHQ WZWYQ UMHUA
QSMND BKJGN RJYSG CUVRS PNSYE GDSMI WKPRE QKSJY BKNPC SWGBF XGMLW
PSYWY RDKYS WMQET OPMQB GYLHO QRZCG MIBFH SAMQI WDIPA XWDUW SUNAR
TTJIP AHILZ SSQFV QNIYC ZKTJI VUVQA LFOET XFHLL UQBQK SDDJO RHFFB
MELCN ZDABW WNFSP OKCSC AQGWZ TXJTT QWKTO FBWDS HOWGX FIQHU JOQIG
LLNLJ OJHKE SRNHP ROEUF LKFJX WEKUD HRKUH YPWRR HXWBQ DGNTU JIUEL
DMIEH ALHGW FNXGU GGLTM TJSMA HNJNT NTYHN VZJTO INEVB QNCVS OAXUO
ZRVHD HZJNH LVOFU RIYJP KMIBW OVGCJ KKJLQ TYZJQ VPOWR RNGLF SFJLT
BCSCS UOZJZ NWTQS BECOE VXFIJ WEQSX SFYNS QRFJP INAPK GFNOJ CRK
```

S.V.B.E.E.V.

C.J.C.

Exhibit 2

PLAIN TEXT IN LATIN OF EXCERPT IN CIPHER FROM
De BELLO GALLICO

```
GALLI  AESTO  MNISD  IVISA  INPAR  TESTR  ESWWW  HORUM  OMNIU  MFORT  ISSIM
ISUNT  BELGA  EYPRO  PTERE  AQUOD  ACULT  UATQU  EHUMA  NITAT  EPROV  INCIA
ELONG  ISSIM  EABSU  NTYMI  NIMEQ  UEADE  OSMER  CATOR  ESSAE  PECOM  MEANT
ATQUE  EAQUA  EADEF  FEMIN  ANDOS  ANIMO  SPERT  INENT  IMPOR  TANTY  PROXI
MIQUE  SUNTG  ERMAN  ISYQU  ITRAN  SRHEN  UMINC  OLUNT  YQUIB  USCUM  CONTI
NENTE  RBELL  UMGER  UNTWQ  UADEC  AUSAH  ELVET  IIQUO  QUERE  LIQUO  SGALL
OSVIR  TUTEP  RAECE  DUNTY  QUODF  ERECO  TIDIA  NISPR  OELII  SCUMG  ERMAN
ISCON  TENDU  NTYCU  MAUTS  UISFI  NIBUS  EOSPR  OHIBE  NTYAU  TIPSI  INEOR
UMFIN  IBUSB  ELLUM  GERUN  TWWWH  ISREB  USFIE  BATUT  ETMIN  USLAT  EVAGA
REENT  URETM  INUSF  ACILE  FINIT  IMISB  ELLUM  INFER  REPOS  SENTY  QUAEX
PARTE  HOMIN  ESBEL  LANDI  CUPID  IMAGN  ODOLO  READF  ICIEB  ANTUR  WPROM
ULTIT  UDINE  AUTEM  HOMIN  UMETP  ROGLO  RIABE  LLIAT  QUEFO  RTITU  DINIS
ANGUS  TOSSE  FINES  HABER  EARBI  TRABA  NTURY  QUIIN  LONGI  TUDIN  EMMIL
IAPAS  SUUMC  CXLYI  NLATI  TUDIN  EMCLX  XXPAT  EBANT  WWWAD  EASRE  SCONF
ICIEN  DASBI  ENNIU  MSIBI  SATIS  ESSED  UXERU  NTYIN  TERTI  UMANN  UMPRO
FECTI  ONEML  EGECO  NFIRM  ANTWA  DEASR  ESCON  FICIE  NDASO  RGETO  RIXDE
LIGIT  URWIS  SIBIL  EGATI  ONEMA  DCIVI  TATES  SUSCE  PITWI  NEOIT  INERE
PERSU  ADETC  ASTIC  OYCAT  AMANT  ALOED  ISFIL  IOYSE  QUANO  YCUJU  SPATE
RREGN  UMINS  EQUAN  ISMUL  TOSAN  NOSOB  TINUE  RATET  ASENA  TUPOP  ULIRO
MANIA  MICUS  APPEL  ATUSE  RATYU  TREGN  UMINC  IVITA  TESUA  OCCUP  ARETY
QUODP  ATERA  NTEHA  BUERA  TWWWH  ACORA  TIONE  ADDUC  TIINT  ERSEF  IDEME
TJUSJ  URAND  UMDAN  TYETR  EGNOO  CCUPA  TOPER  TRESP  OTENT  ISSIM  OSACF
IRMIS  SIMOS  POPUL  OSTOT  IUSGA  LLIAE  SESEP  OTIRI  POSSE  SPERA  NTW
```

CHAOCIPHER
Exhibit 3

```
T H E H I S T O R Y O F W A R T E E M S W I T H O C
O D H S T O C O C P B H R S L T A N U R I C I A V Z

C A S I O N S W H E R E T H E I N T E R C E P T I O
D Q W O C P R I W F L Q X Q P B G R N S J K Z Y R H

N O F D I S P A T C H E S A N D O R D E R S W R I T
O N X X Q H R T V N H N C O X O Q Q L O U N F B W D

T E N I N P L A I N L A N G U A G E H A S R E S U L
G S R H B E S V A C Z K K C X Q K E V T O V Q B F L

T E D I N D E F E A T A N D D I S A S T E R F O R T
B N N A Y B Y G M N U I U E X T N V I J D L B Q T I

H E F O R C E W H O S E I N T E N T I O N S T H U S
I S K P P Q V M F F B B M P M H S P S X R I L K I J

B E C A M E K N O W N A T O N C E T O T H E E N E M
D T N C H B X O B L Y V V F T P P T G N N J V F L O


T H E H I S T O R Y O F W A R T E E M S W I T H O C
C L X R E Z M N X Z T U U W L G S W U E J H Y K R W

C A S I O N S W H E R E T H E I N T E R C E P T I O
V B Q S V K V L P G B E V O Q K P N V L L W A B X R

N O F D I S P A T C H E S A N D O R D E R S W R I T
D Z O D V G B C R J O E X S H B T L X C R J J U K A

T E N I N P L A I N L A N G U A G E H A S R E S U L
C M V T E F E N S R X Y T O L P L E G G R Z R T N F

T E D I N D E F E A T A N D D I S A S T E R F O R T
O G G A B N L V A K M S K P K T D I B F T W D F R E
```

```
H E F O R C E W H O S E I N T E N T I O N S T H U S
W O S U A B U Y I G R S U Q C A I N G K S B R K W Y

B E C A M E K N O W N A T O N C E T O T H E E N E M
V V S Q L F G G M G V J M D F A Z D F Q X M S E G I


T H E H I S T O R Y O F W A R T E E M S W I T H O C
V V V Q M D W H F J P W A G P A M A N H S F Y Y L F

C A S I O N S W H E R E T H E I N T E R C E P T I O
Y B F I X Q L H T F K K E F V E A K U I X M S X S Z

N O F D I S P A T C H E S A N D O R D E R S W R I T
Q N P L D V P H A F L Q N Z R X G R H X Z E B W Q P

T E N I N P L A I N L A N G U A G E H A S R E S U L
Y H I S N Y T L F U H F S M K P O W D G F D L Y Q R

T E D I N D E F E A T A N D D I S A S T E R F O R T
H I V V U J H F B I S O P F K K L Z T A Y Y V A G N

H E F O R C E W H O S E I N T E N T I O N S T H U S
T Q Q E C S F D B V T T M A P O M F N S F L T N M U

B E C A M E K N O W N A T O N C E T O T H E E N E M
P T U H J P U O R Z T I S Y C M Q X E P T K F B S X


T H E H I S T O R Y O F W A R T E E M S W I T H O C
U J A A P G Z N O R Y X N U G T U E S B A B J Z V T

C A S I O N S W H E R E T H E I N T E R C E P T I O
M D L R Y U P S A W C U Q X P W E I Y G F C C P Y N

N O F D I S P A T C H E S A N D O R D E R S W R I T
L R P M Y Z S L M H A R O C P Y F N Q D D V L E G P
```

```
T E N I N P L A I N L A N G U A G E H A S R E S U L
I S K X A S B H M L A N C J A U K M Y W R S U W N R

T E D I N D E F E A T A N D D I S A S T E R F O R T
I O C H Z T X E G W W O R O P G J Q I G N H J L W D

H E F O R C E W H O S E I N T E N T I O N S T H U S
U N R P O G L O W G G R E H M F D P V C T K Q P Y S

B E C A M E K N O W N A T O N C E T O T H E E N E M
A O B N X X U C J G V J E I Z C P G E K W H G U K V


T H E H I S T O R Y O F W A R T E E M S W I T H O C
N J L W Q M F G H Z K Z R P K K D Q I K N O L K T M

C A S I O N S W H E R E T H E I N T E R C E P T I O
P K V B Z M Y Q R S P E A S A Z B N K G Q Y P W V J

N O F D I S P A T C H E S A N D O R D E R S W R I T
E P N Q O W R Q F B S K K Y C J O Y F C P R V J B Y

T E N I N P L A I N L A N G U A G E H A S R E S U L
Y G F S B Q E U K I Y J E L J Z K P H H L S X K N H

T E D I N D E F E A T A N D D I S A S T E R F O R T
X W B O B I B R G A C M U V T Z Y T Q N J W C J F F

H E F O R C E W H O S E I N T E N T I O N S T H U S
S V N I X P B J C S U U O U D S W A G O D E X P B X

B E C A M E K N O W N A T O N C E T O T H E E N E M
K N S G Q V Z Y K C J L P E K X P X S R E X Q L K Y
```

CHAOCIPHER
Exhibit 4

EXACT PLAIN TEXT OF ENCIPHERED EXCERPT FROM CONGRESSIONAL SPEECH BY GENERAL OF THE ARMY DOUGLAS MacARTHUR

Beyond pointing out these general truisms, I shall confine my discussion to the general areas of Asia. Before one may objectively assess the situation now existing there, he must comprehend something of Asia's past and the evolutionary changes which have marked her course up to the present.

Long exploited by the so-called colonial powers, with little opportunity to achieve any degree of social justice, individual dignity, or a higher standard of life such as guided our own noble administration in the Philippines, the peoples of Asia found their opportunity in the war just past to throw off the shackles of colonialism, and now see the dawn of new opportunity, a heretofore unfelt dignity, and the self-respect of political freedom.

Mustering half of the earth's population and sixty per cent of its natural resources, these peoples are rapidly consolidating a new force, both moral and material, with which to raise the living standard and erect adaptations of the design of modern progress to their own distinct cultural environments.

Whether one adheres to the concept of colonization or not, this is the direction of Asian progress and it may not be stopped. It is a corollary to the shift of world economic frontiers, as the whole epicenter of world affairs rotates back toward the era whence it started.

In the situation it becomes vital that our own country orient its policy in consonance with this basic evolutionary condition rather than pursue a course blind to the reality that the colonial era is now passed and the Asian peoples have the right to shape their own destiny. What they seek now is friendly guidance and support not imperious direction.

The dignity of equality and not the shame of subjugation. Their prewar standard of life, pitifully low, is infinitely lower now in the devastation left in war's wake.

World ideologies play little part in Asian thinking and are little understood. What the people strive for is the opportunity for a little more food in their stomachs, a little better clothing on their backs, a little firmer roof over their heads, and the realization of the normal nationalist urge for political freedom. * * *

CHAOCIPHER

EXHIBIT 4

ENCIPHERED EXCERPT FROM SPEECH MADE BEFORE BOTH HOUSES BY GENERAL OF THE ARMY DOUGLAS MacARTHUR

A Glimpse of Chaos

```
 1  PMRGA  HTMRZ  ABMGA  KMAAC  VEHRN  WQSJL  DIWLU  KKTGY  RVSAE  BPWFN  RKPDP
 2  QTQJT  HQEME  ANFNV  PMKRZ  MIGRF  MGBOZ  WPYDK  WQDWO  HCFYL  CIJVV  KXURX
 3  ICFAP  QVZIA  GEPXK  IKOPJ  LJVUW  WXKSN  SYBOB  RDTJF  LDNNS  BMSMR  JDIMJ
 4  FOHKZ  IZADR  JICVQ  QYJTT  MUZUN  UQJNK  BWWCU  MSNSA  VNRPB  YBJLS  WRUEH
 5  KMGQF  UOIID  MZCPT  URRKX  IICXO  AIYIE  CNQYK  GOZOT  SFDYS  ZVREC  ATJRO
 6  ONGEE  WBQZQ  CYCYU  WFCZC  DQTOK  ZUIEZ  PUTLW  ZMQNJ  FRIKF  ZHBAK  ALXKY
 7  FCLVW  XXXFZ  BMOPO  ESYXE  FCZBW  NQKTC  YFBQY  JCUTP  RHOPC  ASGUK  YRHVX
 8  CBPGF  KTXKC  QHIUU  WAZKO  GZCOK  GLEUP  DUBAN  VDZAE  VOAKW  IFHZE  RGPSR
 9  NHCKB  EVEFR  AOMFA  BMQDT  VWBRL  RQUQE  RRGEG  ALISY  EMBDU  KVIVV  OXMED
10  BWXZV  OIVGF  HKDJQ  LVWFY  JOLKH  VHKYP  PIDKI  GNYRE  XDOGV  SPETT  SQWNZ
11  WLJOA  EIFBK  YHNOF  BARDI  EPCHV  HGONV  JHLZH  DRYYF  UXJSZ  DSWIK  REUIV
12  CTVOP  POWWD  KDIFD  YBCEK  LOPMF  SUTRD  ASFCS  EDKDH  BSTKH  PGETY  EOCES
13  NTEXD  AOFPJ  AWPYT  ZXZAD  CQZSQ  BQVHI  GMMOI  YFKQF  HFNNE  ADKGU  KIEIH
14  EAVST  HORHC  UPQHE  FVXRT  LYBZZ  CMHDV  VBXFT  WCSHK  IWAGT  VJVUR  ACNLP
15  IWDVS  BJIVG  UXDPJ  HLVCB  RGJMD  MLOHX  KQQLO  YTQLL  FQMGD  TWPBS  NLPXQ
16  PMQQM  FVLIN  GEPQK  STYHI  TVSGO  EOVZH  RKFZE  TVMSY  XRNIW  NDQRI  NTNYQ
```

```
17  OJSCE XAQOU MZRUM KLMMV XXFPX WZOLL QUSVV OGGUB YIECW WRSTC LYURR
18  DZDGX XLKYJ OOIQY GQMQI SKIPV NAMSU HTVVE TFVZO FPDAL TEAPD AUIOS
19  LRMCA SIWHU GKHSI BRLPY PZDAX GFAKC QGJPW ZSNAV AZTLQ WJTFV HRVRM
20  BVYBC XARBV BALYB ZXSEO FCPPI ILSHM XSZRR EKUUT MDLUO OUKLG ILKJG
21  OFMDN NQTIU UVKCC OLXJP NTFPQ QQOIX DIAHS TRNZK TYVQT WQSTT KRKPR
22  OULYP BRJTL ZGPYX BUNSQ PDTXC GBQYY ZHHFR WHJYC SJHLF TKBBC YSMFT
23  SCVYJ YQAAA HBFHD TTCYJ ZCGLS SAWIF ZGRZS OEJDJ YVDXQ WSRIE NBJYP
24  SQPPG KZUZT HMTWT GLMED JLISA USBLZ XRLXI MPRJU ZVBLR HKOKW VZUWY
25  HBKIS MAAOV FGPTH XQDIN WKESQ HETCI JHWHM AJPAN YDMFR QPZKG CKZED
26  DOXDV DEHQV LJDUD SIVEF NYKGV ETOFX SDCBF XTESJ MUXEW TDWCX TRYLR
27  RMJMM PGHHL SGVDV IJQPZ SDZJR TZVGM APFWD JBANS QVJZL NLMZN RHSXI
28  PPXJL BXBYB ALYZY IAJIV KSQMX PDZNT ZPCFS TZOFE PLGFI HADTY QAAYI
29  YIOMW XYQHP GXTVO FXKHB NOFWL NKEFG JUWWP DHHAJ ARKZJ DVJYO
30  MAEZR GSSTD CUOCE PBYIL UOGBT VHDMR BNIDM GUHWE HZAGR QKOTC QEASC
31  VDECN EPLGG NWTRH XVVHL YLUQL IKHSZ OJEIX BHWPS TAWCE VDYDW ATGQS
32  YRULL WLQGZ RHRZC XDLRV YIAKL DVKKA YNBSJ GBFCZ ERWFS NTCWZ AGSLC
33  HPGVC PXRKI IUMPB CTPER JQXKI WRRXI SUAPW SQWIK VEFBS NCHOT ZBFSE
34  HCYXR XRZWN TXOAI MOWEK PSIXP CPOLZ JJMXS CYLRF UKMYF DPRCO ARREU
35  DGYQH TQCFJ NGNQA DTLBU MYVDM ULXIW XNVHG OIK
```